PSYCHOANALYTIC COUNSELING

WILEY SERIES IN PSYCHOTHERAPY AND COUNSELLING

SERIES EDITORS
Franz Epting, *Dept of Psychology, University of Florida*
Bonnie Strickland, *Dept of Psychology, University of Massachusetts*
John Allen, *Dept of Community Studies, Brighton Polytechnic*

Self, Symptoms and Psychotherapy
Edited by Neil Cheshire and Helmut Thomae

Beyond Sexual Abuse: Therapy with Women who were Childhood Victims
Derek Jehu

Cognitive-Analytic Therapy: Active Participation in Change: A New Integration in Brief Psychotherapy
Anthony Ryle

The Power of Countertransference: Innovations in Analytic Technique
Karen J. Maroda

Strategic Family Play Therapy
Shlomo Ariel

The Evolving Professional Self: Stages and Themes in Therapist and Counselor Development
Thomas M. Skovholt and Michael Helge Rønnestad

Feminist Perspectives in Therapy: An Empowerment Model for Women
Judith Worell and Pam Remer

Counselling and Therapy with Refugees: Psychological Problems of Victims of War, Torture and Repression
Guus van der Veer

Psychoanalytic Counseling
Michael J. Patton and Naomi M. Meara

Further titles in preparation

PSYCHOANALYTIC COUNSELING

Michael J. Patton
University of Missouri-Columbia

and

Naomi M. Meara
University of Notre Dame

with a contribution by
Steven B. Robbins

John Wiley & Sons
Chichester · New York · Brisbane · Toronto · Singapore

Other Wiley Editorial Offices

John Wiley & Sons, Inc., 605 Third Avenue,
New York, NY 10158-0012, USA

Jacaranda Wiley Ltd, G.P.O. Box 859, Brisbane,
Queensland 4001, Australia

John Wiley & Sons (Canada) Ltd, 22 Worcester Road,
Rexdale, Ontario M9W 1L1, Canada

John Wiley & Sons (SEA) Pte Ltd, 37 Jalan Pemimpin #05-04,
Block B, Union Industrial Building, Singapore 2057

Library of Congress Cataloging-in-Publication Data

Patton, Michael J., *1936–*
  Psychoanalytic counseling / Michael J. Patton and Naomi M. Meara.
    p. cm. — (Wiley series on psychotherapy and counselling)
  Includes bibliographical references and indexes.
  ISBN 0-471-93421-6
    1. Psychoanalysis and counselling. 2. Counseling—Moral and
  ethical aspects. I. Meara, Naomi M. II. Title. III. Series.
  BF 175.4.C69P38 1992
  616.89'17—dc20   91–46055
                                                                          CIP

British Library Cataloguing in Publication Data

A catalogue record for this book is
available from the British Library.

ISBN 0-471-93421-6

Typeset in 10/12 pt Times by Photo·graphics, Honiton, Devon
Printed and bound in Great Britain by Biddles Ltd, Guildford and King's Lynn

Contents

Series preface

The Wiley Series in Psychotherapy and Counseling is designed to advance the science and practice of professional psychology in a number of ways. One of these ways is to offer the reader an opportunity to explore one of the classical positions from a new perspective. The present text is such an undertaking. In *Psychoanalytic Counseling*, Dr Patton and Dr Meara have undertaken the task of demonstrating how a psychoanalytic approach can be used in the field of counseling psychology to address not only issues of theory and practice, but also to encourage an active investment in research. They have offered the first modern systematic text in this area, which means that for the first time the student, teacher, and practitioner have a comprehensive single source for this knowledge easily available. Throughout the text, case material is used to illustrate theoretical concepts of personality functioning as well as therapeutic strategies. Patton and Meara have succeeded in presenting this material in such a way that the skills of a psychoanalytic approach are made explicit without sacrificing the rich theoretical context which provides the meaning and significance of these skills. The authors have avoided mechanizing the concepts while still making them explicit and readily available to the professional reader. In the words of one of the reviews of this text, the chapters in this book are both "coherent and prescriptive" in a manner that sets this material apart from anything available in other texts in this field.

The presentation of the theoretical foundation for psychoanalytic counseling is broadly based in a field which includes expansions of the basic theory offered by self theory, ego psychology, and object relations theory. Because Patton and Meara's approach takes the parent theory in the direction of counseling and general humanistic approaches, it is very important that they have taken the time to differentiate this approach from that taken by a Rogerian counselor. This is all the more important since much of early counseling psychology was heavily influenced by the work of Carl Rogers.

In addition, this text represents the very best of a scientist/practitioner model in professional psychology. Attention is not only paid to theoretically based intervention but is also directed at being able to assess these interventions in such a way as to make the whole process accessible to empirical investigation. In fact, one chapter of the text is devoted to research. It may turn out that this text will serve, in the future, as an example for other texts in this area. For example, the authors have included a chapter on women and one on ethical considerations. Other texts in this area have not included these concerns or have included them in a very incomplete fashion.

It is with a great deal of pleasure that I welcome this text to the series and trust that readers will share my enthusiasm for what these authors have offered. They have made some of the most important ideas in psychoanalytic thought available to the counselor.

Franz Epting
Series Editor

Preface

Until quite recently, the professional specialties of counseling in general and counseling psychology in particular were slow to consider and use ideas from classical and contemporary psychoanalysis in the practice of psychological counseling. That this should be so is not surprising. The two fields evolved worlds apart from each other, geographically and philosophically. Psychoanalysis developed first within the Continental European intellectual tradition of the 1800s, and later flourished in the British and American medical traditions. In sharp contrast, professional counseling traces its origins to public and higher education in North America, particularly the United States, where egalitarian ideas of educating the masses and personalizing the educational experience for the individual student were prevalent.

Perhaps because of this separate development, many counselors believe that psychoanalytic ideas are not applicable to persons in a more individualistic and competitive culture where there are increasing opportunities for women as well as men to achieve. One also gets the impression that the reluctance of counseling practitioners to learn what psychoanalysis has to offer them is due largely to the impression that psychoanalytic ideas have relevance only for the treatment of persons with severe emotional or personality problems who are treated in strictly medical or psychiatric settings. Whatever the reasons, it should be recognized that psychoanalysis is also, in the first instance, an evolving general psychology that has substantial relevance for the understanding and treatment of a broad range of problems in everyday life. These problems include not only the all too frequent manifestations of anxiety, depression, vulnerable self-esteem, and interpersonal maladjustments experienced in daily living, but they also include problems related to educational and vocational indecision. At any event, the counseling field has been without a contemporary text on psychoanalytic counseling that is theoretically coherent and clinically relevant to these many concerns of clients. With this book, we attempt to remedy this state of affairs.

One way to characterize this book is to regard it as a translation of psychoanalytic ideas for counselors and researchers who wish to learn about psychoanalytic counseling and use it in their work. It is an introductory text intended for an audience of experienced masters and doctoral level counselors, graduate students in training, and researchers. We attempt, therefore, systematically to formulate and present a theory of psychoanalytic counseling, such that the applications of central concepts and processes to counseling and research situations are made clear. A major intent which has guided our writing is that of illustrating how the counselor, acting as a scientist–practitioner, may use psychoanalytic theory as a schema for understanding the client's interview behavior, as a plan for intervening in the flow of that behavior, and as a means of assessing the efficacy of those interventions.

In this book we stress the importance of the counselor acting as a scientist–practitioner as he or she goes about helping the client. By this we mean that it is both possible and desirable for the counselor to take up a scientific attitude in the process of helping the client. This attitude is manifested in the counselor's use and testing of theoretically derived formulations that are explicitly based on careful observation of client behavior. The scientist–practitioner approach is thus characterized by the counselor's willingness to use observation as the basis of his or her understanding and, thereby, to regard any formulation of the client's behavior as open to refutation by additional observations. Behaving as a scientist–practitioner is an important ethical and professional responsibility which enables the counselor to contribute to our knowledge of the counseling process as well as help the client.

To demonstrate our position, we begin the book with a brief history and analysis of psychoanalytic ideas and trace their development in counseling psychology. We take seriously our own obligation to perform as scientist–practitioners by making explicit the assumptions on which our theory of psychoanalytic counseling is based. We then present our formulations of Freud's classical theory, Kohut's theory of the self, and our ideas about the interview and the working alliance as key elements in the counselor's theory of the client and of the counseling process. This material then forms the theoretical structure to be used in understanding and working with the client.

We then present several technical considerations in the work with the client. We treat these technical matters as problems to be solved by the client and counselor. Introduced here are principles and techniques for assessing the client's readiness for counseling, formulating the client's communications in the interview, understanding the interviewing process itself, and recognizing and dealing with client resistance. The application of these ideas is also illustrated clinically by the presentation of a lengthy case history. Throughout these chapters, we cite the research literature where relevant in order to show the reader what data-based or research support exists for certain ideas or propositions. As well, in the chapter dealing with assessing client readiness for counseling we include a set of rating scales of client behavior and estimates of their psychometric properties that one of us has developed over the years.

The final section of the book contains chapters dealing with the psychoanalytic counseling of women, ethics, and research. In the chapter on the counseling of women, we are concerned to show how psychoanalytic ideas have been applied to counseling women clients without demeaning them. In the chapter on ethics, we present two ways of thinking about the ethical implications of the counselor's work with the client. Our approach has been to address and use both Principle Ethics, as embodied in formal professional codes of ethics, and Virtue Ethics, a point of view that directs attention to the kind of person the counselor is and the kind of virtues he or she possesses, as well as what the counselor does. The book concludes with a discussion of the problems and the methodology of conducting research on counseling. The last chapter also includes a presentation of several studies that report on the construction of psychoanalytically derived instruments to measure client and counselor attributes and elements of the counseling process.

The idea for the book grew out of conversations between the authors that took place over many years. These conversations often occurred in the context of our joint research endeavors, one of which included analysis of natural language in a psychoanalytically-oriented series of 25 counseling sessions. We brought to these conversations a growing appreciation for psychoanalytic ideas, and one of us was able to share early experiences as a psychoanalytic counselor who was then undergoing regular supervised training in a large, psychoanalytically-oriented community mental health center. Much of the material discussed in these conversations and gleaned from clinical experience became the basis for the book.

However, we owe much to a number of colleagues and students, past and present. The influence of two individuals has been especially important in the writing of this book. Norman S. Anderson, M.D., provided important early opportunities for learning and growing in the clinical psychoanalytic setting, and much gratitude is extended to him. Bruce L. Goates furnished many hours of productive supervision in psychoanalytic counseling and gave his valued friendship as well. His formative role is most appreciated.

Beyond these two persons, we express our gratitude to several others. Norma Simon deserves special thanks for her help in reading and making many useful comments on an early version of the manuscript. We also single out Franz Epting, the series editor, for thanks, not only for his assistance in reading and commenting on the manuscript, but for his ongoing support and encouragement. We are also indebted to former students and now our current colleagues Steven Robbins, Richard Lapan, Kathleen Scott, Matthew Davies, Ila Goodey, Linda Charney, Dee Wright, Mitchell Koles, Gary Connor, James Efstation, Douglas Tyler, Barry Shreve, and the late Kenneth Tucker. Each of these persons has been a stimulating co-worker with whom we have exchanged many ideas.

We also thank Aaron Jackson and Amy Kerr for their diligent work in locating references for us and in preparing the reference list. To Judy Letourneau, Jenny Schultz, and Brenda Baker we owe much appreciation for the care they took in preparing our computer diskettes for printing and copying the numerous drafts of the manuscript.

Finally, we are indebted to Harold Brenner Pepinsky, Pauline Nichols Pepinsky, and Lyle D. Schmidt for the example, tutelage, and encouragement they provided for us as psychology graduate students long ago and their generous friendship and support since that time. Their high standards of scholarship and their model as exemplary scientist–practitioners continue to inspire us.

Michael J. Patton
Naomi M. Meara

Part I
THEORETICAL BASES

1 Introduction: historical and philosophical origins of psychoanalytic counseling

This book is about a process of psychological help-giving (see Pepinsky & Patton, 1971) called psychoanalytic counseling. Its focus is the adaptation of psychoanalytic ideas to the practice of psychological counseling. We intentionally attach the adjective "psychoanalytic" to the term "counseling" to indicate that most of our ideas about the counseling process derive directly from the body of thought that has shaped classical psychoanalytic theory, namely the ideas of Sigmund Freud (1916/1961a, 1926/1959a). Although we modify some of Freud's ideas when we develop a model of the counseling interview, the behavior of the counselor in the interview, or the length of treatment, we do use his notions about personality when we construct a theory of the client in conflict.

We also borrow ideas from contemporary psychoanalytic thought (see Robbins, 1989), primarily those of Heinz Kohut (1977) and his psychoanalytic psychology of the self (Patton & Sullivan, 1980). The works of Karen Horney (1937, 1939), her later interpreters (see Westkott, 1986), and others who have focused upon the psychological development of women also contribute to our conceptualizations of psychoanalytic counseling. This blending of Freudian ideas with those of later writers has permitted us to formulate a model of counseling that can be adapted to the needs and circumstances of a large number of younger and older adults who seek the help of the professional counselor.

While we have emphasized in this book Freud's and Kohut's points of view in psychoanalysis, we are well aware that, in recent years, many other modifications of psychoanalytic thinking have been developed. For example, ego psychology (see A. Freud, 1936a,b; Hartmann, 1939; Erikson, 1950;

King & Neal, 1968), the British and American schools of object relations theory (see Klein, 1932/1949; Fairbairn, 1958; Winnicott, 1965; Guntrip, 1961; Kernberg, 1976), attachment theory (Bowlby, 1980), and interpersonal psychodynamic theory (see Strupp & Binder, 1984) are increasingly used as bases for psychoanalytically informed treatment. Our theoretical choices as authors reflect our training, as well as our research and clinical experiences.

In this chapter, we will first provide a brief stage-setting for what follows by defining what we mean by the phrase psychoanalytic counseling. Next, to understand better the ideas we use, we will discuss their historical and philosophical origins in psychoanalytic thought. Last, the source of psychoanalytic ideas in the specialty of counseling psychology will be presented.

Psychoanalytic counseling: a working definition

By the term "counseling" we mean a process of psychological treatment in which one person, the counselor, attempts to bring about a change in the beliefs and/or behavior of another person, the client (see Pepinsky & Patton, 1971). This definition of psychological counseling emphasizes its properties as an instance of the social influence process and makes it interchangeable with the term "psychotherapy". Both counseling and psychotherapy are instances, then, of psychological treatment and are equivalent in this sense. "Psychoanalytic counseling," as we use this phrase, refers to the deliberate use or adaptation by the counselor of psychoanalytic ideas and techniques to assist the client in acquiring increased insight into his or her emotional problems. As an approach to psychological treatment, psychoanalytic counseling places considerable emphasis on the development and mainten-ance of the working alliance (see Greenson, 1967) between the client and counselor. In developing and maintaining the working alliance the counselor endeavors to identify and enlist the intellectual and emotional assets the client brings to counseling. The working alliance makes possible the counselor's ability to influence the client through their ongoing interaction. Thus, the client's active cooperation with the counselor in the working alliance promotes their interactive understanding of the maladaptive factors responsible for the client's difficulties and helps strengthen the client's adaptive capacities.

In psychoanalytic counseling, the counselor and client meet face-to-face in the interview, or series of interviews. The length of the counseling process may be a few sessions or of longer duration. The client's current needs and level of development will dictate goals, specific techniques and the length of the treatment process, as well as the frequency of the face-to-face meetings. In most cases, the work will proceed on a once-a-week basis, but occasionally the client may need to be seen more often, particularly during times of crisis. The perspective of the counselor provides coherence for the process. The counselor listens in an organized way and understands the client from a psychoanalytic perspective and then intervenes in the flow of client material on the basis of that understanding.

The work of psychoanalytic counseling and its outcomes are achieved interactively by client and counselor. The counseling interview is a social situation whose participants actively manage and interpret moment-to-moment events, such that common understanding about their work is made possible. Their concerted interaction occurs in and is facilitated by the working alliance, itself a sector of their overall experience of each other in the encounter (Greenson, 1967; Bordin, 1979; Gelso & Carter, 1985; Kohut, 1984). It is the responsibility of the client to take part in the working alliance the counselor offers and to use it to bring about change.

Several overlapping processes occur in psychoanalytic counseling (cf. Bibring, 1954). The first of these has to do with the ongoing management of the conversation by the participants, such that the client is able to provide material (Patton, 1984). Usually, the counselor shows restraint, interest, and concern, and the client is encouraged to report material as freely as possible, and to follow the direction the thoughts are taking. With some clients, however, the counselor may need to be quite active until the client is, if ever, able to take the lead in exploring his or her inner life. Second, all clients have a readiness to develop a transference relationship with the counselor. In its broadest sense, transference is a normal process in which childhood hopes and wishes are mobilized in response to present interpersonal situations that are similar, or appear to be similar, to the original situation that gave rise to these patterns of expectation (Basch, 1980). The client and counselor attempt to understand the client's faulty pattern of transference because it is central to his or her difficulties.

Third, the counselor uses client material to observe the process, to understand in terms of theoretical knowledge, to listen for his or her own affective or countertransference reactions to the material, and then to intervene. In all cases, the client's material consists not only of manifestly expressed thoughts and feelings, but also of derivatives of his or her unconscious mental life; for example, fantasies, dreams, slips of the tongue, and other parapraxes. When intervening, psychoanalytic counselors may make use of such technical maneuvers as suggestion, support, empathy, questions, and confrontation of resistance, as well as insight-oriented interventions in the form of clarification and interpretation.

Fourth, in response to the counselor's intervention, the client explores the significance of the counselor's statement by filtering or synthesizing the communication, thus shaping it for personal use. Such use may include a more positive or trustful attitude toward counseling or increased understanding and differentiated perception of one's own behavior. Fifth, the client accommodates to new personal knowledge of him or herself by the altering of old approaches to problems and goals.

It is the function of the various counseling processes, therefore, to help the client: (a) bring about a reduction in the complaints and problems for which counseling was sought; (b) acquire knowledge of many of those factors within the self that have led to the present difficulties; and (c) plan how to exercise newly found choices in thinking, feeling, and acting that increased self-understanding makes possible. It will be our task in this book to explain how events in the psychoanalytic counseling process are predictive of these and other outcomes.

Antecedents in classical and contemporary psychoanalytic thought

It is our conviction that the counselor is able to make the most effective use of theory when he or she is informed both about the origins of psychoanalytic propositions and the assumptions that undergird them. When these matters are explicit for the counselor, a deeper understanding of theory is made possible which, in turn, makes its use more thoughtful and precise. To this end, we will consider here some of the historical and philosophical sources of psychoanalytic theory.

Psychoanalysis is a complicated doctrine consisting of a mixture of ideas from the ancient Greeks, the medieval scholastics, the Enlightenment, French and English empiricism and romantic German metaphysics (Sullivan, 1959). Supporting this conclusion is Bordin's (1979) assertion that "psychoanalysis presents many faces," and Sullivan's (1959) contention that psychoanalysis is a "hybrid, hydra-headed doctrine." This rich heritage of ideas also makes it interesting, but contradictory in places. The task of mastering psychoanalytic concepts and principles is a life-long endeavor and is not for the faint-hearted.

Nevertheless, psychoanalytic thought can be organized and presented systematically so that it does not overwhelm the newcomer on first reading. Our way of doing this is to organize concepts according to how close or distant each is from direct experience (see Patton & Sullivan, 1980). We prefer to begin at the top, or the most general level of explanation in Freud's thinking. By doing so we can note that after 1896, psychoanalysis consisted of a complex theory of mind in which the mental act was the fundamental constituent. In other words, at its most abstract or general level, psychoanalysis explains behavior as the product of mental acts. Prior to this time, however, Freud had attempted to construct explanation in terms of the neurophysiology and anatomy of what was then known about the central nervous system. He called this attempt his "Project for a Scientific

Psychology" (Freud, 1954). It was difficult, however, to find physical correlates for the symptoms that he was interested in explaining. He abandoned the attempt to write a psychology in physical terms, although he never gave up hope that one day all psychological phenomena would be explained by reduction to their presumed neurophysiological causes. In the meantime, he proceeded to write a cognitive psychology. For better or worse, doing so put Freud's ideas into the hands of everyone.

In Freud's version of psychoanalysis, the most fundamental and general assumption is that mind exists, and, therefore, the mental act is the central element of the theory. This idea forms the core of what we call the general theory of psychoanalysis, and we introduce it here to alert the reader that, in addition to Freud, several non-Freudian psychoanalytic theorists (for example, Jung, Adler, Horney, and Kohut) share the assumptions of this general theory. Subordinate to the general psychoanalytic theory of mind, and flowing directly from it, one finds the classical psychoanalytic theory of personality, in which the drives (libido and aggression), the macrostructures of the mind (id, ego, and superego), and the psychosexual stages of development are the main elements and processes. It took Freud many years to work out the relations among the key elements of his theory and to specify the major connections between the theoretical concepts and empirical events. To date, no other personality theorist has matched the breadth and depth of the system that comprises Freud's thought.

While psychoanalysis aims at being a general psychology, it is, at the same time, a set of other theories. It is also a theory of personality, emotional disorder, treatment, the interview, mass behavior, culture, religion and other subjects (see Freud, 1961c/1930).

Table 1.1 illustrates the various kinds of theories within the classical psychoanalytic doctrine. To reiterate, all versions of psychoanalytic theory derive from this abstract, general theory of mind, so it will aid our understanding if we consider this matter a bit further. The reader is urged to use an "active" mind in assimilating the following material!

Mind and the defense theory of the neuroses

In the psychoanalytic theory of mind, mind acts on the data the world presents it by cognitively working those data into a re-presentation, or representation. Freud used this humanistic theory of mind to place the person at the center of both his scientific and therapeutic endeavors. We do not believe the person would be as central in Freud's (1954) thinking if he had stayed with his "Project for a Scientific Psychology". This humanistic view of the person found in the representational theory of mind is not as well known to students of Freud as are his more mechanistic ideas. This is

Table 1.1 Scheme of psychoanalytic theories

---

1. *The General Theory of Psychoanalysis* consists of:
    (a) Theory of Mind. The most abstract or general theory. Mind *acts* in terms
        of wishing, defending, perceiving, etc. Mental phenomena (i.e. objects,
        structures, ideas, wishes) occur within and because of mental acts.
    (b) Methodological principles of inquiry and explanation. Subordinate to the
        Theory of Mind; includes determinism, development, motivation,
        empathic-introspectionism, and theory-governed explanation.
2. *Psychoanalytic personality theories derived from the General Theory in 1 (a)
    and (b) above:*
    (a) Theory of Psychosexual Development.
    (b) Theory of Instincts (libido and aggression).
    (c) Theory of Mental Structures (id, ego, and superego).
    (d) Early Ego Psychology, including psychosexual development.
    (e) Contemporary Object Relations Theory.
    (f) Contemporary Self Psychology.
3. *Special theories derived from Psychoanalytic Personality Theory:*
    (a) Theories of Intrapsychic Conflict and Developmental Deficit (e.g., theory
        of development of neurosis; self-pathology; pathological object relations).
    (b) Theory of Treatment.
    (c) Theory of the Interview.
    (d) Theory of Culture.
    (e) Theory of Religion.
    (f) Theory of Group Behavior.

---

puzzling. We think that either most students of Freud are unaware of his
connection to the great nineteenth-century Aristotelian philosopher, Franz
Brentano, or they choose to "resist" such knowledge. Nonetheless, the
humanistic point of view is abundantly clear in his clinical theories, his
personal letters, and his speculative theorizing in later life (see Holt, 1973).

More well known are the mechanistic images about energy and mental
mechanisms and structures that accompany some of his abstract theoretical
propositions. Even so, Freud's commitment to the notion of the active mind
and his use of the idea in his theory building was, we believe, decisively
influenced by his philosophical studies with Franz Brentano, the leading
Continental European philosopher of the 1800s (Holt, 1963, 1973; Sullivan,
1968; Patton & Sullivan, 1980). Brentano was a philosopher in residence at
the University of Vienna at the time Freud was a medical student there.
Freud attended Bentano's seminar for 2 years, from 1874 to 1876, and
translated several books from English into German for Brentano (cf.
Sullivan, 1968).

Brentano was one of the "empirical philosophers" of the middle to late
1800s whose thought helped develop the discipline of scientific psychology

(Boring, 1950). Specifically, Brentano (1955) founded the so-called school of "act psychology", in which he argued that the proper subject matter for psychology was the processes through which phenomena become objects of our knowledge. In other words, our scientific inquiry should not be focused on the phenomenon of redness, for example, but on the *process* of seeing red. The conclusion is that without the mental process or act, there is no phenomenal object. His formulations are one version of the representational theory of mind characteristic of the humanistic intellectual tradition in Western civilization. This theory infuses our literature, art, music and social science in the Western World. Brentano's (1955) ideas about the mental act turn out to be the intellectual link among psychoanalysis, phenomenology and existentialism, all of which assume an active mind and make it the basic element of their theories (Patton & Sullivan, 1980). Perhaps if this common link had been stressed, we might have seen less rancor and more collaboration among the partisan adherents of each therapeutic camp. Be that as it may, Freud's work with Brentano is either largely unknown or has been systematically ignored by many in the psychoanalytic community, as has this intellectual linkage with phenomenology and existentialism.

The centrality of the mental act to Freud's, and, we might add, to our own, thinking about mind is evident in his initial "defense theory of the neuroses" (Breuer & Freud, 1957). This "theory" has some of its own origins in the work of Freud's mentor and colleague, the eminent Viennese physician, Josef Breuer. Breuer had earlier extended the ideas of the French psychiatrists Charcot and Janet (Sullivan, 1959; Freud, 1900/1953a) in explaining how neurotic symptoms originated and how their associated ideas and affects remained unconscious. Breuer argued that ideas which are unacceptable to consciousness originate and become bound up with strong affect when the person is in a "hypnoid state." By this he meant that symptoms can originate and become elaborated in the unconscious when the person is in a passive condition of withdrawal from wide awakeness. Hynoid states occur, for example, during daydreaming or just before falling asleep.

In Breuer's view, symptoms are things that happen to the person. By not invoking the concept of an active mind in this explanation, Breuer (Breuer & Freud, 1957) could remain consistent with his intellectual heritage in the logical positivistic and reductionistic tradition of science then current in the Europe of the late 1800s. Moreover, it follows from his mechanistic theory that the removal of neurotic symptoms involved getting the patient to undergo a catharsis, or discharge of the bound-up affects, while experiencing them under hypnosis.

Freud (1896/1962b) had a different idea and, we think, a better one. He had noted that catharsis, along with other manipulative treatments such as suggestion, electrolysis, and hydrotherapy, were only partially successful for a number of patients. Following hypnosis, the same or different symptoms often recurred. This unsuccessful outcome cast doubt on Breuer's theory about the origins of the symptoms. We should probably point out here that Freud did more of the doubting than Breuer.

Based on his experiences with his patients, Freud made two crucial additions to Breuer's propositions which moved him toward the development of a psychological theory and away from explanations built strictly upon neurophysiological concepts (Sullivan, 1959). First, he reasoned that the affects attached to the unconscious ideas reflected the operation of sexual forces active in the person. As most people know, this idea was to get him into serious trouble with the intellectual community in Western Europe and the United States. Second, he argued that the ideas remained unconscious because of an "act of will." Hereafter, all neurotic symptoms could be explained as due to this active, regressive mechanism of the mind. Symptoms were, therefore, defenses against unwanted self-knowledge, and the work of treatment then is the analysis of resistances to that self-knowledge. This basic conception of the treatment task forms the core of all psychoanalytic approaches, including our own.

At this point, Breuer broke with Freud over his disagreement with the concept of the active mind, as well as over his distaste for Freud's early speculations about the role of sexuality in the development of neurotic symptoms. For Breuer to have accommodated the direction Freud's theorizing about mind was taking would have meant to break with his own scientific heritage and to risk being ostracized by his colleagues. As is well known, Freud soon found himself *persona non grata* for breaking with the positivistic tradition (Jones, 1963).

Sullivan (1959) notes some immediate logical consequences of Freud's initial theory:

1. An explanation was provided about why cathartic therapy and hypnosis failed to remove symptoms; viz, these methods merely by-pass the resistances, which reinstate themselves later on.
2. A new therapeutic strategy was provided; that is, the analysis of resistances. This amounts to helping the client acquire knowledge of how his or her mind works. Rational self-knowledge is still the major goal of a psychoanalytic approach to treatment.
3. It predicted that therapy would be long and difficult as the analyst tried to introduce to the patient the reality of his or her repressed, unconscious sexual impulses. A formal psychoanalysis that aims at fundamental change in the structure of the personality is, indeed, a lengthy and expensive task. Later developments in ego psychology, object relations theory and self psychology have informed newer and briefer psychoana-lytically-based treatment approaches.

4. It predicted that the successful analysis of resistances would result in a cure of symptoms. This appears to be the case. In fairness, however, it should be pointed out that the key phrase here is "successful analysis of resistances." Some clients have greater reluctance or less ability to acknowledge their resistances than others.

The defense theory of the neuroses made possible by Freud's assumption of an active mind marked the beginning of what became some very complex psychological theories of the person and of psychological treatment. Following the break with Breuer, but prior to 1915, Freud began to develop his ideas about the role of the unconscious and sexuality with the publication of *The Interpretation of Dreams* (1900/1953a) and *Three Essays on the Theory of Sexuality* (1905/1953b). At this time, emphasis in theory construction was placed on the intrapsychic ramifications of conflict among opposing forces and its consequences within the mind.

Freud, like other European intellectuals at the time, paid less attention to the potential impact of an external reality on mind. Following World War I, Freud began to take the external world into account in his theorizing. Whether or not the war had a direct impact on his theorizing is not known. One cannot help but notice, however, that following the war he began to incorporate the potential impact of a sometimes painful social world on mind. Thus, the ego is seen to mediate a compromise between the forces of the id and superego and those of the social world (Freud, 1923/1961b). This emphasis became known as the adaptive point of view, and was a basis for the later development of the structural theory with its id, ego and superego (Freud, 1923/1961b). The adaptive point of view was always implicit in Freud's thinking. By elevating it to the level of the metapsychology, or meta-theory, (Rapaport, 1959), it also made possible theoretical extensions to encompass ego psychology (see A. Freud, 1936a, 1936b; Hartmann, 1939; Erikson, 1950; Loevinger, 1976), and later object relations theory (Jacobson, 1964; Mahler, Pine & Bergman, 1975; and Kernberg, 1976).

The early and later writings of Freud, as well as those of the ego and self psychologists, share many assumptions about the nature of the person. These commonalities enable their perspective to be forged into a "General Theory of Psychoanalysis," and have permitted us to maintain logical consistency in our own formulations. However, by a general theory of psychoanalysis we are not referring to the so-called "metapsychology" (Rapaport, 1959). Freud's papers on the metapsychology comprise his views on how to write psychological theory with the use of a set of underlying assumptions about mental events. These assumptions are somewhat more abstract than his theoretical terms of id, ego and superego, for example, and therefore subsume them. He called these more abstract assumptions the topographic, economic, genetic, dynamic, structural, and adaptive points of view. In keeping with his intellectual and scientific background, Freud (1916/1961a) argued that any mental event of interest to the scientist or the therapist should be analyzed into its constituent elements. In the Freudian version of psychoanalysis, there are thus six such elements for the analysis of mental events.

Our use of the phrase "general theory of psychoanalysis" is different from this conceptualization about the "metapsychology." By the general theory of psychoanalysis we refer instead to (a) an abstract set of meta-science principles of empirical inquiry and theory construction, and (b) the theorist's ontological commitments, or beliefs about what is real in the final analysis (Patton & Sullivan, 1980). To clarify our ideas here, we can talk about these principles in the context of science and the philosophy of science. For example, science has been said to consist of three Levels of Explanation: (1) observations; (2) laws; and (3) theories. Beginning with the level of observation, each of these three scientific levels of explanation and their contents is an increasing abstraction from direct experience (Feigl, 1966). Beyond theory, or Level 3, we find more general explanations at Level 4. These we call meta-scientific principles of explanation. Beyond this, and at still a more general level, Level 5, are the theorist's ontological commitments, or assumptions about what exists in the world. Levels 4 and 5 comprise the philosophy of science. It is at Levels 4 and 5 that the general theory of psychoanalysis resides.

The different versions of psychoanalytic theory found at Level 3 are seen to have assumptions in common at Levels 4 and 5. Thus, for example, the variant theories of S. Freud (1916/1961a), A. Freud (1936b), Hartmann (1939), Erikson (1950), Kernberg (1976), Kohut (1977), Jung (1968), Adler (1959), and Horney (1937) all accept the general psychoanalytic Level 5 ontological position about the centrality of the mental act and its intentional properties, the aim and object (cf. Sullivan, 1968). As well, at Level 4, they all accept that behavior is determined, and that early childhood experiences influence adult development. The role of sexual impulse and psychological development may vary or be lessened in the non-Freudian variations, but the only essential difference is that other motivational variables are added, and may receive greater emphasis. Finally, all variations accept the desirability of the use of theory as the preferred explanatory model.

Table 1.2 is a chart of the levels of explanation found in Freud's theory. We believe the counselor will have a greater understanding of Freud's ideas if he or she studies Table 1.2 and learns at which level of abstraction the various concepts in the theory reside. We have already indicated that Freud's primary Level 5 ontological commitment was to the mental act. Secondarily we also find a commitment to the notion that the objects of mental acts, phenomena such as thoughts and feelings, reside in the act. In other words, the act "works on" the stimulus event and re-presents it as an object of our

Table 1.2 Levels of explanation in psychoanalytic theory

Level 5—Ontological commitment
Assumptions about the fundamental reality. In Freud and other psychoanalytic theorists, this is the central notion that the mind acts to re-present what is presented to it. Social and physical reality are, thus, known only through an act of mind.

Level 4—Meta-science principles of explanation
A set of assumptions that guide empirical inquiry and theory construction. In Freud and other psychoanalytic theorists, these methodological principles make possible the less abstract theoretical propositions about behavior being determined; about its being decisively influenced by historical events during childhood; about the source of behavior being sexual and/or aggressive wishes, broadly conceived; about it being possible to have knowledge of the other person's inner life; and about behavior being best explained by the use of theory.

Level 3—Theoretical psychology
The "system" of mind or personality with its elements, processes and relations; with its maintenance and change devices. In the Freudian version, there are two sublevels at Level 3: the so-called, and more abstract, metapsychology with its six principles (viz. topographic, economic, dynamic, structural and adaptive, and then, subordinate to it, the personality theory proper). The theory proper in Level 3 is where the concepts of the id, ego, and superego, and the drives, are introduced and their relations specified. In the Kohutian version at Level 3, the self is postulated as the organizing center of the personality and its development entails the vicissitudes of narcissism.

Level 2—Empirical psychology
At Level 2 are found empirical laws or law-like statements of relations among the categories and concepts of Level 1. In Freud, we find the defenses, psychosexual stages of development, oedipal theory, and other less abstract ideas. The concepts at this level are amenable to use by the counselor because they explain the observable events found at Level 1.

Level 1—Empirical observation
This is the level of scientific protocol terms or the client's phenomenal report. At Level 1 in Freud's theory, we find such concepts as dreams, symptoms, the affects, derivatives of unconscious wishes, slips of the tongue, and the like. It is these events that are explained at Level 2 and then further abstracted into theoretical propositions at Level 3.

---

conscious or unconscious mind. While the existence of a social and physical reality is assumed in psychoanalytic theory, knowledge of them is not direct, but comes through an act of mind.

With these assumptions about what exists and how we know anything, the psychoanalytic theorist is able to formulate a theory of the person at Level 3 as someone who actively constructs the world from experience. In this theory one also finds a distinction between appearance and reality and between conscious and unconscious ideas. These assumptions about mind as a fundamental reality are logically prior in their generality to all other theoretical ideas. They require that the theorist formulate all other ideas in terms that are logically consistent with these ontological assumptions. More than any other theorist, Freud gives the counselor a comprehensive theory of the person as a resource for understanding the client. His assumptions about mind are what make such theory possible in the first place.

Following from the theory of mind at Level 5 are a few ideas at Level 4 that serve as guides both to theory construction and to the further understanding of client behavior in the interview. We alluded to a few of these ideas earlier, but now we will explain them more fully. In our own work with clients, we have found it helpful to operate with these ideas in constructing a hypothetical model of the client. Any theorist is confronted with questions about how to select and then explain the empirical observations at Level 1 that are of scientific interest. The counselor has the same task in understanding the observations he or she makes in the interview. A complex theory like psychoanalysis provides many possible hypotheses to account for a single phenomenon. These explanations are equivalent to a theory about the theory. They are meta-theoretical or methodological principles on which the theory proper rests. Like the theory of mind, they are more general than the personality theory found at Level 3, or the clinical and treatment theories found mostly at Level 2. We examine below the meta-scientific principles of theory construction used by Freud (Patton & Sullivan, 1980).

Some psychoanalytic principles of explanation

Reductionism   Before 1915, Freud could be termed a *physiological reductionist* in that he attempted to write a theory of human behavior that accorded with what was then known about the nervous system (Freud, 1954). Ever since it was learned that the symptoms of alcohol dementia had physical correlates in the form of lesions in some of the neural pathways of the central nervous system, researchers hoped that similar physical correlates would be found for all neurotic symptoms. So, it is not surprising that Freud had wanted to explain mental processes and structures in terms of the mechanistic constructs of physiology. As pointed out earlier, his attempts to do so can be found in his "Project for a Scientific Psychology" (Freud, 1954). The endeavor failed and Freud began to move further away in his explanatory efforts from the use of the assumption that all events can be reduced to strictly physical objects and processes. After 1915, he began to incorporate principles of theory construction that were more or less logically consistent with the assumption of an active mind and its centrality.

Determinism One such principle is that of *determinism*. This is the principle that directs the scientist and the counselor to look for the antecedents or causes of any event of scientific or therapeutic interest. In other words, if the client is depressed, look for an antecedent event that might have triggered it. Freud believed firmly that all psychic phenomena were strictly determined. As long as he hoped for an ultimate causal explanation in terms of physiological processes and structures, his was a kind of "reductionistic determinism." In abandoning explanation via physiology, however, he did not disavow the importance of determinism in explaining mental events. Instead, he adopted the attitude of determinism by looking for the antecedents of any event of scientific interest to him.

His use of the principle of determinism shows the influence of both Aristotle and the Age of Enlightenment on psychoanalytic thinking. Freud believed, as did Aristotle, that the use of reason was a primary source of knowledge. The Enlightenment was an age when previous doctrines were critically examined from the point of view of rationalism. Thus, upon careful analysis, any event could be understood to have many antecedents. It is not surprising then, that psychoanalytic formulations of the person and of treatment place emphasis upon analyzing resistances as a means to the goal of rationally derived self-knowledge. Through Freud's adherence to the principle of determinism, he brought scientific attention to phenomena such as dreams, humor, slips of the tongue, and transference relations (Sullivan, 1959).

Motivation Another principle in the general theory of psychoanalysis is that of *motivation*. This principle asks the question, what is the source or origin of behavior? Freud's answer to this question was that while reason is a source of behavior, so also is emotion or instinct. He proposed that the basic source of thought and conduct was sexual, broadly conceived. As psychoanalytically oriented counselors, we are instructed to try to understand the client's unconscious sexual (and aggressive) wishes that underly his or her conscious thoughts and actions. The concept of motivation as Freud and other psychoanalytic writers have used it comes from the Age of Romanticism. In his use of this principle, one finds the influence of Goethe, Schopenhauer and other romantic German metaphysicians (Holt, 1973). This principle, when paired with determinism, accounts for the psychoanalytic proposition that every idea and its associated affects reflects the pressures of sexual and/or aggressive trends in the person. Through his adherence to this principle, Freud brought scientific attention to and clarified symptom formation, and was able to introduce the concept of opposing motivational forces in the mind.

On the one hand, Freud's use of the principle of motivation at the level of theory is reductionistic in that the body, or instinct, is the source of behavior. On the other hand, however, and at the level of clinical observation and inference (Levels 1 and 2), the client's conscious or unconscious wishes are accorded motivational status. The concept of wish is teleological, in that it assumes that behavior is goal-directed; that is, the client is motivated to act so as to try to fulfill his or her wishes. The client is also motivated to avoid expression of some of those wishes. Freud's use of the motivation principle in his theory is inconsistent. Logical problems do not arise if both senses of the principle are not invoked at the same level of abstraction. Because we will be using clinical theories in this book, we will operate, for the most part, with the version of the motivation principle that assumes that much of the client's behavior is motivated by wishes; understanding the client's wishes, urges, and longings will be seen to become important tasks for both of the participants in counseling.

Historico-geneticism   Freud and other psychoanalytic theorists have also used the *historico-genetic* principle of explanation in their theory building. For example, if the causes of a symptom or complaint are not to be found in the person's immediate situation, they are to be sought in personal past experiences (history), or in the elements of the personality that were laid down in childhood (genetics). When we understand the client's transferential reference to us as a parental figure, we are using this principle. Through adherence to this principle, Freud brought scientific attention to the importance of early childhood experience for adjustment in adulthood. The use of this principle is reflected in Freud's (1905/1953b) theory of psychosexual development, Erikson's (1950) theory of psychosocial development, Horney's (1939) theory of psychic development, and Kohut's (1977) theory of the development of the self. The historico-genetic principle provides for the explanation of human behavior in terms of elaborate and sequential stages of development, during which the emergent properties of mind become progressively organized and complex. This idea of development comes not only from the Age of Enlightenment, the 1600s forward, but also from Aristotle.

Empathic-introspectionism   In the writings of Freud, and even more prominently in later psychoanalytic writers, especially Greenson (1967), Kohut (1971, 1977, 1984) and Arlow and Brenner (1988), one finds the theorist and practitioner's use of the *empathic-introspective* principle of explanation. This principle assumes that intersubjective understanding between persons is possible, and that such understanding is achieved by using one's own subjective interpretation of the other's actions as the basis for common understanding and concerted action (Patton, 1984; Schutz, 1966, 1967). The empathic-introspective principle of explanation is used in psychoanalysis at several levels. At the level of the theory of personality, the use of this principle informs explanations about the nature and effects of the relationship between parents and child.

In Kohut's (1977) use of this principle, for example, the fragile coherence of the child's sense of self is sustained only if the parents empathically understand the child's need for them to mirror its natural exhibitionism and permit themselves to be targets for the child's idealization. At the level of clinical theory and treatment theory, Greenson (1967) uses the principle in his formulations of the "model of the client" as an aspect of the working alliance between analyst and patient. Present-day psychoanalysts (see Arlow and Brenner, 1988) recognize the importance of empathy for the development and maintenance of the therapeutic relationship.

Kohut (1977) again uses this principle when he speaks of self pathology as due to the person's exposure to traumatic or chronic lapses in parental empathy. As well, Kohut's version of psychoanalytic treatment calls for the analyst to prepare the way for interpretation by preceding it with empathic understanding. Empathy, he contends, is an observational stance from inside rather than from outside the client, and is a kind of "vicarious introspection." Kohut's adherence to this principle at the level of theory brings attention to the importance to the child's development of ongoing parental understanding of, or in-tuneness with, the child's infantile need to find a mirror for its grandiosity and a target for its idealizing. As counselors, we use this principle when we imagine accurately how a client reacted in a situation they are describing to us in an otherwise bland fashion.

Theoretical explanation   Finally, all versions of psychoanalytic thinking show adherence to *theoretical explanation* as a principle. This is the Platonic element in psychoanalysis. Adherence to Platonic notions of explanation in science requires a theory or system which relates ideas, and which becomes an apparatus for the analysis of observed events. By theory or system is meant a set of abstract constructs whose relations to each other are specified, and which explain less abstract constructs that are based on observation. For example, in Freud's theory, the ego is a Level 3 theoretical term whose relationship to equally abstract Level 3 terms like id and superego are specified. Moreover, the concept of the ego explains or accounts for less abstract ideas at Level 2 like repression, which is presumed to be one of the ego's processes. In turn, repression is an inference that can explain the analyst's Level 1 observations of the patient who, during the course of an interview, might be exhibiting wishing, apprehension and forgetting. The point is that the principle of theoretical explanation requires that the mental events the theorist is interested in be explained by a system of ideas that has been based on a methodic examination of all of their related components. The principle of theoretical explanation is the *analytic* element in psychoanalysis, viz. the requirement that one analyze a mental phenomenon into its constituent elements and show its relations to other elements. The *general theory of psychoanalysis* as we understand it is comprised of these particular methodological principles, and the even more general ontological assumption about the existence of an active mind that constructs knowledge from experience. For us, these ideas are meta-theoretical, in that they are implicit or explicit presuppositions found in the many variations of psychoanalytic theory. What is "psychoanalytic" about them is their use in combination. They provide for the view that personality is the developing product of the dynamic interaction of varied forces upon the person, and the understanding of that personality is best accomplished by a careful and detailed analysis of events by recourse to psychoanalytic theory. In summary, using these principles of explanation-building leads to the construction of theories of personality and counseling that provide for the client as active agent, and which call for the rational understanding of events through a systematic analysis of them.

Origins in counseling and counseling psychology

The ideas we use to define the counseling process become more understandable if we also trace their origins and current status in the professional speciality of counseling psychology. In an analysis of the cultural factors responsible for the rise of psychological counseling in the United States, Schmidt (1977) lists the following: (a) the American penchant for experimentation and innovation; (b) a high degree of physical mobility and a premium on individual achievement; and (c) a higher, rising standard of living made possible by technological advances.

The institutional locus for the development of the counseling profession in North America was public and higher education. In concert with the aforementioned cultural factors, education shaped the character of the profession by providing both its predominant value orientations and by specifying the early jobs to be performed; for example, the practice of counseling first developed as vocational guidance, testing, and, later, some personal counseling for adolescents and young adults in the educational setting.

By contrast, psychoanalysis has its origins in the Continental European science, philosophy and medicine of the late 1800s. In spite of Freud's (1926/1959a) advocacy of the training of non-medical analysts, "official" psychoanalysis in North America has been closely associated with training and practice in medicine and psychiatry. The specialty of clinical psychology developed a close relationship with medicine and psychiatry, and hence psychoanalysis, early on (Harrower, 1947) as clinical psychological services were provided in mental hospitals and mental health centers. The opportunities for an early interface between psychoanalysis and the counseling profession in the United States were limited by differences in training and value orientations.

In 1949, a conference, spearheaded by Edmund S. Bordin, on the "Training of Psychological Counselors" (Michigan University, 1950), was jointly sponsored by the then Division of Counseling and Guidance (now the Division of Counseling Psychology; American Psychological Association, 1956) of the American Psychological Association and the University of Michigan. The manifest purpose of the conference was "to consider the most desirable plan for the training of counselors whose background is to be primarily psychological." Further, most counselors were not trained at the doctoral level and many did not have an educational background that was primarily psychological (Michigan University, 1950).

The 12 participants were selected to be representative of two very different views about the training and functions of psychological counselors: one group leaned toward an emphasis on informational and personnel procedures as counselor duties, and the other group favored an emphasis "on objectives of emotional and personality development founded in clinical treatment procedures." Clearly, this book represents an extension of the influence of the latter view. The conference recommendations plainly specified training curricula that were almost entirely psychological in nature, and which included substantial hours of preparation in personality organization and development, psychological assessment and supervised counseling practice and internship. The recommendations on personality organization and development contained considerable evidence of psychoanalytic thinking. This training report and several others that followed helped set the stage for the preparation of *psychological* counselors at the master's and doctoral levels. Doctorally prepared counselors were soon to be known as counseling psychologists. The emphasis on psychological training was in addition to preparation in vocational and educational guidance. These are the events that eventually widened the practice of psychological counseling beyond vocational guidance in North America.

In the main, as counselors began increasingly to identify themselves as professional psychologists, they began to relate themselves to one or more of the dominant emphases in American social science, including behaviorism, pragmatism and humanism (Pepinsky & Pepinsky, 1954). In adopting a behavioristic perspective, counselors have usually eschewed instinctual determinism and have been concerned, instead, with identifying and working on the client's modifiable behaviors. More lately, behaviorism has been coupled with variations of cognitive therapy (Corsini, 1989) as a by-product of the "cognitive revolution" in the behavioral and social sciences (Mahoney & Lyddon, 1988). This has meant a more explicit attention to helping the client change his or her faulty patterns of thinking. A pragmatic orientation has guided the counselor in search of methods that are economical and efficient, and in the development of short-term and focused treatments for such things as enhancing educational and time management skills. The humanistic point of view in counseling has emphasized the intrinsic worth of the individual and the importance of a client's subjective point of view and inherent potential for growth and self-cure. Since the 1970s, feminist perspectives have influenced counseling in the United States, particularly the counseling of women. These perspectives emphasize cultural influences as well as intrapsychic ones, and advocate changes in social structures as well as facilitating client change.

Pepinsky and Pepinsky (1954) note that, historically, priorities in counseling have been placed upon concern for the *whole* individual, including the client's social and emotional well-being, and upon training for educational and vocational success. Now, however, and to the dismay of some, professional counselors have moved beyond the educational setting to join other workers in the competitive public and private health care arena (Fitzgerald & Osipow, 1988). The counselor stands somewhat uneasily at the interface between the two domains of education and health care (see Patton, 1982b). The traditional priorities in counseling have been extended today to include helping individuals and groups understand and respond sensitively to an increasingly broad range of individual differences in life style and development manifest among members of the society. This range includes, but is not limited to, mental and physical disability, gender, ethnicity, and associational preference.

The move from vocational guidance to psychological counseling (Super, 1955) was accomplished by a number of psychologists immediately following World War II. One impetus for this transition was the pressure on counselors to become "professional" (Pepinsky & Pepinsky, 1954). Another impetus was the counseling program of the United States Veterans Administration, which made both a title and jobs available. Edward S. Bordin was an early and leading proponent of the movement to upgrade the training of counselors. As noted above, Bordin and others (Michigan University, 1950) worked successfully for extensive preparation in psychology in the overall training of counselors. Over the years, Bordin's (1943, 1948, 1968, 1979, 1981) evolving views of the counseling interview, and of the interaction between the client and the counselor as dynamic psychological phenomena, have been influential in the training of counselors and in research on the counseling process. Bordin (1968) was explicit in stating that counseling is a "process based on psychological foundations." His emphasis on preparing counselors in psychology helped make it possible to introduce them to psychoanalytic ideas as well.

More than anyone else, Bordin (1968) is responsible for having adapted psychoanalytic ideas to counseling theory, research, and practice in the United States (see Bordin, 1955, 1964, 1968, 1979, 1981). Early evidence of Bordin's psychoanalytic thinking can be found in the training reports mentioned above. He was able to see how psychoanalytic theories of development (Freud, 1905/1953b; Erikson, 1950), for example, were logically compatible with the tasks of counselors. From the beginning, those tasks had been defined, variously, as helping individuals in ". . .overcoming obstacles to their personal growth, wherever these may be encountered, and toward achieving optimum development of their personal resources" (American Psychological Association, 1952). The psychoanalytic assumption that development entails the emergence of the child's innate capacities, its increasing mastery of biological, social, and psychological tasks, and its overall adaptation to a context of environmental demands are compatible with the value orientations of counseling psychologists.

Bordin and his colleagues also pioneered in extending psychoanalytic ideas to theory and research in vocational development and career counseling (Bordin, Nachmann & Segal, 1963; Nachmann, 1960; Segal, 1961, 1965). He believes, for example, that vocational development and career decision-making are best understood in light of ongoing personality development. Such development shapes the underlying drive and defense structures so that certain vocational interests are characteristic of the person and certain vocational environments are therefore more appropriate than others (Bordin, 1943, 1979). Through all of this, Bordin (1968) has always insisted that our understanding of counseling be based on observation and research. Thus, the influence of psychoanalytic thinking on his ideas about counseling has been regularly accompanied by an active program of research. His interest in the research endeavor has extended our knowledge of the utility of such psychoanalytic ideas as free association and ambiguity in counseling (Bordin, 1955, 1964) and of the working alliance (Greenson, 1967) in counselor training (Bordin, 1979). His concern for making his own ideas refutable has also served to improve research methods in counseling (Bordin, 1965). Bordin's (1968) theoretical writings on personality organization and on counseling and psychotherapy process have further illustrated how other psychoanalytic propositions can be usefully modified to fit the parameters of the counseling situation. These include, but are not limited to, the notion of the multiply-determined nature of human motives (Bordin, 1968), and the role of resistance and transference in the therapeutic process (Bordin, 1968).

More lately, his evolving views of the therapeutic process have focused on the centrality of the working alliance, and the advantages to the counselor and researcher of a time-limited approach to counseling (Bordin, 1979). His ideas about time-limited approaches to counseling have been influenced by the work of the psychoanalyst James Mann (1973) and his model of time-limited therapy. His conception of a time-limited psychodynamically-oriented counseling process includes the setting up of an effective working alliance that is characterized by agreement upon the tasks and goals of the work and by a firm emotional bond between the counselor and client.

With the working alliance in place, the counselor's interventions are stated in psychodynamic terms and aimed at one of the client's conscious conflicts that have been selected as a focus of the work. The client is understood in terms of his or her position *vis-à-vis* a stage of development. The purpose of counseling is to promote the client's development, rather than to remediate the client's past failures. Hence, the counselor avoids getting drawn into a search of the client's past. The statement of an explicit focus or goal for the work also helps the counselor and the client stay on task.

Psychoanalytic ego psychology (S. Freud, 1923/1961b; A. Freud, 1936a; Hartmann, 1939; Erikson, 1950) has also been another source of extrapolation to the counseling situation. Ego psychologists generally have stressed the adaptive functions of the ego and its role in conscious problem-solving and decision-making. In this way, the task of the counselor involves strengthening the ego's capacities or assets and helping it cope with reality. A leading writer and practitioner of ego counseling has been Paul King (King, 1965; King & Neal, 1968; King & Bennington, 1971).

In King's adaptation of psychoanalytic ideas, the counselor has as the main task the strengthening of the ego. In more clinically based language, this means helping the client develop his or her assets, gain a sense of mastery over his or her situation, and assist the client in viewing his or her impulses as manageable. Intervention in most forms of ego therapy, according to King & Neal (1968):

> ". . . is a direct attempt to understand the basic introjects (usually parental) of the client that are maladaptive and to dislodge or integrate such introjects into the client's everyday emotional life" (p. 82).

Ego counseling techniques (King & Bennington, 1971; King & Neal, 1968) include "echoing," or confronting the client with his or her low regard for self; counselor "self-devaluating," in which the counselor induces the client to let go of hostility toward the counselor; and exaggerating or caricaturing aspects of the client's problems. Other techniques include the analysis in detail of the client's injuries and conflicts, in order to provide the ego with knowledge; and free imagery, in which the client's defenses are circumvented, conflicted wishes are surfaced through fantasy production, and the client is provided with a sense of therapeutic movement (King & Bennington, 1971). The influence of King's contribution to the introduction of psychoanalytic ideas to counseling resides in his presentation of the relevance of ego psychology for counseling. He adapted ideas about the ego and made them a part of an approach to briefer counseling that was successful in his clinical work with adolescents and young adults in the university counseling center setting.

Gelso's (Gelso & Johnson, 1983; Gelso & Carter, 1985; Peabody & Gelso, 1982) work on time-limited therapy and the working alliance has also shown evidence of psychoanalytic thinking. In a major program of research on time-limited counseling at the University of Maryland, Gelso and his colleagues incorporated several psychoanalytic concepts in their research. Notably, these researchers point out that the conception of time-limited therapy itself grows out of the psychoanalytic tradition (see Freud, 1916/1961a; Sifneos, 1972; Mann, 1973; Malan, 1976). Gelso & Johnson (1983) report that Mann's (1973) time-limited model of therapy was the dominant model used by the majority of practitioners who participated in their research. A study of this model focuses upon such phenomena as client intrapsychic conflict, client resistance, client positive and negative transference, and counselor countertransference. More recently, Gelso & Carter (1985) have very usefully adapted Greenson's (1967) ideas about the working alliance between patient and analyst by generalizing it across different therapeutic orientations to illustrate its applications.

Patton and his colleagues at the Universities of Utah, Tennessee, and Missouri have been attempting to define and illustrate the applications of psychoanalytic ideas to theory and practice in counseling through their research and writing for some years now. In a series of writings focused on clinical applications, Patton (1980a, 1980b, 1981a); Patton & Sullivan (1980), Patton & Robbins (1982), and Robbins (1989) have dealt with such topics as alcohol and other drug abuse as narcissistic behavior disorders; the theoretical and philosophical differences between the ideas of Freud and Kohut; the applications of Kohut's ideas to college student counseling; shame proneness, devaluing of the counselor, and adolescent narcissistic vulnerability as applications of Kohut's (1977) self psychology; and the contributions of contemporary psychoanalysis to counseling.

In addition, this group has been conducting research on the measurement of certain psychoanalytic concepts (Robbins & Patton, 1986). To aid in this task, they have developed a multivariate model (Patton, 1981b) of the counseling process, in which the dimensions and their measurable elements (see Chapters 6 and 13) are derived from psychoanalytic thinking about client behavior and the process of psychoanalytic treatment (Patton, 1981b). Part of this effort has included the use of ideas from Kohut's (1971, 1977, 1984) psychoanalytic psychology of the self in constructing client self-report measures and rating scales to assess narcissism variables in the counseling process (Patton, Connor & Scott, 1982; Robbins & Patton, 1985; Lapan & Patton, 1986; Shreve & Patton, 1988). Finally, Efstation, Patton & Kardash (1990) have developed measures of the working alliance (see Greenson,

1967) between a supervisor and a trainee in counselor training and have examined its utility in predicting training outcomes.

Steve Robbins (1987a) and his students at Virginia Commonwealth University have usefully extended psychoanalytic ideas to studies of time-limited counseling (Robbins & Von Galambos, 1988), countertransference in counseling (Robbins & Jolkovski, 1987), and the working alliance (Golden & Robbins, 1990). As well, this same group of investigators have applied some of Kohut's ideas about narcissism to the study of aging (Smith & Robbins, 1988; Robbins, Payne & Chartrand, 1990), career development (Robbins & Tucker, 1986; Robbins, 1987b) and academic adjustment in college (Scott & Robbins, 1985; Robbins & Schwitzer, 1988).

Since 1980 there has been a rapid growth in the applications of psychoanalytic ideas to research and practice in psychological counseling, as evidenced by published articles in the leading counseling journals and by presentations at national professional meetings of counselors and counseling psychologists in North America (Robbins, 1989; Robbins, 1986; Patton, 1987). As noted above, the historical groundwork for this growth has been laid by the seminal work of Edward Bordin and built upon by others. In the following chapters, our debt to this history will become apparent as we explicate our views on psychoanalytic counseling.

A perspective for this book

The remaining chapters of this book contain in greater detail information about how the counselor can function from a psychoanalytic point of view. We approach counseling as a situation in which the psychoanalytically informed counselor works to assist the client to develop insight into him or herself, and to function with a broader range of thoughts, feelings, and actions than had been available previously. We assume that much of the client's emotional difficulty arises from developmentally-based conflicts and that the task of counseling is to help the client resolve these conflicts and begin to grow again.

We have drawn upon psychoanalytic theory as an approach to counseling because we believe it provides a comprehensive and clinically relevant theory for understanding both the client and the counseling process and its outcomes. Within this perspective, counseling will be seen to be a planful process informed by the counselor's careful use of observations and inferences about the client. By emphasizing the counselor's use of observation and inference, we are advocating the counselor's deliberate functioning as both scientist and practitioner (see Pepinsky & Pepinsky, 1954). This means that the counselor will use observation and inference to formulate interventions that test his or her deductions from the psychoanalytic theoretical structure.

The chapters that follow in Part I of this book provide considerable material from which deductions can be drawn to account for the counselor's observations of the client. The clinical vignettes in all the chapters, and the technical material in the chapters in Part II, illustrate in a broad sense the applications of the deductive process. The final chapter on research discusses various methodologies for the conduct of scientific inquiry on counseling and presents several measurement instruments that can be used in both the assessment of clients and research on counseling.

Ours is an evolving understanding of the psychoanalytic counseling process. Much of the material in this book has been written with the hope of making psychoanalytic ideas accessible and useful to professional counselors. We are aware that the approach we have taken in the book is only one among many ways of writing about the applications of psychoanalysis to theory, research, and practice in counseling.

2 The counselor's theory of the client I: intrapsychic conflict and psychosexual development

Psychoanalytic counseling is different from most other forms of counseling in several ways (Corsini, 1989). A prominent way in which it is different is the demand psychoanalysis makes upon the counselor to observe or listen carefully, understand the client's behavior in depth, and then to take action based upon that knowledge, such that it promotes the client's self-understanding and independence. Psychoanalytic counseling requires that the counselor master and then put together the concepts, processes and relations of theories that pertain to the client and to the process of counseling. While the psychoanalytic counselor uses empathic understanding and his or her own affective reactions as important ways of comprehending the client, it is also the case that the counselor does considerable intellective work during the interview. That is, the psychoanalytic counselor uses empathy to think and feel along with the client in everyday terms, but it is also the case that it is critical for the counselor to acquire an objective understanding of client communications by using a knowledge of theory (Greenson, 1967).

In this chapter we will first make a few comments about the role of theory in counseling to help prepare the way for what follows. Then we will present the psychoanalytic theory of intrapsychic conflict and symptom formation. This will be accomplished by defining and discussing the elements of conflict, how they appear in mental life and their outcome as symptoms or compromise formations. Conflict often has its origins during the first critical years of life when the child develops age-appropriate fears about itself and its world. We will also include, therefore, a consideration of the contribution made to conflict by events during the psychosexual stages of development. Last, we will illustrate the foregoing with clinical material taken from an actual case.

The counselor's use of theory in counseling performs at least three important functions. First, theory helps the counselor organize the client's communications and other observations about the client into a systematic understanding of the client's problems (Pepinsky & Pepinsky, 1954; Anderson, 1967; Langs, 1973). In psychoanalysis this sort of theory is the so-called "clinical theory," or, more specifically, the theory about how the person has developed and maintained his or her problems. Psychoanalytic clinical theory is a rich resource for understanding the client's complaints and symptoms, and how they came to be.

Second, theory serves as a guide for the counselor's interventions with the client, both in a single interview and in the overall planning of the course of counseling across a series of interviews. This kind of theory is the treatment and/or interview theory. Interview theory helps account for events in the single hour (Bibring, 1954; Menninger, 1958). Theory that tries to account for the sequence of events over a series of interviews is the theory of treatment which is, of course, more encompassing (Freud, 1913/1958a). Both cases, interview and treatment theory, can help the counselor by aiding in the formulation of desired outcomes and in determining the criteria for assessing those outcomes.

Third, theory serves as a source of hypotheses for the counselor to use in developing and then testing the accuracy of interventions against the client's confirming or disconfirming response (Langs, 1973). In summary, use of theory permits the counselor to frame tentative inferences based on observations of the client which in turn are used to understand and intervene with the client. As a scientist–practitioner, the counselor frames inferences so that they are open to refutation and/or revision based on data the client provides (see Pepinsky & Pepinsky, 1954). Thus, ideally each interview and treatment across a series of interviews is not only clinically beneficial for a client, but also adds to the counselor's understanding of the science and practice of counseling.

In this chapter, we will present our understanding of the classical psychoanalytic theory of the client, or clinical theory. In the next chapter we will present an alternative to the classical theory by including Heinz Kohut's (1971, 1977, 1984) psychoanalytic self psychology. The classical theory of the client (Fenichel, 1945) derives from psychoanalytic personality theory (cf. Freud, 1893/1962a, 1896/1962b, 1894/1962c, 1912/1958b) and is, thus, less abstract or general (see Chapter 1, Table 1.2). It is a theory of the person with emotional difficulties. Theories of the client specify the underlying conditions within the client for which help is needed and how those conditions developed. In the classical theory, the central emotional difficulty is intrapsychic conflict of one or more kinds. An understanding of intrapsychic conflict entails an understanding of symptom formation.

The elements of conflict

The theory of intrapsychic conflict represents the dynamic and developmental points of view in the psychoanalytic metapsychology. The fundamental proposition is that there are emergent tendencies in the mind that strive toward expression and, hence, gratification, and that there are also counter-tendencies that oppose expression. In its simplest form, we have seen in Chapter 1 Freud's (1893/1962a) original explanation of intrapsychic conflict. There, the outcome of the conflict between the unconscious wish and the act of repression that opposed the wish was a recognizable symptom. The symptom was seen as a compromise among the contending forces in the mind. Later formulations (Freud, 1923/1961b; Brenner, 1982) of the classical conflict theory have greatly expanded the definition of what constitutes a compromise formation as the outcome of conflict. Some compromises are seen as healthy adaptations, while others are maladaptive. In the latter instance, character traits, attitudes, perceptions, habitual modes of thought, as well as symptoms, can be maladaptive. The classical theory specifies that all products of mental life are compromises among the forces in the mind. It is important for the counselor, therefore, to recognize which among the many observations of the client are those that deserve attention as maladaptive compromise formations.

From his ongoing observations of his patients and reformulations of the theory of the origin of neurosis, Freud (1926/1959c) eventually assigned the affects and conflict a central place in the theory. The result of his efforts was a more complete formulation of the theory of symptom formation. Symptoms are now to be seen as the maladaptive consequences of conflict. This means that symptoms and other manifestations of emotional difficulty are compromises between opposing tendencies in the mind. Compromises are composed, then, of various elements which have a course of development that is unique for each person. To understand the client's behavior clearly, it is necessary to identify and understand how each of the elements of the compromise formation are present and active in the client, as well as to understand how the compromise formation came about.

As a brief preface to our discussion of the elements of conflict, the counselor needs to understand that symptoms and other compromise formations occur in a dynamic sequence in the person. Knowledge of their formation requires understanding of the role of adaptation (Hartmann, 1939, 1951). In pointing out that symptoms and other disordered behavior patterns of the client are compromises, we are highlighting their function as attempts at adaptation to the demands of internal and external reality. Environmental demands form an adaptive context (Langs, 1973) to which the person must respond. When those demands are perceived as stressful, the person may respond with symptoms. If so, it is because the person perceives the present demand(s) as similar in some way to an earlier traumatic event. Under such conditions, the person regresses to forms of adapting that were used in coping with the original stressful event (Westfall, 1964). In the symptom or other maladaptive behavior may be seen all the elements of conflict. In our discussion of the elements of conflict and psychosexual development, we will draw extensively upon the ideas of Brenner (1982), Erikson (1950), and Anderson (1967).

Drives: the first element

The first element in conflict is the drive or wish. Classical psychoanalytic theory specifies that we are impelled to action by two classes of stimulus events, libido and aggression. Libido is the term used for the sexual drive and it has its source in the regions of the body that can be used sexually. The primary areas are the mouth, anus, and the genitals. However, almost any part of the body can be used for sexual purposes, including the sensory functions of sight, sound, taste, and touch. The aim of the libido is to bring about experiences of pleasure or gratification (Freud, 1905/1953b). Freud (1920/1955) identified aggression as the destructive drive whose aim is the obliteration of self, other, or both. As with the libido, he gave aggression a somatic source in the tendency of the body (as with all organic substance) to disintegrate or die.

In our opinion, the concept of drive is not a satisfactory concept for clinical purposes because it leaves the person and her or his active contribution to the problem out of the picture. It is necessary, however, to think of libido and aggression as having somatic origins, in that the body makes an important contribution to the psychological life of the client. In this way, and closer to the level of clinical observation, libido and aggression manifest themselves as wishes which motivate the client to take action. Libidinous or loving wishes can then be observed directly in the client's actions or inferred through more indirect expressions. In the same manner, aggressive wishes can be noted in the client's self-directed punitive actions or in aggression toward others.

A wish is an unconscious derivative of the drive, and its content is specific to the individual. A wish is something to be gratified, and, in their pure form, wishes press for immediate and unmediated fulfillment. Wishes represent the operation of the pleasure principle in human behavior. In the normal case, the original primitive nature of their sexual or aggressive content becomes channeled and modified in its expression as the person matures. In cases where conflict has reached unhealthy proportions, however, one can frequently observe the expression of primitive wishes in the client's maladaptive compromise formations.

As counselors, we need to learn as much as we can about each client's unconscious sexual and aggressive wishes. It is these wishes that are the first element in creating conflict and compromise.

For example, a 30-year-old male client reports to the counselor that he unwittingly left the front door of his house open when leaving after an argument with his spouse. The effect of leaving the door open creates a large draft that fuels the fire in a free-standing woodburning stove in the living room. We would not be amiss if we inferred that the client harbored murderous wishes about his spouse on this occasion.

Unpleasant affect: the second element

Sexual or aggressive wishes do not trigger psychic conflict unless they arouse sufficiently intense, unpleasant affects. Superego demands and prohibitions accompanied by guilt can also arouse anxiety and depression, which in turn trigger conflict. For now, however, we can note that affects are psychological phenomena that consist of a sensation of pleasure or unpleasure coupled with an idea or memory. Brenner (1982) suggests that affects which activate conflict are of two broad kinds, anxiety and depression. While we will use a broader classification for the affects, Brenner's definition of anxiety and depression are useful for the counselor in their own right. He indicates that anxiety is an affect that is composed of an unpleasant sensation accompanied by the idea that something bad is going to happen. Anxiety can be noted in the client's expressions of dread, foreboding, apprehension, or hesitation. Depression is an affect that is composed of an unpleasant sensation and the idea that something bad has already happened. Among other manifestations, depressive affect is noted when the client experiences such things as hopelessness, loss of love, remorse, loss of self-esteem, and the like. Wishes that are intense in their insistence on gratification and are unacceptable to consciousness in their content evoke anxiety and/or depression, thus setting the stage for intrapsychic conflict.

On his way to work, the client mentioned above in the section on drives or wishes began to experience considerable anxiety whose source or cause was then unknown to him. He was visibly shaking and breathing rapidly. He imagined that some terrible calamity was going to befall him, and he had the urge to turn around and return home.

Ideas of calamity in developmental sequence: the third element

In psychoanalytic theory, ideas always have associated affects. Only when the ideas or the affects are painful is there likely to be an artificial separation or splitting of idea from affect. In this case, the unity of conscious experience is broken apart, and either the idea or the affect, or both, can be split off and rendered unconscious. The ideas with which unpleasant affects are connected are derivatives of the typical fearful situations experienced during the childhood stages of psychosexual development. That is, the ideas associated with anxiety and/or depression have to do with: (a) loss of the object; (b) fear of the loss of the object's love; (c) castration, or more generally, a fear of injury; and (d) fear of punishment. As is apparent, these calamitous ideas parallel the early psychosexual stages of development (Freud, 1905/1953b).

By way of explanation, we will note here that the term "object," as it is used in psychoanalytic theory, refers to the person's mental representation of self, other, and events in the world. An object is a psychological structure through which the person experiences events (Patton & Sullivan, 1980). Objects, then, can be faithful to the reality they represent, or they can be a distortion of it. In either case, objects, once constructed, are the targets of the person's sexual and aggressive wishes. They change or develop over time in accord with the stages of development.

Each of the stages of development can be differentiated according to its own unique features in the manifestations of the sexual and aggressive drives and the organization of mental life. Moreover, each stage involves a set of psychosocial tasks to be mastered and an accompanying crisis to be resolved (Erikson, 1950). The resolution at each stage can have, then, a positive or negative outcome that influences later mental health. The first 5 or 6 years of life are never totally abandoned or supplanted. Experiences during the early years leave their unconscious mark on our attitudes, values, and behaviors. We are not aware of the extent to which we are influenced by our early years because we often do not remember events clearly, if at all, prior to the age of 6. It is as if childhood amnesia divides our life into two parts (Anderson, 1967).

During each stage the child exhibits a characteristic way of thinking and behaving that is superseded by the next stage. Even so, the vestiges of the earlier stage are still be to found in the succeeding stages and throughout life. In fact, early stages can be brought to life again by regression, which is exactly what happens in the development of maladaptive compromise formations. Later stresses and traumatic events can prompt a return to earlier and less mature forms of thinking and behaving, and hence the development of maladaptive compromise formations. It should be noted that, in addition to regression prompting conflict, later difficulties can also be presaged by an arrest in development at any stage. In this way, important aspects of the personality fail to grow and develop. Thus, unresolved crises at each stage are like defects and represent developmental failures or fixation points, influencing development at subsequent stages. Early failures successively diminish the child's chances for healthy development in the later stages. Let us turn now to a consideration of each of the early stages of development and the typical fears associated with them. In doing so, we will adapt Anderson's (1967) characterization of the child's behavior in each of the developmental stages as we present the fears typical of that stage.

The oral stage   Experiences during the first year of life influence how events thereafter will be looked at by the person. The human environment into which the child has been born is experienced as a pleasant place if he or she is cared for and responded to lovingly. The basis for trust and the formation of loving affectionate relationships are made possible in this stage if the above conditions prevail. Moreover, the capacity to tolerate being alone is nurtured during this phase (Winnicott, 1958). The ability to predict when food and attention will be forthcoming, and experiencing it as part of a tie to a loving mother, lay the groundwork for a trusting or mistrusting bond with reality. The child's wishes during this stage are organized around the oral zone because the mouth is the leading organ for gratification at this time. In consequence, early forms of oral gratification leave their permanent stamp on the personality because of their primacy. Consider the following example:

A dentist of one of us who knew his patient was a psychologist once asked why so many people were so protective of their mouths. In reply, he was asked to think about all the things adults did with their mouths that involve gratification or satisfaction. After he thought about it, his list included breathing, chewing, sucking, swallowing, kissing, spitting out, and talking. He said he guessed he had answered his own question.

During the first stage, the child is building up a reservoir of positive memories through the development of mental objects. Infantile objects during the early portion of the oral stage are primitive and incomplete in their features. The infant's representation of the mother or primary caretaker, for example, may consist of fantastic images of power and nuturance, contrasted with equally unrealistic images of aggression. This is a time of "primary narcissism" in the development of libido. Only over time do the child's object representations become transformed into more stable and reality-based percepts in which the child's image of the mother is associated with satisfaction or pain.

Freud's concern with libidinal development is complemented by Mahler's (see Mahler, Pine & Bergman, 1975) more object-relations emphasis on the development of psychological separation and individuation. Here, the first 3 or 4 months of life are known as the stage of symbiosis or "omnipotent fusion" with the care-giver. During this stage there is not a clear distinction between self and other in the infant's mind. Yet, later during the first year, the child becomes differentiated from the mother as it enters what Mahler, Pine & Bergman (1975) call the stage of separation-individuation.

Fear of loss of the object has to do, then, with the child's experience of having been deprived or separated from a loving mother or other care-taking figure. It may also have to do with the child's own aggressiveness, which occurs in the urge to bite, spit out, or refuse to take in. Ideas that one's own aggressiveness may drive away or destroy the mother contribute to loss. During the oral stage the child is just learning how to construct and maintain a mental representation of the mothering figure. Once constructed, and no matter how fragile it may be, the object becomes the inner ideal parent and will be projected to all women if their primary care-giver was a woman. After the object is formed it is, at first, a fragile thing. The cohesion or firmness of the early objects depends not only upon the reliable gratification provided to the child by the parents, but also on their ongoing physical presence with the child. It takes time to be able to keep the object in memory when the actual person it represents is absent. To assist in this process, children often adopt an object, such as a blanket or doll, from which they are inseparable for a time. Such "transitional objects" help the child bridge the gap between mother's presence and absence (Winnicott, 1953). Retaining the gratifying object in memory helps promote patience and trust (Erikson, 1950).

Loss of the mother or care-giver through parental neglect, indifference, abuse, or death is a traumatic experience of catastrophic proportions for the child, given its utter dependence. Loss of the object at an early age can make the person unusually vulnerable to separation and loss throughout life. Such loss seriously undermines the child's trust in self and others, as well as its capacity to develop affectionate relations with others. It weakens the tie with reality, if, indeed, one had been forged in the first place. Therefore, the activation of a sexual or aggressive wish that gives rise to ideas of object loss can trigger anxiety or depression. The following example illustrates how client anxiety can be related to childhood fears of loss.

A 27-year-old female graduate student kept a strict rein on her aggressive thoughts and lived the life of a nurturing, protecting, caretaking person who had nothing but love to give others. Her choice of vocation matched this personality orientation. She just knew that if she ever told her fiancé that she was angry with him he would leave, if not sicken and die. The growing awareness that she was very angry with him made her increasingly anxious. The client's mother had suffered from a debilitating and lingering illness during the client's first 2 years. Because the mother was cared for at home, the client was not permitted to turn to her mother for comfort and attention and also had to curtail many normal childhood pleasures at this time so as not to disturb the mother. She vaguely remembers being angry at her mother on many occasions. The mother eventually died in the family home when the child was 4 years old.

The anal stage   The second stage begins where the first leaves off, around the age of 2 years. It usually extends until about the age of 4. During this stage, it is normal for the child to want to exercise its developing intellectual and motor abilities. This includes exercising control over one's body and its functions. Experience has not yet taught the child that it does not possess magical and omnipotent powers, and it becomes angry, if not enraged, when life reminds it that one has limitations and obligations. The child struggles with both the physical and the social world by saying "No!" or its counterpart in aggressiveness, running away, defiance, or argument. It has been said that the most important task of a 2-year-old is deciding whether to be good or bad; whether to cooperate or to tyrannize (Anderson, 1967; Erikson, 1950). It is not unusual, therefore, to observe 2- and 3-year-olds defying their parents by becoming oppositional. It takes time for the child to learn patience, cooperation, acquiescence, and sacrifice. This is because the child in the second stage thinks in opposite extremes as a way of defending its fragile independence. Things are good or bad, black or white, right or wrong, clean or dirty, and there are no extenuating circumstances.

The development of a negative identity and an oppositional character are possible dangers in this stage because of the child's automatic opposition to any authority. Parental requests of the child are often met with a firm "No!" It takes skillful, patient and empathically in-tune parents to both protect the child from itself and, at the same time, preserve its growing autonomy. This struggle with the parents is important for the development of the child's personality. The struggle focuses upon the child's wishes about how to use its body, and particularly the function, training, and evacuation of the bowels. The quality of the experiences around this important task helps build a sense of autonomy or a sense of humiliation or shame. Thus, the outcomes for the child are either a sense of acceptance or a sense of alienation. In toilet training, the youngster is required for the first time to take personal responsibility and introduce order into its daily routine.

If, however, such occasions become a call to battle between parents and child, the parents are the usual winners because they are bigger and smarter. The child will capitulate because it is willing to sacrifice its autonomy in order to retain the parents' love. The child takes in the parental attitudes and standards as its own. The child likes what the parents like and hates what they hate; their friends are the child's friends, and the like. In the child's mind, as Anderson (1967) notes, there are only two choices: either accept parental authority and direct your hostility elsewhere, and thereby hold in check aggression and rebellion directed to the parents, or be prepared to accept the outcome of conflict with the parents; that is, loss of love.

But, while unthoughtful parents may succeed in coercing the child to change its behavior from defiance to compliance, the child's angry inner thoughts and feelings are likely to remain active, albeit unconscious. When an outward compliance and cooperativeness have been created under duress, an inner life of opposite convictions persists and can erupt with violence under certain circumstances.

The critically important outcome for this stage of development is the phase-appropriate modification of the child's sexual and aggressive wishes. Up to now they are both expressed in direct, primitive form. The child's libidinal, that is, loving, feelings are readily expressed when it is pleased by something or someone; and its aggressive feelings are made very clear when it hates something. The aggressive wishes are particularly ruthless, fierce and punitive. The experiences a child has during this and the previous stage of development are the forerunners of the formation of the superego and the conscience at the next stage. The healthy adaptation of the sexual and aggressive wishes at this stage help create a conscience in the next stage that is free from sadistic and self-punitive trends. Moreover, the child achieves autonomy in the exercise of its mind and body, rather than doubting its capacities and submerging its initiative to the authority of someone else.

With regard to later conflict, the activation of angry wishes from this stage of development can elicit anxiety or depression associated with ideas that the parents will withdraw their love and approval or have already done so because of the child's "badness." The vignette below points out some of the vagaries of a fear of loss of love.

A 37-year-old divorced mother of four children was convinced that she was unlovable because of her badness. In her view, her three failed marriages were evidence of this fact. Hadn't her parents, after all, made it abundantly clear that they disapproved of her? Longer-term work with this client eventually revealed the extent to which she had identified with her parents' negative image of her as a means of feeling connected to them.

The oedipal stage   The fundamental structures of the personality are formed in the third stage, which coincides with the fourth through the sixth year. As well, the characteristic manner of personality expression is accomplished at this time (Anderson, 1967). Whether the person is outgoing or restrained, stability-seeking or change-oriented, will be decided during this period of development. Later modifications and elaborations will occur but, for the most part, the foundations of the adult personality structure are set in place. Certain kinds of observations can regularly be made of children during the third, or oedipal, stage. One can note how play has taken on an interactive and more cooperative tone. The content of the play as well as the child's fantasies at this stage make evident how play serves as a rehearsal for the tasks of later life. As well, the child is preoccupied with what it will be when it grows up, and this indicates how much its play models what the child perceives to be the interests of the adult. One can also observe the child actively comparing itself in size, attractiveness, strength, skill, and intelligence to those around it.

The child becomes notably competitive at this stage and wants to win in the games it plays with others. Both boys and girls cheat and lie to ensure victory. The child's curiosity is strong at this period, and especially so about sexual matters. Oedipal children take rather intense interest and pride in their own genitals and are quite curious about the genitals of the persons around them. When they become aware of the anatomical differences between the sexes, it is often accompanied by fear and ideas of castration and other forms of bodily injury. Masturbation is the center of the child's sexual life at this time. The activity is dangerous in the sense that the fantasies that accompany it arouse fears. Moreover, if the parents curb it in punitive ways, it may be difficult to transfer mature sexual urges to the person's own initiative and control.

During this stage the child finds ways to focus and make known its loving and possessive wishes, especially toward the parent of the other sex. In this way, children take a stand in what Freud (1909/1959b) called the "family romance," placing themselves between the parents. At the same time, however, they develop rivalrous thoughts and feelings for the parent of the same sex. These thoughts give rise to anxiety because they include a wish for the death of the rival parent which is accompanied by fears of retaliation. All of this sets the stage for a conflict of severe proportions for the child. The child's need for the parents, its love for them, and its hatred, jealousy and fear, all lead to a resolution of this complex in which the child represses these incestuous urges and hateful tendencies and identifies with the parents (Freud, 1905/1953b). The repression and identification set up in the child's mind the psychological structure called the "superego."

The child needs considerable help in resolving the crisis at this period. Understanding parents are helpful in preventing the child's further humiliation or deliberate sexual stimulation. They help the child enter into a cooperative partnership with them, retaining tender feelings for the parental love objects, but later the ability to direct sexual interest to persons outside the family. While all persons retain traces of the incestuous and destructive wishes of the oedipal period, most are able to live in harmony with themselves because they have developed a balance among instinctual impulses, their conscience, and the demands of outer reality. The incomplete resolution of the oedipal complex means that the person has not abandoned his or her incestuous or murderous plans, but waits until he or she is old enough to carry them out in direct or attenuated ways. In classical psychoanalytic theory, the maladaptive compromise formations of adulthood are decisively influenced by the oedipal crisis.

Freud (1924/1961d) stated that the superego is the heir of the oedipus complex. By this he meant that the child's resolution of the conflict by means of repression and identification establishes an internal set of standards, values, ideals, and patterns for behavior. But, as has been alluded to several times above, the superego is also a component of conflict (Brenner, 1982). Our concern with it in the context of conflict is that the superego is responsible for the person's tendency to want to inflict self-punishment. A need to punish oneself can have the same function in creating a conflict that a loving or aggressive wish has (Brenner, 1982).

The superego metes out disapproval in the form of guilt and shame. For Freud (1924/1961d), guilt and shame are the same thing as the fear of punishment. In the child, to be good is to do as one is told or expected to do, and is a matter of avoiding the calamity of guilt/shame, or self-inflicted punishment. The important ingredient is what the child believes will bring parental approval or disapproval; what the child fantasizes about in this regard is decisive in determining its behavior.

Thus, for example, the child is willing to suffer if it means that parental love will continue to be forthcoming or that parental disapproval will be forestalled. The intensity of childhood sexual and aggressive wishes toward the parents and siblings is what influences the child to believe it will be punished for those wishes and behaviors. Compliance with parental dictates helps mitigate the anxiety and depressive affect that may be aroused with the wishes. When the child identifies with the parents' real or fantasized prohibitions, such behavior may include becoming strict, moralistic, intolerant, and self-punishing. In any case, the result is that the child is strengthened in its ability to defend against wishes that give rise to painful affects. With regard to the superego's role in conflict, then, oedipal wishes can arouse a need to punish oneself, which in turn elicits anxiety or depression, associated thoughts and, finally, defense. Guilt or shame, that is, self-inflicted punishment, is the last of the childhood calamities.

Unlike Freud (1925/1961e), we do not take the position that anatomy is destiny. A nexus of biological, social, and psychological factors undoubtedly shapes the sexual status and accompanying attitudes that society, for good or ill, assigns to its members at birth (Garfinkel, 1967). Notably, the sequelae of oedipal conflicts for women and men regularly include a sense of inferiority (shame). In the case of women, however, the self-perception of inferiority that regularly accompanies conflict at the oedipal stage has often been intensified by social attitudes, values, and practices that demean women because they are women.

The following vignette illustrates the role of guilt in the attempt to ward off anxiety-provoking thoughts of punishment.

A 32-year-old, divorced, male client reported in counseling that he had become involved romantically with a married woman who, he was quick to point out, had initially approached him to express her interest in him. He reassured the counselor, as well, that he would only engage in sexual intercourse with her if she initiated the activity. Not long after this he reported that they had slept together, but it was her idea. Moreover, he went on to say that what really excited him about being with the woman was the clandestine nature of their relationship, and the possibility that her husband might find out. It was only much later in the work that the client could link his behavior in this instance to his ongoing struggles with his parents. In a word, he had retained an incestuous interest in his mother and expressed it in derivative form through a liaison with a married woman. His rivalrous intentions toward his father were played out by attempting to dupe the apparently unwitting husband. He handled some of the anxiety and guilt these wishes created by assigning responsibility for his sexual and aggressive behavior to the woman.

The latency period Freud did not systematically specify the latency and puberty stages of development. He alluded to them in his writings, but did not detail their contents and functions as he did the preceding three stages. It fell to later psychoanalytic writers to flesh out the characteristics of the later stages (see A. Freud, 1945; Erikson, 1950). The calamitous ideas involved in conflict are those that have their origins in the first three stages. By the time the person reaches the later stages, all four ideas can occur simultaneously and the person can become fixated in or regress to any of the later stages, just as it was possible to do in the earlier stages. For these reasons, it is important for the counselor to understand the latency and adolescent stages as well.

Following the resolution of the oedipal crisis, the drives are relatively quiescent, and the child enters a period of continued growth and consolidation of its biological, cognitive, and emotional functions. Latency begins at about age 6 and ends with the onset of puberty. Repression of the oedipal fantasies and identification with the parents now help the child manage its impulse life. Fear of punishment reflects the influence of the superego on the child's sexual and aggressive wishes at this time.

However, some children enter latency already casualties of the difficulties experienced during earlier stages. Fixations or developmental arrests at the oedipal period can be reflected in the latency-age child by its angry and hostile attitude toward society's expectations. Still other children show disturbance in their capacity to be close to their parents and thereby shun any displays of affection. Some children who enter latency show difficulty in relating to the peer group and prefer to be alone rather than develop friendships. Finally, the child may indicate difficulty by frequent emotional outbursts or delinquent behavior, thus manifesting inability to manage thoughts and feelings.

For most children, latency is a time of productive activity in the home, school, and community. The cessation of the turmoil of the oedipal period is replaced by attitudes of cooperation and willingness to learn. The child concentrates on the development of its skills and talents while it is gathering new experiences. Important experiences include activities with the family and the peer group that assist the child in exercising its developing social, emotional, and physical capacities. Interpersonal skills are developed which, when practiced with peers and adults, lay the groundwork for initiating and maintaining productive and enjoyable relations with others. Children begin to understand the inner life of other persons and to orient their behavior accordingly. The play of the latency-age child takes on more complexity. School experiences are also critical here for their contribution to shaping the rapid growth of the child's intellectual capacities. In all activities the child is presented with the task of learning how to work consistently and with purpose. Erikson (1950) referred to the task of latency as that of industry vs. inferiority. Failure to master the tasks of latency are manifest in such things as lack of ambition, difficulty relating to same-sex peers, school problems, inability to adapt to appropriate social roles, and behavior problems that include lying, cheating, stealing, and fighting. The example below illustrates some of the difficulties that occur during the latency phase.

A 9-year-old boy was referred for counseling by his mother because, increasingly over the last 3 years, he had refused to play with boys his own age, was having serious academic difficulty in school because he would not do the work or participate in play during recess, and had begun to prefer to play alone while dressed in his mother's clothes. Play therapy revealed the boy's intense fear of his father and many of the feminine strategies he had adopted to attempt to placate and please him. He would occasionally verbalize his preference for being a girl, and would add that then his parents would like him better.

From the child's birth on, the parents had used the boy as a buffer in their contentious relationship. The mother actively devalued him and openly preferred his sister, 2 years younger. This youngster had become so frightened of his own normal aggressive and loving feelings, and of his parents' inconsistent and often punitive responses to him during the oedipal stage, that he had carried the conflict forward unresolved. Upon entering school he was especially vulnerable to any event that involved competition or closeness with others, or that required assertiveness on his part. Such occasions triggered a regressive episode in which he became passive and withdrawn. More lately, he had developed the behavior pattern of responding in a flirtatious way around males whenever he felt anxious.

Puberty   Puberty, or adolescence, is the stage of psychosexual development in which the capacity for genital sexuality is reached. It is generally a time of turmoil for the adolescent. It lasts from approximately age 12 to adulthood. Its earlier tasks include establishing heterosexual relationships and gaining control over the sudden increase in sexual and aggressive energy that accompanies the rapid changes in the body. The internal strain the adolescent feels is mirrored in his or her often chaotic and usually inconsistent behavior and attitudes.

The important pyschosocial task of the adolescent is to gain a sense of personal identity. This means, among other things, that as the adolescent struggles to maintain a sense of continuity with its past, it must also try to differentiate itself from the parents and peers. Prior to this time, the adolescent's attitudes about sexuality, anger, society, drugs, competition, marriage, and a host of other issues in everyday life have been mandated or greatly influenced by the parents. Maturation of the cognitive, motor, and sexual equipment, plus additional freedom to come and go, present the teenager with numerous decisions to be made. Each decision the adolescent tries to make is a blend of personal desires and opinions, societal expectations and possibilities that are realistic (Anderson, 1967).

As with previous stages, the young person can enter adolescence already burdened with conflict and/or can fail to master the special tasks this stage of development presents. Adolescent conflicts are manifested in such problems as sexual acting out, asceticism, excessive dependence on or hostility to authority, and problems with the other sex. Fixations may occur at this stage as they can in others. The sexual and aggressive drives may remain untamed in their expressions. The superego may continue to dominate the adolescent's mind with self-punitive consequences. The ego may fail to bring about a synthesis of conflicting elements, such that portions or all of reality is experienced with major distortions. Events may occur during adolescence which trigger previous conflicts and prompt a regression to earlier forms of behavior.

In the normal case, however, the events that have gone before are integrated in the outcomes of this stage. These outcomes, in the form of tasks, include completing education, making career decisions, establishing heterosexual intimacy and learning how to use leisure time (Erikson, 1959). If all goes well, the result is an adult who is independent, has a clear sense of personal identity, is faithful to reality, and assumes responsibility for oneself and others. As Blos (1941) would have it, adolescence presents the individual with a second chance at normal development. Due to the normal loosening of superego prohibitions at this age, the adolescent undergoes a kind of second separation-individuation process (Mahler, Pine & Bergman, 1975), and thereby has an opportunity to repair the earlier failures of the oedipal crisis and the original attempts at separation-individuation.

A case of arrested development characteristic of a fixation to the pubertal stage is illustrated in the example below.

A 28-year-old single woman reports that she regularly fantasizes herself lying naked on a bed being surrounded by a host of admiring men while she masturbates. She says she couldn't imagine being intimate with any of the men. It is merely enough to know that they think she is beautiful and that they want to be near her. This attitude is reflected in her inability to establish and maintain an intimate relationship with men in her everyday life. It is simply too frightening to imagine falling in love with and marrying someone. Instead, she attempts to manage her important needs in this sphere by diluting them through dating several men at the same time. This way, she gains some satisfaction, but avoids the greater fear of making a loving commitment to a man.

Defense: the fourth element

Thus far, we have seen that the child's loving or aggressive wishes can trigger anxiety, depression, or other unpleasant affects, along with their associated ideas of object-loss, loss of the object's love, castration, and fear of punishment or guilt. When this occurs, an internal stage of conflict has ensued. To maintain equilibrium, and to be able to adapt to external reality in the face of intense internal demands, thoughts are censored, impulses to action are blocked, and feelings are blunted or banished from consciousness (Anderson, 1964). It is at this point that the ego has instituted defenses. A partial list of defenses includes repression, projection, denial, identification, reaction formation, intellectualization, undoing, regression, identification, and displacement. Defense is the next element in conflict. In Chapter 9 on Client Resistance, we shall have considerably more to say about the role of defenses in the counseling process.

According to Brenner (1982), defense is any operation of the mind that reduces anxiety and/or depression. This simple definition greatly expands upon the more traditional notion of defenses as ego "mechanisms" (A. Freud, 1936a), implied by the short list of defenses above. The expanded definition allows for the possibility that perceptions, attitudes, character traits, habits of thought, or any other aspect of mental life can function as defense. We identify mental activities by their purpose. In this case, a defense functions to block gratification of a loving or aggressive wish.

Defenses may be directed toward each or all of the components of conflict. They may be directed at blocking or modifying the expression of the wish. That is, they may render it unconscious and keep it that way by forgetting about it, that is by repression. Or they may modify the wish so that it is perceived to belong to some else, as in projection. Defenses may also be aimed at the unpleasant affect that is aroused by the wish. That is, the unpleasant feeling of anxiety, depression, guilt, and the like may be repressed, so that one is unaware of the affect and/or its intensity.

As well, defenses can be directed at the ideas that accompany the unpleasant affect, or at both the unpleasant sensation and the ideas simultaneously. Sometimes, for example, defense may succeed in splitting the affect from the idea, such that only the idea is conscious. Or, the idea or wish may be turned into its opposite manifestation in consciousness, as in reaction formation.

Defenses can also be directed at components of the superego which demand punishment for thoughts or deeds. In this case, defense may operate to block from awareness the person's wish to harm him or herself. Finally, defenses can be directed at the external stimulus event that activated the unconscious wish in the first place. The latter state of affairs can be illustrated by the person who withdraws, avoids, or denies the external event. The role played by defense in conflict is presented in the vignette below.

A 25-year-old woman reports having a heated and painful argument with her husband about sharing a bottle of whiskey between them. The client complains that the husband wouldn't let her have her fair share of drinks from the bottle. As the argument ensues, the client reports that she begins to feel like a small, frightened and helpless child. When the argument is finished, the client says she needed to get up and go outside for a walk in order to clear her head. In doing the latter, the client is defending against the regressive, helpless state she experienced in the argument by turning passive into active. That is, to help her overcome her feelings of helplessness she used physical activity to reassure herself that she was in control.

Compromise formations: the fifth element

To reiterate, wishes and/or certain aspects of superego functioning can arouse unpleasant affects and their associated ideas. These ideas are usually related to the developmental danger points of childhood: loss of the object, loss of love, castration, or fear of injury and self-punishment. In turn, the unpleasant affects and ideas can, if sufficiently intense, elicit defense. This is the chain of internal induction that constitutes intrapsychic conflict. Its outcome is a compromise between all the elements of the conflict. That is, in the client's observable complaints and symptoms are to be found the manifestations of wishes, affects and ideas, superego content and defense.

The consequences of conflict are a set of observations of the client from which the counselor may construct inferences about their possible antecedent elements. It is from these consequences, then, that we are provided with a rationale for counseling and a basis for understanding the client and attempting to construe the client's problems in terms of the classical psychoanalytic theory of conflict. What we may observe in the client are such things as moods, plans, dreams, complaints, symptoms, fantasies, habits, and the like. In the adult, these observations can be simply the result of compromises among the elements of conflict: wishes, affects, ideas, features of superego functioning, and defenses.

Compromise formations are recognizable as maladaptive, according to Brenner (1982), when we observe one or more of the following in the client:

1. The client inhibits the experience of normal pleasures, such that even commonplace, age-appropriate satisfactions are difficult to achieve or are avoided altogether.
2. The client is too often engulfed by painful affects, primarily anxiety and/or depression, and thereby has difficulty using his or her normal intellective functions.
3. The client shows strong tendencies to self-injure or self-destroy.
4. The client is too often in serious disharmony with other persons.

A particularly painful compromise formation in a client is presented in the following example.

A 28-year-old, divorced, male client insists he is dying of emphysema, even though seven complete medical work-ups have indicated he has no evidence of this or any other disease. For this talented man, life has become almost unbearable since his wife walked out on him to live with another man several months earlier. In addition to his breathing difficulties, he is quite depressed. He is unable to work more than a few hours a week at his job and, indeed, has recently had a series of low-paying positions because of his work inhibitions. He is divorced at the time he enters counseling and has been referred by the last physician he consulted for his respiratory "illness." He is unable to see any connection between the onset of his breathing difficulties and the precipitous break-up of his brief marriage, preferring instead a physical rather than an emotional explanation for his condition.

After several months of counseling and against strong resistance, it became clear to the client that the sudden departure of his wife had triggered a regressive slide back to conflict points earlier in his life. He began to recall with pain and fear how, as a very young child, and even later as a teenager, he had been neglected and physically and emotionally abused by his parents. His mother was less abusive than his father, and there was evidence of her occasional closeness and caring for the boy. The memory that stood out from early childhood involved his being shut up in a small, unventilated room for hours at a time while his parents were drinking downstairs or were away from the home. He longed to be with his mother, wanting her to hold and comfort him, while at the same time he smoldered with resentment toward his father for keeping her from him. He remembered quite clearly wishing his drunken father would be killed in an automobile accident while driving to his favorite tavern. The client's psychophysiological reaction (the maladaptive compromise formation) to his wife's departure expressed all the elements of a compromise formation. The "illness" gratified in a disguised way his wish to be taken care of while, at the same time, defended against the anxiety and accompanying thoughts of retaliation that such gratification would bring by portraying himself as weak and incapable of harm. As well, guilt is evident in the self-punitive aspects of the illness.

To further help illustrate the applications of the classical psychoanalytic formulations to clinical material derived from counseling, we turn now to the following case.

A case example

The counselor's task in using the classical psychoanalytic formulations of conflict and psychosexual development is to begin to identify in the client's complaints, symptoms, communications and other behaviors the various elements of conflict and to seek to learn how the client's present circumstances are serving as precipitants for a regression to earlier fixation points. This permits the counselor to begin to construct an hypothetical model (Pepinsky & Pepinsky, 1954; Greenson, 1967) of the client, such that the central or underlying condition for which help is needed can be formulated and tested in the interview and across a series of interviews.

The following case material will help illustrate how the various elements of conflict may be inferred from the observable aspects of a client's functioning. The client was a 23-year-old man who had been in counseling for 1 year at the time of the example reported here. His presenting complaints included depression, loneliness, and anxiety in approaching women and in dealing with his boss. The counselor noted that the client was quite unassertive in his interaction, coupled with a tendency to be stubborn. The most recent precipitants for these complaints were the refusal of a woman to see the client for further dates and an argument with his boss which he had lost.

Pre-counseling data are as follows: prior to counseling he had never been able to develop and sustain a romantic relationship with a woman; and he was angry at, yet intimidated by, his boss at work. His behavior with the woman who refused to see him further had been heavily influenced by the unconscious censoring of: (a) his jealous and hostile feelings toward his father and the counselor; (b) his loving feelings for his mother and his present love interest; and (c) his fantasy that he would become sick if he acted on his wishes. Accordingly, his typical conduct with the women he dated was anxious, ambivalent, rather passive (in that women usually initiated contact with him), and frequently argumentative. Needless to say, his romantic relationships were not long-lasting.

Toward the end of the work in counseling, he had initiated and sustained an intimate relationship with a woman, was able to acknowledge tender feelings for her and engaged in sexual intercourse with her. During this time, his increasingly conscious feelings for her often made him anxious. To ward off accompanying ideas of punishment by his father, he would start a fight with the woman, or become oppositional with the counselor.

The point in time with which we are concerned was taken up with the client's report about a young woman in whom he was interested and was presently dating. He and the woman had begun to experience conflict in their relationship in the form of disagreements about when to go out and where to go. He reported his experiences with the woman in an anxious manner over the course of the next several sessions. In fact, he found it increasingly difficult to talk at all when he came into the session. After observing the client's initially silent behavior on several such occasions, the counselor said at the beginning of the next hour that it looked as though he (counselor) were serving as some kind of stimulus for the client when he walked into the office. The client appeared to be contemplating what the counselor had just said but did not respond.

Presently, his skin tone took on a slightly greenish cast and he began to sweat and squirm in his chair. He looked as though he were going to become sick to his stomach. At this point, he asked if he and the counselor could go outside for a walk in the fresh air. The counselor replied that for the moment it would be all right if the client wanted to walk around the office until he felt better. The client did so for a few minutes and then sat down again.

Now composed and feeling better, the client wondered why he had begun to feel so nauseated. The counselor suggested that the client's body was doing the remembering of something that his mind did not want to acknowledge. This had the effect on the client of triggering a childhood memory. The client recalled that around the age of 4 he had been in the habit of calling out from his bed for his mother to come to him and bring him a glass of water. On the occasion in question his father came instead and told him that this was the last time he could ask for a drink of water in the middle of the night, but that he would take him to the bathroom to get one this time. The client recalled protesting vigorously, but his father picked him up out of bed anyway. At this point the client reported kicking his father and screaming. The client smiled slightly and reported that he next remembered vomiting on his father. Accompanying this memory were other early childhood memories of rivalry with his father and punishment at his father's hands. Toward the end of this session the client was able to link these memories and the accompanying fear with his anxiety about telling the counselor about his present love interest.

This is an example, not only of progress in counseling, but also of conflict and its elements. Before the client recalled the childhood memory he had been unaware of his angry and rivalrous wishes toward his father, his boss, and the counselor. He had also been unaware of the fear and the thoughts of punishment this aggressive wish had aroused in him. The wish itself had been aroused in his mind by the experience of talking with the male counselor about his erotic interests. Talking in this way to the counselor put the client in mind of his father and this had frightened him. One way in which his mind had defended against conscious knowledge of these earlier matters was to simply forget the childhood experiences. As is well known, this defense is called repression. Under the stimulus of talking with the counselor, he experienced a regression to the early childhood experience in which he had coped with his anger and fright by vomiting on his father. The adult outcomes of this and other of the client's conflicts included his compliance and passivity with his father and other men, his argumentative behavior with women, the restrictions he placed upon his capacity to experience pleasure with women, and too much conscious anxiety and depression.

Our report of this client's conflicts and their elements is incomplete. We have included here modifications of the case in order to illustrate the components of intrapsychic conflict. To summarize, in using the classical psychoanalytic theory of conflict, the counselor begins with observations of the client's actual talk and conduct, noting particularly the client's complaints and other aspects of this material that may represent maladaptive compromise formations. Then, drawing careful inferences from psychoanalytic theory, the counselor listens to the client's material for evidence of compromise formations that include: derivatives of loving and/or aggressive wishes; anxiety and/or depressive affect and their accompanying calamitous ideas from childhood; and the defenses which manifest themselves in the counseling interview as resistance to open communication.

3 The counselor's theory of the client II: psychoanalytic self psychology

In recent years a new variation of psychoanalytic theory that places the self at the center of the personality has appeared. Heinz Kohut (1971, 1977, 1984) has written a psychoanalytic psychology of the self, based upon the proposition that the personality develops along two narcissistic or self-expressive lines called grandiosity and idealization. In Kohut's (1977) theory, Freud's (1916/1961a) conceptualization of the drives of libido and aggression, and the id, ego, and superego as macrostructures of the mind, are replaced by a single cohesive psychological structure called the self. In spite of this major theoretical difference with the classical formulations, Kohut's (1977) theory is collateral rather than contradictory to Freud's (Patton & Sullivan, 1980), and thus remains consistent with the general theory of psychoanalysis, as outlined in Chapter 1.

We introduce self psychology here to provide the counselor with additional theoretical options for understanding client behavior. In doing so, we will present some background information to help the reader distinguish between the Freudian and Kohutian versions of theory, as well as to understand where they are similar. Then we will explain the development of the self, and the genesis of disorders of the self. Last, we will present a case example to illustrate the use of Kohut's ideas in understanding the client.

Some distinctions and similarities between Freud and Kohut

Much has been made of the presumed difference between the classical psychoanalytic theory and Kohut's (1977) theory. We contend that this difference is more apparent than real. While Kohut's (1977) explanatory constructs are different from Freud's at the level of theory proper (Level 3; see Chapter 1), he very much remains in the psychoanalytic camp by virtue of his agreement with and use of the same methodological principles of theory construction and assumptions about mind at Levels 4 and 5 found in Freud's theory. It will be recalled that these methodological principles include an emphasis on determinism, motivation, development, and a preference for explanation by recourse to formal theory. Like Freud, Kohut makes the mental act the fundamental constituent of his theory.

Moreover, Kohut's (1971, 1977) recommendations for and descriptions of the conduct of psychoanalysis are identical with the classical formulations. That is, they involve as fundamental elements the confrontation of resistances, and the development and working-through of the transference (Patton & Sullivan, 1980). Kohut's explanation of events in the analysis of disorders of the self varies, however, in that the patient develops a narcissistic or selfobject transference, rather than a classical neurotic transference.

By the same token, some psychoanalytic writers have underemphasized the important differences between Freud and Kohut at the level of theory, and still other writers are apparently confused about these matters. If one reads only Kohut's first exposition of self psychology (1971), it is quite possible to believe that he wrote a theory that stays within the classical psychoanalytic formulations about the personality. That is, in 1971 Kohut argued that the self, as a content of the ego, is the organizing center of the personality, and subject to the vicissitudes of narcissistic libido. It looked, therefore, as if Kohut were writing a variation of ego psychology or object relations theory (see Monte, 1987; St. Clair, 1986). On closer inspection, however, it becomes clear that Kohut was struggling to keep his concepts logically consistent with the drive and structure theories of classical psychoanalysis. We say struggling because his efforts to remain within the classical tradition failed. They failed because at that time his theory contained a logical contrary that undermined its explanatory structure.

According to Patton & Sullivan (1980), the trouble was this: it is not possible to have the self as the organizing center of the personality when, at the same time, it is purported to be an aspect of the ego. This is like saying that the whole is equal to a part. Kohut (personal communication, 1982) has stated that with this analysis "you have put your finger on" an important problem inherent in the conceptual scheme outlined in his 1971 book. In 1977 and in subsequent theorizing, Kohut corrected this logical problem by abandoning the classical formulations of the drives and the macrostructures of the mind. The terms of Kohut's (1977) theory are not reducible to those of ego psychology or object relations theory. Psychoanalytic self psychology stands on its own as a theory that is collateral to the specific

Freudian version, yet it remains within the general theory of psychoanalysis at the higher levels of abstraction (see Table 1.2, Chapter 1).

Still other writers have tended to link Kohut to the humanistic movement in American psychology (see Kahn, 1985) by showing the similarities between Kohut and Carl Rogers (1951, 1957), for example. Because both Kohut and Rogers construct their theories around a putative self, and both make empathy a central theoretical construct, it is concluded that Kohut has either written a latter-day, psychoanalytic version of client-centered theory, or an humanistic version of psychoanalysis. Both conclusions are erroneous.

Kohut's (1977) theory or any other classic psychoanalytic theory cannot be a version of client-centered theory because Rogers (1951) does not subscribe to several of the methodological principles that characterize the general theory of psychoanalysis. For example, Rogers (1951) avoids the troublesome problems that arise when the theorist adheres to a strict determinism. Instead, Rogers (1951) explains behavior by focusing on what he has called the "currency of needs" and the salience of the person's subjective view of events. That is, he believes we can know right now why persons behave as they do, simply by understanding their perception of events. The sources or causes of behavior do not have to be sought in the events that are antecedent to the present. This so-called "subjective" determinism is also found in the theories of Alfred Adler (1959) and Albert Ellis (1962). By contrast, Kohut (1977) is explicit in his typical psychoanalytic use of this principle when he assumes that the antecedents of behavior are the formative causes of adult adaptation, and they reside in early childhood interactions with the parenting figures. Understanding of these experiences is critical for helping the client begin again the process of development.

Rogers' (1951) use of the principle of motivation is quite different from Kohut's. Rogers is a master-motive theorist, in that organismic enhancement, or the tendency to actualize the organism, is assumed to be the origin of behavior. By contrast, Kohut (1977), like Freud (1915/1957b), assumes that there are as many motives for behavior as there are unconscious wishes, and that some of these have little to do with actualizing the person's capabilities.

Because development of the self-concept is implicit with Rogers, he does not use the historico-genetic principle of explanation to construct a stage-sequence theory of development. Kohut (1984), on the other hand, provides for a series of transitions from one general period of development to another. Kohut, it can be noted, is not as explicit as Freud in explicating clear-cut stages of development. Finally, Rogers' theory or system is less abstract and complex than Kohut's because it is not used as a resource for the detailed analysis of events in the client's report to the counselor. Instead, Rogers' theory emphasizes the holistic or synthetic trends in the personality, such that understanding is achieved by grasping the whole and not by analyzing the parts. Kohut's theory has been written in a more scholastic and continental European fashion, with an emphasis on specifying the formal properties of mind and in classifying them.

It also seems apparent that Kohut's writings are not a client-centered version of psychoanalysis. Although, like Rogers (1951), Kohut (1971, 1977, 1984) makes considerable use of the concept of empathy, and believes that empathic understanding on the part of the counselor is critical to the well-being of the client, the similarities end here. Kohut (1977) uses empathy in two additional ways that Rogers does not. First, he incorporates the concept at the level of theory by making it an attribute of normal parenting that occurs through interaction with the child. In doing so, he then details how the parents use empathy to understand the needs that the child's expressive displays communicate through its exhibitionistic and idealizing actions. Second, because Kohut defines empathy and gives it a formal role in the theory of the person, he has elevated the concept of empathy to the level of a methodological principle of explanation at Level 4. That is, empathy is the assumption that knowledge of the other person is possible by means of "vicarious introspection" (Kohut, 1977). It is one thing to argue that the communication of the counselor's empathic observations to the client is critical for all therapeutic relationships, which, of course, it is. It is quite another to work out the theoretical details of how parental empathy promotes the development of the child, as well as how it operates in the counseling situation.

In summary, Kohut is similar to Freud in his acceptance of the same principles of empirical inquiry and theory construction, and in his commitment to the idea of mind as active in the representation of events. He is also similar in the conduct of psychoanalysis. Kohut's formulations differ from the Freudian version at the level of theory by referring all behavior to the operation of the self. In consequence, Kohut's (1977) theory of the person is less complex than Freud's, has fewer theoretical terms, has terms that are less abstract, avoids concepts related to the body and, in consequence, accounts for a smaller range of empirical observations. In spite of Kohut's theory having a narrower "range of convenience" (Kelly, 1955) than Freud's, the terms of his psychology of self provide a clinically useful account of problems in living that are centered around the maintainance of self-esteem.

Kohut's similarities to Rogers are more superficial than actual. Kohut is explicit in his theorizing with respect to the antecedents of adult adaptive behaviors residing in childhood, the interactions with parenting figures, a stage-sequence theory of development, and his conceptualization of empathy as a methodological principle of explanation in development.

The development of the self

Kohut (1971) proposes that we are born with native talents and skills, and with self-expressive or narcissistic trends that occur in two lines of development called grandiosity and idealization. In 1984, a work by Kohut was published posthumously in which he introduced a third line of development called the "alter ego." Because, in our judgment, Kohut (1984) had not worked out the theoretical exposition of the alter ego line of development sufficiently to clarify it and show how it relates to the original two lines, the alter ego line will not be included in our presentation of Kohut's theory. Personality development is, thus, a matter of the genesis and maturation of a bi-polar self and its constituent elements, called selfobjects, along the lines of grandiosity and idealization.

It is assumed that prior to the formation of the infantile self and its grandiose and idealizing selfobjects, however, the child represents its experience to itself by constructing loose, fragmented mental images. As psychological structures, these images are frail, discohesive, unrelated to each other, transitory, and unreliable. The infant lacks the perceptual and cognitive maturity to construct and then arrange these mental objects into reliable, consolidated structures for experiencing and understanding the world. One might imagine, for example, that the infant's early percepts of what will eventually become its representations of self and the mother (or mother figure) are a series of discrete, disconnected, fragmentary images. Such percepts would likely represent various physical features, including mother's face and other parts of her body and those of the child's, the sound of mother's voice, the texture of one's own and of mother's skin and the characteristic taste and odor of each.

The cohesive infantile self and its selfobjects

At about the age of 18 months, these fragmented images coalesce into a fragile, yet cohesive, psychological structure called the infantile self and its selfobjects (Kohut, 1971). The self now serves as the organizing center of the infant's personality, and will continue to do so as long as subsequent events do not weaken it. But the fragile infantile self is subject to a break-up or re-fragmentation unless conditions promote its continued cohesion. Accordingly, the infantile self contains two percepts, or selfobjects, that correspond to the two lines of development of the bi-polar self, grandiosity and idealization. The selfobjects in relation to the self function to maintain the infant's self-esteem and the cohesion of the self. We will explain below how the selfobjects operate to promote cohesion.

For now, we should explain here that a "selfobject," in Kohut's (1971,

1977, 1984) terms, is to be contrasted with an "object" in the sense that Freud (1923/1961b) used the term. An object in the classical psychoanalytic theory is a mental representation of self or other in which the separateness of the self from the other is experienced and maintained. An object is a "whole object," as it were, and one is said to have "object relations." A selfobject in Kohut's (1984) terms is a "part object," not a whole object. This means that in the case of a selfobject, the other is not perceived as separate from the self. Instead, no distinction is made between the self and the other, so that percepts of both self and other are contained in it as if both were one object. In Kohut's terms, one has "self–selfobject relations."

As a preview to the discussion of the development of the self the reader is referred to Figure 3.1. The figure is an illustration of the lines of self development and their maturational features from the fragile, infantile self to the healthy, cohesive adult self (see Kohut, 1977; Patton & Robbins, 1982).

The mirroring self-object At the grandiose pole of the nuclear self, the child constructs the mirroring selfobject which consists of the parent or caretaker as the faithful mirror of the child's greatness. The grandiose child establishes a mirroring self–selfobject relation with the parent. Reliable mirroring of the child's exhibitionistic displays in the grandiose sector requires a parent who understands the child's wish for normal grandiose expression and its need for a mirror in this regard. Moreover, the child needs a parent who takes delight in the child's presence and shows it. Such a parent is in tune with the child's inner life. The child's self-esteem is maintained and the cohesion of the infantile self is fostered in the grandiose sector. Maintainance of self and cohesion are facilitated when the child experiences the mirroring of its normal infantile grandiosity and exuberant exhibitionism through the self–selfobject relation.

For the child, then, the mirroring parent and the grandiose self are experienced as one and the same; that is, the parent is a part of the child and exists only to perform the mirroring function that the child cannot yet perform for itself. The child only becomes aware of the need for the mirroring function when the parent is absent. It is typical for normal parents to occasionally fail to be empathic and to respond to the child's displays with indifference or even disapproval. In this case, the child will also experience the lowering of self-esteem, embarrassment, shame or rage that accompanies a narcissistic injury. These are typical reactions to normal or phase-appropriate lapses in parental empathy.

The idealized selfobject Analogously, the child constructs an idealized selfobject that consists of the powerful, omnipotent parent in relation to

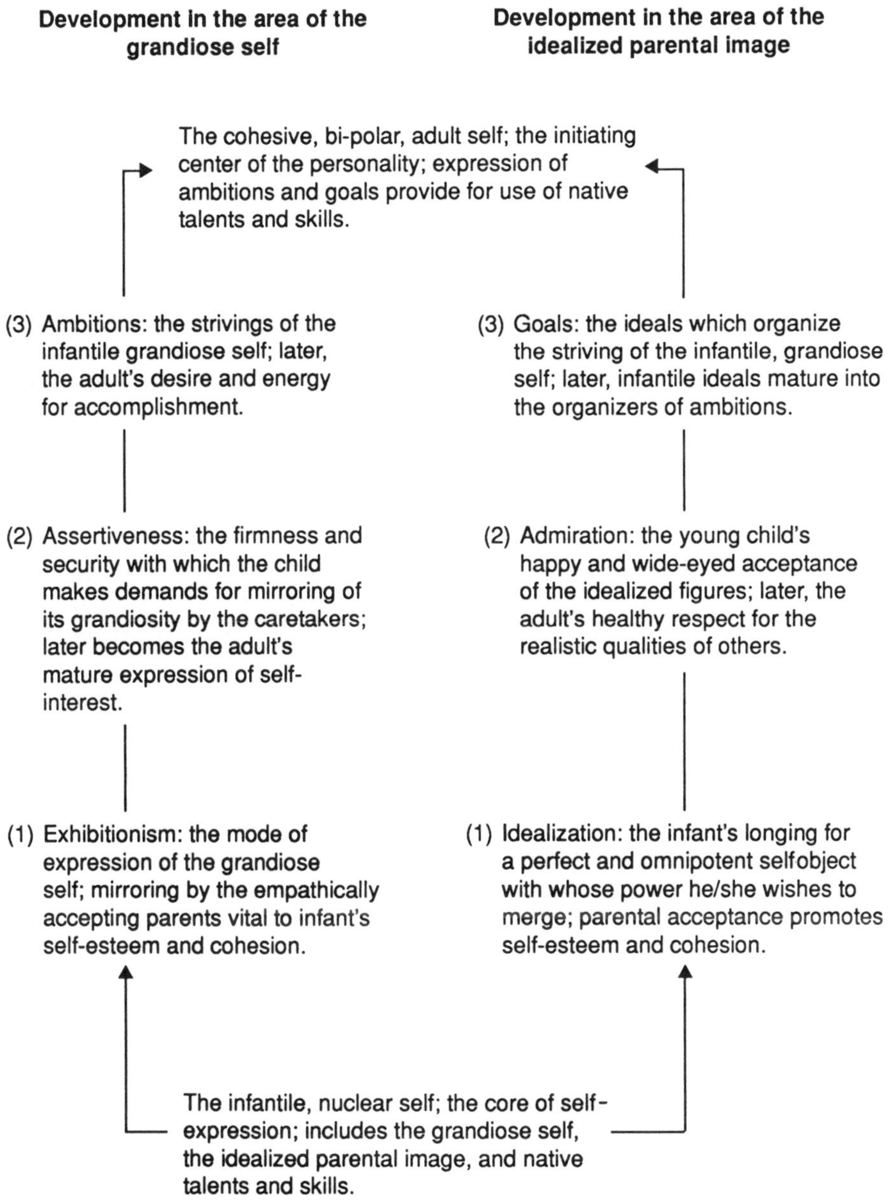

Development in the area of the
grandiose self

Development in the area of the
idealized parental image

The cohesive, bi-polar, adult self; the initiating
center of the personality; expression of
ambitions and goals provide for use of native
talents and skills.

(3) Ambitions: the strivings of the
infantile grandiose self; later,
the adult's desire and energy
for accomplishment.

(3) Goals: the ideals which organize
the striving of the infantile, grandiose
self; later, infantile ideals mature into
the organizers of ambitions.

(2) Assertiveness: the firmness and
security with which the child
makes demands for mirroring of
its grandiosity by the caretakers;
later becomes the adult's
mature expression of self-
interest.

(2) Admiration: the young child's
happy and wide-eyed acceptance
of the idealized figures; later, the
adult's healthy respect for the
realistic qualities of others.

(1) Exhibitionism: the mode of
expression of the grandiose
self; mirroring by the empathically
accepting parents vital to infant's
self-esteem and cohesion.

(1) Idealization: the infant's longing for
a perfect and omnipotent selfobject
with whose power he/she wishes to
merge; parental acceptance promotes
self-esteem and cohesion.

The infantile, nuclear self; the core of self-
expression; includes the grandiose self,
the idealized parental image, and native
talents and skills.

Figure 3.1 The parallel lines of development of the self. From Patton, Connor
& Scott (1982), copyright 1982 by the American Psychological Association.
Reprinted by permission of the publisher

the idealizing child. Idealization of the parenting figures and merger with their omnipotence during times of stress helps maintain cohesion by permitting the child to see itself as part of their calm, power and perfection. In this way, the child "borrows" what it perceives it lacks, and gains strength from doing so. Parents who permit themselves to be used as reliable targets for merger and idealization are empathically in touch and accepting of the inner life of their child. They understand that the desire to merge with the parent helps to calm and soothe the child, and to elevate the child's self-esteem.

It is also normal for the child to occasionally be separated from such powerful figures, or for the parents to reject the child's wishes to merge with or idealize them. Such events make the child experience the same sense of lowered self-esteem and embarrassment or rage that is experienced by a narcissistic injury on the grandiose side. In either case, the self is temporarily weakened and discohesive. The child lets us know this by the sense of pain it communicates with its behavior. Cohesion is restored when the parent is once again in tune with the child's idealizing trends by making him or herself available to the child.

Thus, the consolidation of the nuclear infantile self is sustained by a matrix of parental empathy (Kohut, 1971). As long as the child's parents or caretakers empathically understand the child's needs and make themselves available to mirror the infant's normal grandiosity, and serve as targets for its wishes for merger and idealization, they perform vital functions for the child which it cannot perform for itself. As Kohut (1971) puts it, the child's view of things at this time is something like this: "I am great. You are great; but then, I'm a part of you." Reliable parental empathy grasps this infantile logic. The empathic parental matrix permits the child to construct and maintain the self–selfobject relations that promote the organization and development of the personality along its two major lines.

Kohut (1984) maintains that we have need of self–selfobject relations throughout our lives, because we always have need for others to mirror us and to be available as targets to idealize. The quality of our later self–selfobject relations necessarily changes and matures over time, reflecting changes in the self. If our course of development has been healthy, our selfobjects are more reality-based by reflecting the changing needs that accompany us through the lifespan. The kind of grandiosity an adult expresses, and which he or she expects a spouse or friends to understand and mirror, differs markedly from the exhibitionistic displays of the 3-year-old. Yet the mirroring function performed by the selfobject is the same at both ages. Kohut (1984) argues that the self–selfobject relation is a sector of the overall experience we have with others. As adults, we are able to perform these same functions for others. For these reasons, the early self–selfobject relations are important because they are the prototype for all those that follow. In summary then, out of the empathic matrix of the mirroring and the idealized selfobjects, an independent, self-initiating and cohesive self begins to emerge (Kohut, 1977).

Break-up of the infantile self

In the normal case (Kohut, 1971, 1977), the grandiose and idealizing sectors of the self develop from their fragile, infantile origins into increasingly reality-based formations that provide the adult self with cohesion, firmness, and harmony, and with basic patterns of initiative and inner guidance. Kohut's (1971) technical term for the process of maturation of the self is "transmuting internalization." What this means is that the infantile self and its selfobjects are fragile and prone to discohesion and fragmentation. In development, the elements of the infantile selfobjects break up and are transformed and rearranged into a different psychological structure, which is then internalized as a part of the self. The infantile self and its selfobjects are prone to fragmentation, and it is instructive to examine in what ways these early structures are fragile, and how this break-up comes about.

We mentioned earlier that the infantile self needs a mirror for its grandiosity and a target to idealize. Further, we noted that normal parents are empathically in tune with the child's narcissistic wishes in this regard, and thereby provide the child with these experiences. Each time the child experiences a mirroring of its infantile greatness or is permitted to merge with the soothing, calming caretaker, its self-esteem is strengthened and its cohesion maintained. However, it is normal for the parents to fail to be empathic with their child on occasion. These phase-appropriate lapses in parental empathy disappoint the child. They confront it with the possibility that it is not the powerful center of the universe, and that its caretakers are not perfect. In a word, the child's wishes for the mirroring of its greatness and for a target to idealize are frustrated.

It is the frustration of the child's infantile narcissistic wishes brought about by phase-appropriate failures in parental empathy that promote the gradual break-up of the selfobjects. That is, when the infant's grandiose sense of self is not confirmed by the approving gleam in the parent's eye or by the parent's otherwise delighted acceptance, the selfobject loses its firmness and cohesion. A bit of reality has intruded into the symbiotic union (Mahler, Pine & Bergman, 1975) represented by the grandiose self–selfobject relation. Accordingly, the child's capacity to believe that it is entitled at any time to the adoring and undivided attention of its parents is diminished.

In the same way, the idealized selfobject and its relation with the self breaks up when the parent is not available as a target to idealize or with which to merge during times of stress. The unpleasant reality in this case is that the child cannot maintain or enhance self-esteem through union with the parent. The idealized selfobject thereby gradually loses its capacity to promote cohesion of the self by way of the fiction that the child is fused with the omnipotent parent. On such occasions, the child is unable to perform those functions that result in calming and soothing and is left in a state of tension. A little later, when the cognitive apparatus has matured, the child's self-esteem is injured when it realizes that its idol has feet of clay.

The gradual break-up of the two infantile selfobjects amounts to change in or mutation of the elements of the self. Ongoing phase-appropriate lapses of parental empathy provide the child with opportunities for reorganizing its percepts of self, other, and the world around it. New experiences, appropriately timed, give the child material for the mutation of the self, and therefore the build-up or cohesion of the new percepts, into a consolidated self.

Over time, the infantile selfobjects are gradually replaced with the structures of the cohesive adult self. This process will be expanded upon in a discussion of the development of each of the two lines in the next sections of this chapter. For now, it may help the reader to review Figure 3.1 and to look at the illustration in Figure 3.2, which is an attempt to portray the process of the break-up of the infantile self and the build-up of the cohesive adult self. Later we will return to a discussion of this figure.

Development of the self in the grandiose sector

The grandiose line of development is the carrier of the person's ambition or initiative (see Figure 3.1). Normal development of the grandiose self begins with infantile exhibitionism and the infant's assertive initiative. Later, around the age of 4, 5 and 6, nuclear grandiosity consolidates into the basic ambition of the self. For the infant, nuclear grandiosity *vis-à-vis* the mirroring selfobject is that aspect of narcissism that underlies the person's wish to draw attention to him or herself; to vigorously seek the recognition and approval of others for one's accomplishments. An aspect of self-expression, then, is accompanied by the wish for an approving mirror.

After the consolidation of the infantile self at about 18 months, the toddler comes to perceive itself as the center of the universe and, as such, entitled to the gratification of all its desires. It is carried from place to place by adults, such that it has a commanding view of all that it sees from its lofty perch. Attention is given whenever demands are made known; and the parents take delight in the child's presence and shows it by the gleam of approval in their eyes. These are just a few of the experiences the child has and from which it is sustained in the belief that it is all-powerful.

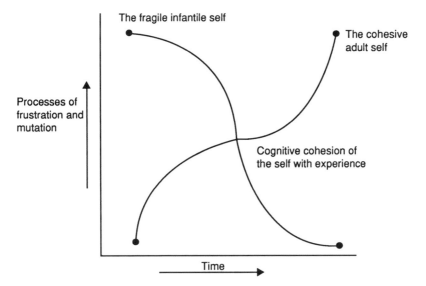

1. Phase–appropriate frustrations of the child's needs for empathy (mirroring of grandiosity and idealizing of parent) is a pre-condition for the decline or break-up of the archaic self.

2. The decline or break-up of the archaic self is a pre-condition for change or mutation in the parts of the self (that is, new concepts of self).

3. Mutation is a condition for the build-up or cohesion of the new parts into a firmly consolidated self.

Figure 3.2 Kohut's concept of transmuting internalization. From Patton & Sullivan (1980), copyright 1980 by the National Psychological Association for Psychoanalysis. Reprinted by permission

Exhibitionism is the mode of expressing childhood grandiosity. The infant and the toddler are in the business of showing off the body and their childish accomplishments to others. At this age, it is fair to say that the child gives a performance in which approval is expected as a matter of course. If it is not forthcoming, it is now demanded with much fuss. The child takes particular pride in its body, which it exhibits in numerous ways, often most noticeably around bath time. Normal parents understand this by praising the child's physical appearance and by stroking, patting, and rubbing its body. It doesn't occur to the young child to be ashamed of its naked body.

As well, the child takes pride in its motor functions and its growing command of language. Both are exhibited with much assertive display or fanfare as the child races from place to place or repeats incessantly its first few words or sentences. The child does not understand the adult meaning of the word "enough," and it expects the same delighted response each time it performs the new accomplishment. Thus, the assertive display of its native endowments and learned accomplishments is an occasion for mirroring. At this age, the child's display is a noisy and diffuse ultimatum for the mirroring approval of others. The healthy exhibitionism of the child includes its sense of omnipotent control over the responses of the mirroring selfobject. As long as this situation obtains, the groundwork is laid for the eventual emergence out of this matrix (see Kohut, 1977) of an independent self, because the child's proud displays have helped promote the security and cohesion of the infantile self.

As the child grows, its demands become more specific and the earlier energetic grandiosity is replaced with increasingly more concentrated assertiveness. The infant's healthy self-assertiveness in relation to the mirroring selfobject is converted into what will become the basic patterns of ambition of the self. That is, the child begins to evidence the ability to eagerly begin or follow through with tasks and plans it has initiated. This consolidation in the nuclear self manifests itself between the ages of 4 and 6 years. Thus, the proud displays of the exhibitionistic toddler gradually transform into the child's strong desire to succeed or achieve. Later, the basic patterns of ambition formed in childhood serve the adult as the basis of its determination or initiative throughout life.

Kohut (1977) believes that the early constituents of the self in both lines of development are derived from the self–selfobject relation with the maternal figure. In the case of the grandiose self, it is the mother's mirroring acceptance of the child's exhibitionistic displays that confirms infantile grandiosity. Later it is the paternal figure's approval and support of the child's exhibitionism and later assertive initiative that strengthens the grandiose self.

Development of the self in the idealized sector

The idealized selfobject formed by the infant when the infantile self becomes consolidated around 18 months of age functions to permit merger with the omnipotent figure. Being held in mother's arms and carried about, or being calmed and soothed at times of stress, help promote the merger experience. The mode of expression in this line of development is, therefore, idealization. The infant longs and searches for an idealized, omnipotent selfobject with whose power it can merge. The infant and the young child may, therefore, select aspects of the idealized selfobject to become preoccupied with as single symbols of its greatness. It may select, for example, the texture of mother's hair or skin, or, indeed, her face, or it may be father's hands or arms, or any other aspect the child selects. The child is enthusiastic and indiscriminate in its idealization of the selfobject.

The idealizing experience requires a parent or caretaker who enjoys and allows her or himself to be idealized by the child; someone who actively encourages the experience by empathic interaction with the youngster. The parent functions, then, as a merger-accepting, idealized imago. Later, this selfobject will influence the organizing of ideals. Such ideals serve as an internalized guiding structure which is a source of sustenance for the person. Initially, however, the process requires a willing and responsive parent, because only in this way will an idealizing relationship with the child unfold.

Later, as the self matures, the child is able to express its idealizing in a more focused way. In the pre-school age child, this occurs as the happy, wide-eyed acceptance and admiration of the idealized figures. Later still, in the adult, idealization is expressed as respect for the realistic qualities of other persons.

As was implied earlier, the idealized self–selfobject relation makes possible the formation of goal-setting ideals that become a part of the structure of the self. Such a structure has an organizing effect on the personality by giving it a sense of direction. The infantile idealized goal structures are acquired in later childhood around the fourth, fifth and sixth years. As was the case with the mirroring selfobject, the idealized selfobject is transformed into a psychological structure that functions in conformity with the pattern of inner ideals.

According to Kohut (1977), the normal developmental sequence of events in this line involves merger with the maternal ideal, later de-idealization and the incorporation of elements of the idealized selfobject into the self as an emerging pattern of goal-setting ideals, and the later integration of these ideals with other aspects of the personality. This same sequence of events is postulated to occur subsequently with the paternal figure.

The growing child learns how to become the center of its own initiative. The cohesive infantile self, and later, the adult, bi-polar self consist, then, of patterns of ambition (rooted in the area of the grandiose self) that function to provide the person with initiative or determination, and patterns of ideals (rooted in the area of the idealized parental image) that function to organize the ambitions and provide a sense of direction. The self also consists of certain functions. The adult with a cohesive self learns to be the regulator of its own self-esteem, the manager of its own tension states, and the introspective/empathic observer of self and others (Patton, Connor & Scott, 1982).

The two poles of the self stand in relation to each other in terms of a "tension gradient" (Kohut, 1977). The tension gradient is conceived as a kind of action-promoting tendency "that arises between a person's ambitions and his ideals" (see Kohut, 1966, pp. 254–255). On the one hand, we are driven by our ambitions, and, on the other, led by our ideals. Both enable the person to harness native talents and skills in initiating action toward the pursuit of goals. Kohut's use of the historico-genetic principle (see Chapter 1) formulates the process of the transformation of narcissism as a normal trend in the personality. In this way, the development of the self is the transformation of narcissism, the growth of the self-expression-seeking sectors of the personality (Patton, Connor & Scott, 1982).

Disturbances of the self

Defects in the self arise from either chronic or traumatic frustration of the child's needs for the mirroring selfobject and/or its wish for merger with the idealized selfobject. Severe empathic failures on the part of the childhood selfobjects promote the fixation of development upon the injured sector(s) of the self, and prompt the self to institute either defensive and/or compensatory maneuvers in order to avoid a painful sense of fragmentation. The earlier the defect in the self, the more severe the adult disturbance. As Kohut (1977) notes, the personality of a client with a narcissistic disorder can usually be characterized by three important features:

1. The client will show evidence of suffering from a defect that is located in either the grandiose or the idealizing sector of the self.
2. If the defect in either sector is unusually severe, the client will have attempted to cover it over with typically inefficient defensive maneuvers.
3. The client will usually have attempted to undertake compensatory maneuvers that increase the activity of the healthier parts of the self and ignore the defective parts.

Disturbances in the cohesion of the self injure self-esteem and threaten the self with painful fragmentation. In order to prevent a sense of depletion or permanent break-up, either or both of the infantile selfobjects may become defensively isolated through fixation. In this way, they are not subject to the influence of other parts of the personality that could help rehabilitate them. The problem is that the infantile structures endure, such that the adult is then subject to the possibility of a break-through into consciousness and action of their contents. In the grandiose line, this may mean that the person seeks, with or without awareness, a mirror for his or her infantile sense of grandiosity. Outward manifestations of the problem may be observed in vain, arrogant, aggrandizing and attention-seeking behavior. As with all weaknesses in the self, the person's self-esteem is extremely vulnerable, such that the failure of others to provide the expected mirroring/approving responses can result in reactive arrogance, shame, humiliation, and withdrawal. When the defect is in the idealizing line, the person seeks other persons or political, religious, or social movements with which to merge. Only then can the enfeebled self feel strong and whole again. Needless to say, the person is prone to disappointment in both arenas and subject to further erosion of self-esteem and cohesion.

Other manifestations of a disturbance in the self can include a tendency toward lying, shame-proneness, restlessness, work or study inhibitions, and hypochondriasis (Patton, Connor & Scott, 1982). In more severe cases, one may also observe alcoholism and drug abuse, psychogenic obesity, delinquency, and sexual perversion (Patton, 1980b). However, Kohut (1971, 1977) contends, and clinical experience verifies, that the most reliable indicator of a defect in the self is the way in which the client relates to the counselor over time. That is, the narcissistically vulnerable client will try to use the counselor as either a mirroring or idealized selfobject in order to resume the process of development. The client is using the counselor as a projected part of the self in order to maintain cohesion and elevate self-esteem. When this manifestation of either a mirroring or idealizing transference relationship is established, the client becomes very vulnerable to the counselor's lapses in empathy. When the counselor fails to understand the client's use of him or her in this way, it injures the client's self-esteem and can prompt a regressive acting out to avoid the sense of emptiness or fragmentation. Thus, the counselor's inevitable lapses in empathy are especially instructive in this regard.

Table 3.1 is a classification of attempts at adaptation by persons with a deficiency in the self in either of the two lines of development (see Patton & Robbins, 1982). The table is organized in terms of adaptive strategies (either defensive or compensatory), lines of development (either grandiose or idealizing), and level of severity (that is, mild, moderate, or severe).

The concept of defensive maneuver (Kohut, 1977) refers to the person's attempts to use ideas, affects, or behaviors as a means of directly defending against or covering over the defect in either the grandiose or idealizing sector of the self. Defensive maneuvers focus directly on the defective area. If, for whatever set of circumstances, the defect were in the grandiose line, the purpose of the person's defensive fantasies or actions is to restore a sense of power or greatness by controlling the mirroring selfobject. Here, the person denies his (or her) sense of weakness and shame by attempting to provide himself with an approving mirror for his exhibitionistic displays. If the defect is in the idealizing line, the defenses against it are intended to restore the sense of merger with, or approval of, the omnipotent selfobject. In this line, the person attempts to supply him or herself with missing confidence, acceptance, and security by merger with perfection. In either case, the more severe the defect, the more pain the person feels, and the

Table 3.1 Assessing the degree of vulnerability and adaptive strategies observed in clients with a defect in the self

Area of vulnerability	Defensive maneuvers Patterns of thought, feeling, and behavior aimed directly at covering over the defect in the self.	Quality of compensatory action Patterns of thought, feeling, and behavior that serve to compensate for the defect in the self through work, study, or leisure.
Grandiose self		
Mild	Occasional fantasies of power and domination with social, religious, or political tones. Autoerotic activities, such as eating or masturbating, may accompany fantasies. Becomes arrogant and aloof when challenged or attacked by others, yet uncomfortable when praised.	Stable, longer-term patterns of work, study, and leisure in which values are expressed; lacks zest for this, however, with episodes in which sense of striving and ambition decline markedly.
Moderate	Extensive fantasy life with themes of power, domination, and sexual preoccupation. Demands placed on partners for an approving mirror. A sense of vanity, self-righteousness and entitlement. Quite sensitive about assertions; seeks out continued approval. Reactive arrogance and lying are a consistent pattern.	A non-stable work or avocational pattern because of severe inhibitions and lack of enthusiasm. Much difficulty in beginning or finishing projects and participating in activities.
Severe	Defends against loss of self-esteem through direct action via addictions, eating disorders, sexual perversions. Focus upon others to display sense of power, aggrandizement. Seeks out continued approval. Reactive arrogance and lying are a consistent pattern.	Stable patterns unlikely; may evidence history of abortive attempts to use native talents and skills that are related to unrealistic goals and a once idealized figure. No energy to act on plans is apparent.
Idealized parental image		
Mild	Some fantasies of closeness with idealized others. Tendency to rely on others for direction and confidence. A need for someone or something to believe in. Becomes withdrawn when an important other leaves.	Relatively stable and productive patterns of work, study, or leisure which reward singularized effort. Enthusiasm may become diminished because efforts are not attached to a system of goals and ideals.

Table 3.1 (*Continued*)

Moderate	Strong fantasies about being inseparable from envied and idealized others, sometimes with sexual overtones. A pattern of ingratiation, charm, and approval-seeking which puts others off.	Solitary patterns of work or direction likely which reward person for singularized performance. Can become completely inhibited when displaying self because of fear of shame and embarrassment.
Severe	Use of addictions, sexual activity/perversions, psychogenic eating disorders, which leave the person "at peace" and with a sense of blissful union with others, and which defend against a sense of aloneness. Experiences an immobilizing depression when disappointed by important others.	Stable patterns unlikely because of lack of goals or ideas to strive for. May evidence occasional crude bouts of center-staging to demonstrate a sense of power which isn't there.

Adapted by permission from Patton & Robbins (1982), copyright 1982 by the American Psychological Association. Adapted by permission of the publisher

more prone he (or she) is to use the environment, rather than his mind, to solve the problem. In a word, the defensive maneuver ignores or denies the defect in the self by covering it over.

Compensatory maneuvers are structures the person develops to strengthen the healthier parts of the self that reside in the developmental line that has been less afflicted with a defect (Kohut, 1977). Compensatory maneuvers in one line of development arise in consequence of the defect in the alternate line. Compensatory patterns usually involve work, study, or leisure. They are related to the infantile selfobject in the same line because it was to this object that the child turned when the selfobject in the alternate line disappointed him or her. Thus, one sees in the pattern of work, study or leisure, remnants of the earlier self–selfobject relation.

The type and effectiveness of the defensive and compensatory maneuvers vary with the level of severity of the defect in the self. Severe defects in the self are usually accompanied by the use of drugs or alcohol, or by sexual perversions, obesity, and delinquency, all of which may be the urgent, yet inefficient and defensive, attempts at self-cure (cf. Patton, 1980b). Less severe defects are defended against by using the mind to create fantasies, or by the incorporation of less socially offensive personality characteristics like vanity, hero worship, ingratiation, and the like.

By the same token, when the defect in the one line is especially severe, compensatory actions in the other line are less well organized and stable. If the defect in the grandiose line is severe, for example, ambition is likely to be intermittent, if not absent. This affects how well the person can compensate by implementing a set of guiding ideals in the other line. By contrast, when the defect is in the idealizing line, the person usually suffers from an absence of a sense of direction and set of ideals to believe in. Compensatory action to strengthen the grandiose sector by developing one's sense of initiative or ambition is likely to be unstable in the absence of inner guidance. In this case, it is as though the person were "all dressed up with no place to go."

When the defect is more moderate, or even of mild consequences, the attempts to compensate for it are likely to be met with greater success in the form of longer-term, stable behavior patterns. There is a simple principle in operation here. Compensatory maneuvers can become effective methods of adaptation in the healthier line of development only if the sustaining contributions of the other line are not too severely impoverished. Everyone has two chances to develop the adult self. The narcissistically vulnerable person may yet develop a cohesive adult self by building up compensatory structures through the more cohesive pole of the self.

A case example

The counselor's task in using psychoanalytic self psychology formulations is to observe how the client's complaints, symptoms, and other behaviors reflect the vulnerability of self-esteem, and either the hunger for a mirroring relationship or the absence of goal-setting ideals (Kohut, 1984; Elson, 1987). However, the way in which the client develops the transference relationship with the counselor over time is the most reliable method for determining whether the client is or is not suffering from a disorder of the self. Clients who have a disorder of the self in the grandiose line will put up strong resistances to becoming aware of their need to use the counselor as an approving mirror. Those who have a defect on the idealizing side will erect resistances against their wishes to become a part of the omnipotent counselor. As with the classical conflict model, the counselor uses his or her own empathic observations and affective reactions in combination with theoretical knowledge to construct a hypothetical model of the client. The model is then tested in the interview with the client and revised accordingly (Pepinsky & Pepinsky, 1954).

The following case material will help illustrate how the propositions of Kohut's (1977) psychology of the self are useful in attempting to gain understanding the client's difficulties. The material reported here is taken from a consultation interview with the client. Although this material was unusually abundant for an initial interview, the client was not motivated for further work and declined to accept additional interviews. Nevertheless, we include this material to show how a tentative working model of the condition for which the client needs help can be formulated from the assessment or initial interview. The client was a young woman, 18 years of age, whose mother had referred her to the counselor. In the initial phone call to the counselor, the mother had mentioned that her daughter "needed to talk with a counselor" because she believed the client had never gotten over the mother's divorce from the client's father. Mother went on to say that the client's father had rejected her and that she felt the client was spending too much of her time with her boyfriend.

During the initial interview, the client's presenting complaints were more specific. She complained that several bad things had happened to her in the past 3 years and that these things kept bothering her because they were always on her mind. By this she meant that she couldn't forget these things and that she was depressed by them. She also stated that her "self-esteem was very low." She said that she and her mother were very close and that if something happened to her mother, she would not want to live. Recently, she had made up with her boyfriend after a break-up that occurred because they were becoming "too serious." When asked if she could tell the counselor about the bad things, she said she did not want the counselor to think badly of her after she had done so.

The first matter she reported was that when she was 15 she had become pregnant by an older man and had obtained an abortion. She went on to say that she still felt very guilty about the abortion. The second problem she reported had to do with her father's ongoing rejection of her. He was remarried and from this second marriage he had children of whom the client felt jealous and envious. The client longed for her father's approval and wanted to be close to him, but whenever she was in his presence, she received his disapproval instead. In the third complaint, the client reported how her step-father had on several recent occasions tried to initiate sexual contact with her when she and he were alone in the home. She had been able, thus far, to successfully avoid such contact with him. His appearance and his daily habits were loathsome to her.

The counselor also noted that she was having trouble in school in that she was not making passing grades at the time, and was a year behind her age-mates in high school. The counselor further observed that she was mildly depressed and displayed a pervasive lack of initiative, coupled with excessive dependence on her mother and her boyfriend. She permitted both of the latter to make most of the decisions for her. The client's appearance was typical of her age and gender.

Her quality of talking with the counselor was rather matter-of-fact, low key. In spite of the traumatic events in her life and her complaints about them, she acted uninvolved or disengaged. She reported that she rarely displays strong feelings about anything. She was quick to use psychological jargon in describing herself or others. In spite of keeping distant from her feelings, she showed some insight into the dynamics of her dysfunctional family and her own difficulties.

To gain an initial, working understanding of this case, the counselor needs an avenue from her presenting complaints and symptoms to her personality organization; that is, the counselor wants to move from clinical observations and the client's self-stated complaints to the underlying conditions for which help is needed (Elson, 1987). Moreover, the counselor needs criteria for distinguishing between whether her depression, lack of initiative, low self-esteem and dependence reflect a disorder of the self, or whether they indicate intrapsychic conflict in which guilt might play a leading role. We have a clue in the nature of the client's dependence on mother and boyfriend. The client seems unwilling to move toward more autonomy and to become more active in completing her education. She attends to her appearance so that she is attractive, but otherwise she is just going through the motions, lacks a sense of direction, and is unhappy. It is as if she is trying to postpone or, perhaps, even avoid the separation from mother and the transition to adult independence as a person with her own ambitions and goals. She relates with her mother more like an obedient latency-age child than an 18-year-old young woman.

Further, she stated how much she wants her father to love and approve of her, even to the point of continually risking his rejection. Thus, she stated that she had recently gone over to his house to see him and he was alternately critical and indifferent to her. Notably, she does not respond with anger. Instead, she complains that she invariably experiences a significant drop in her self-esteem following such encounters with her father. One can well imagine that a young woman of 18 would normally anticipate her father's pleasure in seeing her after a period of being apart. The client quite naturally wants to look good on these occasions and to be admired. When just the opposite occurs, it hurts her terribly and she feels ashamed. These are late experiences and not themselves responsible for the disturbance. Yet, they indicate how vulnerable she is and, therefore, stand for earlier experiences.

The clues we are able to pick up from the limited material we have thus far suggest a young woman who may have experienced a major disturbance in the grandiose sector of the self. At a time when she was still very dependent upon the mirroring approval of her parents, and especially on her father's loving attention, the parents were divorced and the father moved out of the home. Gone was the approving mirror that had taken delight in her presence. This severe phase-inappropriate disruption in the empathic matrix that helped sustain her grandiose self proved too much for her. She turned to her mother, who was too preoccupied with her own concerns to understand accurately how the little girl was experiencing the loss of her father. Still later, when her breasts began to swell as a pre-teen, her father became anxious about and critical of her budding sexuality. These events were major assaults on her as yet vulnerable self-esteem and on the consolidation of the grandiose self.

In consequence of these events, the client relives in her late adolescence the intense need that a little girl has for the unequivocal approval of a doting father. She is strongly and sexually attracted to older men, yet fears rejection by them. She struggles against her fears of separation and her strong need to seek the attention and approval of older men by remaining dependent on her mother, and by clinging to her somewhat immature boyfriend. Mother and boyfriend are the possessions she uses to sustain the conviction that she is a special child who needs and deserves constant care and attention.

With these tentative formulations, the counselor is alerted to a number of technical problems and opportunities in working with a client such as this. First, it is likely that the client's self-esteem would continue to be fragile for some period of time, such that extra care in the counseling interviews would be needed to safeguard it. Second, the client's need for the counselor's unequivocal admiration and approval of her would likely to be a source of considerable resistance for her and a potentially serious threat to a solid working alliance between the pair. If counseling is to help this client grow toward self-understanding and independence, the counselor would need to assist her in using him or her as a mirror for her grandiose strivings. Then it would become possible for her to grow by having these wishes pointed out to her and by learning from the inevitable lapses in mirroring that would occur. These and other client problems will take much tact and patience on the counselor's part.

Clients with defects in the self present the counselor with special technical challenges. The first of these has already been pointed out. That is, their self-esteem is usually extraordinarily vulnerable. Another technical problem these clients present is their tendency to use the counselor for the performance of important self functions they themselves cannot perform; for example, self-esteem regulation. In a word, these clients lack sufficient empathic capacity to become aware of the other person's thoughts and feelings and to take them into account in interpersonal situations. Because of this, the counselor is often not perceived as a whole person with his or her own inner life. Instead, he or she is treated as an object that exists for the client alone. It is uncomfortable for the counselor to be treated in this way on a regular basis. It feels as if one is being devalued. In consequence, the counselor needs to be aware and in control of his or her own negative reactions to the client on this account. The key to the counselor's avoiding a negative intervention with the client is empathy for what the client is doing and a firm sense of one's own worth.

Kohut's theory provides a rich resource for understanding the client. The terms of the theory are "experience-near," yet systematically arranged so that a coherent theoretical structure is evident. Self-esteem is a central feature of Kohut's theory and, as counselors, we are cautioned to attend to and safeguard the client's self-esteem at all times. While we are never far from self-esteem issues with any client, Kohut's theory makes explicit the central importance of self-esteem to the overall integrity of the client's personality, and how lack of empathic understanding of the client is a narcissistic injury of greater or lesser proportions.

4 The counselor's theory of the psychoanalytic counseling process

Our task in this chapter is to introduce the reader to some of the major dimensions of psychoanalytic treatment as applied to the counseling interview. Our conceptual problem involves organizing these ideas in ways that will help the reader understand them. To accomplish our task we will characterize the psychoanalytic counseling process and its desired outcomes by constructing two theoretically derived models. The first model will depict the sequence of important events that make up the psychoanalytic interview process. The second model will consist of several sets of factors that can help the counselor predict the client's responses to the opening phase of counseling.

Psychoanalytic treatment theories include a wide variety of complex ideas and their interaction. Ideas about the counselor's interventions, the client's productions and the sequencing of these two classes of events are best organized, we believe, when they are presented in a structure that helps elucidate their dynamic interaction. We have constructed two models with which to do this. The models are intended to be heuristic devices in helping the reader grasp the central ideas in the treatment process. The models will portray interview events as more orderly than they actually are. Even so, we believe the reader can use the models to help build a conceptual map for recognizing and labeling important events in the interview.

The previous two chapters have dealt with two different psychoanalytic theories of the person to illustrate how disharmonies in the personality arise. This chapter introduces a psychoanalytic framework for thinking about how to manage a course of therapeutic interaction with the client. Subsequent chapters will elaborate the ideas now introduced here in broad outline.

The first model we present will characterize the course of events in a series of psychoanalytic counseling interviews and is adapted from Menninger's (1958) "flow of insight" model. This model is introduced to help the reader understand some of the important events that occur in psychoanalytic interviews with the client, their sequence and their desired consequences. The second model will include a description of factors that help us predict the client's responses to the first or opening phase of counseling (see Patton, 1987; Meara, 1987). We include the second model to highlight the importance of organizing information systematically so that we can predict whether counseling will be of benefit to the client. Both models draw upon concepts from psychoanalytic treatment theory (Freud, 1913/1958a; Berliner, 1941; Greenson, 1967; Brenner, 1982; Langs, 1973).

The path of client understanding: a model of events in the psychoanalytic counseling interview

Our model of the essential components in the psychoanalytic counseling interview is a depiction of their sequential occurrence across one or more interviews. When we speak of sequence we are referring to the order of the ongoing series of interactions between client and counselor. The events that the participants produce as their sequences of interaction, and what they do with them, is the process of counseling and its outcomes. That is, the participants have a relationship of interaction in which they produce and attempt to manage or sequence events concertedly in the interview. Both the way in which certain events are conjointly managed or sequenced by the client and counselor, and the events themselves, are what identify the encounter as an occasion of psychoanalytic counseling. In this case, we infer that the participants' concerted management of interview events (see Patton, 1984) can facilitate a reduction in the client's presenting complaints and symptoms, and his or her attainment of insight or self-understanding.

Client insight and the concomitant reduction of complaints and symptoms are goals of the psychoanalytic interview. In our model of interview events, insight is defined as client and counselor production and understanding of factors within the client that contribute to his or her emotional difficulties. Insight and the reduction of complaints are interactive events. They are, therefore, the joint achievements of the participants.

These achievements depend for their accomplishment on the client and counselor's concerted management of their conversation. That is, the conversation in psychoanalytic counseling is one in which each participant is able to use his or her own and the other's utterances to document and develop an underlying pattern of psychological factors that account for the client's problems. In this sense, then, some of the work of the counselor and the client can be described as documentary work (Garfinkel, 1967).

That is, the counselor and client look for and use portions of the client's verbal and non-verbal behavior as documentary evidence of the existence of a pattern of personality attributes in the client member of the pair. As far as insight is concerned, the counselor's and the client's task is one of finding facts in both the client's current behavior and past circumstances that are interpretable as evidence of a problematic dispositional pattern in the client. The identification of elements of the pattern from the client's material is insight.

The sequence of events that precede the client's and counselor's achievement of insight determine the organization of the interview. One way of describing the structure of the interview is to examine the events contributed by the client and counselor and their interaction. The client's contribution consists of six different events, and the counselor's contribution consists of five events. These events are depicted in Figure 4.1. This figure is adapted from the work of Karl Menninger (1958), whose model of the "flow of client insight" in the interview is a triangle. We have elaborated Menninger's ideas by adding several more features to the client's contribution, and have also added to the counselor's contribution. In Figure 4.1, the events of both participants proceed from the apex of the triangle down the right side, across the bottom and up the left side back to the apex. Our ensuing narrative follows the model by illustrating its events with excerpts from an actual case. The case involves a young married woman with three children who was seen in counseling over a period of 3 years.

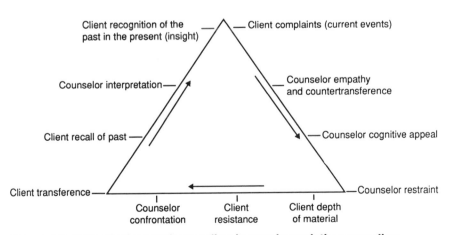

Figure 4.1 Path of client understanding in psychoanalytic counseling

The relevance of current events in the client's life

According to psychoanalytic ideas about psychological treatment (Greenson, 1967), a part of the client's mind wants to cooperate with the counselor, and another part opposes the work of counseling. For these and other reasons, it is never possible for the client to say explicitly, and with conscious awareness, everything that is on his or her mind. Even if the client wanted to do so, resistance would preclude the client's disclosure of all that is on his or her mind. The upshot of this dynamic feature of communication is that some of the meaning of the client's material is manifest and some of it is latent; that is, the latent meaning of client communication must be inferred from the manifest content of the language and other significant client behaviors. The counselor's task in this regard is to try to understand both the manifest and the latent meanings in the client's communications. This is made less difficult when it is recognized that a common, underlying theme connects the seemingly disparate segments of the client's talk during the interview.

The theme that connects each of the events in the hour is usually to be found in the client's initial complaints. The theme, or associative thread that runs through the client's communications in the hour (Langs 1973; Fancher, 1973), is ordinarily a derivative of unconscious material in the client. In attempting to understand the latent meanings in the client's communications, it is important to recognize that the client communicates at several levels. The manifest level is the ordinary, everyday meaning of the language the client uses. The client also communicates latent meanings in terms of his or her longings or wishes. Underlying each manifest communication is the language of desire stemming from the transference and directed both to the counselor and to some significant other person(s) outside the counseling interview. In other words, the client's manifest communications are a derivative of the unconscious or latent communication through which the transference is expressed. This latent communication is present in the client's opening complaints.

For these and other reasons, the client is encouraged to begin the interview by reporting about events that are current in his or her everyday life. Current events in the client's everyday circumstances are items to be understood for their relevance to the client's inner life and his or her manifest problems. The client begins at the surface of his or her mind and tells the counselor the things that are of present concern. When the client reports about current complaints, it helps both participants locate and describe those situations to which the client is attempting successfully or unsuccessfully to adapt (Langs, 1973).

The client's current life situation makes demands on the ego for adaptation. Current events form an "adaptive context" for the client (Langs, 1973;

Hartmann, 1939). The adaptive context contains the stressful events to which the client has responded with the development of complaints or symptoms. It contains, therefore, the client's subjective view of the situation. That is, the client will have his or her own unique way of understanding events in the adaptive context. The ego may perceive the adaptive demand in one of several ways that indicate it is a stressor of some kind and respond accordingly. The event may be interpreted by the ego as: (a) a loss; (b) an injury or threat of injury to the body or self-esteem; or (c) an obstacle to the satisfaction of sexual or aggressive wishes (cf. Westfall, 1964). Each of these three subjective interpretations will have its origins in the client's biography.

We may comment generally, however, in noting that loss, for example, is a ubiquitous phenomenon in our technologically oriented and rapidly changing world. Death and separation from loved ones is all too common in a world with widespread political, economic, and social unrest, not to mention natural disasters. Transportation disasters and terrorism add to the toll. Cultural change in many societies places considerable strain on marriages and families, which seem to dissolve at an increasing pace.

The pervasive competition in work and leisure that is found in most industrialized societies focuses enormous attention on the individual and his or her achievements. When the individual rather than the group is the desired locus of expression in a society (see P. Pepinsky, unpublished manuscript), the risk is greatly increased that the individual will experience serious injury to either the body or to self-esteem, or both. Finally, both the increased numbers of other persons with whom one must interact in daily life and the sheer complexity of modern life in the family, the school, or the workplace practically ensures that the individual will encounter obstacles to the fulfillment of his or her sexual or aggressive wishes. Those not endowed with sufficient intellect or physical strength are especially vulnerable.

When the client responds unsuccessfully to events in the adaptive context and interprets such events in the manner mentioned above, the resulting complaints or symptoms form what Langs (1973) calls the "therapeutic context." That is, the client's resulting complaints and symptoms provide a rationale for the counselor and client's interaction in a given interview. It is the counselor's responsibility to help the client reduce the complaints and symptoms. The therapeutic context is a focus of the client's reporting and the counselor's interventions in the interview. This context also contains the latent communications referred to above. The adaptive context is antecedent to the therapeutic context and gives significance to the latter by making explicit the dynamic relation between the two.

Part of the therapeutic context includes the client's affective response to the events in the adaptive context. That is, for each perceived stress there is a corresponding affect. For example, the affective accompaniment of separation and loss is depression. One laments the absence, however permanent, of the valued object. Shame is the usual affective response to injuries to the body or self-esteem (see Kohut, 1971; Williams, 1940; Shreve & Patton, 1988). Shame has its corollaries in the client's guilt, embarrassment, or humiliation. With shame, one feels exposed and experiences the urge to withdraw from the gaze of others. Anger is the partner of a delay or blocking of one's sexual or aggressive wishes. Anger, like most strong affects, disrupts the client's access to his or her normal intellective functions and is usually accompanied by the conviction that someone needs to pay for the damages.

The client's adaptive and therapeutic contexts consist of those current events that are most salient for the client and the client's responses to them. It is in reference to current events that the participants are able to observe, and later claim, that the client member of the pair has attained a reduction of the complaints and a modicum of self-understanding. Current events are the interpretive background against which the participants may later make the distinction between what was *then* and what is *now*. It should be clear, then, why psychoanalytic counselors are often quick to identify as resistant any client who begins the interview by talking about past rather than current events.

In the example below, the client makes clear what the complaint is. She is currently and has been depressed. However, she and the counselor are not yet clear about what the adaptive context for the complaint is. She has had a depressive reaction to something but is not aware of the precipitating event(s). For this reason, the meaning of the complaint in the client's life is incomplete. At this point, it lacks a background context that would help the counselor understand its dynamic significance.

At the outset of a session, this 25-year-old, married, mother of three small children began by complaining that following several recent sessions she had become very depressed and tearful on the drive home. She also reported that she was feeling despondent now and on the verge of tears. In talking about this matter, she stated that she had felt so dysphoric on one occasion that she feared she would try to drive off the road in an attempt to kill herself. It was all she could do to maneuver the car home following this particular episode. She was very puzzled by this because she could not account for her depressive mood. Because the dark mood occurred during her drive home on each occasion, she wondered whether she was simply anticipating her return to a marital situation that was currently stressful for her. At this point, she also became visibly anxious.

Counselor empathy and countertransference

Social interaction in everyday life, however it is structured and for whatever manifest purposes, typically includes conversational practices that promote not only understanding among the parties to a conversation, but also affiliation among them (see Atkinson & Heritage, 1984). Just as typically, persons evoke in each other a wide range of affective reactions that represent portions of each person's conscious and unconscious inner life. Regardless of the "topic" of their conversation, persons typically avoid talk with each other that is disaffiliative. The ability of persons from the same language community and local culture to engage in commonly understood talk, as opposed to talk that is misunderstood, depends heavily upon each person's accurate, conscious and unconscious interpretation of the other's talk and intentions. Understanding depends, as well, on each person's awareness of his or her own affective reaction to that talk. Common understanding among persons in this regard is, therefore, an intersubjective phenomenon (Schutz, 1967) which is informed as much by one's subjective, affective reactions as it is by our understanding of the manifest properties of language (Garfinkel, 1967). We refer here to the interrelated processes of counselor empathy and countertransference.

Empathy   Empathy has been a much researched topic in the literature on counseling (see Rogers, 1951; Barrett-Lennard, 1981). In counseling, the participants not only use their empathic abilities to understand each other's talk, the counselor often makes explicit that he or she is doing so by communicating this to the client. Empathy has at least three functions in psychoanalytic counseling. First, the counselor's empathizing is a particular form of observation and understanding of the client (Kohut, 1977). In this case, the counselor's observational stance is from within the client's perspective. To obtain this stance, the counselor introspectively uses his or her own inner life as the touchstone. Kohut (1977) refers to empathy as "vicarious introspection." Greenson (1967) refers to empathy as a kind of "emotional knowing." The counselor's understanding of the client in this way is subjective. Counselor empathy is an awareness of the client's thoughts, feelings, and impulses to action. Such awareness leads to the momentary experiencing of them by the counselor. The counselor uses empathy to obtain a momentary experiential understanding of the client's inner life. Later, the counselor shifts to an objective mode by augmenting his or her empathic awareness with knowledge of theory.

The second use of counselor empathy is as an intervention. When the counselor communicates his or her empathic understanding, it conveys to the client that the counselor is in tune with him or her. Thus, counselor empathy can take the form of responding to the client's affect before content. This has effects both on the relationship in counseling and on the client. With regard to the working alliance between the counselor and client, if the empathic communication is accurate and correctly timed, it functions to strengthen the alliance (see Greenson, 1967). It does this because communication based on accurate empathic understanding is affiliative. With regard to the client, to be correctly understood by another person is gratifying and soothing, particularly if the client is suffering. By acknowledging that we are in tune with and concerned about the client's inner state we convey our caring and our humanness.

As the third use in psychoanalytic counseling, accurately timed empathic interventions also help on some occasions to prepare the way for the counselor's later interventions. Empathy can be used to as a kind of stage-setting to precede a cognitive appeal, a question or a confrontation or interpretation. By making an empathic intervention regarding the client's affective state, the counselor helps the client prepare to focus on the painful thoughts accompanying the affect, to do something about them. It does so by helping the client gain greater access to his or her intellective functions. For example, acknowledging a painful inner state can often serve to calm the client. This heightens the client's readiness to think and talk about the material in greater depth, or about the significance of the counselor's later confrontation or interpretation of that material.

Countertransference   In psychoanalytic counseling, we take the position that the counselor's countertransference reactions can be an effective method for increasing one's empathic understanding of the client (see Strupp & Binder, 1984; Jacobs, 1988). This broadened view of countertransference varies sharply from the earlier and more narrow view in psychoanalysis. The earlier view holds that countertransference is exclusively the counselor's edition of a pathological transference. That is, countertransference is seen to be a situation in which the client represents an object from the counselor's past, onto whom are projected the remanants of unresolved conflict. This can be the case and when it occurs, it is antitherapeutic because it produces errors in the counselor's handling of the client's transference (Greenson, 1967, p. 348). Pathological countertransference reactions lead to consistently inappropriate behavior toward the client which, according to Greenson, usually takes such forms as persistent misunderstanding of the client, or some unconscious rewarding or punishing of the client. In this case, the counselor has been unable to set empathy aside in order to reflect on these reactions.

To preclude and/or remedy such persistent errors due to countertransference, psychoanalytic counselors are advised to: (a) seek their own treatment, preferably to undergo their own personal analysis with a qualified psychoanalyst; (b) seek well supervised and organized training in psychoanalytic treatment; and (c) make use of ongoing case consultation with colleagues throughout one's career as a counselor. Even so, there are times when it is very difficult to avoid losing one's objectivity with the client, and, thereby, become drawn into helping the client blindly live out his or her emotional difficulties. There is no substitute for the counselor to remain aware of his or her reactions to the client, and always to keep in mind that it is the client's pervasive sense of vulnerability that prompts his or her attempts to get the counselor to play a role that reinforces faulty relationship patterns.

The topic of countertransference, its definition and significance, remains controversial in the psychoanalytic literature. The debate centers around seeing countertransference as either an exclusively pathological phenomenon in the counselor which is elicited by the client, or as sets of thoughts, feelings and ideas in the counselor which represent conscious and unconscious aspects of the client's conflicted inner life. We hold that countertransference is both of these things. The broader view of countertransference grows out of the object relations point of view (Kernberg, 1980) and reflects the emphasis on the interpersonal aspects of the client and counselor relationship. This emphasis fits nicely with our own stress on the interactive nature of that relationship.

Our view is that the non-pathological, interpersonal element of counter-transference is of great importance to the counselor. It helps the counselor understand more about the client's inner life. Countertransference in this sense is a form of empathy in which the counselor experiences reactions that are evoked by the client's transference wishes and fears. In this way, the counselor's countertransference thoughts, feelings or fantasies are reactions to (are set off by) the client's unconscious wishes transferred to the counselor for fulfillment. By attending to the internal reactions, the counselor can derive clues to the underlying problem for which the client needs assistance.

In the example below, the counselor's use of an empathic intervention helps illustrate the role of countertransference and three functions of empathy. First, the counselor sensed the client's depressed feeling from within her frame of reference. That is, as she spoke, she had momentarily evoked in the counselor a deep sense of sadness and fear. Second, the counselor intervened to communicate awareness of this depressed affect, so that the client would feel understood. Third, the counselor's intervention also had the intention of helping the client calm herself in preparation for later talking about her feelings.

The counselor became aware of the client's blue mood, her possible reasons for it, her anxious discomfort and the effect of these in disrupting her ability to continue talking. The counselor had several purposes in mind in deciding to intervene with an empathic response at this point. First, to demonstrate to the client that the counselor was in tune with her painful state, the counselor responded first to the client's affective state before responding to the content of her communication. Second, it was hoped that the empathic intervention would have a calming effect on the client, such that she could again report more freely. The counselor intervened as follows: "I can tell you are sadder now, and at the same time are also feeling pretty scared. There is no hurry; just talk when you feel ready."

The counselor's cognitive appeal to the client

In the psychoanalytic interview nothing is trivial. Every piece of client material is of potential relevance as a candidate for analysis or understanding. The client begins the interview with complaints that are embedded in the current events of his or her life circumstances. If, however, understanding is an important goal of the work, eventually the client must stop complaining and begin working in order to acquire insight about the complaints. The counsellor's task is consistently to encourage the client to do the work of thinking and talking in the interview, instead of complaining. Such encouragement on the part of the counselor is what Bruce L. Goates (personal communication, February 12, 1980) calls a "cognitive appeal." It is a counselor intervention that aims at mobilizing the forces within the client that are on the side of counseling. In Bibring's (1954) terms, a cognitive appeal is a technical manipulation.

Specifically, a cognitive appeal is a class of counselor intervention that is characterized by the counselor's invitation to the client to use his or her mind. There may be several reasons why the counselor may wish to intervene with the use of a cognitive appeal. A client may not know how to go about reporting in the interview after having mentioned the initial concerns that brought him or her to the interview. In this case, the counselor may ask the client for specific details that will flesh out the complaint. For instance, the counselor may say, "An example of that will help us understand. Does one come to mind?" In another case, the client's mind may try to hide unpleasant thoughts and feelings associated with complaints. When this occurs, the circumstances and the dates of onset for the complaints may be withheld or reported in vague terms. Yet the counselor understands that such information is important and is, therefore, interested in helping the client to use his or her mind to remember, describe, discriminate, and evaluate. In this instance the counselor may say, "Let's see if we can understand what that's about. Please just try to describe what you are feeling."

A counselor's cognitive appeal is aimed at the activation of the client's intellective functions. It is a request to the client to interrupt the stream of experience by observing and commenting on the complaint. When the client is in a complaining mode, he or she is usually living in the experience without much accompanying reflection. Like most of us, the client is not likely to pause to engage in reflection about current experiences unless there is a special reason and assistance in doing so. The counselor's cognitive appeal helps the client activate the cognitive processes that promote awareness and eventual understanding.

In the next chapter we will comment further about how the cognitive appeal invites the client to accept or to restore the working alliance offered by the counselor. For now, however, it is important to understand that a major purpose of the counselor's cognitive appeal is to help move the client out of the complaining mode and into a working mode by requesting the client to think and talk actively about the current experiences with which he or she begins the hour. In doing so, the client begins to provide examples and details from memory, to become curious about these matters and to begin to evaluate the significance of the material thus produced.

The cognitive appeal, when successful, achieves several other accomplishments in the hour. Initially, it assists the new client in learning how to be a client. That is, in making the cognitive appeal, the counselor is asking the client to do two things that are necessary to the work. First, the client is requested to disclose the contents of his or her mind, and to do so as freely as possible. Second, the client is requested to think and talk about current experiences; literally, to "work" in the hour with the counselor. Next, if the counselor's cognitive appeal is phrased such that it is also an invitation to seek mutual understanding, the client is also learning how to collaborate with the counselor. Last, the counselor's cognitive appeal helps set the stage for the next important event in the sequence of achieving client understanding.

The following example illustrates the wording of a cognitive appeal. The reader will note in the example that the counselor deliberately says "us" to emphasize the working alliance or partnership between them. The counselor's intervention also makes a specific request of the client to do the work of remembering and talking by asking for a specific example of one of the times during which she experienced feeling depressed.

Following the counselor's empathic intervention, the client visibly relaxed and began talking again about her depression during the drive home. She began to repeat the complaints with which she had opened the hour. The counselor intervened with the purpose of inviting her to begin thinking about the circumstances of her depression on the drive home as follows: "I believe it will help us understand if you can select just one of these episodes where you felt so depressed on the way home from here and describe in detail what was happening and what you were thinking."

The importance of counselor restraint

When cognitive appeal has been successful, the client has stopped complaining, at least temporarily, and has begun to report in detail the circumstances surrounding the onset of the complaints. Instead of complaining that he or she is depressed, angry, anxious, and the like, the client begins to think and talk about the ideas connected with those feelings by reporting the recent circumstances surrounding their appearance. In doing so, the names of other people involved and dates are frequently mentioned. So is the sequence of events that made up the adaptive situation to which the client responded with complaints or symptoms. It is not easy for the client to report in detail about painful events without re-experiencing some of the pain. The client would prefer not to talk about such matters in explicit detail, and would welcome, therefore, some activity from the side of the counselor. The client would like to be relieved of the burden of continuing to talk about such matters.

The counselor has a decision to make. The counselor's response at this point is guided by his or her evolving empathic and theoretical understanding of the client and by a psychoanalytic principle of counselor behavior that applies at any point in the interview, viz., it is usually better to let the client continue to try to talk than for the counselor to intervene. Therefore, as the client makes the attempt to do what he or she can to work on the complaints, the counselor refrains from intervening in favor of listening. By doing so, the client is tacitly encouraged to use his or her own mind, and to follow as best as possible, the direction his or her thoughts are taking. In this way, the counselor helps the client approximate free association in reporting. Counselor restraint is called for when the client is able to use his or her own mind. Restraint or silence is not appropriate when the client needs to hear from the counselor because he or she is becoming overwhelmed by affect. There are times, then, when silence might be experienced by the client as withholding or otherwise punishing.

Generally, however, psychoanalytic counselors are less active in their work with clients than are counselors from other therapeutic persuasions. The main reason for this relatively greater restraint on the part of psychoanalytic counselors is a technical one. Counselor restraint encourages the client to take the major responsibility for reporting as freely as possible the direction his or her thoughts and feelings are taking in the hour. By counselor restraint, we are referring not only to the decision not to intervene verbally in the flow of client material, or to do so minimally, but also to the counselor's inhibition of non-verbal behaviors as well. This idea follows from Freud's (1913/1958a) recommendation that the analyst be an ambiguous stimulus for the client on which he or she is able to project conscious and unconscious wishes from past conflicted situations. The client cannot do this if the counselor is too active and disclosing of his or her own personal material.

Counselor restraint also functions to place the responsibility for talking on the client. Over the course of the interview, the division of responsibility (see Robinson, 1950) with regard to who does the majority of the talking clearly favors the client. But counselor restraint as an intervention strategy serves still another function that promotes client communication in the interview. Appropriate counselor restraint is mildly frustrating for the client. By being restrained, the counselor is not doing the client's thinking, or is not rewarding or rescuing the client. Instead, the client is tacitly encouraged by the counselor's restraint to consult his or her own experiences in the quest for self-understanding.

With the judicious use of restraint, the counselor helps encourage the occurrence of the next event in the sequence that leads to client self-understanding. That is, counselor restraint mildly frustrates the client's wishes for gratification from the counselor. Frustration helps surface the thoughts and feelings in the client's mind and makes them more amenable to exploration, thus increasing the depth or relevance of client material.

Counselor restraint as an intervention can occur when the client is providing abundant information, or when the client is struggling to communicate. In the former case, the counselor refrains from intervening so as not to distract the client. In the latter case, the counselor avoids intervening to permit the client to work it out on his or her own. Finally, in the example below, the counselor's restraint keeps the responsibility for communicating on the client.

Following the counselor's cognitive appeal to think about her depressive episodes in detail, the client began to describe the events that occurred as she left her sessions, got in the car, drove through town, and finally arrived at her own home. As she talked, she began to recall thoughts and feelings that had been present on her mind as she left the counseling session. She also reported the sequence of these thoughts and feelings. Inasmuch as it was clear that the client had a considerable amount to say and appeared motivated to communicate, the counselor refrained from intervening in favor of listening. The client continued reporting on the example at some length.

Depth of client material

When the client stops complaining, and when the counselor stays out of the client's way, then the client is able to deepen the significance of the material he or she is reporting. This is because, when given the opportunity, the client will experience a pressure to communicate to the counselor what the problem is. It may take 5 minutes or 30 minutes for the client to deepen the material and explore its meaning, but, however long, the meaningfulness of the client's material is gauged by its contents and the client's attitude toward them.

When the client is able to freely follow the direction his or her thoughts are taking, he or she begins to talk about matters that have increasing relevance to the presenting complaints for the hour. Moreover, the client shows some curiosity about these matters. Relevant material is characterized by its association to uncomfortable affects, and by the reporting of detailed and sequential actions in context. Ideas that were preconscious or unconscious are reported along with their implications. Cause and effect patterns may be clarified. New fears may surface, accompanied by new defenses against them.

In addition to curiosity, the client may also evidence a certain thoughtfulness or introspectiveness about the direction the thoughts are taking. Memories may be recalled, details supplied and then the material again worked on by evaluating its significance. Connections to recent precipitants will usually be made. Ordinarily, some recent event serves as a trigger for the internal chain of events that led to the complaints the client mentioned at the outset of the hour. When the client's material has deepened sufficiently, there is usually a clear indication that the client is aware of the role of the recent precipitant in the induction of the succeeding events. The client's material may then cycle back to the precipitant and forward again several times. Each time, some new facet of material is uncovered and added to the growing picture.

All that may be needed from the counselor when the client is reporting freely and in some depth is occasional encouragement to continue. This is because the client is busy exploring the heretofore unseen horizons of the conflictual theme that has been made relevant by the precipitating events. The client feels a pressure to communicate what he or she has discovered. In such circumstances, it is best to continue to stay out of the client's way and to just let the talk continue. Interrupting the client in the middle of a long, but relevant, monologue only serves to disrupt the client's train of associations. Without knowledge of the train of associations in the client's thought, neither the counselor nor the client will grasp, or have evidence of, the underlying condition for which the client needs help.

Each time the client is able to deepen the material he or she is reporting, both participants are given an opportunity to increase their understanding of the client. Each such event is like a "critical incident" that sets up the later possible occurrence of improved reality testing, re-education, insight, or all three events, for the client. When the client is helped to deepen the material around his or her presenting complaints, the way is prepared for the uncovering of troublesome thoughts and feelings that are derivative of the client's central emotional difficulties. Such difficulties invariably involve other important persons in the client's life, such as the counselor in the example below.

With silence on the counselor's part, the client began to deepen her reporting of the one episode she selected. For example, she recalled that after the session in question, she felt happy as she walked to her car. Her thoughts were about what the two of them had talked about on that occasion. As well, she reported feeling grateful for the attention the counselor was paying to her. It had been enjoyable being there working on her problems.

Client resistance

Obstacles to open communication are ever present in the counseling interview. When the obstacles are centered in the client, we refer to them as resistances. We identify as client resistance any aspect of client talk or conduct that opposes the work of understanding. Client resistance may be present from the outset of the interview, or it may not appear until after the client has begun to deepen the significance of the material he or she is reporting. Resistance will inevitably appear whenever the direction of the client's thoughts lead to the counselor. Thus, on the one hand, resistance is an obstacle that must be removed if open communication is to occur. On the other hand, however, client resistance is also an opportunity because it helps the counselor understand how the client's mind works; that is, it assists us in understanding the client's conflicts. Resistance is both a technical problem for the counselor and an avenue for greater understanding of the client. Outside of counseling resistance operates as defense. In Chapter 2 we introduced the role of the defenses in the development of psychic conflict and compromise formations. There, we saw that the defenses are elicited to block awareness of unacceptable ideas and/or painful feelings that threaten to become conscious. In Chapter 9, we will go into greater detail about the topic of resistance. For now, we can note that in the counseling interview, defenses function as resistances that serve to block the kind of free and open communication on which self-understanding is built.

Client resistance will be apparent to the observant counselor as an element of conflict. Client resistance is the language of avoidance. It is also a threat to the working alliance between the participants if it cannot be overcome. The counselor's task is to help the client understand the nature and role of resistance and how the client is resisting. As an important element of our model of the psychoanalytic counseling process, client resistance is a phenomenon of great importance because much of the work of the counselor involves understanding and working with the client's resistances. One method of dealing with those resistances is with the next element of the model, counselor confrontation. Before examining that element we present our example of client resistance.

After the client mentioned how much she had enjoyed the work with the counselor in the session in question, her face began to darken noticeably and she stopped talking for a moment. She then changed the subject and began talking about the trouble she was having with getting her youngest son to mind her. Then she mentioned she had quarreled with her father earlier in the week. Soon she changed the topic again and began talking about how difficult it was to enjoy the little time she and her husband had to be alone together. Finally, she stopped reporting altogether.

Counselor confrontation

A confrontation is an intervention by the counselor that helps the client to become aware that he or she is resisting the experiencing of something. When the client becomes aware of resistance the counselor then helps him or her to understand what is being resisted and why (Greenson, 1967). A successful counselor confrontation promotes the flow of client understanding by helping the client learn how his or her mind is working to hide or say "no" to the expression of certain thoughts and feelings. It prepares the way for the identification of what is being resisted and the clarification of the reasons for the resistance.

The counselor's initial task in dealing with client resistance is to recognize how it manifests itself in the client's behavior. Recognition involves awareness of the mode of resistance. By mode is meant the form taken by the resistance. We believe it is useful for the counselor to learn to identify not only the typical defense mechanisms, but also to understand that any client behavior that reduces unpleasant affect can also serve the purposes of resistance. Thus, for example, both "reaction formation" and an habitual attitude of humility can be resistant behaviors. Clients vary with regard to how easily they can and will recognize resistance. Some clients are aware of even momentary resistance in their reporting of material to the counselor. Others will need strong evidence that they are resisting. The counselor's empathic knowledge of the client will help him or her determine when and how to confront the client's resistance.

With particularly strong resistance, the counselor is advised to let it build (Greenson, 1967), so that when it is demonstrated to the client, he or she is less able to deny its occurrence. Ordinarily, the counselor will confront the mode of resistance in some way in order to demonstrate that the client is resisting. When dealing with the client's reaction formation, for example, the counselor might intervene to demonstrate that the client's positive or negative reaction to something seems unusually strong, if not out of proportion to the circumstances.

In all instances, the counselor waits to confront or demonstrate the client's resistance until he or she is convinced that the confrontation will have significance for the client. Time and material will be wasted if the confrontation is premature, or if the counselor intervenes in a less than tactful way. The later clarification of the resistant material cannot take place unless the client acknowledges that he or she is resisting. Only when the client is in a working mode, that is, in a working alliance with the counselor, is it possible to convince the client that he or she is resisting. The client's recognition and understanding of resistance requires a reasonable ego that can both experience and observe that experience. This process is called "splitting the ego." An example of counselor confrontation to highlight client resistance is presented below.

It will be recalled that the client had become resistant as she began talking about how she enjoyed working with the counselor. The mode of resistance at this point might be called "topic switching." The counselor intervened with the following response in an attempt to demonstrate the resistance to the client: "Are you aware that you have changed the topic three times in the last couple of minutes?" The client acknowledged this behavior but was at a loss to account for it. The counselor went on to clarify the source of her resistance for her by saying: "I suspect you changed the topic because the original talk about how you were enjoying our work together made you anxious." The client confirmed this. The counselor then asked her to elaborate this point and she was able to report that she did enjoy the work but that it scared her to think how gratified she felt after the sessions.

The client's transference

At this point, the path of client understanding has led to the client's transference manifestations about the counselor. Because one of the targets of the client's longings is the counselor, the client begins to make direct or indirect reference to him or her. The client's previous communications as a train of associations have prepared the way for the surfacing of material related to the transference relationship with the counselor. The psychoanalytic model predicts that the client will give expression to the irrational or transference aspect of his or her overall relationship with the counselor. The surfacing and recognition of the more readily accessible aspects of the client's transferential thoughts and feelings about the counselor will help promote later self-understanding.

One of Freud's (1912/1958b) seminal discoveries was that of transference relations among persons. Transference is an intrapsychic phenomenon in which the person transfers to someone important in the present certain conflict-laden ideas and feelings that are more appropriate to someone important in the person's past. The result is that the person brings to an important relationship faulty, that is, inappropriate patterns of expectation and behavior that have originated in an earlier, frustrating relationship in the client's childhood (Basch, 1988). One does not observe transference proper. Instead, we infer its presence and operation from inappropriate or irrational patterns of relating on the part of the client. Thus, a sector of the person's experience of the other in the present is influenced by his or her attributions from the conflicted past. This can make the client's overt reactions to the counselor irrational because the reactions are not based on the reality of the contemporary situation.

Transference reactions to other people occur when those people become important to us as objects for fulfilling longstanding, conflicted childhood expectations. One person does not have a loving or hateful reaction to another person unless, in the first person's view, there is some kind of emotional relationship between them. One reason for an emotional attraction or repulsion between persons is that each reminds the other of an important relationship from the past. When those past relationships have been conflictual, ongoing encounters between persons in the present can serve as a stimulus for the activation of earlier wishes, feelings, and defenses against these. The result is often the reaction of one person to the other that is inappropriate as to time, place, and person (Greenson, 1967).

In counseling, then, the client directs to the counselor loving or aggressive thoughts and feelings, as well as overt reactions that are not based on the real relationship between them. Instead, these phenomena can be traced back to earlier wishful fantasies of the client's that have been involved in conflict and which have, therefore, become unconscious (Freud, 1915/1957b). In the present, the client anticipates the gratification of these wishes with the counselor, and sooner or later, his or her communications reveal them (Freud, 1916/1961a). Counseling presents a new opportunity to repeat either the earlier conflicted situation with the hope that this time, the client will master the trouble (Freud, 1920/1955), or to at least face how the wishes cannot be gratified in his or her adult relationships.

However, as we have seen, the client erects resistances to becoming aware of his or her transference feelings for the counselor. The reason for this resistance to re-experiencing the needs and wishes from the past is the client's fear of again experiencing the painful disappointment that accompanied their original arousal. Much of the work in the first phase of psychoanalytic counseling is directed at helping the client recognize and overcome these resistances to the transference.

In using the transference, the psychoanalytic counselor assists the client in becoming aware of how his or her faulty patterns of relating to others have manifested themselves in the therapeutic relationship. Client awareness of these matters gives the client the opportunity to resolve them or, when this is not possible, to diminish their impact or work around them. The following excerpt helps illustrate a portion of the client's transference.

Following the confrontation of the client's resistance and the partial clarification of its source in her present feelings for the counselor, the client reported how close she had come to feel to the counselor, and how very enjoyable it was to sit here and talk and be listened to. It was exciting, but also a little frightening. It was important to her that the counselor think well of her, too.

Counselor interpretation

Counselor interpretation is an event in the flow of client insight that promotes the client's understanding of the central emotional problems in his or her life as those become manifest in the transference. It is the counselor's formulation of the gist of some aspect of the client's material in the conversation thus far. An interpretation of transference material that the client has just remembered gives the client an appraisal of the relevance of the memories to events in the present. Relevance is established in this case by using the memory as the historical grounds for the client's current motives and conduct. With the interpretation, the counselor attempts to help the client understand how his or her past is being relived in the present in the relationship with the counselor.

Counselor interpretation is the primary intervention technique for helping the client acquire insight. It is used sparingly. Conversationally, an interpretation functions like an assessment or an appraisal given by one speaker to the other (see Atkinson & Heritage, 1984). Such conversational devices call for a confirmation or disconfirmation from the other speaker, in this case the client. Obviously, confirmation is the preferred response. If the intervention is timed correctly and can be heard by the client as a personally relevant inference about the meaning of the current material, it is more likely to be confirmed than disconfirmed. When the client confirms an interpretation, or any intervention for that matter, additional material about the point becomes available and deepens in significance.

All other events in counseling lead to interpretation. The events that have preceded the counselor's interpretation should make it possible for the counselor to time the intervention appropriately and to be correct in framing its content. A period of time and a strong working alliance between the participants are, therefore, necessary to prepare the client for interpretation and to provide the counselor with enough knowledge of the client to enable him or her to understand the meaning of the client's memories. Thus, current events or complaints need to be reported, together with examples of their onset and circumstances. The counselor needs to help the client confront and clarify resistances to reporting this and other conflictual material. Only after the resistances have been dealt with sufficiently will there be a recall of material that the client is willing and able to think and talk further about. When this stage is reached the client is usually ready to hear and work with an interpretation. We provide below an example of counselor interpretation of transference material.

After the client had disclosed that she enjoyed being together with the counselor and looked forward to coming each week, the counselor offered the following interpretation: "It seems that you have to pay for your pleasure. On the one hand, you enjoy our work together. On the other hand, enjoying it makes you feel guilty, so you punish yourself all the way home by feeling terrible and by wanting to kill yourself."

Client recall of the past

Following an interpretation, like a confrontation, the counselor and client may work on clarifying the point. This process may require very little or a considerable amount of time, depending upon the state of the client's ego at the moment and his or her introspective capacity. It is sometimes the case that after an interpretation (or a confrontation, for that matter), the client will recall related material from the recent or remote past. These memories will also be seen to be related to the material that has preceded them in the hour.

All the events in the hour that have gone before have prepared the way for the client's recall of significant events in the past. Those events are related to not only the client's beginning complaints that opened the hour, but also to his or her later report of material flowing from the complaints, and to references to the counselor. Each segment in the path of client understanding thus far has been related to those that have preceded and followed it. Each has contributed its influence to helping the client remember.

The client's report of memories that surface in this way may be brief or lengthy. The counselor should facilitate the client's recall of as much material as is possible, with due attention paid to the client's affective state as he or she does so. If the working alliance between the client and counselor is firm and the resistances have been cleared away on this occasion, the recall of abundant material is usually the rule. The recall of remote memories typically involves the client and members of his or her natal family. Childhood memories of the client's interaction with one or both parents or caretakers is most common. One or more of the childhood calamities of object loss, loss of the object's love, castration or guilt (mentioned in Chapter 2) can be noted in the memories. In this way, there are very often scenes in which the client remembers feeling frightened, anxious, depressed, and/or guilty or angry with reference to the parents or caretakers. The recall of memories of more recent events is no less significant for the client. In this case, the recent event has served as a current precipitant for the client's complaints and symptoms.

In either case, the client's recall of the past is a critical event in psychoanalytic counseling. It is not because the past is of historical interest in its own right. Rather, the client's memories often serve as a lens through which the problematic present can be better understood. The counselor uses the client's past to help him or her learn how and why they are behaving in faulty ways with others in the present. Thus, the client's recall of past material following the confrontation of resistance in the interview, and the confrontation itself, illustrate the principle of determinism mentioned in Chapter 1. That is, the memories are antecedent to, if not the cause of, the unpleasant, associated affect which, in turn, is prior to, or the cause of, the resistance. In the passage below, the client recalls relevant material from her past.

Subsequent to the counselor's interpretation about the client paying with guilt for her pleasure at being with the counselor, the client recalled a memory from early childhood. She remembered sitting on her father's lap in the living room when she was 4, and he was tickling her. She said she could remember clearly how frightened she became and how she had to jump off his lap and run to her room and hide. She had a sense of foreboding that her mother was going to come in and kill her.

Client recognition of the past in the present

The purpose of the counselor's interpretations is to help the client achieve greater understanding or insight into him or herself. One form of insight occurs when the client recognizes the connection between past experiences and their reinstatement in th present. With self-understanding comes the possibility of making choices that were not available previously. In other words, the client is now aware that he or she may make a conscious choice of what to think, feel, or do *vis-à-vis* the conflicted area of experience. In the example below, the client learns how a relevant portion of her past has been reinstated in the present.

The client went on to elaborate the memory of the frightened little girl. She was able to understand for the first time how much guilt was at the heart of her depression. It was as if something bad had already happened and she was forever doomed to pay for it. Simple pleasures were not to be available. She had to be careful around her father lest she experience positive feelings for him. Better to maintain her distance and keep a war going with him. Enjoying her children or her husband too much would bring on depression. Enjoying the work with the counselor was out of the question altogether. These and other relationships began to improve the more she understood about how she lived out the old childhood conflict in the present.

Summary of the interaction sequence

In our model, the foregoing events comprise a sequence of interaction between the counselor and client that leads to client self-understanding. The counselor may occasionally observe this or a similar sequence of events leading to client insight in a single hour. More typically, the sequence occurs over a series of interviews. While we have characterized the sequence as a linear chain of sequential events for the purposes of illustration, it is important to realize that several of the events interact with each other, many are repeated over and over before the next event occurs, a complete chain of events rarely unfolds within a single hour, and, finally, therefore, the sequence is, more often than not, either begun anew each hour, or resumed at the point of interruption from the preceding hour.

Some important experiences in psychoanalytic counseling

Psychoanalytic counseling is hard work for both the client and the counselor. If that work goes well, it is not without pain and frustration for both participants. The counselor can experience frustration when attempting to help the client deal with his or her resistances to experiencing the transference with the counselor. In fact, with some clients, the initial reduction of their presenting complaints after seeing the counselor for a few sessions can prompt a so-called "flight into health," in which the client announces the intention to terminate counseling at exactly that point where the difficult work of understanding is about to begin. Dealing with this kind of resistance is especially difficult for the counselor.

The client's frustration with the counseling process often occurs precisely because the work is going well. In such a case it is not uncommon for the client to experience a temporary increase in turmoil and pain as he or she struggles with resistance or learns painful information. The counselor's humane support, patience, and willingness to explain what is happening are important at such times.

Finally, psychoanalytic counseling requires of the counselor that close attention be given to termination (Anderson, 1966). It is not uncommon for the client who is approaching termination to re-experience some of the complaints or symptoms that prompted the request for help in the first place. Neither is it uncommon for the client, and sometimes the counselor, too, to avoid talking about termination. The reason for these manifestations of avoidance is simple. Termination means separation and loss. The relationship with the counselor has been an important one for the client by virtue of the explicit focus on the transference, with all of its childhood hopes and fears. And, for the counselor, termination means the loss of companionship. The termination process deserves, therefore, to be dealt with openly, sensitively and consistently as counseling approaches the final session. This latter principle holds regardless of the duration of the treatment.

Predicting the client's response to the first phase of counseling

In the remainder of this chapter, we will present another model that involves predicting the client's response to the first phase of the psychoanalytic process. For heuristic purposes, we conceive of the overall counseling process occurring in three phases in its development, much like a well-formed, three-act drama. There is an opening phase of problem definition and relationship-building, a middle phase of working through the problem, and a closing or termination phase.

We single out the first phase of counseling for close scrutiny at this point because of the importance of getting the working alliance established during this phase. We believe that the working alliance is the most important outcome of the successful completion of the first phase of counseling. A firm working alliance (Greenson, 1967; Bordin, 1979; Gelso & Carter, 1985), in which the client accepts the counselor's invitation to collaborate in the work of thinking and talking freely about his or her problems and to evaluate the significance of what has been reported, is seen as essential to movement into the middle and termination phases of psychoanalytic counseling. In Chapter 5, we will have considerably more to say about the working alliance in its own terms. For now, let it be said that the working alliance, as well as other important outcomes of the first phase of counseling, are dependent on prior events involving the counselor and client. We believe knowledge of these events can be helpful to the counselor in predicting whether the client will be able to enter into a working alliance with the counselor.

Figure 4.2 contains three dimensions for the prediction of client outcomes as responses to the first phase of the counseling process. The fourth dimension consists of the desired outcomes of the first phase and are the client's responses. In addition, the model further characterizes the client's response in terms of stress and coping, as seen at the bottom of the figure. Client stress response and type of coping are seen to form three sub-phases within the first phase of counseling.

The first sub-phase

The first sub-phase consists of two dimensions whose individual elements comprise the nexus of psychological, physiological, and social factors relevant to the client. These elements form adaptive and therapeutic contexts (Langs, 1973) for understanding the client's communications over the course of the first phase of counseling. In other words, the elements in the first two dimensions provide the counselor with the means for organizing the client's communications within a psychoanalytic framework, and provide the basis

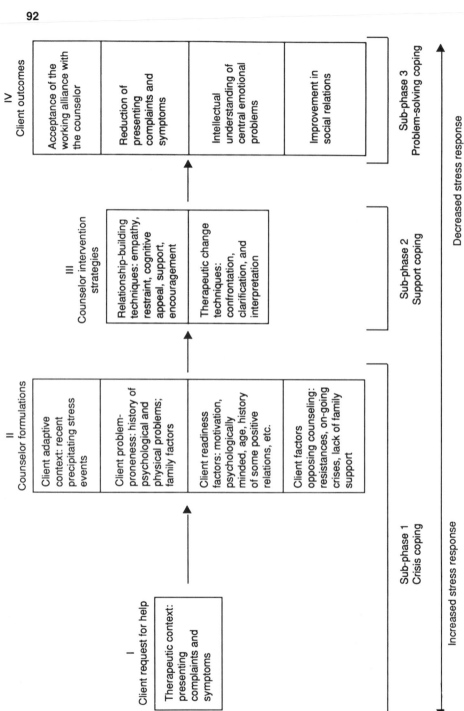

Figure 4.2 Prediction of the client's response to the first phase of the counseling process

for the development of treatment plans. In Chapter 7, we will present a formulation outline that will detail how the counselor uses these elements to organize the client's communications systematically, so that a course of action can be undertaken on the client's behalf. The relationship of these elements to establishing a working alliance and to other first-phase outcomes is mediated to some extent by counselor intervention strategies.

In Dimension I, Client Request for Help, the client's presenting complaints and symptoms are the manifest reason the client is seeking help. They form a therapeutic context (Langs, 1973) in which the counselor will try to intervene. The complaints and symptoms provide the client with motivation for cooperating with the counselor and accepting a working alliance if they are painful for the client. In Dimension II, Counselor Formulations, the recent or recurring precipitating stresses stand as antecedents for the presenting complaints, as does the client's history of problem-proneness. These elements form the adaptive context. In general, the more severe or chronic the stresses and the more extensive the history of previous psychological or physiological illnesses, the more severe the presenting complaints. To these elements can be added a set of client readiness factors that include such things as the client's age, his or her psychological mindedness, history of positive relationships with others, autonomy, and the like. We will also have more to say about client readiness factors in Chapter 6.

Finally, the last element in Dimension II consists of the factors that oppose counseling. Some of these factors can be events that are external to counseling itself. Lack of support for counseling on the part of the family, spouse, or employer can seriously undermine the client's ability to work purposefully in treatment. More commonly, however, are the factors within the client him or herself that oppose counseling. These we refer to as resistance and we will have much more to say about this subject in Chapter 9. In summary, perhaps it can be seen now that the elements in Dimensions I and II are a balance of forces, some of which support the client's acceptance of the counselor's offer to enter a working alliance and some of which oppose it. Obviously, the establishment of a firm working alliance requires that the balance of forces in this regard be on the positive side.

The presence of severe presenting complaints in the face of overwhelming affect would likely describe a client in a phase of crisis-coping and with increased stress-responding (Horowitz, 1976) at the outset of counseling. Regardless of the severity of the presenting picture or the degree of psychological debilitation evidenced by the client, most clients are more or less in a crisis-coping mode when they ask for professional counseling help. We call the first sub-phase crisis-coping to highlight the point that the client's responses to the demands placed by the environment at this time are mediated more by what will reduce pain than by rational self-knowledge.

The client's access to his or her normal intellective functions will either be impaired or intermittent. These observations provide the counselor with a general benchmark against which to measure progress. When they subside it is likely that the client has replaced the presenting symptoms and complaints, at least temporarily, with the working alliance.

The second sub-phase

The second sub-phase consists of the Counselor Intervention Strategies Dimension. We will present interviewing techniques in greater detail in Chapter 8. For now, the elements of this dimension include, first, the techniques that the counselor uses to build and maintain a productive working alliance with the client. Many of these techniques might be called "technical manipulations" rather than strictly therapeutic strategies (Bibring, 1954), in that they are intended to mobilize the forces within the client that support the treatment. For example, the counselor's judicious use of restraint gives the client the opportunity to be heard by a concerned and sympathetic listener. As well, empathy communicates to the client that the counselor is in tune with him or her and understands. A cognitive appeal asks the client to use his or her mind in trying to understand as well as experience. Finally, counselor support and encouragement directly influence the client to cooperate and put trust in the counselor.

The second set of intervention strategies include counselor techniques that are intended to bring about change in the client's knowledge of him or herself. The first set of techniques above help prepare the way for the use of the more therapeutically-oriented techniques. Confrontation, including clarification, and interpretation, are the major counselor techniques for attempting to help the client gain insight. Each of these techniques was discussed in the preceding sections of this chapter.

The use of these techniques is informed not only by the contextual features of the ongoing conversation between the participants in the interview, but also by the counselor's evolving formulation of the client based on the elements in Dimensions I and II. If the client is in a crisis mode at the outset, or at any time for that matter, the counselor is more likely to employ supportive, encouraging, and empathic techniques than techniques that call for the work of thinking and talking. When the crisis subsides, the counselor will introduce techniques that help the client begin to think and talk about his or her concerns, to reduce the sense of urgency and to become curious about those factors inside him or herself that have contributed to the problems.

In the earliest portions of the first phase of counseling, the counselor is more likely, then, to use the relationship-building techniques than the change-oriented techniques. The client will be invited to join in a working partnership with the counselor. At the same time, the client and the counselor will be attempting to gain initial understanding of the client's problems. The counselor may gently confront client resistances at this time, and may even try out a low-level interpretation to determine how the client deals with the counselor's efforts to understand.

The gist of the second sub-phase is that of helping mobilize the client for the later work of treatment. The counselor does this by extending to the client a supportive relationship in which that work can take place. With such support from the side of the counselor, the client does what he or she can to think and talk about him or herself and to then consider the significance of what has been reported.

The third sub-phase

Client Outcomes is the final dimension. Its elements consist of the "immediate criteria" (Robinson, 1950) of counseling effectiveness. By "immediate criteria of effectiveness" we mean those first-phase observations that tell us whether or not the process is working for the client. Long-term criteria, on the other hand, refer to the ultimate outcomes of counseling. In other words, it is a sign of counseling effectiveness, first of all, when the counselor has offered and the client has accepted a firm working alliance. One indication that the client is in a working alliance is when he or she is freely providing abundant information in the interview and is doing what he or she can to evaluate its significance.

Another first-phase outcome is a reduction in the client's presenting symptoms and complaints. The client should be reporting considerably less discomfort. There should be a decrease in anxiety, an increase in self-esteem, and an elevation of mood if the client has been able to enter a working alliance with the counselor. In other words, what the original complaints and symptoms did for the client in the way of gratification and reducing pain, the relationship with the counselor now increasingly does. The relationship with the counselor temporarily replaces the complaints and symptoms.

Another outcome of the first phase includes the client's growing intellectual understanding of his or her central emotional problems. As the first phase comes to a close, the client should have an understanding, in broad outline at least, of the major components in his or her make-up that have perpetuated the problem. But this is only intellectual understanding. The client's central problem, as that is made evident in the transference, remains to be understood in the context of living it out emotionally (working it through) with the counselor and with significant others, and, at the same time, doing so with growing awareness. This is the task of the middle, or working-through, phase of counseling.

Finally, we know the work is beginning to be successful when the client shows some improvement in his or her relations with others. For example, instead of conflict or withdrawal, the client begins to cooperate a little, or sustains contact instead of avoiding others. In any case, it is a positive sign when the client begins to talk with the counselor about his or her interpersonal problems instead of blindly living them out at home or work.

Acceptance of the working alliance and the other outcomes of the third sub-phase indicate that the client has begun to move into a problem-solving mode of adaptation. This is accompanied by decreased stress-responding, such that the client gives evidence of more access to his or her normal intellective functions. We believe that an estimate of the client's status on each of the four broad outcomes in Dimension IV can be made by knowledge of the elements in Dimensions I and II, and the client's response to the counselor's use of the techniques in Dimension III.

5 The working alliance

Steven B. Robbins

The task of this chapter is to describe the central role of the working alliance as a phenomenon in psychoanalytic counseling. To accomplish this, an historical perspective will be provided that identifies the working alliance as a component of the relationship between counselor and client. Within this perspective, a distinction will be made between the working alliance, the transference, and the "real" relationship as aspects of the overall interaction between client and counselor (Greenson, 1967; Gelso & Carter, 1985). The working alliance will then be described from both conceptual and empirical bases. A basic tenet of this chapter is that the working alliance forms the platform from which all interventions emerge. As such, the working alliance can be seen as both a change agent in itself and a necessary condition for the production and interpretation of material related to the client's central emotional problems. The role of the working alliance within neurotic, narcissistic, and borderline conditions will be differentiated. Examples of strategies to strengthen and maintain the working alliance will be provided, along with a discussion of the effect of the alliance, or its absence, within a single interview. Finally, two case examples will be presented that highlight the role of the working alliance over the course of both time-limited and time-unlimited counseling.

An historical perspective

Historically, the cornerstone of psychoanalytically-informed treatment was the interpretation of the transference, or the irrational and unrealistic responses a client would have to a counselor as a result of unconscious conflict. The transference is:

> . . . the experience of impulses, feelings, fantasies, and defenses with respect to a person in the present which do not appropriately fit that person but are a repetition of responses originating in regard to significant persons of early childhood, unconsciously displaced onto persons in the present (Greenson, 1967, p. 362).

From this perspective, the relationship between counselor and client is best served by understanding the developmental and dynamic determinants of the thoughts, behaviors, and feelings manifested by the client. The meaning of client–counselor interactions, then, were to be understood within the context of the client's irrational responses to the counselor and the counseling situation.

Not surprisingly, the non-transferential aspects, or rationally derived aspects of the client–counselor interaction, did not hold much importance for the early analysts. Nonetheless, Freud (1958b) as early as 1912 sensed the importance of what he called "the patient's positive conscious transference" and to a lesser extent the importance of affection and sympathetic understanding of the therapist. He writes:

> It remains the first aim of the treatment to attach (the patient) to it and to the person of the doctor . . . If one exhibits a serious interest in him, carefully clears away the resistances that crop up at the beginning and avoids certain mistakes, he will of himself form such an attachment . . . It is certainly possible to forfeit this first success if from the start one takes up any standpoint other than one of sympathetic understanding (pp. 139–140).

We can speculate that Freud's emphasis on ego functions in the later part of his life (e.g. Freud, 1923/1961b), and the emergence of the concept of a conflict-free or autonomous sphere of the ego (A. Freud, 1936b; Hartmann, 1939) provided the theoretical underpinnings necessary to examine other aspects of the client–counselor relationship. In other words, the construction of a conflict-free zone of the ego shifted the focus from instinctual determinants to adaptive processes, or how a person manages both internal and external life demands.

Sterba's (1929, 1934) work on the role of the ego in therapy is an example of the early efforts to describe the client's ability to (a) observe the process of counseling, referred to as "splitting the ego" (see Chapters 4 and 9), and (b) to identify with the analyst's analyzing ego. Self-awareness is considered a critical ego function when assessing mental health (Bellak, Hurvich & Gediman, 1973). Furthermore, the identification process is a powerful one observed within the counseling setting. This process can also be found with abused children, for example, who take on the characteristics of the abuser as a desperate means of seeking the love that they need (Ferenczi, 1933; A. Freud, 1936a).

Yet it was not until the 1950s that any serious interest in the non-transferential aspects of the counselor–client relationship began emerging. Zetzel (1956), who first used the phrase "working alliance," defined this concept as that part of the analytic relationship that is stable, realistic, and cooperative. Zetzel actually used the terms "working alliance" and "therapeutic alliance" interchangeably. She proposed that the therapist must work through the client's infantile projections onto the therapist in order to secure a working alliance. For some clients, this may be impossible:

> A differentiation is made between transference as therapeutic alliance and the transference neurosis, which, on the whole, is considered a manifestation of resistance. Effective analysis depends on a sound therapeutic alliance, a prerequisite for which is the existence, before analysis, of a degree of mature ego functions, the absence of which in certain severely disturbed patients and in young children may preclude traditional psychoanalytic procedure (Zetzel, 1956, p. 370).

Although Zetzel's ideas did not immediately spark widespread interest in the psychoanalytic community, Gitelson (1962) perpetuated the notion of the working alliance in a paper on the curative factors in psychoanalysis. He suggested that the alliance (characterized by "rapport" and "optimistic hope") would eventuate into transference phenomena.

Despite the efforts of Zetzel and Gitelson within the psychoanalytic school of thought, the focus on the relationship between counselor and client as something apart from the transference was generated mainly from the client-centered therapy approach of Carl Rogers (1951) and his colleagues. This work has inspired several decades of research and writing on the "facilitative conditions" of counseling, namely therapist empathy, non-possessive warmth, and genuineness (Truax & Carkhuff, 1967).

Greenson's tripartite distinction

During the 1970s and 1980s the research on the therapist–client relationship shifted from humanistic notions (as exemplified by Rogers) of the facilitative conditions of counseling to an elaboration of Zetzel's concept of the working alliance. Greenson (1967, 1978) may have done the most systematic work in describing the various components of the counselor–client relationship. He described three components, the transference, the real relationship and the working alliance. We have already described the transference as that sector of the client–counselor relationship determined by early childhood experience and unconscious conflict (see also Chapter 4). The real relationship refers to:

. . . (1) the sense of being genuine and not synthetic or artificial, and (2) realistic and not inappropriate or fantastic (Greenson, 1978, p. 429).

Anecdotally, during Anna Freud's later years, she is said to have pounded on the back of her analysand's couch and complained that she was "too old for you to fall in love with me" (personal communication with Dr Maurice Apprey, March 1986), referring to the realistic qualities of the therapy situation.

Greenson (1978) defined the working alliance as:

. . . the non-neurotic, rational, reasonable rapport which the patient has with the analyst and which enables him to work purposefully in the analytic situation despite his transference impulses (p. 364).

Briefly defined, Greenson's concept of the working alliance incorporates an "observing" self, or the objective, reasonable side of the person that is willing to collaborate with the counselor.

Greenson's distinction between the different aspects of the counseling relationship is important in that one of the major problems in understanding counseling processes comes from confusing the ideas of transference and the working alliance (see Frieswyk et al., 1986). Furthermore, Greenson (1967) provides a clear statement of the rationale behind creating and using the term "working alliance":

The label working alliance was selected because the term emphasizes its outstanding function: it centers on the patient's ability to *work* in the analytic situation. Terms like the "therapeutic alliance" of Zetzel (1956), the "rational transference" of Fenichel (1941), and the "mature transference" of Stone (1954) refer to similar concepts. The designation working alliance, however, has the advantage of stressing the vital elements: the patient's capacity to work purposefully in the treatment situation. It can be seen at its clearest when a patient is in the throes of an intense transference neurosis and yet can still maintain an effective working relationship with the analyst (p. 192).

More recent distinctions

Bordin (1979), following Greenson, defined the working alliance as the fusion of three features: (a) a bond between participants that is emotional in nature; (b) an agreement or collaboration about the goals of therapy; and (c) an agreement about the tasks of therapy. Bordin points out that these bonds and agreements will vary depending on many factors, such as the theory of counseling being employed, the ability of the client to afford time-limited vs. unlimited treatment, and the individual transference issues of the client. Bordin argues for the central role the establishment of the working alliance plays in the counseling change process. He clearly views the working alliance as distinctly separate from the unconsciously derived transference process. One implication is that the working alliance can be observed in a number of ways:

> . . . a working alliance between a person seeking change and a change agent can occur in many places besides the locale of psychotherapy. The concept of the working alliance would seem to be applicable in the relation between student and teacher, between community action group and leaders, and, with only slight extension, between child and parent (Bordin, 1979, p. 252).

Gelso and Carter (1985) adapted and extended the definitions of Greenson (1967) and Bordin (1979) by defining the working alliance as an "emotional alignment" (p. 163), based on the "shared process" of moving between reflection and experience. The realistic and non-transference derived qualities of the relationship described by Greenson allow the counselor's clarifying and interpreting side to connect with the client's observing ego. This promotes a client's ability to stand back and observe him or herself and the counseling process. At the same time, the client is expected to feel and experience unreflectively. The successful work of analyzing these thoughts and feelings creates an emotional alignment based on the working or collaborative relationship. Moreover, this emotional alignment is both fostered and fed by the emotional bonds, agreement on goals, and agreement on tasks described by Bordin (1979). From this perspective, the working alliance is not *defined* as the composite of agreements and bonds but is in part *formed* by this agreement. Finally, this "shared" process was described from a phenomenological perspective by Patton (1984), who stated that the working alliance is an intersubjective phenomenon, evidenced by two people's ability to use their own individual subjective understanding to develop common or shared understanding of the interaction based on both commonsense knowledge and counselor expert knowledge.

Measures of the working alliance

Attempts at theoretically defining the working alliance cannot bear much fruit for counselors anxious to understand its importance in counseling without efforts at operationalizing and testing the construct within the counseling setting. For the purposes of this chapter, four examples of measuring the working alliance will be described as a means of highlighting the range of thinking about this construct.

Penn helping alliance scales

Luborsky and his associates (Luborsky *et al.*, 1983) argue that the working alliance (they call it the "helping" alliance) has two types. In Type I, the alliance is based on the client's perceiving the counselor as supportive and helpful, with the client as receiver of help. In Type II, the alliance is based on the client's feeling of being part of a team, working together with the counselor in a "joint struggle" against the problem. Type I and II dimensions can be calculated through either global ratings or the counting of "signs" based on transcripts. Examples of Type I behavior include the client expressing rapport with the counselor and conveying a belief that the process would help him or her overcome problems. Examples of Type II behavior include the sense that the client and counselor are working together in a joint struggle against what is impeding the client and that there is a shared responsibility for working out the goals of counseling.

Working Alliance Inventory

The Working Alliance Inventory was first developed by Horvath (1981) and later revised by Horvath and Greenberg (1989; see also Chapter 13). It draws directly from Bordin's (1979) conceptualization of the three main components of the working alliance (see also Chapters 4, 6, 7, and 8). Accordingly, there are three, factor-analytically-derived, scales: bonds, tasks, and goals. Client scores on these scales indicate the strength of the alliance, and thereby the likelihood of success in counseling. Examples of items corresponding to the bonds, tasks, and goals dimensions, are: "The client feels uncomfortable with the therapist"; "The client and therapist agree about the things the client will need to do in therapy to improve his/her situation"; and "The therapist and client have a common perception of the client's goals".

Vanderbilt Therapeutic Alliance Scale

This scale was developed (Hartley & Strupp, 1983) to measure the client's perception of the counselor as trustworthy, caring about him or her as a person rather than as a case, and perceiving counseling as helpful. Six scales were derived through factor-analytic procedures that measured global dimensions along six-point Likert rating scales. Two dimensions, positive climate and therapist intrusiveness, were counselor-related variables. Four dimensions—resistance, motivation for counseling, responsibility for problematic and cooperative behavior, and anxiety—were client variables. The authors argued that client characteristics described as hostile, negativistic, and resistive impeded the formation of the working alliance.

The Menninger Therapeutic Alliance Scales

These scales were based on the conceptualization of Frieswyk and his colleagues (1986), who argued that the therapist's techniques and the client's transference should be separated from the actual therapeutic alliance. Thus, they restricted their definition of the alliance to the client's collaborative work in counseling. Two major scales were constructed. The client collaboration scale refers to the client's ability to bring sufficient material to the session, being open to the expression of feelings and information, using the session to change or to clarify problems, working on tasks, generalizing work in session to outside situations, and identifying with counselor values. The second scale measures mediating variables affected by the transference and not considered a part of the working alliance. Expert judges make a global rating on a five-point continuum for each dimension. For example, one dimension of the collaboration scale ranges from 5, "the patient makes optimal use of the treatment," to 1, "the patient sabotages treatment."

Each of the four measures described above attempts to operationalize the concept of the working alliance. All seem to assess that aspect of the counselor–client relationship which can be called collaborative and work-oriented in nature. Two of the scales (Vanderbilt and Menninger Therapeutic Alliance Scales) distinguish between counselor and client contributions to the working alliance.

Summary

The premise of this chapter is that the working alliance is an aspect of the client and counselor relationship that facilitates the client's work of thinking, reporting, and understanding in the interview. As such, it is an index of the degree of purposeful collaboration between the pair in their pursuit of effective client understanding and change in counseling. The working alliance as an interpersonal phenomenon in the interview is a cornerstone of the psychoanalytically-oriented interview because it is that aspect of the client's experience with the counselor in which objective or reality-based observation and reflection can occur.

Observing and promoting the working alliance

What is the working alliance? In other words, how do we *observe* its occurrence? At a basic level, evidence for a firm working alliance is observable in the client's willingness to report relevant material freely and abundantly, and to make the effort to evaluate the significance of that material (see Chapter 8). The working alliance also occurs more subtly. Allen *et al.* (1984), identified eight indicators of the working alliance when it is effectively operating. They are as follows:

1. *Brings in significant issues and material.* A willingness to focus on emotionally-laden material entails confidence that the pain associated with this material will result in positive outcomes. An example will help clarify this working alliance indicator.

   A client appeared for a first appointment and described in elaborate detail the break-up of a first marriage. He was asked when this marriage took place; his answer was, "15 years ago". This unwillingness to present more "experience-near" material will shift as the working alliance strengthens.

2. *Works actively.* A distinction must be made between passively complying with the perceived expectations of counseling and an active commitment to the counseling endeavor. In other words, a client must internalize and feel responsible for the counseling process. Waiting for the counselor to set the "topic" for the hour is an example of a poorly formed working alliance.
3. *Makes good use of the therapist's efforts.* A willingness to "accept" counselor interventions is observed when the client elaborates or discusses an intervention. This is most evident when the client provides other examples and/or memories associated with the aim of the intervention. Simple agreement or acknowledgement that does not result in a deepening of material can be seen as both resistance and an aberration in the working alliance. Even if it takes a client *20* minutes to explore actively a previous interpretation, this is evidence of the working alliance placing unconscious pressure on the client to "yield up" dynamically important material.
4. *Reflects upon the meaning of reactions and behavior.* The goal of psychoanalytic counseling is to help the client to understand those internal factors that are contributing to his or her current maladaptive behaviors. A client who is able to observe and explore these connections within the hour has accepted this goal. A natural curiosity should arise for the client about the symbolic and unconscious meaning of his or her behavior. Resistance (see also Chapter 9) is observed when a client quickly and enthusiastically agrees with what a counselor has said but

is not interested in "Why has this taken place?" With careful listening, the counselor can observe whether a client is drawn to the meaning of an intervention.

5. *Applies work to life outside therapy.* In any counseling experience, a fundamental outcome must include an improvement of attitudes and responses *outside* the counseling hour. This process begins when clients are able to "carry with them" the ideas and insights elaborated within the counseling hour. For example, a client described an irrational response to a supervisor who had reminded her of the previous week's discussion of her harsh and critical mother.

6. *Is motivated to change.* At some point, the client must decide that the cost of his or her neurotic conflict and accompanying symptom formation is greater than the fear and anxiety attached to change. Many clients struggle with their commitment to counseling once the immediate crisis that leads them into treatment has diminished. It is at this point that the working alliance must be firmly established so that an enduring commitment to work can override the desire to avoid the inevitable discomfort that is a result of the counseling process.

7. *Shows resistance.* As will be discussed in Chapter 9, the clarification and interpretation of resistance is the pathway to change within the psychoanalytic counseling process. Overcompliance with the counselor's wishes, difficulty expressing ambivalent feelings, and a hesitation to appear obstinate are all examples of resistance to show resistance. A strong working alliance allows clients to risk displaying the negative attitudes and behaviors associated with resistance to exploration. These counterproductive thoughts and feelings are dangerous to the client, who may fear an angry response from the counselor or who becomes embarrassed by not being able to control the need to prevent being caught with his or her "pants down." In other words, clients experience considerable anxiety when behaving in ways "despite themselves." The working alliance facilitates the ability to reveal troubling attitudes and feelings.

8. *Works with resistance productively.* As was mentioned, clients become uncomfortable when they begin to be aware of previously unconscious material that is uncovered and interpreted within the counseling session. A client will frequently state, "it must have been my subconscious, because I did not mean to . . .." A willingness to manage the embarrassment and anxiety attached to not being fully in charge is necessary for exploring the reasons for resistance. Clients must be willing to treat resistances as important material within the therapeutic process, material that is to be clarified and interpreted.

We can see that when there is a strong working alliance, the client has a level of commitment and motivation necessary to engage productively in the psychoanalytic counseling process. Establishing the working alliance is another matter, however. Both the counselor and client contribute to the working alliance. Turning to the counselor's contributions, these can be divided into *counselor technical procedures* and *counselor qualities*. Examples of these factors are summarized in Table 5.1.

From a technical perspective, a number of counselor actions are necessary to begin fostering a working alliance. These occur both directly and indirectly. More directly, the counselor must invite collaboration and mutual study. The client must begin to understand that nothing too big or small can be ignored. In a sense, a process of educating the client to the goals and expectations of psychoanalytic counseling must take place. A client is entitled to an explanation the first time a response is given or technique suggested. The interaction in psychoanalytic counseling is markedly different when compared with conversation in everyday life.

The counselor must also provide the boundaries or the climate that encourages client self-exploration. This occurs through the counselor's painstaking and steady observation and interpretation of reality and by the premium placed on the client doing the talking and the counselor doing the listening. This is an intensive and at times frustrating process, with the client asked to delay the urge for immediate action. Clients need to be encouraged

Table 5.1 Promoting the working alliance

Counselor's technical procedures
Maintenance of firm boundaries that invite client self-exploration.
Premium on gaining understanding, nothing too small or big.
Regular and orderly work.
Painstaking observation and interpretation.
Invite collaboration and mutuality.
Gratify at appropriate and/or necessary times.
Explain a certain response/technique the first time it is used.
Use everyday language and avoid technical terms.
Ask client how the work is going.
Do not impose rules without an explanation.

Counselor qualities
Allow genuineness and warmth to enter.
Use naturalness and humor.
Admit not understanding when this occurs.
Admit when feeling annoyed or bored.
Acknowledge painful material.
Show interest in and concern for client's well-being.
Straightforwardness and everyday language to avoid demeaning the client.
Maintain ordinary courtesy to communicate the "rights" of the client.
A curiosity and desire to learn that is "contagious" to the client.

in this process. As Greenson (1967) rightly notes, clients must be supported, even if a neurotic wish is gratified as a result.

At the same time, the counselor must provide the type of supportive and empathic environment that enables the client to reveal painful material, to allow transferential thoughts and feelings to occur and resistance to build. The use of natural, everyday language counteracts the tendency of clients to feel demeaned by the boundaries imposed in psychoanalytic counseling. The counselor also must value an openness to feedback and a willingness to express genuine concern. A rigid adherence to "rules of abstinence" can never be an excuse to ignore the ordinary courtesies and "rights" of the client.

Development of the working alliance with the borderline and narcissistic conditions is especially difficult. The role of empathic understanding emerges as central to the formation of this alliance. These clients have difficulty accepting or contributing to a "we" situation. The counselor must patiently and consistently invite collaboration through the use of mirroring and unconditional acceptance. This empathic stance communicates not only a deep understanding of the client, but also an ability of the counselor to help contain the frightening thoughts and accompanying impulses that could otherwise prompt the client to terminate counseling.

An empathic stance entails the ability briefly to experience the client's thoughts and feelings in spite of their disturbing and/or irrational content. Counselors in training frequently underestimate the difficulty of maintaining an empathic observational stance *vis-à-vis* the client, when the result entails the identification and communication to the client of the latter's painful and distorted interpersonal relationships or intense and chaotic affective or cognitive states. An example of an invitation for collaboration and the setting of expectations may best be exemplified in brief excerpts from a first hour interview. In the vignette below (CO = counselor, CL = client), the client sought counseling after acute anxiety attacks forced a temporary leave from graduate school. After reporting in this hour the immediate circumstances around the anxiety attacks and the ambivalent feelings of taking medication prescribed by a psychiatrist, the following interaction took place:

CO. So, at the beginning of the school year, you'd catch yourself starting, dreading the start of the school year.

CL. Always I like finding a situation that I'm good at and getting into and doing a good job. I don't . . . like whenever I'd get a new job in high school over the summer or something, I'd always dread having a new job because I've always felt like it took a while for me to catch on and a lot of anxiety trying to get used to a new job. But once I'd get used to it and learn the new stuff, I'd always do well at it. But it's sort of the same thing with graduate school.

CO. There's a sense that you've had this hidden thought that when you really got into a tough situation, you wouldn't be able to do well enough.

CL. I never really thought . . . I'm not a very introspective person I guess. I just sort of . . . I've always gone through just trying to do my best and not worrying about it . . . .

CO. You haven't exactly had a lot of time to introspect.

The counselor invites the client to see the connection between a "hidden thought" and performance anxiety. The client, who is quite intelligent, immediately sees the role of introspection in psychoanalytic counseling. At the end of the hour, this interaction occurs:

CL. I've always sort of viewed myself as the type of person . . . I think I'm a really nice person and I've got really good morals and I really like helping people a lot, like working hard for people. But I don't think I'm the type of person that you meet the first time and say, hey, he's a great guy. It's more from working with me, working with people you sort of get close to them and they realize you're a good person and then become better friends with them gradually instead of some big . . . .

CO. Well, it takes time to know the true you.

CL. Yeah.

CO. We need to wind up. What I'd like to suggest is that we continue meeting and get a sense of what's behind the attacks and when we get a handle on that, we'll set up a contract with times to meet and take it from there.

CL. Okay.

CO. And so what I'd like to do is offer you a set time that we can meet for 50 minutes.

CL. Okay. One trouble I'm gonna have that I'm gonna try to fight through is that it's not like I'm a college student where I'm gonna have time off. This is gonna be . . . the time that I do my counseling with is gonna be time that I have to leave the office and sort of let other people do my duties and I mean, I'll probably hurt my grades a little bit, but I think it's important enough to get settled.

CO. I know how tight and stressful being in graduate school is, but I also know that this is something that will have to be a priority for you and I'll try to help meet you in terms of times, and if we need to shift times because of your job assignments, we can discuss that.

CL. I just sort of wanted to warn you that . . . and starting in 2 weeks, my next 1-month assignment's gonna be in ————— and I was thinking I'd like to still get the counseling during that but it's gonna be hard. I was thinking either like doing it in early mornings where I could like spend the night up here and come in here and then get down there by noon or late afternoons where I can do my work there in the evening.

CO.   If you're willing to meet me halfway, I can offer an early morning time on Monday, or one evening I am here at night. I could offer you a night time.

CL.   I want to work hard at being able to fit it in because I think it is important.

CO.   We can work around your tough schedule if you're willing to meet me halfway.

The counselor *offers* a time to the client. This act forces the client to decide whether he will commit to the beginning of the counseling process. Anxiety about counseling and performance immediately arise. The counselor purposefully uses the "we" to suggest a partnership and directly states to the client that he must meet the counselor "halfway" to begin the hard work ahead.

Another critical juncture in psychoanalytic counseling is when especially painful and affect-laden material begins to emerge. At this stage, the working alliance is used to help enable the client to overcome fears and resistance to this material. The counselor must combine a genuine concern and understanding for the client's discomfort with a firm, patient expectation that the client and counselor can and will engage in an analysis of the thoughts and feelings that are arising.

Following is an excerpt from the seventh hour with the same graduate student described above:

CL.   Thanksgiving went pretty good. My brother came home. He came home and a bunch of his high school friends met him at the airport and my family met him there. And that went pretty good. He brought me a T-shirt back from Phil's bar, the one with the TV show. We aren't that close in age and we've never really been super confidantes. Never told each other our secrets but I still feel like we're pretty close. I can tell that he cares what I'm doing and I let him know that I care what he's doing. It was good to see him. Still, it got to the point at the end of the weekend I think where I wanted to give him a hug and give my father a hug, but all those emotions got stirred up and I hugged my mother and shook their hands and hopped in the car and drove off before my tears started flowing. I cried for about 2 minutes and Barbara asked me what was wrong and I told her nothing was wrong, it was just something that would go away in a minute. It's almost like a ritual. Now, when I leave my parents, I get upset because I feel like I can't tell them how I feel about them.

CO.   Kleenex is there if you need it.

CL.   No. If I could have seen you yesterday, I probably would have used a lot. Because I feel pretty lost and overwhelmed and useless. Even into last night. But it was sort of like what we were saying. I went home last night and I did work and I did a written assignment that I have to hand in to be graded. Just getting that done. It's not directly dealing with my emotions and dealing with my problems, but getting the work out of the way and getting on top of things a lot of times makes me feel a lot better than anything else.

CO.   Lost and overwhelmed are pretty strong feelings.

CL.   I finally got to the point where, when people ask me how my third year is going, I don't say, "Oh, it's going great." I'll say something like, "It's got its good days and its bad days," or if it's somebody I really know, I'll tell them I'm really having a tough time with it but I'm making it. It feels good to not be taking the time off anymore and feel like I have to explain to everybody that I wimped out and have them give me this look like you couldn't take it. I feel like that's sort of behind me and I can almost be proud in a way of my decision to take time for myself, and realize that I did something for myself, and that things are going better now, and that things are really gonna work out a lot better since I've given myself some time instead of always trying to do what other people think I should do.

CO.   But you're not fully better yet.

CL.   Well, it's sort of . . . it's frustrating . . . it's true but it's frustrating in a way too that . . . I think one thing I've sort of learned through all this is that I'm me and I'm not gonna change who I am. I should just sort of . . . I need to be more aware of myself and be more aware of what I do. But it's frustrating to think that I can't do that homework every week when this happens in class, I can't pull out my little booklet and do number one, two, and three, and that problem will be solved or . . .

CO.   Your feelings are important ones because they give us two clues: first, that you imagined that I could quickly help you get a complete handle on your problems and second, that you're starting to realize today that there isn't a cookbook and that your problems will not quickly disappear.

CL.   I always feel good when I come here and like last week when I came here, things were sort of going rough and on Monday and Tuesday, I felt overwhelmed, but I didn't feel like giving up or anything because I could sort of look forward to this. And yesterday, when I was really down and out and feeling overwhelmed and feeling like I had no free time, I got to the point where I almost called you last night just to tell you I wasn't going well, but I figured I'd see you today.

CO. But you hesitated saying that you felt so badly; you came in saying you had a good week.

The client describes an emotional goodbye with his family. Yet, he is having difficulty discussing these feelings with the counselor and becomes tearful. The counselor uses a combination of empathy and reflection before beginning to focus on the client's wish that these painful feelings could be taken care of without first having to understand their source. The working alliance is evident by the client's description of positive gains before moving to his hesitation about revealing these feelings. The counselor confronts the client's resistance in the last interchange, pointing out that the client stated at the beginning of the hour that he had a good week. The counselor goes on to state that *we* must focus on these feelings and begins moving to analyze the resistances to them.

While Table 5.1 focuses on the counselor's contribution to the working alliance, it is important to point tit that the client must also be capable of forming a working relationship. Chapter 6 will discuss client readiness for counseling in greater detail. For now, this capacity to form a working alliance relates to the ability to *form a firm object relationship* (for discussion, see Horwitz, 1974; Kernberg, 1978). By this, we are referring to the presence in the client of a positive parental image that has derived from a nurturing relationship. A good parental image permits the counselor to build upon and strengthen this ability to attach and accept nurturing from others. The negative or bad image of the nurturing other must not be so strong or powerful as to overwhelm the good image, and thus prevent the development of a working alliance. An example of failure to form a working alliance with a client who was given a borderline personality disorder diagnosis (American Psychiatric Association, 1984) will help to illustrate this point.

A 27-year-old fork lift operator, "Jim," who works a night shift, sought out counseling stating, "My life has become stagnant. I don't feel I can go on with my life being as empty, lonely, and isolated as I feel. I saw a psychiatrist four times but he didn't say anything, all he did was send me a damn bill for $65 an hour. I never went back." Jim further stated that his family is "dumb" and that he felt like he stuck out and he never had any real friends, even as a child. He did feel close to one girl he knew from his neighborhood but was crushed when she married during her senior year in high school. He wished he could go to college, but felt that he doesn't have a "healthy ego."

Jim's demeanor in counseling was aloof and hostile. He became surprised when his anger was pointed out to him. His mood alternated between sad and apathetic and angry and sullen. Whenever positive attributes or skills were pointed out to him, he became distrustful. For instance, Jim was told that he seemed able to get along well at work, recently being promoted to fork-lift operator. Jim responded, "I should have been, I've been there for 4 years and there was no one else to do it."

The counselor attempted slowly to build the client's confidence in the counseling process by patiently pointing out the client's hypervigilence at being criticized and his discomfort with positive feelings. A strong feeling of anxiety and dread filled each hour. During the third hour the client bitterly complained of not feeling any better and requesting immediate action. By the fifth hour this "wound-licking" stance became increasingly apparent, where the client constantly complained of feeling distraught, of being angry at those who did not appreciate him, and of not trusting the counselor. The client stated "I am not getting anything out of this, I can't continue." The client did not return or respond to a follow-up letter.

A working alliance can be formed with those clients who maintain a "split" or separation between good and bad images. It is extremely difficult, however, to do so. The counselor's use of need gratification, such as acknowledging the client's hard work, interpretation of the splitting defense mechanism, and understanding of the client's devaluing of counseling and the counselor, can help to counteract the forces opposing the establishment of a working alliance in borderline clients.

The working alliance as change agent

The working alliance is the platform that allows for a number of therapeutic processes to occur. When the goal of counseling is confronting resistances and interpreting unconscious conflicts, the working alliance enables the client to regress in a controlled way, such that the relevant material becomes manifest. The working alliance also provides the environment necessary for clarifying and interpreting the transference material once it has been uncovered. As Bordin (1979) notes, the working alliance also can be a curative agent in and of itself. Bordin (1979) suggests that the client's experience of a working alliance with the counselor results in improved client self-esteem and interpersonal relations. In other words, the working alliance "is not only a prerequisite for therapeutic work, but often may be the main vehicle for change" (Horwitz, 1974, p. 255).

To explain this point, we will use the model in Figure 5.1. The model was developed by Horwitz (1974) to summarize some of the findings of the Menninger Foundation psychotherapy research project, and is modified here for our purposes. The model highlights the "internalization of the therapeutic alliance and its accompanying part-process" (p. 256). The internalization process, or the incorporation of the attitudes and feelings associated with a collaborative relationship, creates a number of by-products that interact to enhance the counseling relationship. In other words, these by-products both facilitate the working alliance and in turn are enhanced by a growing positive relationship.

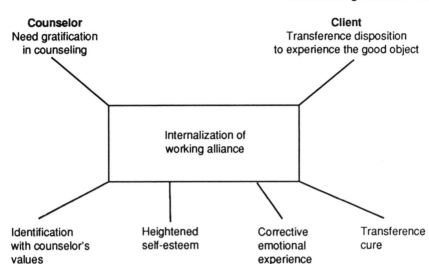

Figure 5.1 A model of the working alliance as therapeutic change agent

As can be seen, the client and counselor each make a contribution to the establishment and maintenance of the working alliance. Need gratification by the counselor occurs through encouraging and actively soliciting the client's participation in a partnership of mutual study. He or she must also work to safeguard the working alliance from threats to its dissolution and give such work a first priority in intervening to counter such threats. The client must have the capacity to accept the working partnership the counselor is offering, the ability to distinguish between experiencing and observing, and the desire to overcome his or her emotional difficulties. These qualities refer to the ability to experience the "good object."

The working alliance, in turn, serves as an impetus for four separate but related client outcomes of counseling. The first, identification with the counselor's values, refers to the process of taking on the characteristics that the counselor had demonstrated, such as a commitment to understanding and a concern for and empathy with the client. The client begins to incorporate certain ego (Sterba, 1934) and superego (see Strachey, 1934) values of the counselor. This process has also been called the client identification with the counselor's analyzing ego (see Greenson, 1967).

The second client outcome is heightened self-esteem, or more positive feelings about self, including greater self-respect and self-regard. This occurs as a result of the client experiencing the counselor as caring and accepting, even of the "bad" elements of the client. The third component is the corrective emotional experiences that occur as the client realizes that the counselor has not reacted to the client's behavior as expected. The frustration of neurotic expectations and the resulting need for new responses modifies misperceptions and defenses against them. Finally, the transference cure, or the changing of behavior to gratify the counselor rather than due to underlying structural change, is an effective means of helping the client rapidly engage in adaptive behavior. These changes can be surprisingly stable (Horwitz, 1974), and are consistent with outcome research on the role of counselor suggestion and modeling in counseling (Garfield & Bergin, 1986).

A case example will help to describe the beneficial process of internalizing the working alliance.

A client feels a pressure to create change in an unsettling work situation. She openly expresses frustration and disappointment with the counseling process for not helping her figure out what to do about her job situation. She openly challenges the counselor, in part due to the "safe environment" created by the working alliance. The counselor's acceptance and tolerance of the client's frustration and anger helps to modify an overstrict superego that tells the client that she is an "ingrate" for challenging authority, in this case the counselor. The client feels good about herself because she has "worked through" these distressing feelings with the counselor. Moreover, the client's self-perceived "weaknesses" have not alienated the counselor. The firm but understanding reaction of the counselor, that he can not make decisions for her, comes as unexpected and provides a "corrective emotional experience." The client, in turn, senses the need to discuss directly with the supervisor her concerns with the work load. All these outcomes further strengthen the affective bond between client and counselor, i.e. the working alliance.

The working alliance through the course of counseling

A strong initial working alliance is an important marker for positive outcome in both time-limited and time-unlimited counseling (Frieswyk et al., 1986; Luborsky et al., 1985). The working alliance has been found to strengthen quickly during the early phases of successful treatment, and conversely, to be weakly formed in unsuccessful cases (Hartley & Strupp, 1983). As a process variable, differences emerge between time-limited and time-unlimited counseling. The degree to which the working alliance stays within the "foreground" of counseling depends on the goals and parameters of the counseling; as Gelso and Carter (1985) point out, counseling can be time-limited or time-unlimited, expressive or action-focused, and geared toward developmental or more serious personality issues.

The model presented in Figure 5.1 underscores the primary importance the working alliance can have in time-limited counseling or problems resulting from stress due to life transitions (developmentally-oriented). In this case, the interaction between the working alliance and these four change processes results in a powerful mechanism for ameliorating client difficulties while creating an atmosphere for growth and development. In more intensive, longer-term counseling, where the goals include the partial uncovering and interpretation of unconscious conflict, the primacy of the working alliance waxes and wanes, depending on the severity of client resistances and the disturbing nature of client material. The working alliance, in other words, not only becomes the necessary springboard for later uncovering and interpretive work, but also serves to bolster the client at frightening times.

Golden & Robbins (1990) examined the working alliance within time-limited treatment, using a case study approach. They hypothesized that as clients begin to realize that the counselor and counseling will not solve all their problems, the working alliance weakens. Working through these frustrated wishes for immediate cure and relief creates a more realistic and positive atmosphere for the client to separate from the counselor. The termination process can help to recreate the independence–dependence conflict typically associated with late adolescence and young adulthood.

Golden & Robbins (1990) used a case study approach to study this process. They first determined through independent raters that the counselor maintained a consistently high level of warmth and exploration with low levels of negative attitude in two cases of 12-session, time-limited counseling. As can be seen in Figure 5.2, for both clients, the client's perception of the working alliance was relatively strong in the beginning, dropped in the middle, and began strengthening during the ending phase. The counselor, in turn, as depicted in Figure 5.3, rated the working alliance as increasing through the course of treatment. This finding suggests that the highly specified 12-session time limit may create doubts within the client about the bonding aspects of the working alliance that the counselor does not experience. "Working through" these ambivalent feelings was a central part of the counseling.

As has been mentioned, the duration of counseling, the frequency of contact, and the seriousness of client difficulties interact with the nature and development of the working alliance within the counseling process. The initial bonding that occurs in all forms of psychological treatment must develop even more deeply and intensely in psychoanalytic counseling, where an exploration of unconscious material is required. Bordin (1979), notes:

> Some basic level of trust surely marks all varieties of therapeutic relationships, but when attention is directed toward the more protected recesses of inner experience, deeper bonds of trust and attachment are required and developed. (p. 254).

As yet, there has been very little research on the "waxing and waning process" (Gelso & Carter, 1985, p. 167). However, it can be hypothesized that the working alliance recedes into the background once the initial goals and tasks of counseling are agreed upon, and the immediate fears of

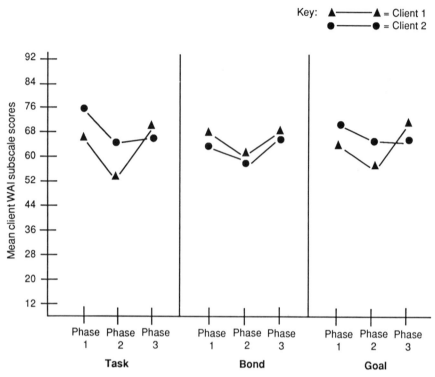

Figure 5.2 Client ratings of the working alliance across three phases of treatment

counseling diminish. The working alliance moves to the foreground and is buttressed at difficult times, such as the emergence of the negative transference, painful early childhood memories, or heightened resistances. "The strong alliance allows the client to feel trusting enough to experience support during difficult times, and to maintain faith in the counselor's effectiveness and good motives during periods of negative transference" (Gelso & Carter, 1985, p. 169).

Case examples

To highlight the use of the working alliance at different phases of treatment, two cases will be presented. The first is a life or developmental adjustment case with a pre-med student, seen at a university counseling center for 18 sessions. The second case is an intensive long-term case of a man seen twice

Key: ▲————▲ = Client 1
      ●————● = Client 2

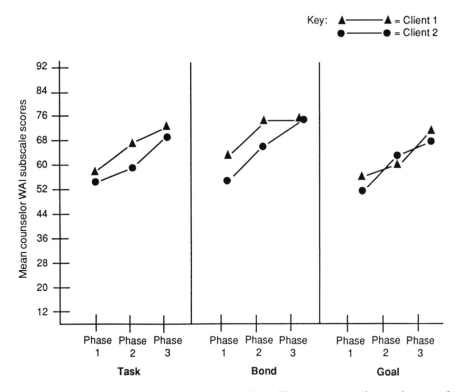

Figure 5.3 Counselor ratings of the working alliance across three phases of treatment

weekly over 2 years at a mental health center. In both cases, a description will be provided of the centrality of the working alliance, technical interventions aimed at strengthening and maintaining it, and criteria for its presence. The cases will also be reported in terms of early, middle, and termination phases (see Golden & Robbins, 1990).

In the time-limited case, the client was a 22-year-old single woman in her last year of college. She sought out counseling after the abrupt termination of an affair with an "abusive" man. She stated that she was "only attracted to mean men and was not attracted to nice men." The client was a talented and resourceful person who was accepted to medical school during the course of treatment. Her primary difficulties centered around close relationships, as she had a stable school and work history.

During the early phase of treatment, the client manifested considerable resistance, as evidenced by lateness, eating lunch during the hour, and an inability to report thoughts and feelings naturally. At one point, she threatened to quit because she was not being more actively helped. The working alliance necessarily became the primary focus of treatment, due to the possibility that the client might terminate. Early confrontation of these resistances, including the interpretation of fears of treatment and a supportive stance about the trying nature of counseling, resulted in reduced anxiety and a freer reporting of thoughts and feelings. These interventions, in turn, improved the quality of the working alliance.

During the fifth session, the client's anxiety had visibly risen again. A simple acknowledgement of the difficulty she was experiencing being in treatment and a technical manipulation (Bibring, 1954) of the resistance, in this case stating that the counselor would only move at a pace that was comfortable for her, resulted in the reporting of the circumstances related to her father's death when the client was 12 years old. This marked the beginning of the working alliance phase.

Generally, the need to focus directly on the working alliance lessened as the client began to question the relationship between her inner life and her reactions to the world around her. The denial and repression employed by the client were gently confronted and clarified, which helped her bring to the surface strong feelings about her father's death and fears of men. A history of promiscuity and self-destructive relationships was understood in the context of her confused and ambivalent feelings about her father. The non-judgmental stance of the counselor, the increased self-awareness of the client, and the premium placed on understanding resulted in improved self-esteem, diminished feelings of guilt and worthlessness, and greater control of frightening affect related to fears of loss of important others.

During the 11th session, the client reported a new dating relationship with a "nice guy." Concerns over engaging in sex right away, fears of having to leave him, and the everyday difficulties of deciding on what to do and where to go were discussed. In other words, the client was learning how to be close to someone. These discussions helped to strengthen the client's capacity for direct expression of caring and closeness. This marked the beginning of the termination phase.

As spring approached, the client was able to report curiosity about the counselor's plans for the summer. The ending of the school year would also mark the ending of treatment. Both positive and negative feelings about counseling were reported. Considerable frustration with not having "moved fast enough" was expressed. Feelings of sadness and loss were surfaced, both in terms of counseling and the end of an "important period in [the student's] life." The client was able to anticipate the stresses associated with moving and with entering medical school without losing enthusiasm for the coming year.

To summarize, the working alliance served a pivotal role in engaging and maintaining this client in a process of exploration and self-understanding. The working alliance was strengthened through the direct appeal to the client to do the work of thinking and talking before acting. Such methods included the explicit statement of what was required of each participant in the work, the confrontation of the client's ambivalence and fear of counseling, and the judicious use of support and encouragement that also serve to foster a sense of working collaboration or partnership. While the working alliance was not a central focus of the middle phases of treatment, the gains made by the client would not have occurred without it. The termination phase marked the re-emergence of the working alliance as a central issue. Expression of ambivalent feelings toward the counselor and the counseling process and the ability to say goodbye helped to consolidate and maintain the gains already made by the client.

The second case to be presented concerns a 31-year-old man who sought counseling after he broke up with a woman. He stated, "I don't know how to talk to people. I don't have any ambition or confidence in myself. I'm tired of relying on others to keep me going." The client had a history of cross-dressing, excessive masturbation, and masochism. He reported chronic feelings of loneliness and emptiness. After four treatment sessions, the client and counselor agreed on a twice-weekly schedule due to the reaction to stress the client was experiencing.

The client's urgency in wanting solutions was reduced by the counselor early on. The client was helped to understand that "answers" did not have to arrive quickly and that a partnership of mutual study would result in self-understanding. Fears of treatment, confused feelings about twice-weekly contact, and hesitancy to report material freely were continually clarified and confronted (for discussion, see Masterson, 1983). Toward the sixth month of treatment, the client was able to obtain an intellectual understanding of his fragile self-esteem and his strenuous efforts at protecting himself.

At this time, the client underwent a drastic revision in appearance, cutting his long, bushy hair short and neatly trimming his beard. An atmosphere of empathic reliability and trust was created, which allowed for the free reporting of thoughts and feelings that would have otherwise been disavowed. The relationship between current feelings and behaviors and the emergence of past memories and hurts began surfacing and marked the middle phase of treatment. The client began to master feelings of insecurity and vulnerability, rather than being overwhelmed by them.

A sudden set-back during the second year of counseling was evidenced by the client's suddenly regressive behavior. This included lateness to appointments, difficulty in the reporting of thoughts and feelings, and reports of increased masturbation. A combination of empathy, encouragement, and mild confrontation resulted in the client blurting out that he had heard the counselor would be leaving the mental health center. The following exchange occurred at the beginning of an hour where the client was able to overcome a strong affective state of sadness to confront the counselor:

CL.   Gosh, I didn't want to come in today (*tearful silence that continued for 4 or 5 minutes*).
CO.   I get the sense that you are mourning something.
CL.   This is really hard to talk about (*pause*). I don't know if I can (*tearful silence*).
CO.   We will go at a speed that is comfortable for you. I can see how overwhelmed you feel at the moment.
CL.   I don't know (*silence*) . . . I have benefited so much by our work . . . (*silence*). You're leaving now . . . (*tearful silence*).
CO.   The thought of my leaving must be both frightening and angering to you. Let's understand what it is all about.
CL.   Oh, I don't like this . . . . The nurse said you would be leaving . . .

A clear disruption in the working alliance had occurred, based on what turned out to be misinformation. Although the counselor had no idea of what had precipitated the client's strong emotional reaction and difficulty in communicating, the counselor's steady, patient and empathic stance allowed the client to begin talking about his overwhelming reaction. It became clear that what had led to the break in the working alliance was the client's fear that the counselor would abandon him.

The working alliance was repaired, especially when the counselor clarified that he was being transferred to another unit but that it would not mean they would have to stop. During this period the client stopped cross-dressing, which had been a chronic pattern of behavior dating back to early adolescence. He also began working again in the occupation for which he was trained.

The working alliance again subsided into the background, but the emotional bond between counselor and client was strong. The uncovering of urgent wishes and needs of the client led to the reporting of a sad history of neglect and abuse as a young child. The desperate efforts of this child to fulfill unmet needs, to ward off terrifying fears, and to control intense anger and rage were clarified and understood within the context of current behaviors, including his excessive masturbation.

The termination phase was marked by increased resistance, a renewal of old complaints, and hopeless and sad affect. This time, though, the client was able readily to surface feelings of appreciation, fear, anger, and sadness. The ability to report and manage these feelings marked both the increased maturity of the client and the stability of the working alliance. The use of encouragement and support were kept at a minimum, at which the client was able to engage in a process of self-understanding without the counselor's constant encouragement. At the same time, both counselor and client shared the realistic sadness that comes from having worked hard together and having enjoyed each other's company. The acknowledgement of the importance of this relationship was another part of the working alliance.

Concluding comments

This chapter was based on the premise that the working alliance is a central vehicle for change in counseling. It has emerged as our understanding of the counselor–client relationship becomes more complex (see Gelso & Carter, 1985; Robbins, 1989). As a process variable, the working alliance serves as the necessary springboard for the uncovering and interpretation of unconscious conflict. As an outcome variable, it is an important consequence of collaborative interpersonal relationships. Whether the working alliance is a non-specific factor found in all positive counseling relationships, or is the result of specific counselor techniques, it is, like transference, at the center of therapeutic change (Strupp & Hadley, 1979).

Part II

TECHNICAL CONSIDERATIONS

6 Client readiness

The client's initial responses to counseling reflect his or her state of preparation. Whether or not the client is prepared to take advantage of the opportunity that psychoanalytic counseling provides depends upon a number of factors. We have organized the material in this chapter around four broad dimensions that we and others in counseling have argued are important in determining the client's readiness for either longer or shorter-term forms of insight-orientated psychological treatment (see Kokotovic & Tracey, 1990; Barth et al., 1988; Moras & Strupp, 1982; Keithly, Samples & Strupp, 1980; Sifneos, 1972; Kernberg et al., 1972; Greenson, 1967; Malan, 1963; Robinson, 1950). These four dimensions of client readiness are: (a) motivation; (b) ability to accept a working alliance with the counselor; (c) certain cognitive functions; and (d) level of adjustment. We introduce each briefly below and then move to the first major subsection on motivation and its elements.

Perhaps the most commonly mentioned and studied dimension affecting the client's readiness for counseling is motivation. On the one hand, motivation refers to the client's desire to overcome his or her ehttional difficulties (Greenson, 1967; Robinson, 1950). On the other hand, motivation also denotes the client's ability to become involved in the work (Keithly, Samples & Strupp, 1980). We will refer to this latter sense of the concept of motivation as the client's capacity to trust. In either sense of the concept, motivation is one of the core ingredients of the working alliance.

The second readiness dimension is the client's capacity to engage in a working alliance with the counselor. We regard the working alliance as a particular relationship of interaction between the client and counselor, one that is characterized by, among other things, cooperation, purposefulness, positive feeling, and rationality (see Chapter 5). Although the client can also be seen to engage in a transference and a real relationship with the counselor (see Greenson, 1967; Gelso & Carter, 1985), the working alliance is the primary relationship between the pair and the vehicle through which the counselor attempts to influence the client in the interview (Greenson, 1967; Bordin, 1979; Moras & Strupp, 1982; Gelso & Carter, 1985; Robbins, 1989; Kokotovic & Tracey, 1990). The client's capacity to accept help and the quality of his or her interpersonal relations will be seen to be important elements of this dimension. These elements affect how well the client can enter into a working alliance with the counselor. In this section on the client's capacity to accept a working alliance, we will present a set of 10 empirically derived interval rating scales for assessing the quality of the client's interpersonal relations (Patton, 1978, 1981b; Charney, 1982; Tucker, 1982; Goodey, 1985; Efstation & Patton, 1985).

The third dimension of client readiness consists of certain cognitive functions that enable the client to participate meaningfully and actively with the counselor in the interaction (Patton, 1981b; Koles, 1981, 1982; Zetzel, 1956). We have in mind here such cognitive functions as the client's accessibility of memory, judgment, regulation of affect, and control of stimulation. Cognitive or ego functions also refer to the client's capacity: to think and remember; to put one's feelings and thoughts into words; to tolerate delay and to prefer thinking and talking before acting; for "psychological mindedness" and the ability to stand strong affect (Keithly, Samples & Strupp, 1980; Robinson, 1950). In this section, we will present nine empirically derived interval rating scales to assess some of the cognitive functions we believe are important in psychoanalytic counseling.

The fourth and final dimension of client readiness for counseling is the quality of the client's adjustment or level of experienced distress (Kokotovic & Tracey, 1990; Robbins & Patton, 1986; Patton, 1981b; Robbins, 1980; Robinson, 1950). The severity of the client's problem and level of overall adjustment are related to the ability to profit from an insight-orientated approach to treatment (Gelso & Carter, 1985). Clients whose problems are evident without explicit origins and are long-standing and severe, and who need to be seen more than once a week, will likely first do better in a more active and supportive form of counseling based on psychoanalytic principles. If and when such clients have then developed tolerance for delay of gratification and the capacity for reflection, counseling can become more insight-orientated. With clients whose level of adjustment in everyday life is quite marginal, such that they require a high degree of direction and active support from the counselor (see Howard, Nance & Meyers, 1986), it is necessary to spend a period of time actively helping them develop the necessary motivation, interpersonal skills, and ego strengths necessary to work in an insight-oriented form of treatment.

Motivation

Psychoanalytic counseling, like other forms of psychological treatment, requires not only a skilled and sensitive counselor, but also a client who is motivated for the work in two important senses. First, the client must have the desire or motivation to surmount his or her emotional problems. The desire to overcome one's problems by seeking a professional counselor requires that the client be sufficiently uncomfortable or unhappy about them to take such action. Second, the client must be motivated to understand and adapt to, i.e. trust, the various requirements that make up the organized structure of the ongoing interview situation. This is the second sense in which we use the concept of motivation.

The desire to overcome one's problems

Robinson (1950) singled out motivation as the first attribute to consider in assessing client readiness for counseling. For Robinson, motivation referred to the extent of the client's interest in working on his or her problems. For the client who is in considerable distress, this kind of motivation is often not a problem. A motivated client will try to keep the interview focused on the problem even if the counselor is avoiding it or just misunderstands, as illustrated by the client's responses to the counselor's interventions below:

CL. You should have seen me last night. I had cried like a baby all day. When evening came, I felt even worse and couldn't even get out of my chair.

CO. What time did you finally get to bed?

CL. About 1.00 a.m. But, it just seemed like there was no hope for me. I felt so bad inside, I couldn't stop shaking.

CO. Did you finally get to sleep?

CL. I don't know how to handle my feelings, they overwhelm me. That's my problem right now.

We can depend on the motivated client to make attempts to "cure" the counselor (see Langs, 1973) when the counselor is not tracking the material correctly. Even if not consciously aware of the nature of the problem, the motivated client will try to tell us in several ways what it is. Thus, we can count on the reasonable part of the client's mind to try to cooperate and communicate with us about the problem.

The extent of the client's comfort with his or her problem is a major factor in client motivation. When the problem is "ego-dystonic," that is, when the client is aware of the problem and is uncomfortable with it, we can expect the client to seek out help and to cooperate with the help-giver. This is because the problem appears as alien to the client's ego. When the problems are "ego-syntonic," however, they appear less troublesome or even natural to the client. To increase motivation in these cases, we have to try to help the client recognize the maladaptive features of the problem, such that the client becomes uncomfortable enough to continue in counseling.

Trust

Motivation as trust refers to our second meaning of the term. In this case, motivation is the client's compliance with whatever are perceived to be the "demand characteristics" of the counseling interview (see Garfinkel, 1967). Trust, then, is a person's motivated cooperation with the required features of a situation. As counselors we want to know, therefore, not only whether our clients are motivated to overcome their problems, but also whether they will be motivated to comply with the conditions under which counseling will occur. In a word, can the client understand and place trust in the essential features of the counseling situation?

Earlier, we mentioned how the client's problem may be ego-dystonic or stressful and appear to the counselor, therefore, as though the client is sufficiently motivated to work to overcome those problems. As the following example illustrates, however, distress is not always a good measure of motivation and is not necessarily the reason a client seeks help.

The client was a 35-year-old, married man who presented himself to the mental hygiene clinic because he said he wanted to work on his sexual problems. The young intake worker assigned to him reported that the man seemed genuinely distraught and eager to work on his long-standing habit of exhibiting his genitals to little girls. The client was embarrassed to report that little girls made him "feel sexy." He was cooperative in supplying plentiful details of his abusive behavior, appeared remorseful about it and was willing to come in for regular counseling interviews to work on the problem. The intake worker felt that the client was sufficiently motivated to work constructively in counseling and recommended to the clinical supervisor that he be assigned a regular counselor. Upon hearing the intake worker's recommendation, the supervisor asked if inquiries had been made into the reason why the client had sought help *now* for a long-standing problem. The intake worker replied that it appeared the reasons for seeking help were obvious. The supervisor then informed the intake worker that the client had appeared at the clinic only as a consequence of his most recent conviction for child abuse, because he had been ordered by the court to either enter counseling or serve a jail term. The supervisor tactfully suggested that, in future, it would be wise for the intake worker to inquire about the reasons and current circumstances surrounding a client's distress. Some motives for counseling are appropriate and others are less so!

The client's capacity for honesty makes up an important aspect of this element of motivation. Lying is a grave prognostic sign. It destroys the working alliance between the client and counselor. If the counselor does not confront the client's lies when they become apparent, he or she tacitly colludes with the client and gives approval to the dishonesty. Moreover, such counselor collusion creates sectors of the client's experience that are off limits for examination and understanding in counseling. Lying demonstrates the client's inability or unwillingness to trust or take for granted the requirements of the counseling situation.

Other aspects of client motivation

Motivation for counseling is also influenced by the client's ongoing life circumstances and by the amount of support the client's family, spouse, partner, or friends lend to the endeavor. When the client is facing a chronically stressful home situation, or a catastrophe at work, for example, motivation for doing the work of reporting and understanding in the interview is usually absent. Instead, crisis intervention rather than counseling is called for. On such occasions, the client's overburdened ego needs support. In a crisis situation, matters have some urgency about them and call for more activity on the part of the counselor in offering supportive services to the client. When the crisis subsides, the client can then re-establish a working alliance with the counselor and begin to think and talk reflectively again about him or herself.

Support of family or significant others is also important in helping sustain the client's ongoing interest in counseling (Gaston *et al.*, 1988). Family members who themselves have confidence in professional counseling services are able to convey their trust to the client. Supportive family members or friends accept the client's need for help, welcome its availability and respect the confidentiality of the client's relationship with the counselor. By contrast, the absence of support for counseling from family and significant others often manifests itself in the client's sense of ambivalence, guilt, or anxiety about seeing the counselor. When family members feel threatened or resentful about the client's participation in counseling, their attitudes can directly or indirectly undermine the client's motivation for the work. The following example illustrates this kind of difficulty.

The client, a 30-year-old male, had been making good progress in counseling for about 5 months, when he announced one day that he would have to stop coming because he needed to find a couple's counselor for him and his partner. At this point in counseling, the client's sense of independence and self-worth vis-à-vis his partner had increased, some of his long-standing anger had surfaced, and his depression had lessened and was accompanied by more energy for work and leisure.

These improvements in the client's well-being had discomfited his partner. Her response was to insist that he now pay attention to their relationship instead of exclusively to himself. She demanded that he find a couple's counselor they both could see, so that she could tell the counselor how badly he had mistreated her over the years they had been together. Inasmuch as the client's dependent and hostile manner of relating to his partner was central to his core emotional conflicts, he had, as yet, little insight into either her motives or his reactions. In consequence, he could not help but feel extremely guilty under the stress of her insistence. In a word, she wanted him to feel as badly as she did, and he thought he deserved to. To manage his unpleasant feelings, he terminated with his present counselor.

Some examples of research on client motivation

Researchers have defined motivation in many different ways and the concept is complex and is composed of many elements. Even when defined in simpler terms, researchers and theorists have found contradictory results. We have already seen that both Robinson (1950) and Greenson (1967) defined motivation more simply as the client's interest in working to overcome his or her problems. More lately, however, researchers have recognized the complexity of the concept and have begun to specify the elements of motivation more precisely. Perhaps the first attempt of this sort in research on psychoanalysis was in the classic Menninger Foundation study (Kernberg *et al.*, 1972). In this complex study of the efficacy of the long-term effects of both psychoanalysis and supportive psychoanalytic psychotherapy, clinicians assessed patient motivation in terms of indication of willingness to change, willingness to pay for the treatment, honesty, and absence of benefit (that is, secondary gain) from their emotional problems. The results of the Menninger study indicated that highly motivated patients had better therapeutic outcomes in both forms of treatment than did less motivated patients.

Extending the research on motivation to shorter-term, dynamically orientated treatment, Sifneos (1972) listed seven client characteristics as elements of motivation:

1. Ability to recognize problems as psychological.
2. The inclination to be introspective, as well as honest in accounting for one's difficulties.
3. A willingness to participate actively in the treatment situation.
4. Curiosity and interest in understanding oneself.
5. A willingness to change.
6. A reasonable expectation of the results of the treatment.
7. A willingness to make reasonable sacrifices.

Earlier studies by Sifneos (1968, 1972) indicated that clients higher on these measures did better in treatment than clients who were rated lower.

Sifneos (1972), like most psychoanalytic writers, recognizes that the psychoanalytic treatment situation makes several difficult demands on the client. These demands amount to expectations we have for the client's acceptance of, or trust in, those characteristics that, in our view at least, constitute a psychoanalytic counseling situation. Keithly, Samples & Strupp (1980) followed up on Sifneos' (1972) work and devised a rating scale consisting of nine items that represent client motivation. These items refer to both senses of the concept of motivation as we use it here: (a) the desire to overcome emotional difficulties; and (b) trust in the features of the counseling situation. The rating scale was devised for use in a study that attempted to determine whether scores on a measure of client motivation would be related to measures of counseling process and outcome. If such scores were significantly related, then the variable of client motivation might be used as a criterion in selecting clients for short-term dynamically oriented treatment. Thus, the nine items were used by counselors and other expert raters in judging the extent to which a client possessed the attribute named in the item.

The Keithly, Samples & Strupp (1980) list of items was as follows:

1. Ability to recognize problems as psychological.
2. A tendency to give an honest and truthful account of emotional difficulties.
3. Willingness to participate actively in the treatment situation.
4. Curiosity and willingness to understand oneself.
5. Willingness to change and experiment.
6. Appropriate expectations of the results of counseling.
7. Taking personal responsibility for seeking help.
8. Level of felt distress.
9. Post-interview expectations.

Items 7, 8, and 9 were added by Keithly, Samples & Strupp (1980) to the original seven items in Sifneos' (1972) list. Item 9 was included because the researchers had noted a tendency for clients to undergo either a positive or negative change in attitude toward counseling following an intake interview.

In using these items, Keithly, Samples & Strupp (1980) were interested in predicting the relation of the level of motivation in 18 male clients to certain process and outcome variables in short-term psychotherapy. Using a Pearson product–moment correlation coefficient to estimate inter-rater reliability for the motivation scale, the authors reported moderate to high estimates ($r = 0.62$–0.84) for the nine items. In using the scale, their results indicated that the motivation items related significantly and positively to the process variable of patient participation, and negatively to therapist negative attitude and patient hostility, for the early sessions of this 25-interview study. Moreover, therapists' and clinicians' ratings of global change, as an outcome variable, were significantly related to the client's initial level of motivation as measured by the items.

In keeping with our earlier definition of motivation as trust, we can note that Keithly, Samples & Strupp (1980) also pointed out that low levels of initial client motivation were significantly related to the counselor's negative attitude toward the client. It is as if, through an attitude of detachment and/or outright hostility, the client influences the counselor's personal attitude toward the client. The counselor's perception of the client's non-compliance with valued routines is not only potentially disconcerting of stable, ongoing interaction in the counseling interview, it may also induce some troublesome negative affect in the counselor. This, the authors conclude, may well have an influence on the quality of the subsequent interaction between the participants and on the outcome as well.

The conclusions reached by Keithly, Samples & Strupp (1980) about the effect of client motivation on the process and outcome of short-term psychotherapy would also seem to pertain for longer-term work. They point out, as well, the counselor's need to continually assess the client's level of motivation and to try to help increase that motivation if it is low.

In the overall assessment of the client's motivation, it is important, then, to keep several elements in mind. We need to learn about the support the client has from family and others for counseling. It is also important to assess the degree of stability in the client's current life circumstances. Finally, the counselor is advised to continually monitor the level of the client's desire to overcome his or her difficulties and to work cooperatively and purposefully with the counselor in a partnership of mutual endeavor. A high level of motivation means that the client has invested trust in the conditions or requirements of the counseling encounter.

Capacity to accept a working alliance

Earlier, we stated that the working alliance is the primary relationship of interaction between the client and counselor, and that it is the vehicle through which the counselor attempts therapeutically to influence the client. It is important, therefore, that the client be able to move into a working mode in counseling by accepting the counselor's invitation to form a cooperative alliance with him or her. Unless the work is to be of longer duration, it is also important that the client form the working alliance with the counselor fairly early in the process. Unless the client is able to trust and to relate effectively and quickly with the counselor, time must be spent either teaching the client the necessary interpersonal skills that are missing, or slowly building the client's trust that the counselor or the counseling process will not hurt the client. Occasionally, it is necessary to do both of the latter tasks before the client is able to work productively in, and benefit from, an insight-orientated approach to counseling.

The alliance from the client's perspective

The client's half of the working alliance, as a central ingredient of the counseling situation, consists of an orientation to the interaction that is reciprocal and complementary to the counselor's. The client's task involves learning and then trusting both the counselor's and the client's working orientation in order to understand what is expected of each in the social situation. Elsewhere, one of us (Patton, 1984) has attempted to describe the client's perspective on the working alliance. From the client's perspective, the working alliance is a helping relationship that can be defined as follows:

> . . . any occasion in which it can be observed that the client acts either to (1) elicit by complaining the counselor's support in mitigating the client's present sense of dis-ease, and the counselor reacts by doing so, or (2) elicit the counselor's construction of the meaning of the client's thoughts, feelings, motives, and actions, and the counselor reacts by doing so (p. 453).

The client's capacity to accept and participate actively in a working alliance with the counselor depends upon a number of elements. It goes without saying that there will be no working alliance unless the counselor is able to offer one to the client. On the client side, the definition above implies that the client must learn to do at least two things in order to receive the counselor's help. He or she must learn that making complaints is a legitimate claim on the counselor's time. Clients who cannot overcome their sense of embarrassment or dislike for asking for help will have difficulty carrying out this aspect of the working alliance. The client must also go on to learn that he or she must manage to talk to the counselor in such a way that it invites the counselor to comment on or reconstruct the meaning of the client's material. In this sense, the client must learn to become an object of study, curiosity, or discovery for both self and the counselor. These, then, are modes of interaction that make up the social requirements of the client's half of the working alliance.

The client's ability to participate in the ways required above depend heavily upon the quality of the client's previous interpersonal relationships. In the next section, we will discuss some of the elements that go into making it easy or difficult for the client to accept the working alliance as a way of relating to the counselor. The elements to be included here are: (a) the potential for receiving help from others; and (b) quality of prior interpersonal relationships. We will conclude this section with a research example of the relationship between client interpersonal relations and the working alliance.

Potential for receiving help

Another way of phrasing this element is to ask whether the client is able to accept the good that the counselor has to offer. Not everyone is able to ask for help or to receive it. Sometimes it hurts to know you need help. If self-esteem is especially vulnerable, accepting help can lower it. Moreover, to let the counselor in may mean that vulnerable hopes and longings will be experienced and this will be intolerable. Once again, we see how the element of trust contributes to stable, concerted interaction (Garfinkel, 1967).

Our definition of the client's perspective on the working alliance cited above suggests the situational requirement of active participation on the part of the client. Indeed, a readiness to accept help in this way necessitates active collaboration with the counselor. In terms of the social requirements of the working alliance, the client must actively inform the counselor what the trouble is by disclosing private matters about him or herself. Doing so demonstrates that assistance is needed and welcome. Then, he or she must make it clear that the counselor's perspective on the material provided thus far is invited. Once the counselor offers his or her perspective on the client's material, the client is expected to actively consider and talk about it. The working alliance requires the client to collaborate actively with the counselor in these ways.

The client's capacity to receive help also implies a willingness on the part of the client to experiment with new ways of thinking, feeling, and acting. The client's participation in the working alliance in psychoanalytic counseling involves him or her in an ongoing process of change through re-education. It involves the construction of new, rationally derived knowledge of the self. This process, which takes place through the working alliance, presents the client with new ways of understanding him or herself.

The experience of knowing oneself in a new way frequently involves increased awareness of the self and others, and the expanded recall of the past with new understanding of the influence of past events on one's life. New knowledge brings with it increased awareness of choices to think, feel, and act. To accommodate this process, the client must be willing to invoke at least a minimal need for change, as opposed to a need for stability (see Kunce, Cope & Newton, 1988). Hence, the capacity to receive help through a working alliance with the counselor also involves a willingness to experiment with one's habitual ways of thinking, feeling, or acting.

Quality of prior interpersonal relationships

Most psychoanalytically orientated counselors advocate assessing the quality of the client's interpersonal relationships as a criterion of suitability for treatment. It is assumed that the client's ability to enter a working alliance with the counselor is based on the experience of having had a history of at least a few stable, trusting, and intimate relationships with significant other persons. As counselors, we are concerned with whether the client's behavior promotes or disrupts collaborative interaction with others (see Charney, 1982). Moras & Strupp (1982) note that in the psychoanalytic literature certain qualities of a client's interpersonal relations have been regarded as important indicators of suitability for, in this case, short-term dynamic therapy. They emphasize the presence in the client's life of relationships that involve mutuality, emotional relatedness, trust, and positive transference attitudes. By contrast, prominent attitudes of mistrust and hostility are usually regarded as negative indicators.

A set of 15 client interpersonal relations rating scales were developed by Patton (1981b), Charney (1982), Goodey (1985), and Efstation & Patton (1985). The scales were developed as part of the Utah Counseling Outcomes Project (UCOP) (Patton, 1978), in which a multivariate model of the counseling process was constructed and further developed by Patton (1981b) and his colleagues. The scales to be introduced here comprise one dimension of that model called Client Improvement in Social Relations. The scales in this dimension, and all other scales in the model, are to be used at various points in the counseling process to assess the client's status on the construct being measured. The constructs from which the social relations scales are derived are elements of the client's interpersonal functioning that we believe are important for assessing the client's capacity for working cooperatively in counseling. The scales can also serve as informal criterion measures of client change or improvement.

The scales are interval measures that were developed by using Thurstonian methods of scale construction (see Robbins & Patton, 1986). Each of the attributes of The Client Improvement in Social Relations dimension is placed on a continuum of severity represented by eight anchors descriptive of the attribute. A rating of 8 represents the high or positive end of the continuum, and a rating of 1, the low or negative end. The interval values for each of the eight anchors, along with initial estimates of scale reliability (internal consistency), and estimates of inter-rater reliability and agreement, have been established in previous research (see Chapter 13) (Charney, 1982; Tucker, 1982; Goodey, 1985; Efstation & Patton, 1985). The scales that proved to have the most suitable initial psychometric qualities are presented here as an example of one way a counselor might go about assessing the client's interpersonal readiness for counseling. The 10 scales listed in Table

6.1 are not intended as a device for selecting clients for counseling, but as a means of appraising the client's status *vis-à-vis* interpersonal relationships. The scales should not be used as a device for selecting clients for counseling because they have not been developed for this purpose.

Table 6.1 contains the definition and the anchors for each scale to illustrate their content. The scales are: Trust; Altruism; Role Flexibility; Self-management; Supportiveness; Dependability; Intimacy; Acceptance; Mutuality; and Maintenance of Long-term Relations. The rater's task in using the scale is to select that anchor in each scale whose interval best appears to represent where the client is on the continuum at the present time.

Trust   We have already seen in the previous section on motivation the important role of trust as a readiness factor. The association of trust with interpersonal relations, as measured by the first scale, focuses on the client's faith in other persons. A client who is rated at the high end of this continuum is like someone who shows exceptional faith in others in situations of risk. This is simply another way of speaking of the client's capacity to take on faith and comply with the requirements of the counseling situation. At the negative end of the Trust continuum is a client who is so devoid of trust that he or she is like the person who never lets a spouse or partner out of sight.

Altruism   The second scale measures that characteristic of a person which is reflected in acts of kindness or mercy to others. The scale is centered on the client's capacity to understand and meet the needs of other persons. The client who is rated at the negative end of this scale is judged to be similar to someone who is totally self-centered. The high end of the continuum describes behavior that is self-sacrificing for the sake of others in need.

Role Flexibility   The third scale measures an attribute that we believe is an increasingly important characteristic of interpersonal relations in a complex world. This scale taps the client's capacity, or lack of it, to adapt to changing role requirements that characterize a person's daily life in contemporary society. If the client is rated at the maladaptive end of the scale, it is because the rater believes the client is not able to adjust to important changes in his or her life. The positive or adaptive end of the scale is represented by demonstrated role versatility in the client's behavior.

Self-management   The attribute measured by the fourth scale is closely related to role flexibility as an attribute of client interpersonal relations.

Table 6.1 Client improvement in social relations scales

Trust
Scale definition: the client's belief in the character, integrity, strength and/or truth of others.

8. Shows exceptional faith in others in situations of risk.
   GREATEST
7. Never has problem loaning money to friends when needed.

6. Considers letting children take trip on their own.
   MODERATELY HIGH
5. Disclosing fears to others causes him/her anxiety.

4. Insists on watching mechanic tune car.
   MODERATELY LOW
3. Behaves suspiciously whenever new neighbors move in.

2. Makes children account for every minute they are out of the house.
   LEAST
1. Never lets spouse or partner out of his/her sight.

Altruism
Scale definition: client behaviors that display kindness and devotion to the interests of others.

8. Would risk his/her own life for someone in need.
   GREATEST
7. Outstanding example of someone who is charitable.

6. Has had rewarding experiences in Volunteers in Service to America (VISTA), Peace Corps, or other service organizations.
   MODERATELY HIGH
5. Has concern for others but has some trouble giving help.

4. Believes people should help themselves rather than ask for help.
   MODERATELY LOW
3. Lets others know their requests are a burden.

2. Is stingy to the point of meanness.
   LEAST
1. So self-centred that others' needs are totally ignored.

Table 6.1 *(continued)*

Role Flexibility
Scale definition: the client's versatility in assuming a variety of roles with an adequate degree of comfort.

8. Has no difficulty taking care of and being taken care of by intimates.
   GREATEST
7. Equally effective in being both firm and friendly with children.

6. Is not lost when spouse goes on a business trip.
   MODERATELY HIGH
5. Has some trouble seeing alternatives in his/her educational goals.

4. Does not know how to act when he/she meets colleague away from work.
   MODERATELY LOW
3. Cannot stop thinking about children while at work.

2. Sees opposite sex only as sexual object.
   LEAST
1. Refuses to consider any change in lifestyle.

Self-management
Scale definition: the extent to which the client takes care of self with appropriate amounts of assistance and direction from others when needed.

8. Resourcefully uses all available means to care for self.
   GREATEST
7. Looks after own health by a routine of daily exercise.

6. Promptly fixes household items when they break.
   MODERATELY HIGH
5. Often asks spouse's opinion of what s/he should wear.

4. Would rather depend on others than learn to drive.
   MODERATELY LOW
3. Neglects bathing until body itches.

2. Sleeps on street if not accompanied home.
   LEAST
1. Must be taken to toilet or will soil self.

Table 6.1 (continued)

Supportiveness
Scale definition: the extent to which the client gives help and encouragement to the efforts of others.

8. Assists people by helping them to use their own resources.
                              GREATEST
7. Makes time available to attend children's performances.

6. Shovels neighbor's sidewalk when it snows.
                              MODERATELY HIGH
5. Sometimes offers assistance to new workers.

4. Gives advice instead of listening.
                              MODERATELY LOW
3. Prefers not to give directions to strangers if asked.

2. Refuses to listen to others' problems.
                              LEAST
1. Is always a hindrance to others in need of help.

Dependability
Scale definition: the degree to which the client can be counted on to carry out responsibilities.

8. Is completely reliable in doing both the expected and beyond.
                              GREATEST
7. Can be counted on to work extra hours in times of crisis.

6. Always pays rent on time.
                              MODERATELY HIGH
5. Is usually a little behind schedule.

4. Tells friends will call later but doesn't.
                              MODERATELY LOW
3. Arbitrary in showing up for business appointments.

2. Forgets to get weekly groceries for an invalid relative.
                              LEAST
1. Didn't show up to take sick grandmother to doctor's appointment.

Table 6.1 *(continued)*

Intimacy
Scale definition: client capacity for warm, unreserved, personal expression, rather than cold, distant, or formal involvement with others.

---

8. Fosters mutually close relationships by sharing deepest feelings.

    GREATEST

7. Openly expresses feelings of affection with loved ones.

---

6. Can quickly establish close friendships.

    MODERATELY HIGH

5. Only shares self with people who like him/her.

---

4. Does not look at people when s/he talks with them.

    MODERATELY LOW

3. Changes subject when people talk about their feelings.

---

2. Shudders and moves away when touched.

    LEAST

1. Insults people who ask about his/her feelings.

Acceptance
Scale definition: refers to the client who is receptive, non-judgmental and valuing of differences in others.

---

8. He/she actively involved in work to overcome racial prejudice.

    GREATEST

7. Active as foster parent for retarded children.

---

6. Would like children to meet others from different backgrounds.

    MODERATELY HIGH

5. She/he feels uncomfortable associating with unwed mothers.

---

4. Is not openly hostile, but will not associate with persons of different ethnic background.

    MODERATELY LOW

3. Frequently condescending to people with less education than he/she.

---

2. Will not allow children to play with those who do not attend his/her church.

    LEAST

1. He/she belongs to group that persecutes minority group members.

Table 6.1 *(continued)*

Mutuality
Scale definition: client's cooperative interaction with others to promote common goals.

8. Even during conflict, always finds point on which to cooperate.
                              GREATEST
7. Always offers help before asked.

6. Is usually available to help neighbors with their projects.
                              MODERATELY HIGH
5. Occasionally offers ideas into ongoing conversations.

4. Collaborates with others for only short periods of time.
                              MODERATELY LOW
3. Others must always finish his/her portion of group project.

2. Never shares talents or ideas with others.
                              LEAST
1. Never offers help, or even thinks to.

Maintenance of Long-term Relationships
Scale definition: client behaviors which sustain social relations with others during both times of change and periods of routine.

8. Outstanding example of someone who nourishes his/her relations with others.
                              GREATEST
7. Adapts exceptionally well to the give-and-take of long-term relationships.

6. Sustains friends in times of trouble.
                              MODERATELY HIGH
5. Although frightened by trouble in relationships, can work to repair damages.

4. Doesn't seem to know how to use courtesy to help keep friends.
                              MODERATELY LOW
3. Lets others know that a relationship of any length means too many hassles.

2. Abandons friends at the slightest sign of trouble or dissatisfaction.
                              LEAST
1. Actively provokes others to break off relationship.

This scale has implications for, among other things, the ease with which the client can adapt to the role of asking for and receiving help from the counselor, and the extent to which the person is self-sufficient in caring for him or herself. The client who is rated at the maladaptive end of the self-management continuum is seen to be at level of severity comparable to someone who has to be reminded to eat daily. The adaptive end is represented by the client's resourceful use of all appropriate means of caring for him or herself.

Supportiveness This scale measures a quality which is a characteristic of those persons who give encouragement or inspiration to others, as opposed to standing in the way of or hindering others. The counselor may wish to know the extent to which the client has been or is capable of supporting his or her spouse, children, subordinates and the like. The level of severity at the negative end of this scale is characterized by someone who is always a hindrance to others. The adaptive end of the supportiveness continuum describes someone who assists others by helping them use their own resources.

Dependability This scale assesses the client's ability to live up to his or her responsibilities to others. Again, the counselor may wish to know how much he or she, and others, can depend on the client to keep regular appointments, to arrive on time, and to discharge other responsibilities. If the client is rated at the negative end of this scale, it means the level of severity is comparable to someone who willfully ignores his or her responsibilities to others. At the high end of the scale, we find the person who is completely reliable both in doing the expected and going beyond that.

Intimacy This scale assesses the client's capacity for sharing him or herself with others in close relationships. Intimacy involves the willingness to disclose deep feelings about oneself. If the client is rated 1 on the intimacy scale, it means his or her behavior could be likened to a person who shudders and moves away when touched by someone else. By contrast, a rating of 8 on this scale means the client is like someone who fosters mutually close relationships by sharing deepest feelings.

Acceptance This scale assesses that feature of the client's interpersonal relations that is marked by non-judgmental attitudes toward other persons. The accepting person values individual differences and is receptive to them. If the client is rated at the maladaptive end of the scale, the level of severity is assumed to be comparable to that of the person who ridicules or persecutes those who are different from the client. The adaptive or positive end of this scale describes the person who actively supports the expression of individual differences among persons.

Mutuality   This is a measure of that characteristic of interpersonal relations important to the building of the working alliance in counseling and in cooperating with others outside of counseling. Mutuality is realized in the sense of cooperation in working toward common goals. The absence of mutuality is found at the negative end of this continuum and is characterized by the person who, for example, works with others only for personal gain. By contrast, the adaptive end of the scale describes the behavior of someone who consistently promotes cooperation among others.

Maintenance of Long-term Relations   The client's capacity for the Maintenance of Long-term Relations is the tenth scale. The capacity for such relationships is apparent when the client works to sustain or conserve relationships, even during times of conflict. This is the client who promotes, rather than disrupts, stable concerted action among persons. The client who is rated at the maladaptive end of this scale has a level of severity like someone who abandons friends at the slightest sign of trouble or dissatisfaction. The adaptive end of the scale is characteristic of persons who can endure considerable frustration for the sake of a friendship.

The counselor's rating of the client on these 10 scales can provide useful information for later follow-up with the client. Ratings made by a single person, however, are not sufficiently reliable to warrant using them for clinical decision-making about the client. Hence, the counselor is cautioned to treat his or her own ratings as suggestive of possible trends in or as a working model (Pepinsky & Pepinsky, 1954) of the client's approach to interpersonal relationships. The reliability of the ratings increases to acceptable levels, however, when the scales are used by three or more trained raters (Efstation & Patton, 1985). If an improvement in the client's social relations is considered an appropriate outcome of successful counseling, it becomes possible to use the scales with three or more trained raters to assess formally the amount of change or improvement over time in client social relations as an indication of the efficacy of counseling.

Some examples of research on client interpersonal relations

Not a great deal of research has been conducted on the relationship between the quality of the client's interpersonal relations and the client's ability to enter into a working alliance with the counselor in dynamically oriented forms of counseling. In one case with elderly depressed clients, Gaston *et al.* (1988) did not find that pretreatment quality of interpersonal functioning was related to the client's contribution to the working alliance in behavioral, cognitive, or brief dynamic psychotherapy. However, as Gaston *et al.* (1988) point out, this negative finding may be related to the fact that the clients presented with depression rather than with difficulties in interpersonal functioning.

Moras & Strupp (1982), on the other hand, had found just the opposite. These authors designed their stueh to test the proposition that the quality of interpersonal relations prior to treatment was significantly related to whether the client would form a working alliance with the counselor. The subjects were 33 single college males who were selected from persons referred to an ongoing research project by the university counseling center, and from respondents to a letter sent to a random group of undergraduate males soliciting participation in a counseling program for problems with anxiety, shyness, and interpersonal relations. To assess interpersonal relations, the authors devised a rating form that assessed: (a) current social relationships; (b) family relationships; and (c) prominence of hostile or resentful attitudes toward others. Clinicians' ratings on these items were summed to obtain a global index of adequacy of interpersonal relations.

The results supported the psychoanalytic assumption that a client's interpersonal relations prior to counseling are predictive of the ability to form a working alliance with the counselor in short-term treatment. These results were seen as extending those of Gomes-Schwartz (1978), who found that a client's active, positively-toned involvement in counseling was more predictive of outcome than was counseling technique. However, not a large amount of the variance in the working alliance measure was accounted for by the supportive results, so caution in generalizing these results is in order. In light of these results, Moras & Strupp (1982) raise the further important question of the extent to which significant client behaviors related to the working alliance are a function of the counselor's behavior, and which are related to pre-existing client attributes.

We have tried to point out in this section our conviction that the client's capacity to accept a working alliance depends both upon the client's attributes, including a history of prior positive relationships, and upon the counselor making such a relationship available to the client. A set of scales for assessing the quality of, and change in, the client's interpersonal relations has been presented.

Client cognitive functions

Greenson (1967) has noted that in classical psychoanalysis:

The patient is asked: (a) to regress and to progress, (b) to be passive and to be active, (c) to give up control and to maintain control, and (d) to renounce reality testing and to retain reality testing (p. 361).

Accomplishing these tasks requires reasonably strong and flexible ego functions, particularly in the conflict-free spheres (cf. Hartmann, 1951). In classical analysis, the patient is expected to have each of these ego functions intact. Only when one or more of these functions becomes involved in the neurotic transference to the analyst is the patient expected to exhibit a loss of ego functioning, and then only temporarily.

Psychoanalytic counseling does not make as many demands as classical psychoanalysis on the client's ego, nor are these demands as severe. For example, because the client is typically seen on a once-a-week basis, he or she is not expected to be able to regress in the direction of primary-process thinking in free association for extended periods of time. Rather, the client is expected to remain understandable or coherent in his or her communications, to remember, and to provide accurate information. Moreover, the client in counseling is expected to understand and identify with the counselor's function in the interview; that is, to form a working alliance with the counselor through which transference manifestations can be examined, ameliorated, or accommodated if necessary. Thus, in broad outline, the psychoanalytic counseling situation requires of the client that he or she: (a) try to report freely and honestly thoughts, feelings, and action tendencies and to censor nothing; (b) have the capacity to both experience and to observe and reflect on what he or she has experienced; (c) be able to take responsibility for thinking and talking, rather than blindly living out his or her emotional problems; and (d) have reasonably effective management of his or her feelings.

We believe it is possible to identify and measure some of the cognitive demands which the psychoanalytic counseling situation makes on the client's ego. To this end, Koles (1982) and Patton (1981b) developed a set of nine rating scales to measure client change in cognitive operations as one of the five dimensions of the multivariate model of the counseling process from the Utah Counseling Outcomes Project. For the client to participate meaningfully in psychoanalytic counseling, we think it is important for him or her to give evidence of the capacity for exercising the following cognitive operations, listed here as scale names: Control of Stimulation; Regulation of Affect; Perceptual Attention; Accessibility of Memory; Judgment; Exploration; Recognition; Mode of Conflict Expression; and Revision of Concepts of Self and Other.

Like the rating scales in the previous section on Client Improvement in Social Relations, the Client Change in Cognitive Operations scales are interval measures developed along Thurstonian lines (Robbins & Patton, 1986). Each attribute is placed on an eight-point continuum of severity with a descriptive anchor located at each of the eight intervals. A rating of 8 represents the high or positive end of the continuum, while a rating of 1 represents the low or negative end. As was the case with the previous scales, the eight interval values for each of the nine scales have been determined, and initial estimates of overall scale reliability (internal consistency) and inter-rater reliability and agreement have been obtained (see Chapter 13). These estimates are in the moderate range, suggesting the scales are useful for further research purposes involving three or more trained raters, but should not yet be used as a sole basis for clinical decision-making. Instead, the counselor may find it useful to rate the client on these scales to gain information that can be used in follow-up with the client. Table 6.2 contains each of the Client Change in Cognitive Operations scales and their descriptive anchors. On some of these scales, one, and in some cases two, anchor statements are missing because the derivation of interval values for that point on the scale could not be determined statistically with the original data set of judges' ratings. New statements can be selected and their interval values determined through a "mini-rank" order procedure. Because a missing anchor statement is bounded by other statements along the scale, it is still possible to use the scale point adjacent to the missing anchor.

Control of Stimulation   The title of the first scale refers to the process of controlling or regulating internal and external stimulation. A client at the maladaptive end of this scale might, for example, be someone who is hypersensitive to even a slight increase in the level of stimulation. In this case, the person's response to such stimulation might be maladaptive, such that he or she cycles between becoming numb on the one hand, or swamped by excitement on the other (see Horowitz, 1976). Persons who are rated at the adaptive end of this scale give evidence of the effective control of stimulation by engaging in appropriate activities.

Regulation of Affect   This is a cognitive function that controls and modulates the intensity and experiencing of affects. It is often the case that difficulty in regulating painful affect is a presenting complaint and the reason for seeking help by many clients. At the maladaptive end of the scale we find clients who are swamped by their affect and have no access to their normal intellective functions. At the adaptive end of the continuum we find the client who is able effectively to regulate the intensity of affective experiencing. For example, disappointment replaces devastation, anger replaces rage, or mild and realistic anxiety replaces panic.

Table 6.2 Client change in cognitive operations scales

Control of Stimulation
Scale definition: the regulating and organizing of internal and external stimulation; sensitivity to the sensory modalities.

8. Jogs to release the day's tension.
                        GREATEST
7. Concentrates well and is not easily excited.

6.
                        MODERATELY HIGH
5. Is uncomfortable with the excitement of competitive athletics.

4. Becomes over-excited at parties and outings.
                        MODERATELY LOW
3. Is startled by even slight sounds.

2. Skin is so sensitive, he/she hurts when touched.
                        LEAST
1.

Regulation of Affect
Scale definition: control of the intensity and experiencing of affective states.

8. Feelings do not interfere with her/his ability to think and decide.
                        GREATEST
7. Is rarely overwhelmed by feelings.

6. Says he/she gets a little blue now and then when disappointed.
                        MODERATELY HIGH
5. Is somewhat bothered by guilt feelings when expressing anger.

4. Gets so hurt by break-up of romances she/he stays at home and broods.
                        MODERATELY LOW
3. Feelings are so intense he/she leaves the situation to avoid facing them.

2. So plagued by strong feelings, she/he can't think of anything else.
                        LEAST
1.

Table 6.2 *(continued)*

Perceptual Attention
Scale definition: attending to and organizing stimulus information; ability to concentrate and attend to information.

---

8. Excellent concentration even in times of conflict and stress.
GREATEST
7. Puts aside thoughts of conflict and trouble when concentration is needed.

---

6. Is able to direct attention but with some difficulty.
MODERATELY HIGH
5. Sometimes has difficulty staying involved in everyday conversation.

---

4. Has considerable trouble paying attention.
MODERATELY LOW
3. Even the simplest statements of others confuse her/him.

2.

LEAST
1. Is completely immobilized and doesn't respond to any stimulus event.

Accessibility of Memory
Scale definition: ability to retain, recall, and use significant memories.

---

8. Memory for even painful events is continuous and complete.
GREATEST
7. As he/she talks, there is full recovery of memory for relevant events.

---

6. Often remembers a significant event on the way to the session.
MODERATELY HIGH
5. Remembers important events but not their sequence of occurrence.

---

4. Some memories on the "tip of her/his tongue", but still not accessible.
MODERATELY LOW
3. Sometimes cannot recall what has happened between certain periods of time.

---

2. When reminded that something has happened before, he/she often says, "I don't remember."
LEAST
1. Mind is a complete blank.

Table 6.2 *(continued)*

Judgment
Scale definition: decision-making through the comparison, discernment, deliberation, consideration, and anticipation of a possible future state of affairs.

8. Is giving careful and realistic thought to planning her/his career change.

GREATEST

7. Can see that planning the budget for the year paid off.

6. Considers it risky to get married at present.

MODERATELY HIGH

5.

4. Is overtly seductive with colleagues at work.

MODERATELY LOW

3. Is deep in debt because he/she is always giving expensive gifts.

2. Is convinced she/he will never get caught stealing.

LEAST

1.

Exploration
Scale definition: examining and searching of own reported attitudes, feelings, and behavior with positive interest.

8. Actively monitors and pursues own thoughts and feelings.

GREATEST

7. Questions the discrepancy between compliments and how she/he felt inside.

6. Is becoming curious about why he/she felt threatened by spouse.

MODERATELY HIGH

5. Is now able to talk about two people: one good, one bad.

4. Downplays the importance of painful arguments with his/her spouse.

MODERATELY LOW

3. Feels few events are important enough to discuss in therapy.

2. States that she/he is only in therapy due to spouse's wish.

LEAST

1.

Table 6.2 *(continued)*

Recognition
Scale definition: client insight and understanding of the relations between thoughts, feelings, and past and present events.

---

8. Understanding that feeling repugnance when with mother is a protection against his/her own desires.

GREATEST

7. Sees idolizing the therapist as a replacement for her/his own mother/father.

---

6. Missed sessions remind him/her of parents' long absences during childhood.

MODERATELY HIGH

5. Is astonished by the connection between having a good time and feeling guilty.

---

4. Thinks it is silly to react with a headache to the departure of a close relative.

MODERATELY LOW

3. Explains that his/her exhausting daily routine is only to be of help to others.

---

2. Is quite unaware of his/her longing for his/her parents.

LEAST

1.

Mode of Conflict Expression
Scale definition: primary means by which client expresses thoughts and feelings that are painful or conflicted (e.g. words, movement, images).

---

8. Conflicted material gets labeled accurately.

GREATEST

7. Clear report of ongoing thoughts.

---

6. Talks about how her/his dress and gestures are seductive.

MODERATELY HIGH

5.

---

4. Wraps arms around self when he/she starts to talk about divorce.

MODERATELY LOW

3. Makes rigid stereotyped gestures when feeling frightened.

2.

LEAST

1. Urinates without comment when trying to talk about painful matters.

Table 6.2 (continued)

Revision of Concepts of Self and Other
Scale definition: methods of maintaining or changing enduring images of self and other.

---

8. Shows balance in evaluating and accepting own positive and negative qualities.

GREATEST

7. Shows care and concern for others whom she/he has wronged.

---

6. Can entertain the notion that family members have good and bad qualities.

MODERATELY HIGH

5. The idea that father is different from mother has begun to dawn.

---

4. When annoyed, gives the impression that his/her needs should take priority.

MODERATELY LOW

3. Usually becomes self-righteous and moralizes after sex.

---

2. When frustrated, others are seen as trying to destroy her/him.

LEAST

1.

Perceptual Attention   This scale refers to the cognitive process of attending to and organizing stimulus information. The client at the maladaptive end of this continuum has extreme difficulty concentrating on information. The adaptive end of the scale represents the person who has effective concentration even during times of stress or conflict.

Accessibility of Memory   At the adaptive end of the scale, Accessibility of Memory refers to the client's ability to retain, recollect, and actively use past experience and significant memories. The client whose memories are continuous and complete, even though they are painful, might be rated at the high end of this scale. On the other hand, the client whose mind is blank, or whose memories are essentially mostly incomplete and sketchy, is at the maladaptive end of the scale.

Judgment   This concept refers to the cognitive function of decision-making through the comparison, deliberation, consideration, and anticipation of current events or a possible future state of affairs. The maladaptive end of this scale might be characterized by the client who shows a lack of consideration or awareness for the consequences of his or her actions. The adaptive end of the continuum characterizes the client who is able to postpone action where appropriate and who is aware of, and deliberative about, potential decisions.

Exploration   This concept is defined as the cognitive process of examining one's attitudes, feelings, and behaviors. The adaptive end of the scale is represented by the client who accepts responsibility and is willing actively to probe or investigate. The maladaptive end of the scale is characterized by the client who is unable or unwilling to question or become curious about him or herself.

Recognition   This concept refers to a cognitive process that facilitates the acquisition of insight by enabling the client to discern the relationships or patterns among his or her thoughts, feelings, or between present and past events. At the maladaptive end of this scale is the client who has difficulty making changes because he or she is unable or unwilling to understand the design or pattern that has connected important past events in his or her life.

Mode of Conflict Expression   This concept refers to the process whereby clients express thoughts, feelings, or action tendencies which are painful or conflicted for them. At the maladaptive end of this scale is the client who, for example, may use his or her body as the sole means of expressing conflict. It is assumed that accurate labeling and verbal expression are more adaptive than the unconscious expression of conflict through symptoms and other compromise formations. Thus, the adaptive end of the scale is characterized by the client who is able to provide full and accurate verbal reports about what he or she is experiencing.

Revision of Concepts of Self and Other   The ninth and last of the Cognitive Operations scales attempts to assess the flexibility or rigidity with which such concepts are held by the client and the methods by which they are maintained or changed. At the maladaptive end of this continuum one finds the client who, for example, refuses to change and, thus, desperately clings to and maintains an unrealistic image of self or other by refusing to discriminate the accurate perceptions that are available. It may also characterize the client who works hard to keep separate in consciousness contrasting good, and bad images of self and other. The adaptive use of this cognitive process includes changing the images of self and other by evaluating and accepting both positive and negative qualities.

These nine scales may be used for research or employed informally by the counselor to gain information about those client cognitive functions thought to be important in an insight-orientated approach to counseling. As has been mentioned previously, they are not intended, neither are they appropriate as, the sole basis for clinical decision-making about the client. The reliability of these scales increases to acceptable levels when three or more trained raters use them. In this case, they are a useful means of assessing the extent of change in the client over time.

Client adjustment

The client's overall adjustment or adaptation also affects how he or she responds to counseling (Robinson, 1950). For example, the client's level of felt distress (Keithly, Samples & Strupp, 1980) or vulnerability (Kokotovic & Tracey, 1990) have been shown to be related to a variety of counseling process and outcome measures. Yet these are very general terms and do not help to pinpoint the precise kind of distress or maladaptive behavior the client is experiencing. For example, the counselor will want to know whether the client is experiencing unpleasant affective or physical states; whether there is any evidence of inhibitions, phobias or compulsions; or whether the client's behavior is limiting socially or interpersonally. These and a host of other problems influence the way in which the client responds to the counseling process.

In keeping with our assumption about symptoms or compromise formations being attempts at adaptation (see Chapter 2), we will present in this final section of the chapter a method by which the counselor might assess the extent of the client's unsuccessful adaptive response patterns. Such an assessment should be an ongoing practice throughout and following counseling. As with the two previous sets of rating scales for Client Improvement in Relations and Cognitive Operations, the scales in the Client Reduction of Unsuccessful Adaptive Response Patterns dimension (Robbins, 1980; Robbins & Patton, 1986) were developed as part of the Utah Counseling Outcomes Project. These 10 scales are empirically derived interval measures, placed on an eight-point continuum of severity with descriptive anchors at each interval. In a few cases, the anchor statement adjacent to a given scale point is missing, but it is still possible to infer the level of severity for that point on the scale by extrapolation from the immediately surrounding statements. Initial estimates of scale reliability (internal consistency) and inter-rater reliability and agreement have been obtained for all 10 scales (Robbins, 1980), and validity estimates have been obtained for a subset of them (Robbins & Patton, 1986) (see Chapter 13).

Table 6.3 contains each of the scales from the Client Reduction of

Unsuccessful Adaptive Response Patterns dimension. The 10 scales are labeled as follows: Somatization; Hypochondriacal Preoccupations; Hysterical Style; Sexual Dysfunctioning; Obsessive Qualities; Anxiety; Addictive Style; Reality Orientation; Anger; and Depression. The counselor may find that his or her own rating of the client will provide information useful for observing and following up with the client. Again, the counselor is cautioned against using the scales to make clinical decisions about the client, given the low reliability of the ratings when using only one rater. Three trained raters improve reliability to acceptable levels, however, and provide a means of evaluating the efficacy of counseling by measuring the progress or change in the client's unsuccessful adaptive response patterns. Again, the scales are appropriate for use in counseling outcomes research.

Somatization   This is a rating scale that assesses the extent to which the client tends to respond to stress and tension with physical complaints. At the negative end of this scale is the client who develops crippling physical symptoms following stressful events. At the positive end is the person whose physiological functions remain within normal limits even during stressful periods. Clients who somatize their problems are frequently difficult to work with because they would prefer a physical to a psychological explanation for their troubles. A period of time has to be spent helping them accept the contribution made by the emotional side to their problems.

Hypochondriacal preoccupations   The second scale measures the extent to which the client adapts by showing an exaggerated concern with mental or physical functioning. A client at the negative end of this scale shows the level of severity like someone who becomes so panicked over a headache that he or she rushes off to the emergency room. The absence of such preoccupations is characterized by the client who has realistic confidence in the functioning of his or her mind and body.

Hysterical style   This scale assesses the degree to which the client is prone to adapt to stress with histrionic behaviors, amnesia, sensory and visceral distortions, or intense, dramatic, and inevitably painful romantic involvements. At the negative end of this continuum is the client who, for example, cannot remember stressful events in which conflict involving guilt is present. The adaptive end of the continuum is represented by the client who is comfortable with his or her sexual responsiveness.

Sexual dysfunctioning   This scale refers to a pattern of impaired sexual functioning, inability to participate in sex, sexual acting out, severely

Table 6.3 Client reduction of unsuccessful adaptive response pattern scales

---

Somatization
Scale definition: responding to distress and tension with physical or psychosomatic reactions.

---

8. His/her blood pressure stays normal even during stressful times.
LEAST
7. Because of the strain of changing jobs, he/she is careful to get enough rest.

---

6. When dirty jokes are told, he/she blushes deeply.
MODERATELY LOW
5. At parties she/he hiccups when asked to dance.

---

4. After learning about the friend's love life, a splitting headache developed.
MODERATELY HIGH
3. The thought of giving birth makes him/her break out in hives.

2.
GREATEST
1. Emotional events are followed by crippling physical conditions.

Hypochondriacal Preoccupations
Scale definition: endless preoccupation, worry or panic about bodily or mental dysfunction.

---

8. Seems to have confidence in the functioning of his/her body.
LEAST
7. Shows normal concern for self when physically ill.

6.
MODERATELY LOW
5. Likes to discuss health-related matters.

---

4. Tends to dwell on reporting the physical sensation being experienced.
MODERATELY HIGH
3. Worries constantly about developing hemorrhoids.

---

2. Anxiously gives the descriptions of the illnesses he/she anticipates getting.
GREATEST
1. Gets so panicked over headaches, he/she goes to the hospital.

Table 6.3 *(continued)*

Hysterical Style
Scale definition: display of histrionic behaviors, stormy relationships, denial, sensory and visceral distortion, or unmanageable emotional episodes.

---

8. Comfortable with his/her sexual responsiveness.

LEAST

7. Says he/she feels strong inside.

---

6. Handles romantic break-ups with resignation.

MODERATELY LOW

5. Calls self a big flirt and enjoys it.

---

4. Jumps quickly into new love relationships after a break-up.

MODERATELY HIGH

3. Occasionally he/she can't stop crying.

---

2. After times of stress, he/she often can't remember the next several hours.

GREATEST

1. Often has episodes of jerking convulsions.

Sexual Dysfunctioning
Scale definition: inability to participate in sex, a pattern of sexual acting out, a pattern of severely inhibited sexuality, or very unusual sex practices.

---

8. Sex is a joyous and happy experience for him/her.

LEAST

7. Enjoys own body during sexual intercourse.

---

6. A little difficulty initiating sex, but is responsive once begun.

MODERATELY LOW

5. Troubled by unwanted thoughts during sex.

---

4. Only sex really wanted is frequent masturbation.

MODERATELY HIGH

3. Has an orgasm only when wearing clothes of opposite sex.

---

2. Can't resist the urge to try to urinate on partner during sex.

GREATEST

1. Likes to hurt partner during sex.

Table 6.3 *(continued)*

Obsessive Qualities
Scale definition: intrusive thoughts, repetitive acts or urges, or over-concern with the issues of control and autonomy.

8. Can enjoy just letting his/her thoughts go.
LEAST
7. Enjoys cooperating with others.

6. Has a fairly relaxed attitude toward disciplining the children.
MODERATELY LOW
5. Is bothered by his/her stinginess.

4. Gets uncooperative if it isn't his/her idea first.
MODERATELY HIGH
3. If the house is not cleaned daily, he/she gets upset.

2. Can't get rid of the thought he/she could kill spouse.
GREATEST
1. So afraid of dirt, he/she stays in bed all day.

Anxiety
Scale definition: painful, apprehensive state of mind, as evidenced by fearful concern or worry, marked physiological symptoms, or feelings of uneasiness and self-doubt.

8. Is a peaceful and calm person.
LEAST
7. No signs of uneasiness or dread have been reported.

6. At times feels pressured to get things done.
MODERATELY LOW
5. Becomes "nervous" after arguments but quickly calms down.

4. While talking, his/her face and neck frequently flushes.
MODERATELY HIGH
3. Leaves the scene whenever panic hits her/him.

2. Can't stop trembling and shaking.
GREATEST
1. Is so scared, thinks he/she is dying.

Table 6.3 *(continued)*

Addictive style
Scale definition: compulsive use of substances such as drugs, alcohol, or food in response to stress caused internally or externally.

8.

LEAST

7. Reports no uncontrollable urges even when upset.

---

6. Rarely drinks to excess.

MODERATELY LOW

5. Gets drunk once in a while to let off steam.

---

4. When has to wait, constantly snacks on food.

MODERATELY HIGH

3. Doesn't seem to have fun without being intoxicated.

---

2. Her/his hands start to shake without a drink.

GREATEST

1. Is afraid he/she will die without drugs.

Reality Orientation
Scale definition: ability and preference for differentiating between fantasies, wishes, and external events and for maintaining realistic contact with others.

---

8. Shows good grasp of even the more subtle aspects of a social relationship.

LEAST

7.

---

6. In spite of her/his handicap, is making realistic plans for employment.

MODERATELY LOW

5. Saves money but only daydreams about spending it.

---

4. Has difficulty talking and eating in front of others.

MODERATELY HIGH

3. Has strong and pervasive feelings that people "look" like him/her.

---

2. Becomes agitated and begins seeing things that aren't there.

GREATEST

1.

Table 6.3 *(continued)*

Anger
Scale definition: attitude or mood of rage, hostility, bitterness, or enmity toward self or others.

8.

LEAST

7. Seems even tempered in most situations.

---

6. Gets mildly annoyed when stuck in long lines.

MODERATELY LOW

5. Can be sarcastic when talking about her/his family.

---

4. Shows pleasure when the ex-lover or ex-spouse has misfortune.

MODERATELY HIGH

3. Seems cold and nasty to whomever he/she talks to.

---

2. Seems so angry none of the co-workers will go near him/her.

GREATEST

1. Rage can be so intense, she/he feels ready to explode.

Depression
Scale definition: dysphoric affective state as evidenced by a dejected mood, feelings of hopelessness, or difficulty in performing daily activities.

8.

LEAST

7. Usually he/she is feeling good inside.

---

6. Gets blue now and then.

MODERATELY LOW

5. Has occasional restless nights feeling lonely.

---

4. Sounds low in energy and slowed down.

MODERATELY HIGH

3. Feels sad almost all of the time.

---

2. Doesn't think life is worth living any more.

GREATEST

1. Tried killing him/herself recently.

---

inhibited sexuality, or very unusual sexual practices. At the maladaptive end of the scale, we might find the client who, for example, enjoys hurting his or her partner during sex. At the positive end of the continuum is the client for whom sex is happy experience.

Obsessive qualities This scale assesses the extent to which the client complains of intrusive thoughts, repetitive actions or urges, or concern with issues of control or autonomy. The maladaptive end of this scale is characterized by a level of severity suggested by the client who is so frightened of germs that he or she refuses to leave the house. At the adaptive end, we find persons who enjoy cooperating with others.

Anxiety This term refers to the client's painful or apprehensive state of mind. The anxious client may exhibit worry, evidence notable physiological or behavioral symptoms or voice self-doubt and feelings of uneasiness. The most severe level of this scale is characterized by clients who are so frightened they think they are dying. The adaptive end of the continuum is represented by someone who is calm and peaceful.

Addictive style This scale attempts to assess a client's compulsive use of substances such as drugs, alcohol, or food in response to stress. The greatest level of severity on this scale is characterized by the person who is afraid he or she will die without drugs. Adaptiveness on this continuum would be represented by the absence of any uncontrollable urges.

Reality orientation This scale assesses the client's ability and preference for distinguishing between fantasies, wishes, and external events and for maintaining realistic contact with others. To score at the most maladaptive end of the scale, the client's behavior would have to be as severe as someone who is afraid he or she is merging with the walls when stressed. Adaptation at the highest level is characterized by the client who is able to discriminate even the most subtle interpersonal cues when interacting with others.

Anger This scale assesses the client's rage, hostility, bitterness, or enmity toward self or others. If the client were to be rated at the most maladaptive end of this continuum, he or she would need to be similar in level of severity to the client whose rage has completely dominated his or her intellective functions. The absence of maladaptive anger is represented by the client who is likely to be even-tempered in most situations, but who can become annoyed when appropriate.

Depression   The tenth and last scale in the Client Reduction of Unsuccessful Adaptive Response Patterns dimension refers to the client's dysphoric affective state, as evidenced by a dejected mood, feelings of hopelessness, or difficulty in performing daily activities. The maladaptive end of the scale suggests the client who may think life is no longer worth living, or who may have attempted suicide. The adaptive end of the depression continuum is characterized by the client whose mood is usually elevated and who feels good inside.

As was the case with the other two sets of scales, the rater's task with the scales in the Client Reduction of Unsuccessful Adaptive Response Patterns dimension is to find that anchor on the continuum of severity that best represents the client's current status or level of severity on that scaled attribute. A client's pattern or profile of ratings across these 10 scales gives an indication of the current level of distress.

In this chapter, we have argued that there are four broad dimensions that make up the client's readiness for psychoanalytic counseling: motivation; capacity to accept a working alliance with the counselor; certain cognitive functions; and level of adjustment. We have attempted to explicate these dimensions by highlighting their specific elements. In the case of motivation, we saw that both the client's interest in overcoming his or her problems and the ability to trust and take for granted the requirements of the counseling situation are the necessary ingredients. For the working alliance dimension, the client's capacity for receiving help and the quality of his or her interpersonal relations were seen to be important. We presented a set of cognitive operations that we felt were important for the client if he or she were to participate meaningfully in psychoanalytic counseling. Finally, we argued that the level of the client's adjustment is important in determining how he or she responds to counseling, and we introduced several ways in which clients adjust to stress.

We also provided three sets of rating scales for the counselor's use in informally assessing the client's interpersonal relations, cognitive operations and level of unsuccessful adaptive response patterns. We want to emphasize here that it is the specific elements in each of these four dimensions that point the counselor to the observations about the client that are important in determining his or her level of readiness for psychoanalytic counseling.

7 Guidelines for organizing client information

Psychoanalytic counseling is a planful enterprise. It is not accomplished by moment-to-moment improvising. Certainly, it consists of the counselor's humane concern, good intentions, and respect for the client. These are necessary and helpful ingredients, but alone they are not sufficient to bring about constructive change in the client. In addition to these therapeutic attitudes, effective psychoanalytic counseling requires the counselor's deliberate and planned use of knowledge and skill. The counselor listens carefully and patiently to understand the psychodynamic meaning of the client's communications and then intervenes on the basis of that understanding.

The knowledge the counselor acquires about the client comes from two important and different sources. The application of that knowledge depends upon making it relevant to the ongoing interaction in the interview. First of all, the counselor's knowledge comes from empathic observation of the client, from awareness of his or her countertransference reactions, and from a developing hypothetical model of the client built upon both of these. The counselor's subjective grasp of the everyday meaning of the client's behavior is the raw material out of which later objective or theoretically driven understanding is acquired. Second, the counselor has, as a background of more or less tacit knowledge, a general understanding or mastery of the concepts and principles of psychoanalytic theory as presented in the preceding chapters. Finally, application of theoretical/technical knowledge depends upon the counselor's ability to make it relevant to the client's material on a given occasion.

This chapter is about a method and guidelines for organizing the client's ongoing communications so that their psychodynamic relevance is clear. Even the most resistant client provides a considerable amount of information.

Our set of guidelines is based on the work of Anderson (1964). We use many of his ideas about organizing client material and modify others to fit our purposes. The theories of the client and of the treatment encounter presented in earlier chapters assist us in the task of organizing information systematically. Organizing client information according to its psychoanalytic significance helps us do several things. First, when we operate in the interview with a method for organizing information systematically, we are alerted to listen for information that has special relevance. Second, when we have gathered sufficient information, we are able to state the client's central emotional problems. Third, once the central problems are defined, we are able to plan a course of action in counseling based on that definition.

The guidelines offered here are intended to help the counselor organize client information after listening to it. They are not intended to be used as a list of questions as part of some interview schedule. An attempt to use the guidelines as a device for structuring the interview will preclude the client from reporting in his or her own natural way. It is our experience that the client's spontaneous and unforced reporting of material provides the most useful information. It is best for the counselor to use these guidelines for organizing client information as soon after the interview as is possible. In this way, the events of the hour are fresh in the counselor's mind and can be recalled with more reliability. The counselor should make a habit of sitting down and using the guidelines after every interview to formulate the case material. After every twelfth interview or so, it is recommended that the counselor do a longer formulation of the material to date. Frequent use of the guidelines helps the counselor revise his or her conceptualizations according to new information. As with the counselor's interventions in the interview, the counselor's formulations of the case are tentative propositions that are open to refutation in the light of new information.

Whether the guidelines are used to organize information systematically from the first interview or the fiftieth, the principles that undergird their use are the same. The guidelines can be used, therefore, to formulate a single interview or a series of interviews. In any case, over the course of counseling it is important to reformulate the information provided by the client on a periodic basis.

The remainder of this chapter is divided into three sections. The first two sections comprise our set of guidelines for organizing client information, and the third section illustrates their use with a case example. The first section deals with the dynamic elements of the client's communication, including the client's presenting concerns or complaints, their immediate and remote antecedents and the pattern of defenses the client exhibits. The second section concerns the counselor's response to the material gathered in the first section. That is, this section begins with guidelines for defining the conditions for which the client needs assistance. It is followed by a consideration of the goals that will be set for the work, along with the intervention strategies that will be used to meet those goals and the means for assessing client progress. Table 7.1 includes the entire set of categories that make up these guidelines for organizing client communications.

Understanding the dynamics of client communication

As we have noted in preceding chapters, external events and a person's responses to them are in a dynamic relation to each other. The client's communications to us in the counseling interview will show this same kind of dynamic relationship if we listen for it. It will be important to locate the various components of this relationship because each adds information necessary to a full understanding of the client's problem. The categories in this section each deal with a component of the dynamics involved in client communication.

The client's complaints

We assume that the client seeks professional help and comes to counseling because of personal distress. If the client is not experiencing some kind of personal pain, a legitimate motive for counseling does not exist. The counselor is advised to take special note of the client's complaints. Their psychoanalytic relevance is that they function in the client's life as compromise formations or as the failure of such formations (see Chapters 2 and 4). They are the outcome of a sequence of events and they signal the presence of intrapsychic conflict and/or vulnerability of the self structure.

Table 7.1 Outline for organizing client communications

Part 1: Understanding client communications
  1. The client's complaints
  2. Dates of onset and precipitating events
  3. Defenses
  4. Predisposing influences
  5. Unanswered questions

Part 2: Acting on the client's communications
  6. Conditions for which the client needs help
  7. Counseling goals
  8. Intervention plan
  9. Criteria for progress

The purpose of this category is, then, to provide the counselor with a means for compiling a careful list of all the client's complaints. We say careful because it is often the case that the client will mention some complaints in passing, or minimize their relevance in some other way. The counselor needs to be watchful in recognizing such instances. On the one hand, hearing the client's complaints informs the counselor just how the client hurts. On the other, keeping a record of the complaints provides the counselor with important information for diagnostic purposes.

The content of this category consists of several kinds of observations made by the counselor. First, it consists of the concerns mentioned by the client as the reasons he or she has sought professional help from the counselor. These may be complaints about negative affects, well-developed symptoms or whatever the client alleges that others have done to harm him or her. Second, it includes the counselor's observations of those things the client does not complain about, but which are nonetheless regarded as noteworthy. We mean here observations that indicate there is some difficulty that the client is either not aware of, is not concerned about, or is deliberately avoiding. Third, it includes the manner in which the client makes the complaint. The client may express a concern with appropriate affect, for example, or he or she may minimize its significance by mentioning it in passing, laughing about it, or otherwise downplaying its importance and the pain it causes. Fourth, it consists of the counselor's recognition of the context in which the client mentions the complaint. A complaint that surfaces each time the client talks about a spouse, a parent, or the boss, for example, is providing important information.

We saw in Chapter 4 how the client's report of current events provides the counselor with information about how the client is adapting to the demands of the environment. Complaints or symptoms are the client's responses to the adaptive context in which he or she lives (Langs, 1973). Complaints arise in the client's life when adaptation to a particular situation becomes problematic. The demands of that situation exceed the capacity of the person to cope successfully with it. In the optimal case, there is a balance between the person's biological and psychological needs and his or her satisfaction in the environment. This balance permits the individual to experience congruence in the exercise of intellective functions, affects, and actions. It provides for a sense of freedom and enjoyment.

In the client, however, the relationship to the environment is accompanied by a more or less painful sense of strain. The balance between need and satisfaction has been breached. The results of this breach are to be noted in the constrained way in which the client must now manage thoughts, feelings, and actions. Gone is the spontaneity and pleasure that marked a conflict-free relationship with the environment. Instead, the client's complaints and symptoms now signal the presence of conscious or unconscious controls on thoughts, feelings, and actions. The client now censors thoughts, holds back feelings, and inhibits actions.

The same sequence of events is mirrored in the interview. At some point in the conversation with the counselor, the client stops reporting freely about experiences and begins complaining about his or her condition. This change occurs because the reporting of an experience has become pervaded by conflict and pain. In other words, the client no longer talks about the experience or discusses it with the counselor because it is too unacceptable to deal with consciously, even if it is acknowledged. Instead, the client will now mention new or previous complaints, or talk about the need for rest, vacation, or a prescription. It is instructive, therefore, to note the context in which complaining arises in the interview. It will be preceded and followed by references to people and events that are associated with pain in the client's mind. The report of a symptom or complaint is bounded on either side by information that is indispensable for understanding its meaning. In the same way, what the client says before and after voicing the complaint is also informed by the complaint itself.

Clients also often voice their complaints in subtle ways, such that it is not clear just what the problem is. To help recognize a complaint as such, Anderson (1964) advises the counselor to adopt the definition of complaint that is used in a court of law. That is, the person who makes a complaint is called a plaintiff. Notably, there can be no plaintiff without a defendant, who is the person being held responsible for the alleged injury. As Anderson (1964) notes, in the counseling setting, the client is accusing someone of an injury and is making a claim for damages. More often than not, the client's accusations will be directed to those with whom he or she has an emotional bond; that is, partners, spouses, parents, children, or close friends.

Dates of onset and precipitating events

After the client has voiced a complaint or complaints, we want to know: (a) how long he or she has been suffering; and (b) what was going on at the time the complaint first appeared. We combine these two events in the same category and place them immediately after the section on complaints to emphasize the close connection each of these events has with the other. Complaints, their onsets and the circumstances associated with their occurrence are very important in understanding the client and how he or she handles stressful events. Just as complaints are usually multiple, so are the dates of onset and their circumstances.

The complaint is a response to the demands of the adaptive context, to one or more circumstances that the client has difficulty mastering. Complaints, then, are in a dynamic relation to the circumstances that mark their onsets.

The client may or may not be consciously aware of these antecedents to the complaints. Lack of awareness in this regard is simply one way the client protects him or herself from the pain that is experienced when details of the past are recalled. Part of the work of the interview entails helping the client clarify the connections among the complaints and the circumstances of their occurrence.

Dates of onset   Often, it is as easy for the client to report the date of onset for a complaint or symptom as it is to report the complaint itself. There are other times, however, as Anderson (1964) points out, when the client's mind acts to separate suffering from the circumstances of its arousal. For this reason, it is sometimes difficult for the client to be specific about the dates of onset. Instead, what the counselor hears when the client is asked for a date of onset is a failure to remember, or, more often, a general reference to a year, time of year, anniversary, holiday, birthday, and the like. Clients have many ways that are both vague and detailed of providing information. The counselor needs to be observant so that no date of onset will be passed over. Both the date of onset and how the onset is mentioned by the client are a part of the context or meaning of the complaint.

Dates of onset for the occurrence of complaints may be recent or remote. In using these guidelines for organizing the client's communications, it is helpful to proceed from the recent to the remote past in listing complaints with their dates of onset and precipitating events. Information will be more abundant for the more recent onsets. Usually, it is advisable to actively pursue information about the most recent dates of onset if the client does not offer this information. There are two reasons for doing so. First, the client will likely be able to recall the particulars of a recent onset much more clearly than those of a more remote onset. The names and personalities of persons involved, the precipitating circumstances, and the client's associated thoughts and feelings will be more accessible. Second, when we seek to understand the most recent complaints and to locate their dates of onset, we set in motion an organized plan for counseling. That plan begins with current events (see Chapter 4) and with that portion of the client's mind which is most accessible to both client and counselor.

Precipitating events   Our interest in precipitating events illustrates the use of the psychoanalytic principle of determinism introduced in Chapter 1. We are prompted by psychoanalytic principles to look for the events that precede the occurrence of the complaint in time. Such events are the antecedents for which the complaints are the consequents. We understand the meaning the complaint has in the client's life much more fully when we know the circumstances surrounding its development. The complaint is the client's attempt to master or adapt to a perceivedly difficult set of recent circumstances. Hence, we need to know what was happening at the time the complaint or symptom occurred. We may also wish to know if anything important was happening, both at the time the client first thought about asking for help, and when he or she actually decided to seek it out. Often, these latter two events are different from the precipitating events, and knowledge of what prompted the client to decide to seek out a professional counselor can be very important.

When we ask the client to tell us what was happening at the time the complaint or symptom first appeared, we are making a cognitive appeal (see Chapter 4) to the client to do the work of remembering and talking instead of complaining. We are requesting specific information in this regard. It will be recalled from Chapters 1 and 2 that, according to psychoanalytic theory, ideas and affects are closely associated in the client's mind. Because of this, the client may sense, consciously or unconsciously, that providing the details surrounding the onset of a complaint will elicit pain. That is, by remembering and telling the counselor what was happening at the time, the client is likely to re-experience the painful feelings and thoughts he or she has had difficulty mastering.

Accordingly, the counselor may notice, for the first time, an attitude of opposition on the part of the client. The topic is changed, memory fails, the client falls silent, or some other manifestation of resistance occurs (see Chapter 9). Often, the appearance of this form of resistance early in the work is a kind of fear of treatment as well as of the client's own painful affects and ideas. Anderson (1964) recommends that the counselor needs two things to help counter the resistance to the question, "What was happening at the time?" The counselor needs both the technique and the accompanying attitude of persistence in eliciting the information. Techniques for eliciting information about precipitating events from clients who oppose providing it vary according to the counselor's preferences. A possible list of such techniques might include the following sequence of imaginary counselor interventions, which are ongoing responses to a reluctant client:

1. We first ask the client, "Just tell me what was happening at the time?"
2. Then, if the client says, in effect, nothing was happening, counter by stating, "Something was going on. Try to remember the details."
3. Next, if the client still can't remember, try saying something like, "I recognize that this may be unfamiliar to you, and you may be uncertain about what to say. Don't try to judge what may be important or unimportant, simply talk about what you were doing or what was happening at the time."
4. If the client still can't remember, suggest that "If you take a little time

to think, I'm sure some thoughts will come to mind and that will give us a beginning. I'll just wait while you think about it."

The second component of the counselor's strategy for intervening with the client who is reluctant to disclose information about precipitating events is attitudinal. As the above illustration of counselor interventions attempts to convey, the counselor tries to be patient, gentle, and yet firm in seeking the information about precipitating events. The counselor conveys the impression that he or she expects to get an answer and will be disappointed until one is forthcoming.

At any point in the counselor's quest for the information, the client may or may not show annoyance at the counselor's persistence in this regard. Knowing how to be persistent is as important as knowing when to stop persisting. Information that cannot be provided at the moment may well be disclosed later in the interview. Once this kind of resistance to talking is overcome, the client will usually provide extensive information.

Defenses

We saw in Chapter 2 that the ego institutes a defense to counter the expression of sexual or aggressive wishes, or the ideas of calamity and the painful affects associated with those ideas. The purpose of the defense is to lessen or avoid altogether the experience of pain. Any mental event, character trait, perception, attitude, or belief that achieves this end can be called a defense. The effect of the client's defenses in the counseling interview is the blocking of open communication and the willingness to change. For this reason, defenses are referred to as resistance when they occur in the interview (see Chapter 9).

Defenses are part of the response the client makes to the precipitating stresses that occur. The client's complaint or symptom is a compromise formation which is the outcome of intrapsychic conflict. The defenses are an aspect of that outcome. It is important for several reasons for the counselor to recognize and to keep a list of the defenses the client uses. First, as mentioned above, defenses function to block the free flow of communication in the interview. For this reason, the counselor may find it necessary to help the client understand and modify those defenses. The counselor's technique of confrontation is intended for this purpose and it will be considered in Chapter 9.

Second, recognizing the defenses assists the counselor in building a comprehensive understanding of how the client's mind works when stresses are responded to with conflicting thoughts and feelings. More precisely, awareness of the client's pattern of defenses enlarges the counselor's understanding of the central emotional problem. Thus, for example, if the client seems unduly ingratiating and charming, one might begin to suspect that these are traits and behaviors aimed at getting the counselor to like the client in order to protect vulnerable self-esteem against the pain of possible rejection. In this case, ingratiation and charm are long-term behavior patterns that serve defensive purposes. They oppose communication in the hour because such a client is reluctant to disclose negative experiences that are perceived to reflect badly on him or her.

Another example would be the client who seems to react unusually strongly to the expression of sexuality in others, and who argues for stricter laws against the public display of such behavior. In this case, the counselor might guess that the client is protecting him or herself from engaging in the same behavior. Such a defense is usually called a reaction formation. It opposes communication by keeping the client unaware of the underlying conflict that contains a wish for sexual gratification.

Finally, the client's defenses provide additional reasons for counseling. In the ordinary case, defenses operate in a flexible way to help the person adapt to the ongoing demands of the environment. When the person is working, for example, repression assists in keeping unwanted and irrelevant thoughts from consciousness so that he or she can focus attention on the demands at hand. By the same token, there are occasions when the person can relax his or her defenses to enjoy harmless pleasures that are reserved for special occasions. In Western culture, dressing up for a Hallowe'en party comes to mind as one such occasion.

When the client is under considerable stress, however, one of two things can go wrong with the defenses. Either the defenses are not working effectively, such that the person is overwhelmed by negative affect, or they are applied so rigidly that the person is unable to express him or herself in constructive and satisfying ways. In the former case, one goal of counseling includes helping the client reinstate the defenses so that he or she once again has access to the intellective functions. In the latter case, the goal is to help the client become aware of a defense and how rigidly it is applied, so that he or she can decide to modify or replace it.

A convenient list of defenses and their definitions is included in Table 7.2 on the opposite page. This same list of defenses will be further elaborated in Chapter 9.

Predisposing influences

This category alerts the counselor to the need to understand the historical context that has helped predispose the client to respond to stress with a specific combination of complaints and symptoms. Every person is vulnerable

Table 7.2 Some common defenses

Repression   Certain unconscious wishes, memories, affects or action tendencies are selectively blocked from expression in awareness.

Denial   The refusal to believe that an event has occurred or that he or she is currently experiencing certain wishes or affects.

Regression   The handling of conflict by returning to earlier, less mature forms of adaptation.

Reaction formation   A defense that converts an unacceptable, unconscious attitude into its opposite when expressed consciously.

Projection   The disowning of unacceptable thoughts and feelings, or responsibility for one's actions, by imputing them to someone else.

Isolation, or splitting the affect   The separation of affects from their associated ideational content.

Undoing   A good deed unconsciously corrects or cancels a prior wrongful act.

Reversal   Doing to someone else what the client wishes would be done for him or her.

Turning around on the self with love   Gratifying oneself following an episode in which one experiences a narcissistic injury.

Turning around on the self with anger   Injuring oneself in some way for a perceived transgression.

Introjection   The person's incorporation and expression of the perceived, often negative, opinions, attitudes, or expectations another person has of him or herself, usually to retain the other's love.

Identification   A means of surmounting anxiety and other painful affects and ideas by adopting the attitudes, values, and behaviors of a feared other person.

Passive into active   The use of action rather than thought to avoid dealing with painful affects and ideas.

Active into passive   The use of withdrawal from activity to avoid unpleasure.

---

to stresses of one kind and not another. This statement merely reflects the fact each of us has weaknesses that are tied to specific experiences from our past. Those experiences are usually of two kinds. Either a present circumstance is similar to an earlier traumatic event in the client's life, or the present setting confronts the client with a situation for which the past did not adequately provide preparation. The former case suggests intrapsychic conflict, while the latter may represent developmental deficit. It is not unusual for the client both to be burdened by intrapsychic conflict (see Chapter 2) and to experience a disharmony in the self structure (see Chapter 3) in his or her attempts to adapt to present circumstances.

It is often the case that the client will decide to linger on and report past events. In this instance, the reporting will usually be dry and without emotional substance. When this happens, the counselor needs to take special action to ensure that a full reporting of current events is not being sacrificed. It is a sign of resistance on both the client and the counselor's part when the present is avoided. The model for balanced reporting in the interview occurs something like this: first, the client begins with reporting current events of increasing significance. These are the events that are at the surface of the client's mind. Getting a full report and understanding of the client's current situation is the necessary first step in undertaking a plan for counseling. Next, the client's report brings in significant events that are further removed in time from the present. Finally, in a successful course of psychoanalytic counseling, the client will quite naturally bring in the childhood experiences that are among the predisposing influences for the current maladaptive responses. Sometimes the above sequence occurs during the initial interview, but more often than not, it is rare in the early phases of counseling. In any case, it will never be a frequent occurrence because the client's defenses oppose such a sequence of reporting.

Several kinds of information are important in building an understanding of the predisposing circumstances. Chief among these are the personalities of the client's parents, siblings, and other significant persons. What is important about the parents and others is not what they do, but who they are (Kohut, 1977). How they responded to the client, including how well they understood and cared for him or her, are the relevant factors here. The quality of the client's relationships is the important factor. The counselor needs full descriptions of the important persons in the client's early life. What is helpful is a description of an episode of interaction between the client and the family members. Both personal opinions and factual material are relevant here. What is needed is an answer to the question, "What are the factors that have influenced the client's vulnerability?"

Beyond this, it is helpful to know some general factors such as the size of the family; their socioeconomic status and educational background and the ages and genders of its members. It is also important to learn about any stressful or traumatic experiences for the client before the age of 6, and extending through adolescence. Such events may well prove to be the predisposing event. Serious illness or death of a parent or sibling, parental divorce, physical or sexual abuse of the client by older family members, or prolonged absences by significant members of the family are examples. How the important persons in the environment responded to these events is critically important information to learn about.

Information about predisposing influences comes over time. It is not recommended that the counselor deliberately interview the client for such information. The client's natural way of reporting his or her own biography will provide much more relevant information than if a "social history" is taken. When such information is relatively complete, the counselor is in a position to link it with the preceding categories for a more complete understanding of the client's central emotional difficulties. As more information from this category is added by the client over time, it acts as an ongoing corrective for the counselor's developing formulations of the client. But, because our information is always in some stage of incompleteness, we turn now to the next category on unanswered questions.

Unanswered questions

As mentioned above, the list of predisposing influences is an expanding one. The counselor needs to remain curious about facts in the client's history that are currently obscure or the relevance of events that are, as yet, vague. The client's report is necessarily incomplete. He or she cannot be expected on any occasion to give a full report on those predisposing events that have brought about the current pattern of vulnerabilities.

This category encourages the counselor to build a list of questions. We do not, however, encourage the counselor to frequently interrupt or question the client. Moreover, if information is requested out of context from the client's way of reporting it, much of relevance will be lost. Rather, we propose that the counselor be patient and wait until the information surfaces on its own, or until an appropriate occasion arises in the conversation for asking a question.

Acting on the client's communications

The previous section on the dynamics of client communications contained several categories with guidelines for organizing information about the client. This section is about guidelines for using the information from the preceding categories to take action with and on behalf of the client. The first category is about the conditions for which the client needs help. It is followed by guidelines for developing the goals of counseling, and the intervention plan to reach those goals. The guidelines conclude with a category for specifying how client progress will be identified.

Conditions for which the client needs help

The contents of this category serve as the counselor's set of tentative inferences about the client's underlying or central problem(s). The underlying causes are to be distinguished, therefore, from the client's complaints and symptoms. While the relief of these complaints and symptoms is an intermediate criterion of successful counseling (see Robinson, 1950), the longer-range criterion is client insight into the underlying factors that sustain the complaints. In psychoanalytic theory, the central problems are either some form of intrapsychic conflict or developmental deficit, both of which produce specific kinds of observable complaints, and which manifest themselves through the transference. It is about these underlying conditions that we hope to help the client achieve insight. The counselor's proposed statement of these conditions is best couched in everyday language that remains close to the client's reality. Extensive reliance on the use of theoretical terms is, therefore, usually not helpful. The definition of the conditions for which the client needs help assist the counselor in formulating the goals of counseling and the intervention strategies for reaching those goals.

The counselor's task in this category is to explain the client's complaints, precipitating events, defenses, and predisposing influences (if available). The counselor does this by recourse to his or her knowledge of psychoanalytic theories of the client. That is, the counselor uses the observations of the client to propose an underlying pattern that operates to produce and sustain the client's complaints. The work of psychoanalytic counseling consists of discovering this pattern and working out solutions to the conflicts and/or disharmonies in the self.

There is only one requirement for arriving at a statement of the conditions for which the client needs help. That is, the counselor should be clear about how the observations of the client relate to the counselor's statement of the underlying problem. One approach would be to review the complaints, precipitating events, defenses and predisposing influences and ask what factors within the client could produce this particular set of observations. This would include observations of the client's in-session behavior in both the working alliance and transference. Another approach might consist of first selecting both a conflict or self psychology formulation as the underlying problem, and then determining with which formulation the observations are most logically consistent. In terms of classical psychoanalytic theory, certain kinds of wishes, together with the anxiety- (or depression-)provoking thoughts they elicit, are posssible factors (see Chapter 2). Psychoanalytic self psychology would select certain kinds of vulnerabilities in either the grandiose or idealizing line of the self as candidates (see Chapter 3).

If the counselor were proposing that the client's problem were conflict-related, the core of the material in this category might sound something like this:

The client appears to have an obsessive pattern of defenses with which she attempts to minimize her anxiety and guilt. These defenses, along with her pattern of uncooperativeness with others, including the counselor, and her long history of intruding herself into intact marriages, suggests an arrest in her development at an early point in the oedipal period.

Alternatively, the nucleus of a formulation that draws upon Kohut's (1977) Self Psychology might read as follows:

Given the client's prominent defenses of withdrawal following criticism, his shame-proneness and reactive arrogance, along with his wish to have the counselor admire him unreservedly, it is likely that the client is suffering from a weakness in the grandiose sector of the self.

As they are written here, these examples are elliptical in that they are not preceded by the observations that would make them plausible or followed by material that amplifies them. In any case, we re-emphasize the tentative nature of the counselor's statement of the conditions for which the client needs help, and the need to state it in terms that allow it to be refuted by evidence from the client. In a word, the counselor's statement of the client's central emotional problem is an hypothesis to be tested in subsequent interviews.

One other point is important to make about this category. Because the client usually comes to counseling for the relief of symptoms and the reduction of complaints, it is not easy to convince him or her that what is needed is a method for discovering the causes of those manifest problems. The client would prefer to rely on the counselor for direct answers and a quick cure. Indeed, it is when the client's presenting complaints have been replaced by the working alliance and he or she feels better that the client may manifest a "flight into health" and abruptly terminate. It takes time to prepare the client for the work of thinking and talking in order to gain insight about the factors within him or her that have contributed to the problem. It is important that the counselor take time to prepare the client for this.

Counseling goals

The statement of the conditions for which the client needs help provide the counselor and the client with a means for determining the appropriate goals or outcomes for the counseling that the two will do together. Such goals may be general or specific, and intermediate or long term. In any case, it is important for the counselor to state the goals clearly.

A partial list of goals is as follows:

1. A very important intermediate goal is that of establishing a firm working alliance with the client. Counseling will not proceed effectively without such a partnership. As has been noted in Chapters 4 and 5, establishment of the working alliance marks the end of the first phase of counseling, and much of the counselor's efforts in this phase are directed toward building the relationship, as well as beginning to demonstrate the client's resistances to experiencing the transference. Difficulties to be expected in establishing the working alliance could be stated here.

2. As a longer-term goal, determine whether it will be a goal of psychoanalytic counseling to: (a) return the client to a previous state of adjustment by focusing primarily on present circumstances; or (b) try to bring about constructive changes in the client through insight by focusing on both the present and the past. In order to accomplish (b) above, it is sometimes necessary to first achieve (a).

3. Goals that are specific to the individual client include discovering the personal meaning of symptoms or complaints, reducing or eliminating them, stating what attitudes or relationships would be altered, and defining how work or career circumstances will change.

Intervention plan

Each goal needs a plan for its accomplishment. This section of the guidelines also needs to be written out. Doing so will help the counselor generate alternatives. Intervention plans are the blueprint for completing the work. They are the pragmatic scheme whereby the counselor manages the course of counseling. Intervention plans refer to both general considerations, like the type or intensity of the counseling, and to specific counselor interventions.

If, for example, the goal of counseling is to help bring a client back to a former state of adjustment following a traumatic episode of some kind, the type of treatment will likely be more supportive than expressive or uncovering (see Bibring, 1954), and interviews may be more frequent until the client is no longer undergoing a stress response syndrome (Horowitz, 1976). Moreover, the focus of the work would likely be on the present, and would be geared to helping the client manage the memories of the event and their meaning for him or her. Work that aims to provide the client with understanding of self entails a study of the past as well as the present. Interviews can occur on a once-a-week basis, and presumably the counselor will have determined that the client is able to respond to an insight-orientated approach to counseling.

When the type of counseling to be offered has been determined, the counselor needs to decide on the content of the ideas to be presented to the client, in what sequence, and in what grammatical format. In the case of the latter consideration, it is often more appropriate to convey an idea as tentative or even in question form to the client whose self-esteem is quite fragile. This gives this client the opportunity to say "No" if he or she needs to in order to protect self-esteem. This example simply highlights the importance to the counselor of trying to predict the client's response to any event in treatment.

Criteria for progress

Once the goals and the intervention plan are stated, it remains for the counselor to decide how progress in reaching those goals will be measured. What is needed are criteria that can be observed so that the direction of change can be noted. A set of scales for measuring client readiness was presented in Chapter 6. These scales can also be used to assess client progress.

When the goals include helping the client return to a former level of adjustment, the reduction of presenting complaints and relief of symptoms are outcome criteria. These events can be measured by the scales from the Client Reduction of Unsuccessful Adaptive Response Patterns dimension, noted in Chapter 6. Progress can also be noted by the client's own report and augmented by the counselor's observation of the number of times it occurs. For example, other indicators in this context would include days missed from work, school, or home responsibilities, and the number of times that the client has visited a physician or has sought other help. Such outcome criteria and observational examples of it also pertain to the client for whom the goals also include insight or self-understanding.

Part of the context of the client's precipitating events includes persons who, in the client's mind, were the origin of personal pain. The ways in which the client is now interacting with these persons can also serve as criteria for progress. Scales for measuring changes in the client's pattern of social relations have been presented in Chapter 6. Generally, we take it as a sign of progress when the client moves to establish relationships instead of withdrawing in isolation, or disrupting them with conflict, and when those relationships are marked by cooperation, communication, and mutuality.

A final set of criteria pertain when the goals of counseling include increasing the client's understanding of his or her past. On the road to greater understanding of the contribution of the past, the client's defenses have been altered or eliminated, thereby giving the client more choice in thinking, feeling, or action. In addition, the client becomes aware of the important persons in the past and is able to locate how the emotional problems of these persons have had a negative impact upon his or her life (cf. Anderson, 1964).

Case example

The case presented below is included to illustrate how the organization of client communications according to a set of systematic guidelines can be accomplished from the outset of counseling. In Chapter 10, we will present this case in more detail and will include there a more complete formulation based on material from all the interviews during the first phase of counseling with this client. For the example in this chapter, we have selected material only from the first hour. Even so, this limited amount of material will demonstrate the large amount of important material that can be provided by clients at the outset of counseling. Organizing client communications from material collected in a first hour also highlights how limited the early interviews are and how cautious we need to be in drawing inferences about the meaning of the client's communications based on these early observations.

Identifying information

The client is a 30-year-old, married male who is employed full-time in the field of personnel management. He and his wife of 10 years have no children, and socialize with other persons of their age and circumstances very little. The client is of medium height and has an athletic build. At the time of the initial interview, the client was attending graduate school part-time at a nearby university. The client had been referred by another psychologist who was seeing the client's wife at the time. After about four or five interviews, the referring psychologist reported that the client's spouse declined any further interviews, either by herself or conjointly with her husband.

The client's presenting complaints

During the assessment, or initial interview, the client complained of depression, of being tired, of feeling anxious, and of feeling as though he had no sense of direction. Later in the interview, he reported feeling guilty, and this followed upon his account of a recent sexual liaison with a woman other than his wife. He also became tearful and cried during the first hour.

Dates of onset and precipitating events

The client mentioned the most recent onset for the complaint of depression within the week prior to his first appointment. Two weeks previously was identified in the client's mind with the feeling that he lacked a sense of direction. He identified a date of one month previously as the onset for his anxiety and guilt. He went on to mention other dates of 1 year, 4 years and 8 years previously. These latter two dates are not directly associated with the presenting complaints, but are included here to point out the importance of the counselor eventually identifying the precipitating stress events and the client's maladaptive responses to them.

Within the past week the client had moved out of his house, leaving his wife to move into an apartment by himself. On doing so, his depression deepened markedly. The client's remarks made it clear that there had been strain in the marriage for a number of years. The week prior to this, he and his wife had talked of separating and eventually divorcing and he had become confused and seemed to lack direction following this conversation. He reported that 1 month previously he had been attracted to a young woman who was attending the same professional meeting in a distant city. The two of them went out for drinks and dinner one evening, and ended up having sexual intercourse that night. The next morning he reports that he shook visibly and began to feel very guilty about his behavior the previous evening. A year previously he had turned down a lucrative professional opportunity to advance his career that would have entailed moving to a larger city. Four years earlier his father had died of a lingering illness. Ten years ago he and his wife were married.

Defenses

The leading defenses displayed by the client in the initial hour were splitting the affect, regression, undoing, turning against the self with aggression, passive into active, and reaction formation (see Table 7.2). Splitting the affect is another name for isolation, or the separating of affects from ideas, such that the feeling is out of awareness while the idea remains conscious, or *vice versa*. The client manifested several versions of this defense. Intellectualizing is indicated in the client's highly abstract and often pedantic way of talking, such as "I begrudged my father's absence as an adolescent; I needed a role-model." Minimizing can be seen in the client's frequent assessment of a problem with the statement, "But it was not important to me." Conclusion-giving is suggested when the client fails to tell the counselor how he arrived at a judgment about some problematic set of circumstances: "I decided that this was not worth pursuing."

Regression is evident in the client's tearfulness when he is talking about thoughts, feelings, and actions about which he feels guilty. Undoing is notable whenever the client begins talking about his anger toward his wife or his father, and then concludes by taking back that anger; for example, "It made me furious when my father would try to tell me what to do. All in all, though, my father was a good provider." One of the ways in which the client managed his guilty thoughts was to inhibit their direct expression by punishing himself in one way or another. His depression was one prominent example of this because it was accompanied by thoughts of how worthless he was. Another way was to engage in long-distance jogging until he hurt physically.

As an example of the defense of turning passive into active, the client also used strenuous physical activity. That is, when the client felt vulnerable or weak, he would often attempt to reinstate a sense of strength and competence by leaving such a situation to go to the gym to "work out." And finally, the defense of reaction formation is evident in the client's overt attitude toward those, in this case, males who were in a position of authority over him. His teachers and his boss at work were responded to with an unusual amount of cheerfulness and cooperation. His underlying attitude was one of anger and resentment.

Predisposing influences

The client was the second of four children. He has two sisters, one older and one younger, and one younger brother. He states he feels closest to the oldest sister because "I can call her any time just to talk." The client described his father as a stern disciplinarian who was frequently absent from the home on business when the client was growing up. Father disapproved of the client's high school friends and recreational activities, but most of all, father disapproved of the client's growing sexual interest in young women. The client learned early on that father's approval depended upon compliance with his wishes regarding school performance and sexual abstinence. While the client's external behavior accommodated father's wishes, his internal thoughts and feelings remained the same. An example of his long-standing resentment of his father can be noted in the defiance with which the client allotted very little time to visit his father when it became known the latter had a terminal illness.

The client described his mother as a patient and kind woman who suffered much deprivation as his father's wife. Nevertheless, she always sided with the father against the client in decisions affecting the client. Both parents are said to have encouraged the client's entry into a church-related job following his graduation from high school, rather than going directly on to college. The father also encouraged the client's marriage soon after his release from church service.

Unanswered questions

Specific information about the personalities of the client's sisters and mother would be useful at the inception of counseling. Additional details about both parents would also be welcome. What was the quality of their marriage?

Was the client's marriage similar to his parents? Why did the client and his wife elect not to have children? Is the older sister available to provide emotional support for the client? Who are the client's friends? Are these persons able to respond if the client turns to them?

It would also be helpful to learn about any significant events in the client's childhood, so that the genesis of his current pattern of handling stress with depression, anxiety, and guilt can be noted. What was his reaction to the birth of his younger sister? How did he respond to the several moves the family made to accommodate his father's career? What was the client's reaction when the father returned home after his frequent and long absences?

Conditions for which the client needs help

The underlying conditions for which the client needs help can be stated only tentatively at this time. Further details provided by the client will either alter the content of this tentative statement, or replace it with another. The client's pattern of obsessive defenses, his bitterness, and the leading role that guilt appears to play in his problems suggest that his emotional development may have been interrupted at the oedipal phase. That is, the client is extremely guilty about his sexual interests and urges *vis-à-vis* women, has experienced difficulty with his sexual responsiveness in his marriage, and fears conflict with other males in authority and tries to defeat them by indirect non-compliance with their legitimate requests. It is as though the client's mind took a regressive step in response to his oedipal fears, such that he now seeks to keep tight control on his thoughts, feelings, and actions, and on other persons as well. Hence, issues of autonomy and cooperation become salient in this case.

It is inferred that the pattern of containing conflict, wherein the client complies with his father's wishes by restricting his sexual pleasures, marrying the woman his father approves of and cooperating with his bosses and teachers, is a compromise formation. It is further inferred that this formation has, in the past, helped contain his aggressive longings to defy his father, including his experience of pleasure at his father's death, and his sexual interest in using his body for pleasure with women. In accord with this reasoning, these wishes have elicited anxious thoughts that he will be punished, and the depressive and guilty thoughts that he is currently being punished for his bad deeds and deserves to be. His pattern of obsessive defenses against the underlying wishes and their accompanying thoughts and unpleasant affects operate primarily either to remove the unpleasant affect from the associated ideas, or to change the underlying affect and/or idea into its opposite. At the present time, this long-term pattern of thinking and behaving is not working effectively for the client.

Counseling goals

The goals of counseling, which can only be stated in broad outline at this point, include:

1. Establishing a firm working alliance with the client.
2. Elevating the client's mood, reducing his anxiety, and diminishing his guilty feelings.
3. Helping him understand the factors within himself that have contributed to his emotional problems.
4. Assisting him in expanding his interpersonal relationships and in learning how to cooperate with others.
5. Enabling him to complete his graduate education.

Intervention plan

The first attempt will be to offer the client a working alliance in which he will be encouraged to use the counseling relationship to understand the reasons for his emotional difficulties. Then, an attempt will be made to help him build upon his already growing understanding of the relationship between recent precipitating stresses (the one-night affair with another woman, his asking his wife for a divorce, and moving out of the home) and the increase in his depression, anxiety, and guilt. The client's tendency to resist open communication by eliminating his feelings, avoiding details, and pseudocompliance will be made topical early in the work by helping the client become aware of how his mind works in these ways.

Because the client shows a good capacity for insight and is highly motivated to work on his problems, it is expected that he will accept an extended series of interviews. In this case, every attempt will be made to assist the client in evaluating the significance of the material for himself. It is anticipated that, because of the client's need to be in charge, he will welcome taking the initiative in this regard. Thus, it is further predicted that, after the initial phase of counseling, the client's presenting complaints will have abated and have been replaced by the working alliance. The counselor will be able to rely, therefore, on counseling techniques that emphasize the appropriate use of restraint, cognitive appeal, confrontation, clarification, and interpretation. It is also predicted that through the transference, the client will attempt to obtain the counselor's approval, as well as attempt to conceal, but finally express, his fear and resentment of the counselor. Finally, it is anticipated that very little use will need to be made of the techniques of suggestion or direction.

Criteria for progress

The first criterion to be looked for will include a firm working alliance. This will be evident if the client is talking relatively freely, if the information is extensive and if he is working to understand it. Next, a reduction in his presenting complaints will be counted as a criterion of progress. As well, when the client shows awareness of the sources of his guilty feelings and the wishes that underlay them he will also evidence altered thinking, feeling, and behaving *vis-à-vis* women and men in his life. He will begin to take appropriate pleasure in the use of his body without guilt and anxiety, will establish long-term, satisfying relationships with others, will move ahead in finishing his education, and will be able to establish and tolerate a sustained and intimate relationship with a woman.

8 Principles of interviewing

In whatever other ways the discourse in an actual counseling interview might be construed by an observer, it is also a conversation between two persons. Moreover, that conversation, like all conversations, is locally created and managed by the participants on a given occasion to further their interactive purposes (see Sacks, Schegloff & Jefferson, 1974). The management of a counseling conversation presents the participants with very specific kinds of practical problems. The client must find a way to talk such that he or she elicits help for the complaints that brought him or her to counseling (Patton, 1984). If help is to be provided, the psychoanalytic counselor has the pragmatic task of managing the interview so that the events of the conversation and their unfolding sequence are in accord with psychoanalytic principles (Patton, 1984). These two tasks are unlikely to be problematic for the experienced client and counselor, but can be especially troublesome for beginners.

This chapter is primarily about ways to assist the counselor in learning how to manage the conversation in a psychoanalytic counseling interview. In this way, any list of interviewing principles or techniques whatsoever can be seen as a set of methods for managing the conversation in counseling and bringing about change in the client. The principles we will discuss in this chapter are those that permit the counselor to give events in the interview a psychoanalytic "hearing" (see Turner, 1972). Our organization of this chapter and our inclusion of certain principles owes much to the thinking of Robinson (1950), Bibring (1954), Greenson (1967), Kohut (1977) and Goates (1972). Table 8.1 contains a list of practical principles of interviewing that is adapted from the work of Goates (1972). Much of this chapter is an elaboration of these simple principles

Within a context of humane concern for the client, the psychoanalytic counselor operates with some basic interviewing principles in attempting to

Table 8.1 Principles of interviewing

1. Keep the client talking. The client can't talk while you are talking.
2. Help the client begin the hour with the report of current events and listen for the complaints that arise from them.
3. Ideas, generalizations, and summaries are the way the client's mind hides important feelings and experiences.
4. Let past events come into the conversation naturally. Be curious about the reasons a client may have if he or she dwells a lot on the past.
5. Listen carefully for the point in the conversation where a client introduces important figures in his or her life. What is the broader context in which these figures are being introduced?
6. Be alert to how a client does the same thing in talking with you that he or she describes doing with other people in his or her life, either past or present.
7. When you do say something to the client (that is, intervene in the natural flow of his or her reporting), make your comment short and to the point.
8. Avoid introducing a lot of different ideas into the conversation. Even if the client introduces many ideas, limit your interventions to the selection of a central idea.
9. Ask for the details of something only when the client has brought the subject up, and the details would clarify the central issue you are exploring.
10. When you interrupt a client to clarify a fact or detail, help the client pick up the thread of his or her thought.
11. Always be ready to assist the client in talking about actual experiences in a concrete way. Help the client provide examples.
12. Have a good reason in mind when you intervene in the flow of client material. Just because the client stops talking doesn't mean you need to say something. Wait for the client to begin talking again unless you have a significant observation to introduce.
13. Make an effort to assess the client's reaction to any intervention you make. The immediate reaction is often not the most important feature. Listen for the later reactions as well.
14. Except where there is a special reason for doing otherwise, let the client open and close the conversation. Make sure you are tracking with the client's material.
15. Information obtained from the client's natural way of reporting is most instructive. Therefore, encourage the client to let his or her thoughts come naturally without forcing the direction they will take.
16. When the client appears to change the subject, look for the connecting idea or common thread which relates events that appear to be different.
17. When the client apparently changes the subject, ask yourself why the client needed to do this. What is the client avoiding when he or she needs to change the subject?
18. Notice what the client was talking about before he or she stopped talking and asked a question. What is being avoided now by asking a question?
19. Notice the point in the conversation when the client stops talking about events in his or her life and begins describing symptoms or refers to complaints.
20. Encourage the client to be active in evaluating the material he or she brings to the session.

Table 8.1 *(continued)*

21. The working alliance is firm and effective when the client shows a willingness both to provide abundant information about him or herself and to do what he or she can to evaluate its significance.
22. Help the client understand that it isn't necessary to arrive at answers quickly. Reduce the sense of urgency about solutions. Create an atmosphere of patient exploration. Help the client understand that answers are achieved by a partnership of mutual study.
23. When you intervene to offer an interpretation of the client's reasons for doing something, make sure the working alliance is in place, prior interventions have helped clarify the point, and elements of the client's material support the formulation of your interpretation.

Note: Adapted from Goates (1972), with permission.

accomplish the goal of client insight or self-understanding. These principles underlie the counselor's endeavors to build and maintain a positive relationship (that is, a working alliance) with the client, and his or her efforts to promote client insight. The chapter is organized in two sections to correspond to these two counselor endeavors. In the first section, we will present a set of principles for developing and maintaining the working alliance in the psychoanalytic counseling interview. In the second section, we will illustrate the principle of promoting client insight by discussing the role of confrontation and interpretation.

Counselors have the responsibility of helping the client mobilize his or her resources for doing the work of counseling (Bibring, 1954). They are also responsible for helping develop and maintain a positive working relationship with the client over the course of counseling (Robinson, 1950). The techniques or methods the counselor uses to build a productive relationship with the client are the same as those which help the client participate meaningfully in counseling. In either case, the counselor's purpose in using these methods is to create an atmosphere in the interview in which the client is able to report freely and the counselor is able to understand the client.

Helping the client talk

Counselor restraint

In Chapter 4 we introduced the concept of counselor restraint within the context of the counselor's theory of the psychoanalytic counseling process. There it was given definition as one of the important events in a sequence of events that promote the client's self-understanding. In this chapter, we will emphasize the importance of counselor restraint in the interview, as well as its relationship to the working alliance.

Counselors have the responsibility of helping the client engage in ongoing talking. They also have the responsibility of listening respectfully and with interest to what the client has to say. The client can't talk when the counselor is talking. Restraint is one of the methods the counselor can use to manage the conversation with the client. In this way, it is a good idea to let the client open and close the interview, unless there is a compelling reason that requires the counselor to select the topic. These thoughts underscore the principle that the counselor needs to have a good reason for intervening in the flow of client material. Therefore, it is not necessary to say something every time the client stops talking. The point is that in response to the counselor's restraint, the client is encouraged to make known his or her complaints and their related thoughts and feelings.

Clients often enter counseling with a sense of urgency. They want the counselor to give them answers to their perceived problems, much like a physician would prescribe medicine. Counselor restraints helps create an interview climate in which urgency is replaced by exploration. The leading characteristics of such a climate are patience and curiosity. In this way, the counselor helps the client learn that solutions to problems are found through collaboration and a partnership of mutual study.

Counselor restraint is also an attitude or orientation. Contained in the counselor's reticence is the expectation that when clients are given the opportunity to communicate their concerns or problems, they will usually do so (Langs, 1973). Just as there are forces within the client that oppose open communication and change, there are forces that press for expression of the problems that brought the client to counseling in the first place. This expectation expresses a faith in those forces within the client that are on the side of change and growth. The counselor's reluctance to intervene helps the client mobilize those forces that can overcome the resistance to communicating. In the face of the counselor's restraint, or even silence, the client has the opportunity to become aware of and/or reflect on the events of his or her inner life.

Additionally, the counselor's restrained approach in the interview expresses faith in the client's capacity to use his or her own mind, and suggests that in doing so, solutions to the client's problems will be found. The counselor's attitude of restraint also expresses a respect for the client's autonomy to think and talk as he or she chooses. In order for the client to use his or her own mind to evaluate the significance of the material that is produced in the interview, counselor activity needs to be at a minimum. The right of the client to draw his or her own conclusions about events in the interview is never in dispute. The division of responsibility (see Robinson, 1950) for talking in the interview is clearly tilted in favor of the client.

Counselor restraint, then, is both an attitude and a technique. As a technique, it consists of silence or a minimum of talking. Restraint is also a technique for managing the conversation in counseling. That is, counselor restraint places pressure on the client to do the majority of the communicating. As an attitude or orientation, counselor restraint conveys faith in the client's ability to think and talk productively and respect for the client's freedom in doing so.

The features of counselor restraint mentioned above also help develop and maintain the working alliance. Appropriate counselor restraint develops the alliance by the example it sets. Thus, the client is encouraged to be active in evaluating for him or herself the material in the hour, rather than the counselor doing it for the client. With a restrained approach in the interview, the counselor encourages the client to take responsibility for doing the work of thinking and talking in the hour. Without counselor restraint, there is less room for the client to do this. Restraint tells the client that the counselor wants to hear what is on the client's mind. Restraint encourages the client to do his or her own evaluating of the relevance of the material in the hour. Once the working alliance is established, counselor restraint helps maintain and safeguard the alliance by the counselor's ongoing consistency in this regard. In other words, at all times the counselor conveys the attitude with his or her restrained approach that it is the client's responsibility to do what he or she can in the hour to work with the counselor toward the goal of understanding and change. The working alliance is firm and effective when the client readily furnishes extensive information about him or herself and willingly works to try to understand that material.

When silence is contraindicated   As we have noted earlier in Chapter 4, there are times when it is not in the client's best interests for the counselor to be silent. One such occasion is when the client is on the verge of becoming overwhelmed by his or her affect, or is already overwhelmed. Here, the counselor needs to become active in attempting to soothe and calm the client, and take the time necessary to ensure that the client does not leave the session upset. Only when affect is under control will the client be able to regain a sense, however tenuous, that he or she is competent to function outside the session. Failure to help the client regain control of affect is harmful.

Another occasion for greater activity on the part of the counselor is with those clients whose development in the affective realm has gone awry in some way. After Basch (1988), we may identify three such types of clients. The first group are those clients who become easily over- or understimulated, both of which are very painful states. These are persons who were never able to learn basic tension tolerance as infants and young children. They make their problems known to the counselor almost immediately because they often appear hostile, mistrustful, or unable to delay gratification. A second group consists of those clients who chronically overcontrol their affect for fear of being otherwise shamed for its expression. In this instance, they defend themselves from relating to the counselor by withdrawing from feelings or their arousal. The third group for which greater activity is called for are those clients who rather urgently need to know the counselor is in tune with them. These are persons whose sense of self or competence was not validated by those most important to them, and too often, they have thus learned to disavow such needs.

With each of these types of clients, too much counselor silence can exacerbate the client's existing disorder. Counselor errors in recognizing and responding appropriately in these cases are usually due to a failure in empathy arising from the counselor's own unrecognized countertransference problems. By contrast, then, appropriate counselor interventions that communicate structure, patience, concern, soothing, and understanding help promote in the client, over time, greater tension regulation, trust, tolerance of affect, and the capacity for curiosity and self-exploration. These developments can take considerable time but, as the client matures in these ways, increasing counselor restraint can be introduced as a technique to promote the client's autonomy and use of his or her own mind.

Specificity and brevity of interventions

Related to the attitude of restraint is the counselor's use of specific and brief intervention comments. When we do say something to the client during the interview, we are intervening in an ongoing flow of thoughts and feelings experienced by the client. For this reason, our remarks should be concise.

We should also try to avoid introducing a lot of new thoughts into the conversation. Sometimes it is the case that clients do a lot of topic switching from one idea to another in quick succession, such that in a short space of time they have introduced many ideas into the conversation. Our task in this case is to settle on one main idea expressed by the client and respond in terms of it.

Helping the client communicate naturally

While there is a place for the counselor's questions in the interview, the client's report of his or her experiences, thoughts, and feelings are more meaningful when they are conveyed in the client's own natural way of reporting. The client's uninterrupted and normal style of reporting will provide a meaningful and ongoing context for understanding the material. This principle emphasizes the importance of letting the client determine the pace, form, and direction of the conversation in the interview. The reason for this is that the meaning of the client's utterances are informed, not only by the words the client uses, but also by: (a) their placement in the ongoing conversation (that is, where they occur); (b) by the utterances that have preceded them; and (c) by what the utterances anticipate about the future of the conversation (see Sacks, Schegloff & Jefferson, 1974). These features of context are the necessary resources on which the counselor makes his or her empathic observations and theoretical inferences about the client. Each client has his or her own way of talking about the events that are important. A great deal can be learned about the client from the style with which he or she reports in the interview

Beginning the interview with recent events

In the typical case, it is usual for the client to begin the hour with a consideration of recent events rather than past events (see also Chapters 4 and 7), but, as will be seen later, there are exceptions to this. Beginning the hour with current events is preferable from a psychoanalytic standpoint. The client lives his or her life moment to moment in the present. It is the client's present life circumstances that present the client with exciting and rewarding challenges as well as stressful demands. It is to those present circumstances that the client makes the attempt to adapt. The process of adaptation (see Hartmann, 1939) will be more or less successful for the client. If the client's attempts at adaptation to stressful events have not met with success, he or she will likely develop symptoms or have complaints to voice. In other words, we may observe in the client's maladaptive responses any or all of the following: an ascetic attitude in which pleasure is to be avoided; a tendency to hurt him or herself; serious conflict with his or her environment; overwhelming anxiety; or some variety of depressive affect (see Chapter 2).

In spite of this, there is not always a readiness to report about recent events that are associated with pain. Our minds have a natural tendency to separate suffering from its precipitating circumstances. Consequently, the client can use abstract ideas, generalizations, summaries or conclusions to avoid experiencing strong feelings. Amnesia can be used to hide from the memory of a recent painful circumstance.

The client lives in the present. The client's thoughts and feelings about the present are important clues to how capable he or she is of responding to stressful events. The client's responses to recent events are the outcomes of a process of development. When those responses are maladaptive, we infer the presence of emotional conflict and/or disharmony in the self. The journey toward self-understanding and behavior change begins with knowledge of how the client is managing his or her current circumstances. For these reasons, we want to hear what the client has to report about the recent events that have occurred in his or her life since the last session.

The natural emergence of past events

Sometimes the client begins the early hours in counseling, and sometimes the later hours as well, with a report of past events, or stays exclusively in the past. When this happens the counselor needs to be curious about why the client lingers on the past. As with summaries and generalizations, the past can also be used to hide from pain in the present. Pain is the primary motive for this form of resistance, as it is with all forms of resistance (Greenson, 1967). The problem with a report of past events under such circumstances is that it is elliptical. Some of the meaning that helps us determine the importance of the past event is omitted when its report in the hour serves a resistive function. Usually, what is not clear is whether or how the past event has relevance for the problems the client is experiencing in the present. The connections to recent events in the client's life are not evident.

Even so, there are occasions when beginning the hour with past events, or lingering on the past, is not resistance. It is not uncommon for a client for whom the work is going well to begin the hour by stating that they want to pick up the thread where the last session ended. This can indicate that, during the period between sessions, the client has done some work thinking about the material from the preceding session. Usually this is a positive sign, because it implies that the client is beginning to deepen the material and strengthen the working alliance with the counselor.

In all cases, it is important for the client to let past events enter the conversation naturally. The meaning of past events will be clearer when their report arises as the result of a chain of associations from the present. For this reason, counselor restraint is intended to permit, indeed encourage, the client to freely follow the direction his or her thoughts is taking. Very often, that direction leads to thoughts and feelings about important people and experiences in the client's past.

Listening to events in context

The psychoanalytic point of view assumes that no thoughts are random. Rather, every mental event is determined (Freud, 1957a). We ask the client to report as freely as possible in the attempt to approximate free association. By doing so, we hope to facilitate the client's calling to mind and reporting chains of related ideas. The network of relations among the client's thoughts is the most informative context in which to understand the meaning of any event of interest.

Thus, it is important for the counselor to be especially alert to those points in the conversation where the client begins talking about important persons in his or her life. Our awareness of the connectedness of the client's thoughts will help us understand why these persons are being introduced now, and what current meaning they have for the client. The preceding topics will help provide a clue to both the client's motive for introducing this new topic and its present meaning.

For example, imagine that a client begins the hour by reporting about and describing in considerable detail how unfairly she has been treated recently by the boss. The client sounds very sad as this complaint is related at some length. Then the client begins to talk about a memory of how she came home one day to find her mother in considerable distress at having ruined the dinner she was preparing for company that evening. The client further reports putting an arm around her mother's shoulder and comforting her. It is not unreasonable to infer that the client's recall of the episode with her mother on this occasion was prompted by the recent difficulty with the boss. Moreover, its meaning expresses the client's wish that someone would put their arm around her shoulder. The upshot of the principle of interviewing presented in this section is that the counselor should look for the common thread that relates events when the client appears to change the subject.

Using empathy and countertransference to understand and communicate with the client

Effective counseling depends upon a number of critical factors. At least two of them include the kinds of knowledge the counselor has of the client. Another is responding empathically to the client when it is called for. On the one hand, it is important for the counselor to have knowledge of psychoanalytic theory and to have an intellectual or objective understanding of the client that derives from knowledge of theory. On the other hand, such knowledge is not enough. It must be supplemented by knowledge of the client that comes from an "emotional knowing" (Greenson, 1960) or "vicarious introspection" (Kohut, 1977) of the client. Empathically derived knowledge of the client permits the counselor to perceive the client's inner life, and to be aware of the affective (countertransference) reactions evoked by that knowledge. Communicating that knowledge to the client when appropriate helps prepare the client for insight or self-understanding.

Empathy as an observational standpoint

Empathy is one of two important observational standpoints the counselor can take toward the client. The other standpoint is the objective or more experience-distant stance. It is observation from the outside. Empathy, on the other hand, is observation from the inside, as it were (see Kohut, 1977). Empathic observation permits the counselor to remain in tune with the client's moment-to-moment experiencing. Empathically derived knowledge of the client remains close to the level of experience. Understanding of the client in experience-near terms comes from the counselor's use of everyday knowledge of self and the world, including affective reactions to others. Empathic observation is the counselor's vicarious introspection of the client's inner life and incorporates awareness of the affective reactions such observations evoke. Such knowledge of the client originates in the counselor's own knowledge of how others typically think, feel, and act in given situations (Patton, 1984).

With the ongoing use of empathic observation, the counselor builds an hypothetical model of the client (Greenson, 1960). The model serves as a resource for further understanding the client. Over time, the model becomes a complex and reliable guide to understanding the client's reactions to the numerous situations he or she reports to the counselor. For example, clients often report on stressful experiences, but leave the counselor puzzled as to why they reacted as they did, or why they didn't react more strongly. The counselor's empathically derived models can be used to flesh out how the clients probably felt or what they thought or why they did what they did in the stressful situations. A model can also be used to predict what a client will do and how he or she will feel in future situations that are typically problematic for him or her.

Empathic and objective theoretical knowledge are the two sources of information about the client that the counselor uses consistently. The counselor listens to the client from the empathic standpoint, experiencing briefly and in abbreviated form the client's feelings or having the same pattern of thoughts. Then, the counselor steps back from this immersion in the client's world and tries to understand the behavior from knowledge of psychoanalytic theory. It is from the theoretical stance that the counselor will identify elements of intrapsychic conflict or developmental arrests, and will ultimately derive reasons for the client's conduct.

Empathy and disclosure of feeling as features of the counselor's communication

Communicating our empathic understanding of or affective reactions to the client's longings, fears, plans, or ideas not only helps maintain the working alliance, but it also prepares the way for later confrontations and interpretations by the counselor. For the frightened or enraged client who feels as if he or she is flying out of control, the counselor's communication of his or her awareness of the terrible feelings helps soothe and reassure the client. When the counselor states his or her awareness of a client's strong loving or hateful feelings for the counselor, it helps de-intensify and objectify such feelings. Finally, to be able to tell a very anxious client that the counselor is aware of how terrible she is feeling inside right now lets the client know that the counselor is in tune with and is tracking the client.

Because countertransference reactions can provide clues to what the client is trying to communicate, it can be helpful on occasion to tell the client about them. Disclosure of the counselor's feelings, however, needs to be done judiciously with regard to tact and timing. The purpose of such disclosure is to promote client understanding and to help strengthen the working bond between the pair. Imagine, for example, that a client is extremely guarded and essentially unaware of her affect when reporting an incident involving her parents and her own children. It seems her parents on this occasion pre-emptively took charge of her children and hit them to punish them for some minor transgression. On hearing the report the counselor becomes aware of feeling angry and decides to tell the client about this reaction. The counselor believes the client is angry too, but was then and is now too frightened to express it herself. On hearing about the counselor's reaction, the client is able to recognize and label her own angry feelings, thereby validating her experience.

There are also occasions on which a disclosure of the counselor's feelings would be both tactless and harmful. This would be the case with a narcissistically vulnerable client who has finally been able to act on strong wishes to be mirrored by the counselor. The fact that the counselor has an inner life is irrelevant. What is important is that the client knows the counselor understands the client's wishes to use him or her as a mirror for grandiose fulfillment. Telling the client about the counselor's affective reaction could very likely intrude on this process and injure the client's already fragile self-esteem. Only later, when the client's self is more cohesive, will it be possible to intervene in this way.

Communicating empathy also helps in another way. Regardless of what theory we select to construe the client's behavior, we will need to acknowledge that the self-esteem of most clients is vulnerable. Whether we posit that vulnerability as a central defect in the personality, as in Kohut's (1984) theory, is beside the point. It will always be important to safeguard the client's self-esteem by framing and delivering our interventions with tact. For example, our knowledge that the client feels stupid and humiliated whenever someone conveys something about them that they had not realized helps us frame our interpretations so as to be more tentative. In this case, the client has the opportunity to reject the intervention if he or she is not ready to deal with it.

Finally, it is often important for the counselor to precede interventions that are intended to promote insight with an empathic observation. Interventions like confrontation and interpretation aim at bringing the underlying pattern of feelings, thoughts, and motives, which is believed to be the main contributor to the client's emotional problems, to greater awareness in the client. The client, of course, has attempted to remain largely uninformed about the problematic aspects of his or her inner life. Conscious recognition of such matters has been opposed by resistances because they are associated with pain.

At any time, the counselor's communication of an empathic observation about the client shows the latter that the counselor is trying to understand by tracking the client's material, and is in tune with the direction in which the client's thoughts and feelings are heading. At times of stress, an empathically stated intervention can have the effect of calming and soothing the client. When an empathic observation precedes an insight-oriented intervention, it helps prepare the way for the client's consideration and elaboration of that intervention. Clients who are particularly vulnerable in the area of self-esteem are often those persons who, as they were growing up, had insufficient understanding of their needs and wishes by their parental caretakers (Kohut, 1971). These clients are hungry for the attention and acceptance important others might provide them. Yet these same needs can be painful to acknowledge, and it can be still more painful to learn where and how they have arisen. When the counselor indicates an understanding and acceptance of the client's needs and wishes in a timely manner, the client is also prompted to understand and accept.

The following example is presented to help clarify how the counselor's empathic observation can precede an interpretive intervention.

The client was a 21-year-old college senior who came to counseling at his mother's suggestion because of his anxiety about graduating the following spring. He was a quite pleasant but compliant young man who had yet to conquer the oedipal fears that accompany the move to assertiveness and independence. During the first hour, the client was visibly shaking and barely able to speak. The counselor attempted to help the client relax by asking him simply to describe a typical day. This had the effect of calming the client sufficiently for him to be able to get through the interview. In the second interview, the client was considerably less anxious and was able to say that he could not pinpoint the reason why he should be so afraid of finishing his education and entering the world of work. However, he could not bring himself to go to the Placement Center on campus and interview with representatives of various companies. He had tried to do so on one occasion and had fled in near panic shortly after walking through the front door of the agency. After several more sessions, in which the client described the current events that made him anxious and reported something of his past life, he reported that he was considering dropping out of college.

At this point the counselor intervened with the observation that it was clear how very frightened the client felt about graduating and that it seemed he wished to return to the safety of home. The client responded that this was indeed what he had been thinking about. He added that the counselor's remarks made him feel better; it was comforting to know that someone understood him. The counselor then continued with the interpretation that the client's wish to return to the safety of home was motivated by a fear of competition. Graduating meant the client would be in the thick of competing with other men for a professional position, and the thought of this terrified him.

The counselor's empathic intervention in the preceding vignette had the effect of calming the client and preparing the way for the interpretation that followed it. In this case, the client was now able to reflect on the meaning of the interpretation and elaborate its significance.

Promoting the client's understanding

The aforementioned principles are intended to help marshal the client's resources for doing the work of counseling. They make use of the assets or natural talents the client brings to counseling. That is, their use by the counselor takes advantage of the client's capacities to think and talk before acting, to accept help and to cooperate with the counselor. In one sense, the principles that have been discussed up to now help lay the groundwork for the implementation of principles that aim at changing the client through greater self-understanding.

Confrontation

Psychoanalytic approaches to treatment stress the importance of understanding and dealing with client resistance (Greenson, 1967) and ego dysfunctions that result in impairments in the client's controls, intellective functions, and relations with others (Langs, 1973). These are problems that are apparent in the manifest content of the client's communications and are usually dealt with by confrontation. We will have a great deal more to say about both confrontation and interpretation in Chapter 9. For now, we can note that the purpose of confrontation is to demonstrate to the client that resistance is operative, and to make clear other impairments in dealing with a current problem. If confrontations are used correctly, they point out to the client that he or she is resisting or that there are certain ego dysfunctions exhibited in his or her approach to the problems in a current situation. Ego dysfunctions, acting out, and habitual patterns of defense are all obstacles (resistance) to open communication and change in counseling. By confronting these aspects of behavior, the client has the opportunity to modify them.

Confrontations also encourage the development of the central theme of the hour and help to surface or make conscious the derivatives of unconscious conflicts. In this latter regard, confrontations lay the groundwork for later interpretations.

Confrontations differ from interpretations by their focus on more manifest or conscious material. They do not focus on genetic or historical material in the client's biography because they are directed to the reality-based conflicts and problems the client brings into counseling. Both client and counselor are aware of the matter that is being confronted. The confrontation asks the client to split the ego, stand back, and observe what he or she is thinking and doing. When a confrontation is successful in this way it also helps strengthen the working alliance.

Other approaches to treatment can be differentiated from those informed by psychoanalytic principles by how they deal with resistances. For example, the several varieties of American Humanistic therapy (see Corsini, 1989) generally strengthen resistance by supporting and accepting the client's manner and mode of resisting. Approaches like these "cover" over the resistance. Still other approaches bypass the resistances through didactic instruction, prodding the client to accept the counselor's explanation of how he or she has come to feel badly, hypnosis, group persuasion, or drugs. By contrast, psychoanalytic approaches attempt to surmount the resistances by identifying and understanding them. Thus, confrontations are used to help the client and to deal with the technical problems created in the interview by defenses, acting out, habitual maladaptive patterns of behavior, ego dysfunctions, and threats to or disruptions in the working alliance.

When confrontation is used to bring to the client's awareness that he or she is resisting the conscious experiencing of painful affects and ideas, it does so by demonstrating to the client the reality of that resistance. According to Greenson (1967), the counselor's task is to help the client "understand that he (sic) is resisting, why he is resisting, what he is resisting, and how he is resisting" (p.104). This set of guidelines applies equally to any piece of client behavior the counselor decides to confront.

In the case of resistance, the counselor must first notice its occurrence before it can be confronted. Recognition of resistance requires that the counselor understand the many modes and methods in which client opposition to communication can become manifest (see Chapter 9). Again, restraint is indispensable as the counselor patiently listens to and observes the client. When the client is trying to let his or her thoughts come naturally by setting aside the conscious attempts at censorship, the counselor is able to observe the struggle between the more powerful unconscious resistances and the wishes that seek expression. Often, the client's material will not be clear until we have waited a sufficient amount of time.

Except for gross forms of acting out and emergency situations, Greenson

(1967) suggests that the next task in using confrontation is to allow the resistance or other behavior to manifest itself several times, in order that it will be more apparent to the client when the counselor does intervene. As we have already seen, a primary motive for resistance is the avoidance of painful feelings. Adult clients very often have well-established, habitual patterns of resistive and other maladaptive behaviors. If, for example, the client uses intellectualization to stay distant from his or her feelings, the counselor waits until there is sufficient evidence of this mode of resistance. By intervening with a confrontation, the counselor hopes to demonstrate to the client the occurrence of intellectualizing and help it become ego-dystonic.

The client was a 42-year-old professional man with a moderate characterological problem who came to counseling because he was undergoing a divorce from his second wife and was both depressed and anxious about it. Initially, counseling went well, revealing an ambivalent, masochistic interest in older women. As counseling progressed, he became increasingly distant from his feelings and generally guarded in his reporting of material. A pattern of resistance emerged in which he would allude to an experience with colleagues or with a woman he was dating at the time, but would provide only the conclusions he had reached about the experience. In one session, the counselor confronted the client with his avoidance of reporting details and his conclusion-giving. This reminded the client of having to report to his step-father when he came home from school each day. He then went on to report in considerable detail how hurt and angry he had been during the past week when his male employer had questioned him about some of his work.

This is not an atypical response to a confrontation of resistance in the hour. The confrontation of his resistance to a portion of the transference brought attention to a pattern of reporting that was immediately modified, with the result being both the recall of a memory from his adolescent years and of the detailed report of a more recent experience during the preceding week. Later, the counselor and client could explore the clarify the transference connections between the client's recall of reporting to his step-father and reporting to the counselor. Still later, the unconscious determinants of his fear of reporting to step-father/counselor and their relationship to his ambivalent feelings for his mother could be surfaced and interpreted.

In summary, confrontations help the client become aware of, and modify, resistances to reporting in the interview and maladaptive behaviors outside of counseling. Confrontations help the client become more self-observing by splitting the ego into experiencing and observing sectors. In all, confrontations that are correctly timed promote and strengthen the working alliance. The first step in dealing with material that needs to be confronted is to become aware of the problematic behavior, letting instances of it accumulate and then finally intervening with a confrontation. The next step is to confront it to demonstrate its occurrence. This is followed by seeking to clarify what is being resisted. Finally, when these matters are understood, the motive for the resistance can be interpreted.

Interpretations

A pyschoanalytic counselor's use of the term "interpretation" refers to his or her intervention in the flow of client material that calls attention to unconscious affects, ideas, and wishes that are components of infantile intrapsychic conflicts or developmental deficits. The purpose of any interpretation, then, is to bring to awareness for the client repressed, unconscious motives and wishes on which troublesome thoughts, feelings, and action tendencies are based.

The precipitating event for the client's complaints (see Chapter 4) is the place we begin the interpretive process. It is the precipitating event that has mobilized the client's maladaptive reactions, unconscious fantasies, troublesome feelings, and resistances. As we saw in Chapter 2, the client's compromise formations contain elements of unconscious loving and aggressive wishes, ego operations such as defenses/resistances and object relations, as well as superego derivatives in the form of guilt and standards. The client's communications about these phenomena are directed to significant persons in the client's remote past, to significant persons outside of counseling in the client's present life, and to the counselor. The interpretation draws upon these elements in the client's communication by attempting to explain the resistance to understanding how the determinants of conflict from the client's past are being reinstated in the present.

It is useful to speak of two kinds of interpretation, the unbounded and the bounded (Langs, 1973). Unbounded interpretations are only loosely circumscribed with regard to a particular content, and are comparatively manifest to both the client and the counselor. This more general type of interpretation is important clinically to promote further specific communication from the client. It is most often used when the client has begun to talk about a resistant point, or report a dream or stressful current event, but does not give these matters specific definition or content or make mention of their origins. In other words, the client is not verbalizing the wishes underlying his or her communications and is only vaguely aware of their existence. In using an unbounded interpretation the counselor calls attention in a general way to the feelings and wishes that are implicit, yet unreported, by the client. If the unbounded interpretation is accurate and timed correctly, it will be confirmed by the client's providing more specific and relevant information, thus making it possible for the counselor to provide a bounded interpretation if necessary.

Bounded interpretations, on the other hand, convey specific information to the client about the motives for resistance or the problematic determinants of conflict and address their interconnections with current events. Bounded interpretations specify for the client the less manifest or unconscious determinants in terms that are particular to the client. They are stated in terms of either the client's recent or remote history and current circumstances. Bounded interpretations are the central therapeutic intervention in psycho-analytic counseling. By identifying the manifest elements of the client's associations and formulating from them the latent wishes, the counselor's interpretations help promote the client's greater awareness of his or her central emotional conflicts. An accurate interpretation by the counselor expands the ego's control of the unwelcome effects of the emergence of those conflicts. The following vignette will help distinguish between the two types of interpretation.

Mrs. D. was a young, married woman with three small children, who came to counseling because she was depressed, angry at her parents and her husband, and prone to forget to take the daily medication that was required to keep her chronic illness under control. As has already been described in Chapter 2, she also had difficulty enjoying herself without feeling guilty about it. She came to one session in which she reported that she had left her parents' home in a huff one day the previous week. In a lengthy report, she described how anxious it made her to be in her parents' home and how it filled her with a sense of foreboding. Her father asked her to stay longer on that day and tell him how she was getting along. He invited her to sit with him in the living room and talk while her mother watched her three children in another part of the house. The client reported that her father was too inquisitive about her and she had decided she would not say anything personal about herself. He became annoyed with her about her being closed and again voiced his criticism about her being in counseling. At this point, she became angry, got her children and left. She talked about having left because she didn't trust what would happen if she stayed longer. Then, she began to ruminate about this episode for some time. The material became flat and she began to complain of feeling depressed, guilty, and uncertain about what to talk about.

Mrs. D. fell silent for a considerable length of time. At this point the counselor intervened to say that the client appeared to be shutting down, possibly because she was struggling with some strong feelings and did not trust to express them. She agreed and then recalled a memory from the age of 3, which she was seated on her father's lap in the living room of their home and he was tickling her. She further reported that she became frightened and ran to her room to hide. The counselor commented that Mrs. D viewed the situation in counseling in much the same way as she experienced closeness in some of her interactions with her father. On the one hand, she enjoyed her sessions and the closeness with the counselor, but on the other, they frightened her and made her feel guilty, just as did her loving feelings for her father so long ago. The client agreed and went on to recall additional details of the early experience and to relate them to some of her current work with the counselor. She remembered fearing her mother's reaction and that running to her bedroom was an effort to escape her mother's presumed vengeance. She went on to describe ways in which she would try to put her medicine in a place where she would remember to take it, and then promptly forget to do so.

In this vignette, there was one unbounded interpretation. In this case, the counselor interpreted in a very general way the client's wish to avoid closeness with the counselor. This wish had not been articulated by the client. Instead, it was repressed. In making this interpretation, the counselor drew upon the manifest communications and feelings of the client to infer the presence of a fantasy of withdrawing from the counselor to protect herself from her own feelings. The interpretation is unbounded because it lacks precise definition and/or specific content and does not contain any clues to the possible sources of the fantasy.

The bounded interpretation, on the other hand, points out the unconscious fantasy that counseling is specifically like closeness with her father, that she longs for this, but that she will end up being excited, frightened of her mother's wrath, and feeling deserving of punishment. The ingredients of this interpretation were not directly manifest in the client's communications following her confirmation of the unbounded interpretation in which she recalled the early memory. The interpretation was formulated from both the report of the memory and her later associations, in which she reported her fear of her mother and of "arranging" to forget to take her medicine.

We conclude this chapter by pointing out a few additional principles in the use of interpretation. Timing is an important consideration in this regard. Interpretations follow upon the development of the working alliance and the use of prior confrontations of resistances. Interpretations that occur before these events are likely to be premature. An interpretation can be premature when it is either too deep or is provided before there are enough clues in the client's material to warrant it. Such interpretations can also be experienced as tactless by the client. Bounded interpretations that link early material to the client's present are inappropriate at the beginning of counseling, in any case.

It is also important for the counselor to assess the client's reaction to every intervention, including interpretations. Only by listening carefully to the client's reactions to an interpretation will we know whether it is correct or incorrect. Failure to detect incorrect interpretations can have widespread influence over the efficacy of the work in counseling. Finally, every counselor will miss an opportunity to make an interpretation. As long as this does not become a chronic under-usage of interpretation, little harm is done. It is the counselor's awareness of having missed the opportunity that is the important antidote in this case. If, after each session, the counselor uses the guidelines for organizing client communications presented in Chapter 7, or some other method of organizing the material in the hour, the missed opportunity will be apparent and can usually be remedied in the next session.

It goes without saying that problems in the use of all of the techniques mentioned, including interpretation, can stem both from the counselor's unfamiliarity with the principles of psychoanalytic theory as presented in Chapters 2 and 3, or from the counselor's own unresolved emotional (countertransference) problems. In the first instance, the remedy is study and ongoing, supervised experience with clients. In the second instance, the solution requires that the counselor ask for professional help in surmounting his or her problems.

9 Client resistance

The topics of defense and resistance are closely related and we have encountered both of them earlier in this book in the context of other material about psychoanalytic counseling. In Chapter 2, the defenses were seen to be an important element of intrapsychic conflict in the way they serve to protect the ego from painful affects and awareness of unwelcome ideas and memories. The defenses are part of the maladaptive compromise formations which are the manifestations of the client's symptoms and complaints. In Chapter 4, resistance was seen to be one of the several events in the interview that make up the sequence leading to client insight. There, it was noted that resistance is frequently encountered when the client begins to describe the recent circumstances that make up the current events serving to precipitate the onset of complaints and symptoms. In Chapter 8, the intervention of counselor confrontation was identified as an interviewing technique for dealing with resistance. In this chapter, we will consider confrontation more thoroughly.

We devote a separate chapter to the topic of client resistance because this phenomenon plays such a significant role in the competent conduct of psychoanalytic counseling. On the one hand, the presence of client resistance in the interview is a major technical problem for the counselor and the client to solve because resistance blocks open communication upon which client insight is built. On the other hand, the client's and counselor's recognition of resistance is one of the salient keys used in counseling to understand the client's personality. In the latter case, awareness of client resistance informs the counselor of how the client manages conflict by minimizing the effects of painful affect and warding off unwelcome thoughts. The counselor's task is to identify the resistance and help the client become aware of how and why it is happening. The goal of such procedures is to promote client insight. Client resistance is, then, both an obstacle to the work of counseling and an opportunity to further that work.

Over the years a great deal has been written about resistance in psychological treatment. As Greenson (1967) has noted, psychoanalytic approaches to treatment, including psychoanalytic counseling, can be distinguished from other approaches by the emphasis given to understanding and dealing with client resistance. Other counseling methods may attempt to strengthen the resistances by supportive techniques, or by accepting the client's modes of denying to awareness certain thoughts and feelings. Still other approaches may circumvent or attempt to overcome the resistances by the use of advice, persuasion, role-playing, behavioral enactment, or other directive strategies. In psychoanalytic counseling, an attempt is made to recognize the resistances and to clarify their functions and origins. Our intention in this chapter is to present the reader with a general introduction to the topic, along with some examples of resistance and some suggested procedures for dealing with it. For a more comprehensive treatment of the topic the reader is referred to Breuer and Freud (1957), Freud (1958c), Fenichel (1945), Greenson (1967), Langs (1973), and Brenner (1982).

We will first present a theoretical account of resistance and consider the role of defenses in resistance. This will be followed by a section on manifestations of resistance during the counseling interview in the client's fears of counseling, in general behavior, and through the use of the defenses. The last section of the chapter will take up some of the precedures for dealing with resistance.

Theoretical considerations

A usually punctual client arrives 20 minutes late for her counseling session. Her manner is tense and her appearance somewhat disheveled. Without remarking on her lateness, she begins by announcing that the man with whom she had been intensely romantically involved for several months has just left her for another woman. She reports, in very vague and general terms, the episode in which the relationship ended. She states, "I really don't care that he's gone. I have no feelings about it one way or the other." She goes on to describe other events during the week and then lapses into a prolonged silence. A psychoanalytic counselor will mark as possible instances of resistance several features of the client's language and actions. First, she is late for her appointment. Second, she is vague and general in reporting the circumstances surrounding this current stressful event. Third, she claims to have no feelings about the break-up with her lover. Fourth, she changes the subject and reports on events far removed from the event itself. And fifth, she stops talking altogether. Which, if any, of these behaviors are confirmed as resistance, and whether to deal with them at all, are matters of counselor judgment. For our purposes at the moment, we may note that the effect of the client's resistance is clearly to inhibit the conversation in counseling. The resistance stands in contradistinction to open communication and blocks the client's conscious intention of cooperating with the counselor in thinking and talking freely. As such, resistance presents the counselor and the client with technical problems in their management of the discourse in the hour. Before we proceed in our consideration of resistances, it is essential to consider the concept of defense and to make a distinction between resistance and defense.

Resistance means opposition (Greenson, 1967). Freud's (1962a, 1962b, 1962c) discovery of this "regressive mechanism" in the etiology of symptoms signaled the beginning of psychoanalysis. The theoretical yield of this discovery was the early "defense theory of the neuroses" (Freud, 1962b). The important idea here is simply that the ego is active in defending against the conscious experiencing of unacceptable ideas and painful affects (see Chapter 2). The function of the client's defenses in the interview is the same as it is outside of treatment: namely, to minimize psychological discomfort. In a word, the defenses function as resistance in the interview. It follows, therefore, that one of the analyst's most important tasks in classical psychoanalysis became the analysis of resistances. The understanding and dealing with resistances is no less important in psychoanalytic counseling. Client resistance is common to both forms of treatment.

For the client, defenses operate in the counseling interview in many of the same ways they do in everyday life. On the one hand, the client hopes for relief and tries to cooperate with the counselor. On the other, forces within the client oppose cooperation. When the client is cooperative and is talking freely, the working alliance is effective. When the client is resistant, the language of negation is manifest. Thus, defenses operate to oppose or repress the client's awareness and expression of certain thoughts, feelings and action tendencies.

Because the client's defenses function as resistance in the counseling interview, it will help us to consider more fully the topic of ego defenses. In Chapter 2 we saw that anything the client does to minimize the effects of painful affect, particularly anxiety and/or depression, may be considered a defense (see Brenner, 1982). This general idea has its roots in Freud's (1962c) early observation that his patients had enjoyed good mental health until an "occurrence of incompatibility took place in their ideational life" (p.47). By this he meant that these patients were now faced with ideas that caused such distressing affect that they made the decision to forget them. He ascribed their unconscious decision to forget these ideas to a lack of confidence in their ability to use their intellective functions to resolve the conflict between the troubling idea and the ego. Resistance defends the client's maladaptive solutions to problems and opposes the disclosure of these problems in counseling. Needless to say, resistance interferes with the client's capacity to understand and to change.

It is useful to think of defenses as the methods the person regularly uses to respond to the stresses to which he or she is especially sensitive. But when defenses are weakened, such that the person cannot find ways for self-expression that are satisfying, or when defenses are applied too rigidly, the client loses an important part of the ego's coping repertoire. Like defenses, the resistances operate primarily through the ego. They do so to safeguard against danger. In contrast to the client's loving and aggressive wishes, which seek expression, resistances are a force against expression. Here, they operate unconsciously in the ego and manifest themselves in the counseling situation as opposition to some aspect of the counseling process. In Chapter 2 we saw that the danger situations that may evoke later resistance evolve in a developmental sequence during childhood. These danger situations are fear of the loss of the object, fear of the loss of the object's love, fear of castration, and the fear of one's conscience (guilt and/or shame) (Brenner, 1982). Thus, in counseling when thoughts, feelings, or action tendencies stimulate a painful affect, some amount of resistance will be manifest. What ultimately lies behind the painful anxiety or depression is some dangerous loving or hateful thought which is connected to a painful event corresponding to one of the phases of the client's childhood development.

Freud's early definition of defenses clearly identifies them as cognitive operations. When looked at as a cognitive operation that manifests itself in the language the person uses, all defenses can be seen to use negation as a grammatical operation (Fisher, unpublished manuscript). Linguistic or otherwise, defense is, thus, a statement which contains a negation of facts. For example, in the vignette above, the client claimed she had no feelings whatsoever about the break-up of her romance. This example illustrates how the defense is a person's vested belief. Notably, the belief itself is a contradiction to an experienced fact. In this case, the client was hurting. Ego defenses are, thus, the person's typical cognitive patterns of responding by (a) negating wishes and affects from within the person, or (b) contradicting events from without (i.e. those in the person's external environment).

As a cognitive operation, the defense affects the person's use of both logic and language with reference to the ideas with which he or she is struggling. This is to say that the use of defense restricts the client's use of the intellect in some way. Either a portion of reality is denied or distorted, or the client or some other significant person is removed as the source or target of some action. In this sense, Fisher identifies defenses as negative transformations of logic and language. In consequence, the person's perception of self and world is restricted and so are the person's transactions with others.

The ego plays an important dual role in the defenses. When a danger situation is signaled (Freud, 1964b), the irrational ego institutes defense to protect itself and this manifests itself as resistance in the interview. At the same time, however, the rational processes of the ego, the so-called "secondary process," prompt the recognition and understanding of the danger. As we try to help the client overcome the resistance, we appeal to the rational ego through the working alliance. It is the rational part of the ego that cooperates with us as we try to understand and modify the resistance. It is important to keep this distinction about ego processes in mind as the counselor works to understand the client (see Fenichel, 1941; Gill, 1963).

One implication of this view of the ego is that there is a layering of defenses and resistances. While resistance operates unconsciously, some resistances are more primitive and closely connected to deeply repressed material and, therefore, less amenable to becoming conscious. Other resistances are closer to consciousness and operate more in line with the secondary or reality-based processes of the ego, making them more amenable to awareness. In psychoanalytic counseling, our work with the resistances will more likely involve those that are less deeply embedded and which are more accessible to the client's observing ego.

In the foregoing material, we have implied that the cause of defense or resistance is some danger perceived by the ego. Specifically the immediate cause is the variety of painful affect represented by anxiety and/or depression that elicits the resistance in order to avoid or minimize the effects of the affect. This is why we are advised to deal with the resistance and the warded off affect before dealing with content. But we also know from Chapter 2 that the unconscious loving or aggressive idea with which the painful affect is associated is also a cause of the resistance, albeit a more distant cause. In this instance, the unacceptable ideas are what evoked the painful affect the first place. Finally, we also saw in Chapter 2 that the unacceptable ideas are connected to one or more of the childhood calamities. It is the original childhood misfortune or traumatic situation that is the ultimate reason for the resistance. Some event stirs up an unconscious wish that is associated with an early traumatic situation, and then painful affect ensues as a threat and a signal to the ego.

The causes of resistance are, therefore, the same as those for defense. They are nothing less than the elements of compromise formations (Brenner, 1982). In the interview they act to keep conflicted material out of the conversation. They are part and parcel of the client's conflicts. Thus, working consistently in identifying and helping the client clarify resistance is one of the most important methods in psychoanalytic counseling for promoting an understanding of the client's central emotional difficulties. Working to understand the elements of resistance helps modify the defenses that have held the client hostage to the painful adaptations in the client's life. Such modifications help free the client to think and act in more satisfying and constructive ways.

Manifestations of resistance in the interview

Resistances are ubiquitous in the life of the client. Any material reported by the client or any enactments of the resistances from everyday life can be used as a means of opposing openness and change in counseling. It is important, therefore, that the counselor be able to recognize the appearance of resistances in order to assist the client in dealing with them. We seek a way of organizing our discussion of resistances to facilitate their identification. However, because of the variety of modes of thought, feeling, and action that clients can use to manifest resistance, there is no easy way to categorize them. Any classification scheme that attempts to organize the resistances is going to be incomplete, its categories to some degree not discrete, and some categories will not be of the same species as the others.

With these caveats in mind, we organized our classification scheme into three major parts for this section of the chapter. Because of its importance, we will present some thoughts in the first segment on the client's fear of counseling as a form of resistance. In the second segment, some general behavioral indications of resistance will be discussed. In the third segment, we will consider the appearance of resistance through the use of the defenses.

Fear of counseling

The most noticeable form of resistance is opposition to the path counseling takes to bring about constructive change in the client. This kind of resistance is manifest over the duration of counseling. At the outset of the work, however, resistance can also be motivated by a fear of counseling. We have found it useful to think about resistance due to fear of counseling as consisting of three elements: (a) fear of the counseling process; (b) fear of the counselor; and (c) fear of the reasonable ego. When, at the outset of counseling, resistance to these elements is motivated by a fear of them, there is a special reason to work to identify such resistance and to overcome it. The reason is that if the client's fear of the counseling process, the counselor, or the client's ego cannot be overcome, a working alliance with the client will be difficult or impossible to establish, and thus little or no positive change can be accomplished on the client's behalf. Bringing the client's fears about counseling to awareness and discussing them openly takes precedence over other kinds of interventions when the counselor identifies this form of resistance.

A lack of success in helping the client identify and overcome fears of counseling often results in the client's premature termination. That is, if the client's resistance is not recognized and dealt with when it manifests itself in the early sessions, the client is quite likely not to return for additional sessions with the counselor. The literature on premature termination in counseling is replete with the investigation of counselor and client characteristics or agency practices that are thought to be related to premature termination or continuation in counseling (see Tryon, 1990; Tracey, 1986; Epperson, Bushway, & Warman, 1983). Curiously, however, investigators rarely construe the problem of premature termination in terms of the client's fears of counseling, or the counselor's failure to recognize and deal with this form of resistance.

Resistances due to a fear of counseling manifest themselves in the same ways as any other resistances. After identifying the resistance, it is important, therefore, to ascertain whether it is prompted by a fear of counseling or some other motive. In any event, resistances due to a fear of counseling often appear at the outset of counseling as: requests to reschedule the initial appointment; reluctance to provide more than limited, cryptic information; asking the counselor for direct advice; excessive questioning of the counselor about the counseling process; statements that indicate the client is not prepared to spend more than a few sessions with the counselor because he or she wants a "quick fix"; enactment of inappropriate behaviors in the belief that this is what is expected in counseling; failure to keep the initial appointment; lateness; broken appointments; and client-initiated, premature termination. Let us turn now to a consideration of the three elements or targets of resistance when the reason is a fear of counseling.

Fear of the counseling process   This form manifests itself as resistance in several ways. By process we are referring to the counseling situation itself with its procedures and requirements. For example, a client may be uncooperative in providing the counselor with information because the fear is that counseling will not be of enough help. In this case, the client is less likely to have faith in the efficacy of the procedures. Another client may be resistant for fear the process requires the counselor to assume a critical attitude toward the client. Still another client becomes resistant because of the belief that the client's role requires rigorous preparation for each session, and the client fears such preparation or the personal or motivational abilities to engage in it.

The client's fears of the counseling process are often rooted in faulty expectations about what happens in counseling and what is required (see Tinsley & Harris, 1976; Goldstein, Heller and Sechrest, 1966). In other cases, the client may be fearful through lack of information about what to expect. In the case of faulty expectations, the client frequently possesses misinformation or mistaken beliefs about what a client is supposed to do in counseling (that is, how to be a client), what the counselor does and does not do, who does most of the talking about what, how long the process will take and what outcomes can be reasonably expected, and the like. In other words, the client may misunderstand or have faulty expectations about counselor and client role requirements, discussion topics, duration of counseling, or client prognosis (see Lennard & Bernstein, 1960).

Often, resistance due to a fear of the process can be managed quickly and successfully once it is identified as due to faulty expectations or simply lack of knowledge. The antidote is providing the client with correct information about what to expect in counseling. But, in such cases, it is well to let the resistance become manifest before trying to counter it. In other words, the correct information has a better chance of being assimilated by the client as the need for it is encountered.

At other times, however, the client's fears of the counseling process are more deeply related to the client's central emotional difficulties. For example, it is not uncommon for clients to resist the process early on because it is perceived by them to require cooperation with authority, or to require passivity in the face of intimidation. The process of disclosing oneself to the counselor can remind the client of what it felt like to be required to undress in front of a parent. Anger, shame (i.e. a sense of inadequacy) and fear are the normal accompaniments of such memories. It may take a while longer for the client to recognize that his or her fears of the present counseling situation are due to a contribution from the distant past. The counselor's clues about this are taken from the strength of the client's reaction to the counseling process. The stronger the client's reaction to the requirements of the process, the greater the likelihood that something in the client's past is making a contribution to that reaction. The following vignette will help illustrate resistance due to fear of the counseling process.

A 25-year-old unmarried woman came to her first counseling session 20 minutes late. She nervously reported that she had just broken up with a man she had been seeing for several months and was feeling sad and guilty about this. She had considerable difficulty speaking freely and spontaneously. Over the next four sessions, she broke one appointment, and came running breathlessly in several minutes late to the other three. Again, she was very anxious and halting in her manner of reporting. When the counselor suggested that she was experiencing some fears about counseling, she confirmed this and reported that she was very afraid that she would have to blurt out some things that were embarrassing to her. The counselor reassured her that she was in charge of what she communicated and when she did so. Moreover, while it would be helpful to both of them if she could report all of her concerns, there was no urgency for her to do so. The counselor would take the cues from her about when she was ready to disclose painful material.

Fear of the counselor   Often the client's fear of the counseling is specific to the person of the counselor. It is common for the client to come to counseling with pre-formed expectations about how the counselor will behave, even if the client knows nothing about the counselor. On the one hand, the client hopes or wishes that the counselor will behave in a manner congruent with those wishes, and on the other, fears that he or she will not. Research on client expectations of counseling and the counselor (see Lennard & Bernstein, 1960; Tinsley & Harris, 1976) suggest that clients have very well-formed ideas about these matters. That is, clients want their counselors to behave toward them in specific ways. One set of client expectations for counselor behavior includes hoping the counselor will be either critical, nurturant, or act as a model. Thus, client fears about the counselor can relate to anxiety that the counselor will not meet the preformed expectations. The example below describes the client's fear of the counselor.

A 29-year-old divorced mother of a young son reports that she left her last counselor, a psychiatrist, after one session because he wasn't "friendly to me." "He just sat there in his chair, and I did all the talking. When the session was over, I was ushered out the back door which opened onto the parking lot. He was just too cold for me, so I never went back."

Another type of resistance based on fear of the counselor can manifest itself in the client's habitual behavior patterns of acting or speaking. In such cases, the resistance is usually so ingrained and natural that it is not at all problematic for the client. That is, the resistance is "ego-syntonic," or compatible with the ego. In this case, it is not likely to be something that can be approached at the outset of counseling. Rather, it will be necessary to establish the working alliance and to have successfully dealt with resistances that are "ego-alien," or problematic to the client, before the client is amenable to working on resistances that are more comfortable to him or her. This state of affairs is illustrated below.

A male client, 23 years old, had been in counseling for several months when the counselor attempted to deal with his habitually nice or compliant manner. This resistance would often manifest itself in the client's agreement with the counselor's assessment of something, rather than actively evaluating its significance for himself. At other times, the client would have only positive comments to make about something disagreeable the counselor or other persons had said to the client. The counselor attempted several times to help the client look at the resistive purpose such compliance and niceness served, but to no avail. The client simply said that this was his natural way of dealing with things and that there was no need to talk about it. Besides, being nice and polite was helpful to others.

Finally, the counselor persisted in confronting this resistance until the client became annoyed, and then enraged. In an angry outburst, he told the counselor that he had no right to force him to be unfriendly. "When I'm nice," he said, "you can have no reason to try to hurt me." He then became sad and silent, later indicating that he was now aware that he was afraid of the counselor, just as he was afraid of his father and the other men he worked with. Later, he was able to look at his habitually "nice" demeanor and to consider it as a form of resistance.

Fear of the reasonable ego   Insight in psychoanalytic counseling depends upon the reasonable ego. It is one of the counselor's tasks to assist the client in expanding and then sustaining a reasonable ego. Resistances are evidence of the distorting, defending part of the ego. As such, they oppose the work of the reasonable ego. For this reason, it is a primary task of the counselor to confront and help the client understand the resistances which interfere with the operation of the reasonable ego. Once established, the reasonable ego is amenable to insight.

We have emphasized in earlier chapters the importance of the client's capacity to "split the ego" in counseling. By this is simply meant that the client is asked to observe and report on his or her ongoing experiences; to stand back from the stream of experience, as it were, and observe him or herself in the act of experiencing. It is necessary to ensure that the client possesses a reasonable ego in order to do this. Thus, the client's capacity to split off ego functions into experiencing and observing sectors is critical to the formation of the working alliance between the two participants. It will be recalled from Chapter 5 that the counselor depends on the client's ability within the working alliance to use the rational or reasonable portion of his or her mind to think, judge, evaluate, remember, and talk, rather than blindly living out emotional problems.

The client's reasonable ego has, then, the task of observing the resistances when they are pointed out by the counselor, or later self-discovered by the client. Such observation and understanding by the reasonable ego results in knowledge or insight about oneself. Because of this, the client's reasonable ego is one of the targets of the defensive activities of the mind. Resistance to the reasonable ego manifests itself as a fear of counseling because the client can become afraid of what will be learned about self through the process. Hence, another way of describing the function of the resistances is to say that they oppose understanding or knowledge. Indeed, the defenses provide the client with methods for "not knowing" something, for denying the facticity of an experience. Fear of the reasonable ego is illustrated in the following example.

A 40-year-old married male client had developed the habit of immediately forgetting his frequent sexual experiences and fantasies upon their completion. The next day, he would even go so far as denying the fact that a sexual experience had occurred when the matter was brought up by the partner with whom he had been intimate the previous evening. Little by little, he would regain a portion of the memory of these experiences in the next few days, but memory for the entire experience as a sequence of meaningful actions and feelings remained inaccessible. When asked about the amnesia, the client would shrug it off with "I don't know why I can't remember, I just can't. What's the big deal with forgetting about it anyway?" In this way, the client expressed his further resistance to understanding that and how the amnesia was a resistance. Hoping to help the client to become curious about his resistance and uncomfortable with it, the counselor indicated that his forgetting served a purpose for him; but forgetting on such a scale was also a dangerous alteration of his perception of reality.

The client's use of amnesia continued to oppose understanding of this matter for some period of time. Finally, the counselor suggested to the client that he was forgetting about his sexual encounters so as not to have to feel guilty about them. The client responded angrily that the counselor ought to mind his own business! Following the angry outburst, the client began talking about how he was afraid he was going to have to "pay" for his pleasure. The forgetting seemed to help him assuage his fears of retribution.

In summary, resistance due to a fear of counseling can manifest itself in opposition to aspects of the counseling process, to the person of the counselor and to the expansion and use of the client's own reasonable ego.

Some general indications of resistance

Greenson (1967) has formulated a useful list of the most obvious indications of resistance in the psychoanalytic interview. We might add that the resistances named in the Greenson list can be found in all forms of psychological treatment that mobilize forces within the client that are opposed to change. It should be remembered that anything the client thinks, says, does or feels can serve the purpose of resistance. That is, it can function to minimize the discomfort of painful affects and ward off awareness of unwelcome thoughts. According to Freud (1960) and Brenner (1982), all psychic phenomena are compromise formations and consist, therefore, of elements of instinct and defense. Here we identify only some common forms of resistance that are manifest in the counseling interview. For the sake of clarity, we have organized our discussion of general forms of resistance into three categories: language, discussion topic, and behavior.

Language   The client's task in psychoanalytic counseling is to use everyday language to talk as freely as possible to the counselor. As we have seen, opposition to this requirement can be prompted by many motives, and resistances that can be detected through the client's language take many forms. The most common form of such resistance is silence, and its close variant in which the client announces that he or she does not feel like talking. In the former case, the client may or may not be aware that he or she is not willing to communicate thoughts and feelings on this occasion. In the latter case, awareness of not feeling like talking is followed by silence.

The result is the same in both cases. In any event, the client says he or she has nothing to talk about today, or that nothing comes to mind. The task the counselor faces is to try to determine the motive for the silence.

Greenson (1967) provides a number of useful questions the counselor can ask which help the client recognize the resistance and which invite the client to search for its causes. In other words, the psychoanalytic counselor operates with the principle of determinism (see Chapter 1) in assuming that the "nothing" is caused by "something." To paraphrase Greenson (1967), we ask the client: "What might be making you run away from counseling at this time?" Or, "What might be creating the nothing in your mind?" Or, "You seemed to have turned something into a nothing, what might it be?" (p.61).

In each instance, the counselor has the task of helping the client explore and understand why or what the client does not want to talk about. The client is asked to recognize that the client is resisting and is then invited to work on understanding the causes of such resistance. From an understanding of how silence is used as a resistance comes the client's awareness of the conflict between an urge to communicate the unconscious thoughts or feelings and an opposing urge to hide them. Silence can also have other meanings. On some occasions, the client's silence indicates working (e.g. evaluating or thinking about something). This would be a productive use of silence. On other occasions, the silence can also mean that the client is literally reliving some earlier traumatic event in which silence played a part. In the latter instance, silence is both a piece of content and a resistance. On most occasions, however, the client's silence is resistance and needs to be dealt with as such.

Another way in which resistance manifests itself in language is by splitting the affect. Here, the client avoids experiencing painful affect by talking in such a way that ideas and feelings are kept apart. There are many ways to do this. For example, instead of reporting a detailed sequence of events to the counselor, the client may instead summarize the events, or minimize their importance or significance, or only give conclusions, but not the thoughts that led the client to those conclusions. Finally, the client may also generalize an experience by stressing in the account of it how commonplace or typical it is. Summarizing, conclusion giving, minimizing, and generalizing each use language to hide from the pain that a fully detailed or specific accounting would entail.

In summarizing, the client glosses over sequential details and reports events in only the broadest outline. The resulting account is usually quite vague and the particulars of who did what to whom are ambiguous. Conclusion giving also involves hiding the painful details and the client's thoughts about them. It reports on the end result of an unknown chain of reasoning the client has used to arrive at the conclusion. In this case, the omitted details and thoughts are the unknown antecedents. By reporting only the conclusions the client has reached about these matters, pain is lessened. When the client uses conclusion giving, he or she is saying, in effect: "The details are unimportant; I've decided to think (or do) this about that."

Minimizing is a use of language to obscure the personal significance of events. By minimizing an experience, the client downplays or mitigates its effects. When the client says, "It's not important," or "It's no big deal," resistance in the form of minimizing is present. Finally, generalizing is a way of glossing an account so that its personally relevant or subjective meanings are obscured by highlighting only the common meanings. When the client uses generalizing, he or she is saying, "My experience is just like everyone else's," or, "That's typical, isn't it? Doesn't everybody do that?" We will have more to say about splitting the affect as a defense in the next section.

Language can also be used to avoid by the selection of words and phrases that are sterile, dry or technical. The use of truisms, cliches, and sayings also fall in this category. The client's natural way of using the language in everyday life involves words and phrases that bring to mind visual images. Colorless terms or jargon avoid bringing to mind such images. For example, the client says "I stayed at her place last night," when he actually means, "We made love." The words "stayed at her place" helps the client avoid the memories and the feelings that would be recalled with the words, "We made love." Many clients will use childhood or scientific terms to refer to their own or the genitalia of other persons, rather than use penis or vagina. In everyday life, the words penis and vagina evoke clear-cut imagery when used. The counselor should remember that it is important to use everyday, expressive language with the client. This will not only communicate the counselor's thoughts more reliably to the client, it will also help the client by serving as a model of how to talk in counseling.

Another way of avoiding through language is through the use of terms and phrases such as "maybe," "I guess," "really," "you know," "honestly," "et cetera, et cetera," or by repeating troublesome thoughts and questions. The use of cliches and lingo are among the most frequent manifestations of resistance, yet their use can go unrecognized by the counselor. "Maybe" and "I guess" usually mean "I am certain, but don't want to admit it." The use of "honestly" or "truly" often indicates that the client is aware of his or her ambivalence so that he/she is saying, in effect, "I wish all of what I'm telling you were true."

Discussion topic Resistance can also be recognized in relation to the topic or manifest focus of the client's remarks. In other words, some topics are avoided in favor of others. Topics that clients appear to have a particularly difficult time talking about in a direct way are sexuality, aggression, and their feelings about the counselor, that is, the transference. In the realm of sexuality, it is the sexual zones or body parts and the sexual sensations associated with them that are the most painful and difficult for the client to mention. Aggressive or rageful feelings and fantasies are muted with expressions of feeling miffed or annoyed, when, in actuality, the client would like to blow someone's head off. The same resistances are at work when sexual or aggressive feelings are directed to the counselor, but here such feelings are avoided even more strongly. It should be pointed out, therefore, that when an important topic does not become a part of the work at least once in a while, resistance is at work. Topic avoidance is a resistance that must be pursued.

Topic switching is another form of avoidance. Here, the client changes the topic frequently in the space of a few minutes during the course of his or her remarks. Topic switching occurs when the client senses that the current material he or she is talking about is getting too close to painful thoughts and feelings. With the use of this form of resistance, a theme never develops, the personal relevance of the material remains obscure and the deepening of emotional awareness is absent. Each new topic may be explored by the client until the point at which further exploration threatens to lead to awareness of what is being avoided. Then, the subject is changed and a new direction ensues for a while. The counselor's task is to help the client stay with a relevant topic by first confronting and helping the client become aware of the need to run away, which is being experienced at each topic shift.

Externalizing and talking about trivial events are two other forms of resistance related to how the client selects topics for discussion. Beginning counselors are often heard to complain that their clients are engaging in excessive "storytelling." That is, the client is heard to be talking for prolonged periods of time about superficial and relatively unimportant events. Talk about trivial and/or external events for any length of time, and without awareness that one is doing so, is an indication of resistance. It is an indication that the client is avoiding something.

Ordinarily, when the client is reporting freely the material leads to an internal state of affairs. This is what is meant by the "deepening of the client's material" in Chapter 4. When the client is reporting in a meaningful way, there is evidence of introspection and thoughtful consideration of issues. Over time, there will be an increase in affect, possibly accompanied by insight. These characteristics suggest that the client is in a working alliance with the counselor. As Greenson (1967) points out, if talk about trivia or external affairs does not lead to an increase in emotional awareness, the recall of new memories, or expanded insight, we are dealing with resistance. Therefore, in externalizing or speaking of trivial events, the client is demonstrating a preference to place the spotlight away from self.

The final type of resistance with respect to discussion topic that we discuss here is preoccupation with the past or present. This form of general resistance when noticeable in the client's talk exhibits a rigid focus on past or present events. When the client is able to talk freely without undue restriction, events from the past and present as well as those in an anticipated future, are coherently interspersed with each other, and the client's utterances move back and forth among various time periods. That is, past, present, or future events enter the conversation naturally. But, when resistance is operative, the client gives evidence of a preoccupation with the past or present by sticking to a specific time period. For example, it is an indication that some resistance is operative when the client begins the hour by talking about past events and continues to do so in a superficial or complaining way rather than reporting current events. By remaining exclusively in the past, the client avoids a painful present situation. By sticking to the present the client avoids recall of a painful past as well as the knowledge of how that past is reinstated in the present.

Behavior   The third and final general form in which resistances are manifest is that of overt behavior. This is the form of resistance in which the client lives out personal emotional problems in some way, rather than attempting to think or talk about them. Behavior serves a resistive purpose when the client uses actions instead of talking or remembering, feeling or thinking.

Acting out is a common form of resistance which is:

> . . . . the enactment of a past event in the present, which is a slightly distorted version of the past, but which seems cohesive, rational and ego-syntonic to the patient (Greenson, 1967, p. 92).

When acting out occurs, the client engages in a form of gratification which is difficult to consider productively during the interview. This is particularly true when the acting out is repetitive and drawn out, as in romantic attachments, or when the client has learned to take direct action to achieve impulse gratification rather than delay it by thinking and talking. In acting out, then, the client takes conflict-laden thoughts, wishes, and affects and displaces them onto someone or something outside the counseling relationship. Doing so means that the client can avoid talking about the conflicted material in the interview. The vignette below attempts to illustrate the use of resistance through action.

After she had been in counseling for about 6 months, a 38-year-old female client developed a close relationship with a younger woman who was also in counseling with another counselor. The client would spend hours with the younger woman tutoring her in the politics of their mutual profession. Often, they would spend time together rehashing the material of their most recent sessions with their counselors. The client's reporting about this special relationship with the younger woman was usually guarded and cryptic. When the counselor interpreted her motives for developing the relationship with the younger woman, the client was able to bring it into the sessions and talk more freely about it. By developing this relationship with the younger woman, the client was able to avoid dealing with her wish for closeness and mentoring from her own counselor. Memories of longing for closeness with her father and the latter's rejection of her surfaced and were worked through in the context of the client's transferential thoughts and feelings about the counselor.

Acting out is experiencing without reflection. The more the pattern of acting out seems natural (i.e. ego-syntonic) to the client, the more difficult it is to get the client to recognize and work on the problem. By contrast, the more alien (i.e. ego-dystonic) the acting out is to the client, the easier it is to point it out and to engage the reasonable ego in understanding and modifying it. In the example cited above, the client was uneasy about her acting out, and readily accepted the counselor's invitation to explore this behavior.

Broken appointments, lateness, and frequent requests to cancel or change appointments are resistances that indicate the client's hesitation about coming to counseling. Sometimes such resistances are motivated by a general fear of counseling. After the client has been in counseling for a period of time, however, such resistances are more likely motivated by the client's reluctance to reveal specific wishes and feelings that have become active in the course of counseling.

If the reasons for the resistance are unconscious and not readily available to awareness, the client will usually provide ready rationalizations to account for the behavior. This makes the oppositional behavior much more difficult to confront successfully in the interview. Only when there are multiple instances of the behavior is there a reasonable chance of convincing the client that he or she is unconsciously attempting to evade something. By contrast, then, when the motives for such resistances are more readily available, the cause of the resistance can be worked with sooner.

Any repeated behaviors the client engages in without any change during counseling should be regarded as resistance. Such patterns of behavior are defensive character traits, i.e. something is being avoided or held in check by the trait. Such repeated behaviors include, for example, always beginning the hour with a recitation of one's complaints, always coming early or late, consistently trying to be "interesting" to the counselor, leaving the session with never saying good-bye to the counselor, never changing one's position in the chair hour after hour, or continuous excessive movement during the hour. It is generally understood that when a client sits with arms folded tightly across the chest, ankles glued together or legs tightly crossed, he or she is holding something back. By the same token, the client who moves excessively in the chair but talks of innocuous matters is not telling the whole story. Again, when the client is able to talk freely, resistance is not interfering with the natural flow of thoughts, feelings, and behaviors.

Appearance of resistance through the defenses

Thus far we have seen that resistance can make use of the client's fears about counseling, as well as language usage, discussion topics, defensive traits, and other overt behaviors. Another useful way of understanding resistance is through identification of the defenses engaged by resistance in opposing the work of psychoanalytic counseling. There is no "official" list of defense mechanisms. We will identify twelve such defenses here. For a more complete discussion of defense mechanisms, the reader is referred to A. Freud (1936a), Laughlin (1979), and Valliant (1977).

1. *Repression* opposes the work in counseling when the client forgets an appointment, is confused about what happened to him or her in a recent experience, or when the client's mind goes blank about key people or important experiences in the past. During counseling, client lapses in memory, confusion, and blank spots are key indicators of repression functioning as resistance. In repression, certain unconscious wishes, memories, and affects are selectively blocked from expression in awareness. *Amnesia* is a special form of repression in which whole lived-through experiences are forgotten.
2. *Denial* occurs in counseling when the client refuses to believe that an event has occurred or that he or she is experiencing certain wishes or affects. As Fisher (unpublished manuscript) notes, when a person uses denial, he or she negates the existence of a fact. When denial is used excessively, other related facts (experiences) tend to be negated as well. If denial remains unchecked, it eventually immobilizes the client and the discourse in counseling can become stalemated.
3. *Regression* is a defense in which the client falls back on earlier, more immature forms of dealing with conflict. Regression manifests itself as resistance in counseling when, for example, the client undergoes a prolonged crying spell. Regression is also evident when the client is unable to speak and rocks rhythmically back and forth in the chair, sucking on a finger or thumb. It occurs when the client abandons his or her attempts to cooperate with the counselor in evaluating the material and simply waits to be told what to do. All of these forms of regression act as resistances in counseling because they oppose the client's use of the reasonable ego.

4. *Reaction formation* is a defense that turns an underlying, unconscious attitude or feeling into its opposite when expressed consciously. When this defense is used, the client's behavior has about it the quality of forced expression. Examples that come to mind include the person whose underlying homoerotic wishes are betrayed by a militant stance against homosexuality; or the individual whose aggressive wishes are belied by an excessively nurturant demeanor. In these examples, it is as if the client were adamant in denying homosexual longings, and displaying only disgust for such behavior, or feels only love for others, not hate. In any case, a clue to the client's use of reaction formation resides in the way the behavior suggests too much of an objection, as if he or she "doth protest too much." The client's purpose in using this defense, as in denial, is to posit the non-existence of something. Reaction formation goes a step further in that the client believes that "because I love, I cannot feel hate" (see Fisher, unpublished manuscript).

5. *Projection* is a defense in which the client disowns unacceptable thoughts and feelings or responsibility for actions by placing them on someone else. Projection helps to remove the client as the center of responsibility for the experiencing of something or as the cause of something that has happened. In this way, a part of the self is denied and therefore diminished. Projection is evident when the client insists that "it is others who hate me or want to do something against my will. It is their hate that causes me" to break off a romantic relationship, withdraw and become depressed, overeat, drink to excess, and the like. The resistance manifests itself, then, in talk about the intentions and behaviors of others rather than on the client's own inner signals. In projection, the clients dangerously perceived loving and/or aggressive wishes are transferred to others and the client's behavior then becomes very subject to external determinants. The client believes that personal happiness or freedom from pain depends upon the beneficence of others.

6. *Isolation,* or splitting the affect as it is sometimes called, manifests itself as the separation of affects from ideas in the client's associations. As with all defenses, the purpose of isolation is to avoid experiencing the full weight of a painful affect or idea. As we saw earlier in this chapter, there are many variations of this defense. Summarizing, generalizing, intellectualizing, minimizing and conclusion-giving are all instances of isolation. In conclusion-giving, the counselor can observe this form of resistance when the client reports a judgment about an experience but avoids reporting the steps that led to that judgment. When a vague outline is provided rather than explicit detail, the client is generalizing. Intellectualizing is evident when abstractions or pedantry

are offered in place of an account of the specifics of an event. Minimizing is apparent when the client portrays otherwise important and impactful events as insignificant. In isolation, the reporting of the specifics of an occurrence are avoided because the client senses that in reporting them, one risks experiencing again the painful feelings that accompanied the event.

7. The defense of *undoing* unconsciously rights a wrong in the client's mind. A subsequent action cancels a prior action. With this defense, the client expiates a sense of guilt. The hand-washing of Lady Macbeth or Pontius Pilate come to mind in connection with this defense. A common way in which clients manifest undoing is by taking back their just-expressed angry or loving thoughts about someone. For example, the client says: "I resent the way my stupid parents neglected me when I was growing up. But, then, they had such a hard life; they did the best they could." Anger is expressed in the first sentence and negated in the second.

8. *Reversal* is a defense that permits the client to do for others what the client wishes they would do for him or her. The wish to be taken care of is strong for many clients, yet it can be accompanied by fears of helplessness. In such a case, the counselor may note that the client is an exceptionally diligent and caring person when it comes to discharging responsibility for children or other loved ones. Such an attitude becomes unrealistic when the client steadfastly refuses to let others help when help is clearly called for. It is as if the client were saying, "I am doing for others what I wish they would do for me."

9. *Turning around on the self* has two forms. In the first case, the client turns around on the self with love, and in the second, with anger. Turning around on the self with love usually occurs following a narcissistic injury of some sort. Here, the client engages in self-gratification in some way following an episode in which shame, humiliation, or embarrassment was experienced. Actions are engaged in the attempt to restore self-esteem. Depending on the extent of the narcissistic injury, such behaviors can range from buying a new outfit, or engaging in leisure pursuits, to binge eating, sexual promiscuity, or delinquency. By contrast, turning around on the self with anger is usually motivated by guilt. In this case, the client attempts to inflict an injury on him or herself for some perceived transgression. Such behavior can range from disparaging him or herself verbally, to self-mutilation and suicide.

10. *Introjection* is a defense in which the client incorporates the opinions, attitudes, and expectations another person has of him or her. Negative introjects are especially troublesome in this regard. Some clients cling to a conception of themselves as essentially unloved and unlovable.

The roots of such a belief are found in the client's childhood interactions with its parents. In order to retain the parent's love, the child introjects what it perceives to be the parent's negative image of itself and lives out this image accordingly. By believing about itself what the child thinks the parents believe, the child retains a connection with them. To believe otherwise is to risk loss of the par ts. Only when the fear of such loss can be faced by the client is it possible to modify this defense in counseling.

11. *Identification* occurs as a means of surmounting anxiety and other painful affects and ideas. The prototype for this defense is the oedipal child's identification with the attitudes, values, and sex-role behaviors of the same-sexed parent. Along with repression, identification serves as a means of resolving the crisis of the oedipal period that has been triggered by the child's fears, incestuous desires, and humiliation. Through close affiliation with the perceived features of the feared aggressor, the child borrows strength to overcome its sense of helplessness. Later, the adolescent again uses identification with the activities and values of the peer group to help establish independence from the parents. The same process of surmounting fear can be seen to occur in adults as when, for example, prisoners of war, concentration camp victims, and institutionalized mental patients adopt certain attitudes, behaviors and even the clothing of their captors/caretakers. In the counseling interview, identification can serve as a resistance when, for example, the client uses conscious identification with a perceivedly strong person or group as a defense against unconscious identification with another person or group that is perceived to be weak and helpless.

12. *Passive into active* is a defense that is characterized by the client's use of action rather than thought to avoid dealing with painful affects and ideas. The counterpart of this defense is active into passive, a defense that uses withdrawal and inactivity to avoid feelings of distress. In the former case, passive into active, the client may first experience a sense of fear or helplessness and then avoid this painful inner state by taking action that removes the client from the uncomfortable situation. For example, rather than stay and deal with personal feelings that have arisen in consequence of a heated argument with a marital partner, a spouse leaves the house and goes for a long walk. Another example is the abusing adult who, as an abused child, had passively experienced such trauma.

Conversely, with the defense of *active into passive*, the client deals with painful thoughts and feelings by becoming submissive or simply inactive. For example, another client may deal with angry thoughts and aggressive impulses that have been aroused by a marital argument by becoming compliant and unassertive. Rather than risk giving in to the urge to say or do something that expresses the unacceptable feelings and thoughts that have been evoked in the situation, the client becomes passive.

In summary, client defenses operate as resistance when they become operative during the counseling interview. As with all forms of resistance, the counselor's task is to help the client recognize and identify the client's habitual pattern of defenses, and to further help clarify their effects and the reasons for them.

Some technical procedures in dealing with client resistance

We again remind the reader that client resistance presents the counselor and the client with both a technical problem to be solved in the interview and valuable information about the dynamics of the client's personality. Thus, the counselor works with client resistances to achieve two important purposes. First, the effective confrontation and understanding of resistances helps the client communicate more freely in the interview. Second, successful confrontation of the resistances promotes client insight or self-understanding. In other words, understanding of the resistances provides the client with deepened knowledge of how his or her mind works.

It should be noted at the outset of this discussion of technical procedures in the handling of client resistance that there may be many good reasons for accommodating the client's resistance rather than attempting to confront and modify it. One such reason is the present state of the client's ego or ability to manage affects. If the client rigidly employs defenses to avoid experiencing even milder forms of affect, or if the defenses have been weakened by current stresses to which the client is especially vulnerable, the client may be struggling against becoming overwhelmed by affect. In such cases, supportive rather than uncovering procedures are called for until the client has been restored to a stronger state of well-being. The counselor's ongoing empathic understanding of the client's inner state will provide the clues about the appropriateness of confronting or accommodating client resistance.

There are several principles and procedures for attempting to understand and deal with client resistance. The foremost principle is that *we help the client understand resistance before we give the client assistance in understanding the content that is being warded off by the resistance* (see Freud, 1958b). The reason for this principle is simple. An interpretation of the client's repressed memories and affects is ineffective if the resistances have not been dealt with first. The client is not able to integrate the memory and use it for change if the resistances are still intact because the memory will still be subject to the forces of resistance (see Fenichel, 1941). We want the client to understand and learn about the memories that resistance has served to screen off because insight will be longer lasting and change more effective when such knowledge is available to the client. But such memories will avail us nothing unless we have effective procedures for dealing with resistance.

A second principle is but an extension of the first: *begin with the surface of the client's mind when intervening.* We saw this principle in Chapter 4 where it was called "current events." We want to permit the client to select the topic for the interview without interference from us. It can be noted as well that the client also determines the content for the hour by what he or she avoids talking about. When the client selects the subject matter for the hour, or avoids selecting, we can be assured that we are dealing with what is manifest and psychologically important to the client at the time. These will be contemporary matters that contain derivatives of the client's central emotional difficulties and the resistances against them. We can learn very little about such matters if we determine the topic of the hour.

What is needed are procedures that help us illuminate and modify the resistances so that we can help the client surface repressed memories and their associated affects. Several psychoanalytic authors have written generally about how to deal with resistance (see Freud, 1958b; Fenichel, 1941; Langs, 1973). Very few have written detailed and clinically useful guidelines. Greenson (1967) is an exception in that he has provided a very useful outline of the technical steps involved in this procedure. Those steps are:

1. Recognize the resistance.
2. Let the resistance build.
3. Demonstrate the resistance.
4. Clarify and interpret the resistance.
5. Repeatedly work through the resistance in subsequent interviews.

We will modify Greenson's recommendations for our purposes in presenting a set of technical procedures for dealing with client resistance in psychoanalytic counseling.

Identifying resistance

First of all, the counselor must recognize the resistance in order to deal with it. The immediately preceding section of this chapter was written to assist the counselor in learning to recognize various manifestations or modes of client resistance. When the client is in a working mode or alliance with the counselor, the resistances take a back seat to the production of relevant content. That is to say, derivatives of unconscious material are less disguised and the client is willing to explore and deepen the material. But, when resistance predominates, the client becomes silent, or the material becomes dry and repetitious, or there are frequent topic changes such that the client's productions do not come to focus upon some important problem. In this case, the task is to establish that resistance is occurring. When the resistance is obvious in the client's material, the task is less complicated. Often, however, the client's manner of expressing resistance is more subtle or ego-syntonic. In such cases, it is important and necessary to supplement one's theoretical understanding with empathic awareness of the client's inner state at that moment.

A 28-year-old, married woman who had been in counseling for about 6 months began her weekly hour with a recitation of how unhappy she had been during the preceding week. She felt overburdened with the care of her 5-year-old son. Her husband was neglectful of her sexually, and was not helpful with the household chores. She had had an argument with her mother on the telephone. She was worried about her mother's ill-health. Her father's recent death had also been on her mind this week. His death had relieved her mother of a considerable burden in caring for him. Her boss was not giving her good assignments at work. She went on like this for several minutes without settling on any one topic. The counselor felt that she was struggling to both express and avoid expressing some important ideas and decided not to intervene until the material became clearer. It was not clear, for example, whether she was angry primarily at her son, husband, boss, mother, or the counselor. The counselor felt that she was also depressed about something.

Two features of the client's material suggested the presence of resistance. First, no particular content seemed to predominate. Rather, the client went from one complaint to the next, interspersed with ruminations. Second, the longer the client did this, the more the counselor got the feeling that the client was struggling with some thoughts and feelings that were threatening to break through into consciousness. Third, the counselor tentatively identified the resistance as topic-switching. The decision was made, therefore, to delay intervening until this conflict between the resistance and the unconscious material became clearer.

Allowing the resistance to increase

After recognizing that the client is resisting something, the counselor is advised to allow the resistance to increase. This is another illustration of the principle of counselor restraint mentioned in Chapter 4. Usually, little is gained by trying to confront resistance at the first sign of its appearance. First of all, the counselor may well be mistaken about the meaning of the client's communications. Additional observations of the resistance lend credence to the counselor's initial hunch. From the counselor's point of view, time and additional evidence are needed to verify, or to disconfirm, the inference that the client is indeed resistant about something.

Second, when the counselor confronts the client at the first sign of resistance, the client may become confused or perceive that the counselor is being arbitrary. Moreover, the client can easily deny or rationalize that he or she has reason to be avoiding something when the counselor's attempt to demonstrate the resistance is ill-timed. Thus, the counselor allows resistance to manifest itself several times before attempting to demonstrate it. The client will be more likely to acknowledge and deal with the resistance when examples can be readily demonstrated from preceding material.

There are still other reasons why it is usually important to let resistance build before intervening. Later in the interview, the client can gain benefit from the opportunity of having struggled earlier with tendencies for and against expression of conflicted and painful material. Such an experience can facilitate client's readiness to work on the resistance when it is brought into awareness. The client's recognition of the resistance provides not only some relief from the pressure of expending energy to maintain the struggle, but also some hope which is prompted by the counselor's display of understanding of the client's struggle. In addition, the material that the client has communicated as he or she struggled with the resistance provides the grounds for its later clarification and interpretation. Both participants will use this material as they later work through the resistance.

The clinical example in the preceding section on identifying resistance also demonstrates counselor restraint in letting the resistance build.

This 28-year-old woman continued her topic-switching by next mentioning that her son had dashed out into the street after a ball and was barely missed by a passing car. Thus, she had once again changed the subject. This last item seemed particularly difficult for her to express. As she spoke she closed her eyes, screwed up her face, and practically spat the words out. She then fell silent. Had the counselor decided to intervene earlier in the client's litany of complaints, the mention of her son's near miss with the automobile might well have remained unexpressed.

Demonstrating the resistance

The technical term for the counselor's attempt to demonstrate resistance to the client is *confrontation*. Counselor confrontation is an intervention that can take many forms. Its major purpose is to show the client that, in the way he or she is communicating, there is evidence of opposition to the expression of some painful thoughts and feelings. Not all clients will need to be confronted with their resistance in all instances. If resistance is obvious to the client, his or her reasonable ego will become aware of it, and we do not have to take this step in helping the client. In many cases, however, the counselor will need to confront the resistance by trying to make the client aware of its presence.

We have seen that a period of preparation may be necessary before confrontation is effective. We should attempt to confront resistance only when we have determined that the client's ego is in a position to make use of this knowledge. In other words, the client needs to be able to split the ego to be able to observe the resistance and to work cooperatively with the counselor in dealing with it. Unless the counselor's confrontation of resistance is meaningful for the client, it will have been a waste of time to intervene. It is important, therefore, that the counselor determine the state of the client's reasonable ego before intervening. Correct timing of confrontation will preclude the client's attempts to deny or otherwise avoid its meaning.

As Greenson (1967) points out, there are several ways in which the counselor can help make the resistance easier to demonstate. One is to use silence and let it build or intensify, which was the subject of the preceding section of this chapter. A result of our silence is that the resistance will increase and its presence will have more of an opportunity of becoming apparent to the client. The second method involves asking the client to explain the matter which indicates the resistance. This has the same effect as our silence in that it highlights the client's avoidance. An example will best serve to illustrate this second approach:

A young married woman, Mrs. D., has been in counseling for about 7 months. In several of the immediately preceding sessions, she has made vague and hesitant references to the enjoyment she feels in coming to counseling. On this occasion, she begins by commenting in a timid manner on the counselor's new office: "I really like how your office looks. I guess it reminds me of my mother's living room." She then proceeds to talk anxiously about how important furniture is in making a room feel good, and then moves on to inconsequential matters. The counselor intervenes shortly thereafter and says to her: "Just a minute ago you mentioned that you liked my office. Please help me understand what you mean by 'you like my office'." At this point, the client reddens, stammers and begins to explain, but stops and says: "I know you want me to be specific, but I don't know how to talk about this." The counselor says in reply: "I can see that you are shy when it comes to talking about the pleasure you take in the work we are doing here." This intervention helped the client go on to speak at some length about the difficulties she experiences whenever she tries to talk about enjoying something. While she is not yet ready to explore the resistant point, she has begun to work productively on her avoidance of doing so.

A third method of highlighting the fact that the client is resisting is to mention some or all of its indications. With the 28-year-old female client who had ended her list of complaints with the brief account of how her son had run into the street after a ball, the counselor had waited until then to intervene. Doing so at this point gave the counselor several instances of resistance to point out to the client. The counselor said:

I think you may be struggling to keep from telling me something. You mention a list of grievances that includes the burden of childcare, a neglectful husband, a boss who gives you unwelcome assignments, your mother's 'phone call, and your son's dash into the street without looking, but you haven't elaborated any of these. And now you are not talking at all.

If this client is in a working alliance with the counselor and is able to split the ego, she will be able to recognize that she is avoiding something. In the example above, the counselor is pointing out the evidence that comprises the conclusion that the client is resisting. This method of demonstrating resistance provides a conclusion, assembles the evidence in support of that conclusion and, thereby, attempts to engage the client's reasonable ego in the process of recognition. The counselor's manner of confrontation is not demanding. Rather, the confrontation invites the client to consider the possibility that she is resisting and to think and talk about it. Intervening prematurely, or with less evidence, or by insisting that the client acknowledge the resistance, makes it easy for the client to deny or rationalize the avoidance. After recognizing that resistance is occurring, confrontation is the first active step the counselor takes in helping the client to recognize its presence. Analyzing the resistance is the next step.

Analyzing client resistance

Analyzing resistance is the process that helps the client achieve further insight. This process usually consists first of clarifying or sharpening our understanding of the immediate reason for the resistance and the manner in which the client is resisting. Usually the reason the client is resisting initially is because of some painful affect. The client's mode or manner of expressing the resistance informs the counselor as to the form the resistance is taking. The process of clarifying the reason and manner of expressing the resistance continues as we try to understand or interpret the content or ideas that have evoked the painful affect. The process is repeated as the client and counselor work through these various steps during one or more sessions.

Clarification   The clarification of resistance is undertaken for the purpose of illuminating the motive for the resistance. Some painful affect is most often the primary motive. The more distant reason usually has to do with the specific loving or aggressive wishes and/or traumatic memories that have triggered the painful affect. Pursuing the affect first is recommended because it is closer to consciousness than is the content associated with the affect. Sometimes the client's non-verbal behavior will give a clue to the affect that is being warded off. Clenched fists suggest anger. Silence, sighing, and a gloomy tone of voice may indicate depression. Agitation, trembling, and hesitancy are clues to fear. Covering the face or closing the eyes may indicate the wish to hide and the feeling of shame.

If the non-verbal cues are relatively obvious, the counselor may suggest to the client: "I wonder if you are running away today because you are embarrassed (or scared, or angry or guilty)?" The use of phrases such as "I wonder whether," or "You seem," are preferable to declarative statements about the client's affect. As Greenson (1967) notes, tentativeness is advised for two reasons. First, the counselor's inference about the nature of the painful affect might be incorrect. Second, the client may need room to deny and run from the affect on this occasion. Thus, our interventions in regard to clarifying the motive for resistance need to provide the client maximum latitude in choosing to confirm or run further from the painful affect.

On many occasions, the counselor may be unable to detect the nature of the painful affect. In this case, it is best simply to ask: "What troublesome feeling are you trying to stay away from today?" or "What did you feel when you described your son running into the street?" or "What are you feeling as you sit there in silence?" In any case, the simpler and more direct the counselor's language the better. The counselor's use of abstract words do not portray what the client feels concretely. If, for example, the counselor is trying to help the client recognize a sense of shame underlying avoidance, words like shy or ashamed are probably better suited than words like chagrined or mortified. By the same token, the intensity of the client's affect is a clue to the wording of the counselor's intervention. If the client is mildly depressed, the counselor might say "You seem blue today." Or, if the client is very anxious, the counselor might comment: "I can tell you are feeling terrible inside." To illustrate the clarification of the underlying affect or idea that prompts the resistance, we return to the example of the client whose little boy had run into the street after a ball.

After the counselor had highlighted the fact that the client was resisting, she began to speak, paused, and then said:"I guess I just want to skip over things rather than talk about how I really feel. But, Oh God! Now I know what's bothering me. I feel so badly because when my son dashed into the street, I wished that he had been run over! I saw him run after the ball and I knew he was going to go into the street. I didn't even try to stop him. I even had the urge to push him in front of that car. I have been so angry with him lately because he won't listen to me. I just wanted to hurt him in some way."

In this example, the mode of the resistance, the guilty feelings and the angry wish are clarified somewhat. The angry thoughts about her son had made her anxious and guilty. These feelings prompted the resistance in the form of topic-switching in this hour. The client had centered her angry fantasies on her son but was at a loss to understand why she should be so angry with him.

Interpretation   When the motive for the resistance has been demonstrated and clarified, our next task is to help the client understand the content that is prompting the painful feelings. This involves interpreting the unconscious elements of the material. Usually, the clues to the unconscious content that elicits the painful affect become apparent when the motive for the resistance has been clarified. At this point, the counselor can begin to assist the client in analyzing the resistance. In doing so, it is often useful to ask the client to follow his or her thoughts in reference to the resistant point. In this way, the client's material leads to connected feelings, loving and/or aggressive wishes, fantasies, and memories.

When in a working mode, it is common for the client to proceed from the affect or experience that triggered the resistance to the history of the affect or experience in the client's life. In this way, it is possible for the counselor and client to link the history of the feelings, ideas or experiences that emerge with the current resistance. Such linkage furthers the process of self-understanding or insight on the part of the client. In proceeding to analyze the resistance, our question at this point is to wonder what has happened in the client's life to prompt such a reaction. Consider again the client who wanted her son to be run over by the car.

She had been troubled by her reaction and was unable to account for it. Moreover, she was very reluctant to continue talking about it. The counselor knew, however, that she had formed a good working alliance, so he asked: "What comes to mind when you think about telling me of your angry wishes toward your son?" She began by saying that she had not been permitted to express anger as a child and had been told by both parents that good girls did not act that way. This prohibition on expressing anger had carried over to her girlhood and adult friendships. She generally avoided telling anyone if she became angry and actively avoided situations where she thought she might be involved in an angry conversation. Yet, she complained that there were many things she should be angry about. The recent 'phone call from her mother was just one in a long series in which her mother was critical of her for working and having to place her son in day-care. This led to a series of painful memories of her mother's critical and neglectful treatment of her as a child.

She lingered on one memory in which, at age 5, her mother had caught her masturbating, had slapped her on the face and severely reprimanded her for it. She wondered whether the counselor were equally displeased with her. She knew intellectually that the counselor was not displeased with her, but she feared this was the case anyway. The counselor interpreted to her that whenever she felt angry, he had become her mother and she was once again a small child. She agreed and further confirmed the intervention by recalling that earlier in the day on which her son ran into the street after the ball, she had seen him playing with his genitals and had been both fascinated and furious with him.

These are just a few of the motives for the client's resistance to talking about the episode of her son running into the street, and this report is a considerably shortened account of the analysis of them. In later hours, the client continued to work through the material surrounding the event.

In still other instances, understanding the resistance is facilitated by analyzing the mode or manner of its expression rather than the affects, ideas, or memories. This is particularly the case when the mode of resistance is repeated on numerous occasions by the client. In such cases, its is likely that the mode of resistance is a character trait. These phenomena are considerably more difficult to deal with because they are habitual and ego-syntonic. The counselor's task is to try to make the resistance ego-dystonic or uncomfortable by getting the client's reasonable ego to see the phenomenon as resistance. Greenson (1967) notes that the demonstrability of this form of resistance depends upon how ego-syntonic the resistance is and on how effective the working alliance is:

> The more coherent, adaptive, and successful an activity appears to the patient, the more difficult it will be to persuade him (sic) this activity is a resistance (p.118).

In any event,the steps for dealing with character resistances are the same as those for other forms of resistance.

A final note about resistance is in order here. Resistance has many sources both in and outside of the counseling relationship. Events in the client's everyday life are a frequent source for the arousal of resistance that is expressed in the session. The client's transference relationship with the counselor is the major source. It is always important for the counselor to be alert for transference reactions as the source of resistance. Because the transference is a central element of psychoanalytic counseling, care must be taken to help the client work through any defense against the transference, The purpose is, of course, to help the client begin to relive in the counseling situation those faulty patterns of relating to others that indicate both when and how the painful affects and ideas began that interfered with the client's development (Basch, 1988). As well, interpretations of resistance to the transference can also be linked to the other persons in the client's current life circumstances, toward whom similar affects and wishes are manifested.

The interpretation of resistance in psychoanalytic counseling is necessarily less extensive than in classical psychoanalysis because the client is not seen as frequently or for as long. In consequence, there is less opportunity for a thorough working through of the resistance to all of its genetic roots in the client's history. It is more often the case that the client will gain understanding of the more immediate sources of resistance (i.e. the warded-off content and affect) and how they manifest themselves in the present. Insight achieved in this way is necessarily less pervasive, but often sufficient to promote a marked increase in the client's adaptive capabilities.

10   Case example of psychoanalytic counseling

In this chapter we will attempt to illustrate further the use of some of the concepts related to psychoanalytic counseling, with a case example of a counselor and client. Summary statements of the case will be augmented by the inclusion of verbatim sequences of client and counselor remarks from the initial interview, and from an interview midway in the treatment. We have elected throughout the book to include vignettes of actual client and counselor behavior because we believe that the clinical material itself can be an effective, and often the best, teacher. The case example in this chapter will be necessarily abbreviated and otherwise edited to preserve space and to protect the identities of the participants involved.

We have introduced many concepts about psychoanalytic counseling in this book. The organization we have placed upon these concepts and our particular definition of them represent our approach at this point in time. The entire book is, therefore, a compilation and integration of our growing understanding and experience in working with clients, and in conducting research using a psychoanalytic framework. This effort is ongoing, our ideas are tentative, and we hope that much of what we have said here will be improved upon over time.

In using an actual case to illustrate our ideas, it becomes immediately apparent to us as authors that aspects of the case could have been understood differently at the time and, accordingly, particular counselor interventions might have been framed differently as well. Such considerations indicate our evolving understanding of these matters. Understanding the client from a psychoanalytic perspective and attempting to conduct counseling in line with psychoanalytic principles involves the counselor and the researcher in a never-ending process of learning. Freud (1964a) underscores this point very well in his essay entitled "Analysis: Terminable and Interminable." The lesson to keep in mind here is that we treat our formulations of the case as tentative hypotheses that are open at all times to refutation by observable events in the interview, and by increasingly more precise empirical and theoretical knowledge of the counseling and psychotherapy process.

We have divided this chapter into three sections to accord, more or less, with the three phases of counseling: the opening phase, the phase of problem solving or working through, and the closing or termination phase. In the first section, using the guidelines for organizing client information presented in Chapter 7, we will present a formulation based on the first phase of the work with this client, and will include excerpts from the client and counselor's conversation in the first hour. In this way, we hope to establish the observations on which certain inferences have been drawn about the client, and why the specific goals for the work and the plan of action for intervening are stated as they are. In the second section, we will attempt to illustrate the model of the "path of client understanding" introduced in Chapter 4. We will include excerpts of the counselor's and client's dialogue taken from an interview during the beginning of the middle phase of this case. In addition, we hope to illustrate the use of certain counselor intervention techniques and the importance of the working alliance. Finally, we will conclude the chapter with information about the termination phase of the case and attempt to match client behaviors with criteria for progress.

The first phase

We begin by providing identifying information about the client. The client was a man in his early thirties who had been married for 10 years and who had just separated from his wife. The couple had no children. He was currently employed in a full-time technical position, a job he had held for the past year and a half. At the same time, the client was enrolled as a student at the local university, where he was pursuing a graduate degree in the field associated with his career interests and present job. At the time he began counseling, he was working on the final requirements for his degree. The client was a handsome man of shorter than average height whose weekly routine at the time he began counseling consisted mainly of work and exercise. He spoke in a generally rapid and articulate manner, except when his affect threatened to overwhelm him.

The client had had no previous professional counseling. He was highly motivated to begin work in counseling, appeared to have a history of several stable and supportive relationships with others, and showed evidence of the ability to be curious about himself and to think and remember. Finally, he was clearly in considerable psychological discomfort from which he desired relief.

In addition to some of the above-mentioned readiness factors, another factor initially presented itself in the decision about whether to accept the client for treatment. The client had been referred by another of the counselor's current male clients with whom the new client was well acquainted. Because the counselor did not know the nature or the extent of the relationship between these two men, part of the initial interview was devoted to ascertaining the appropriateness of accepting the new client for further work on these grounds. After listening to the new client, the counselor decided that the relationship between these two clients would not preclude accepting the former in counseling. Further warrant for this decision was taken from the fact that the client who made the referral was in the termination phase of his own work and would likely be finishing in the near future. As it turned out, he did terminate within a short time after the new client entered counseling.

The client was accepted into counseling and appointments were set up on a once-a-week basis. Each appointment lasted for 50 minutes. Throughout the course of counseling, the client proved responsible in keeping his appointments, and gave advance notice when he needed to cancel a session. Moreover, he was generally willing to accept the responsibility for working in the hour, except when his emotional problems spoke more strongly than his intellect. The work with this client lasted for almost 100 sessions over a period of 2 years and 3 months.

During the initial or assessment hour, the counselor attempted to determine the client's state of readiness for counseling and to listen for information that would help contribute to a tentative dynamic formulation of the case. Moreover, because the client presented with considerable anxiety and depression, the counselor took care to help the client avoid becoming overwhelmed by his affect. Throughout the first phase, the counselor continued to offer the client a working alliance and to assess the client's responses to this offer. The following verbatim sequences of counselor (CO) and client (CL) dialogue, taken from the first hour, are included below to illustrate the observations from which some of the information was gathered for later completing a formulation of the first phase of the work. The formulation will be presented following the material from the initial interview.

Excerpts from the initial interview

CO.   Why don't you go ahead and tell me what your concerns are and we'll see what we can put together to help.

CL. Okay. Uh. . .I'm just recently separated from my wife which is, uh. . .I really don't think. . .is not a part of the cause, not the real cause. What happened, uh. . .(*sighs, sounds very sad and is near tears*). . .just trying to piece together things from my own mind. I used to work for a private large company. I was having some problems there realizing I just personally didn't want to put up with the pressures and the tensions that went along with the job. It was a well-paying job, paying far more than I could make anywhere else in this town. And, my wife and I were in some disagreement over a decision to leave, and, uh, my present employer called me up and offered a job that I'd held prior to leaving them, plus a few new responsibilities, a little more money. Uh. . . (*sighs, struggles to control affect*). . . but, anyway, I'd made a decision to leave, and there was some friction there [with his wife]. We [he and co-workers from the previous job] went on an out-of-town assignment and that was my last job for them. I work in the technical end of the business producing marketing materials. We'd been working with people from New York for some time and while I was there, I mentioned I was leaving. One of these people offered me a job to work with him in the New York area for a very substantial sum of money and I turned him down. I didn't have to think about it. I know (*laughs*) I couldn't work in New York. But at the same time I was down there, uh, there's a secretary that's worked for a manager there for some time. We have known each other casually. . .(*pause*). . . We got to know each other a little better while we were on this trip. On the way back home we drove together and she just made me realize that. . .(*sobs*). . .something was. . .was wrong somewhere.

CO. Um, hmm.

CL. Just in talking about hopes and aspirations and that sort of thing. Oh, we had talked down there as well, and, uh, I mean there was a strong physical attraction. . . and up until this time I never really considered that I would ever have an affair, but there was one night on the trip that. . .(*sighs*). . .I don't know how those things happen. I guess they just do. I've really stopped trying to figure that out for now. Uh. . . then when I got back home, I just all of a sudden realized that, uh, I'm just kind of. . .going along, just going along, just day to day.And, uh. . .(*big sigh*). . . I've really kind of, I guess, lost myself. I got up one morning right after I got back. . .(*long pause, struggles to hold back tears*). . .

CO. I can see you're feeling kind of blue. . .so take your time.

CL. (*Several sighs*) May I borrow one of those? (*subdued laugh; asks counselor for a cigarette*).

CO. Yes.

CL. When I looked in the mirror, I realized I really didn't know who I was any longer.

CO. When was this?

CL. About 3 weeks ago.

CO. Oh.

In this opening sequence of dialogue, the counselor attempts to stay out of the client's way so that he can report his concerns in the way that is most natural for him. At the same time, the counselor is in tune with the client's struggle to control his nearly overwhelming affective reactions and how he attempts to do so with externalizing, intellectualizing, and summarizing, and activity (asking for the cigarette). The counselor decides to accommodate the resistances in these opening exchanges. In addition, the counselor tries to communicate directly understanding of this struggle when acknowledging the client's depression. While noting the client's presenting complaints and some of the apparently recent circumstances that precipitated them, the counselor also takes the opportunity to ask how long the client has been feeling so badly. The client continues to describe these circumstances and does what he can to communicate his feelings about them.

CL. This all happened very fast, all within the month of April. We went down to the out-of-town job on the first, and here it is the thirtieth. And I tried to live with it, to sort it out for myself, a couple of weeks after I got back, but it kept getting worse. I found myself unable to. . .have any kind of emotional attachment to my wife. I just mean I felt more towards her like you would feel towards, maybe a sister or something.

CO. Um, hmm.

CL. Then, all of a sudden it bothered me. As much as I tried to. . .as hard as I tried to remedy that, nothing's happening. You know, it was getting to a point I was having huge emotional highs and lows and it was extremely tough on her. And about 2 weeks ago, I. . .I guess, this is what stimulated me to. . .to something was wrong, and I seriously considered committing suicide. I don't think I would have, but just the thought that I gave it more than just a passing thought made me realize that, uh, I, you know, was not in command of my. . .I wasn't in control of what was going on. And so we talked one night. . .*(long pause)*. . .and I told her I'd met someone else that really made me feel like I hadn't, you know, felt in a long, long time. I didn't mention to her about the one night out of town, but, uh, I did tell her, that. . .that I was sorry. It's just that I met somebody that just had made me, you know, dream again, if you will. Uh. . .*(long pause*). . .kind of rekindled, if you will, a lot. . .of things I thought I would like to do 10 years ago, and they've just gotten lost.

CO. Um, hmm. What was her reaction to your saying this?

CL. Well, she was shocked and hurt, and then after a while she realized that maybe she was right, that, you know, like we've been having some problems for some time and neither one of us were willing to admit it. And personally, I think. . .well, we'd moved into a house several years ago and we sold that and moved into a condo not too far from here, just last year, and all of a sudden I realized I've been trying to find something in material things that I didn't have.

CO. Yes.

CL. And that she hasn't been able to give up until this time. Uh. . .and she is quite material and she asked me, "Do you think I've been placing too much value on material things?" And my answer was, "Yes." She asked me if I wanted a separation and I said, "Yes." I moved out this weekend, and I have felt somewhat better for it, and I (*nervous laugh*) feel bad because of that, and, uh,. . .in fact it's better than somewhat better.

CO. Uh, hmm. You felt some relief from the pressure.

CL. Oh, definitely. Just like, I mean, she was gone for a week, and in that week I couldn't even stay in. . .in the same place that she had been, or surrounded by a lot of the things we'd had.

CO. What was your reaction?

CL. Hers?

CO. No, yours?

CL. Mine? When I moved?

CO. No. That she was gone. What was going on? What were the signals inside you?

CL. I realized I didn't love her any longer. I called Sandy one night and we got together for dinner. In all honesty, I mean, the same thing I had felt when we were out of town together was still there and she reciprocated. So, we just had a nice dinner, and she went her way and I went mine. The only peace I've really felt, I realize now, not just in the last several weeks, but for a long time is, uh, you know, when she's been around. Now, I don't know if I, it. . .it's because of her or because of what happened. I look back and, uh, in trying. . . . .(*long pause*). . . .to figure out what happened, I think too much happened at one time. There is my wife and her family telling me I was crazy for quitting a job, uh, they saw as having much more future; and then almost disbelief when I mentioned to my wife the thing about the New York position. And yet, when I told them no, I looked them right in the eye (*laughs slightly*), I didn't feel bad about it at all, because I felt it was a decision I had made before. So, I can accept less money to work under less pressure and be around people I enjoy being around.

co. Um, hmm.

The client continues to struggle with his feelings, particularly the guilt and depression. He has taken a stand about what he wants to do with his life and tries to keep it from eroding under the onslaught of his conscience. The counselor tries to help him surface some of the feelings he is having by asking him about his reaction to his wife's leaving for a week. At first, he misunderstands because he thinks he is being asked about his wife's feelings, and then about his reaction to his own moving out. He responds with his thoughts rather than with a description of his feelings because he is not yet able to manage them sufficiently well in the interview. He proceeds, however, to give more helpful information.

CL. I was headed into a managerial position in my former job, but I found out from the 12 months I spent there, I just didn't want to be there. It really bothered me because most of the things I can remember from my whole life, from my father telling me, well, "You have to be a manager, let the other people dirty their hands. You want to be a manager." And, so here I am trying to rationalize that, and, uh. . .(*long pause*). . .and having somewhat of a difficult time with that part. People telling me, "This is not the way this is supposed to work; you're not supposed to do this sort of thing. No, you're supposed to get out there and strive and achieve, no matter what the cost."

co. Yes.

CL. I guess the bottom line is that the personal cost is too high. I couldn't pay that price. I wasn't going to pay that price. And then the emotional and personal side combined. That's almost like a focal point when I look back. So many things seemed to be going on that I didn't really feel good about.

co. Um, hmm. The job and marriage being the two prominent ones for you?

CL. Oh yes. Definitely. And realizing that there was something wrong, I mean. I'd been working for the last couple of years to finish my degree and it's progressing pretty well, but hadn't been really going . . .I've never had trouble with writing assignments before. While I was working for the church, I wrote quite a bit and for about the first 2 years after I was married, I wrote quite a bit and then just seemed to stop. It was hard to be, I want to call it, inspirational.

co. Um, hmm.

CL. I can't concentrate.

co. Are you finding that kind of interruption in your work also?

CL.   Oh yeah. Fortunately, I have a very understanding boss. He knows something is wrong and wants to ask if he can help.

CO.   Any trouble sleeping?

CL.   Oh yeah.

CO.   Can you describe that?

CL.   (*Sighs and pauses*). Well, the whole thing. I was having some physical problems. I have problems with my urinary tract. The doctors don't really know if it's, uh, I have a very good doctor that I've seen. It happened a couple of years ago, right after my father died of cancer of the bladder and I am kind of convinced. . .I don't know. . .if it's a psychosomatic type of deal or not. They are not willing to lay odds one way or another. It's just flared up again about the first week into the month. I look back and it's coming and going at times with what I would call very high stress, anxiety for me.

CO.   Do you think there's a contribution from the emotional side?

CL.   Oh, it's probable that there is.

CO.   What symptoms are you experiencing?

CL.   Oh, it's just a frequent burning sensation, feeling like I would have to urinate; like when you would get nervous anyway.

CO.   Are you feeling a lot of anxiety during the day?

CL.   It comes and goes. I find, uh, it's there most of the time. If it goes away, it's only for a short period of time.

CO.   How long has this been going on in a constant way?

CL.   Well, since the first week of classes. I think since I drove back home with Sandy.

In the material above, the client provides considerably more information about his complaints and he dates the onset of the increase in his physical and psychological symptoms to coincide with his return home after his liaison with Sandy on the out-of-town business trip. His depression also increases over the course of relating this material. The sequence of the client's thoughts and their context are helpful for understanding more about how the client's mind works to try to protect himself from pain. Notably, his thoughts began with his thinly disguised rationalization of his guilty pleasure about the affair with Sandy, proceeded to his wife and job, continued on to his almost defiant stand about how he would not live his life, then on to his father and the latter's unacceptable career aspirations for him, and finally to his physical symptoms. The client concludes that his present state is due to a combination of events, but has not made clear yet just what the specifics are that led him to this conclusion.

However, from a psychoanalytic perspective, it is assumed that the sequence of this material is not random. For example, the counselor suspects that enjoying himself sexually with Sandy induced guilty thoughts related to his father, which in turn aroused his fear, anger, and defiance. Indulging his angry thoughts about his father elicits further guilt and somatic symptoms as a way of atoning for his misdeeds. In any case, the client is not well defended against any of his painful thoughts or feelings at the present time, and it remains for the counselor to help him manage this in the interview so that he does not become overwhelmed.

In response to the obvious difficulty the client is having in talking about his actions and the events that have made him feel so badly, the counselor decides to help him focus on something else for the moment. Implicit in the client's material is his idea of how he would rather be living his life if he had the opportunity. The counselor therefore asks him to describe where he wants to go or where he wants to be with his life. The client responds by talking about how he has always wanted to be a writer. He goes on to mention that he would like to move to a remote, less populated part of the country and settle down to write stories. He continues in this vein for a short period of time and then returns, once again, to the problem of justifying to himself his decision to leave his wife.

CO.   You seem to be doing a lot of blaming yourself right now.

CL.   I think so. No, I don't think so. I mean. . .

CO.   What's that about?

CL.   Oh, I think it's all tied in the same thing. Uh, like a lot of it right now is I really don't have a desire for reconciliation with my wife, at all. I just, I don't even see it. I don't even want it and that bothers me. I think it was reinforced when I finally moved out. I felt better (*sighs*). . . . .I guess I realized what I was letting happen.

CO.   With Sandy, you mean, or. . . .?

CL.   No, with my wife, 'cause I was letting her lead my life for me. It had gotten so difficult to fight her, I just stopped.

CO.   She was the one who'd make most of the decisions then.

CL.   Oh, a lot of them. I found myself over the last year or so starting to resent that. The friction was growing all the time. I think she had got used to that. The bottom line was it just became easier to stop fighting her all the time. I blame most of this on me, just letting her do it.

CO.   An example would help us here. Does one come to mind where you were having an interchange with your wife?

CL.   Oh, I guess that's hard. I can't put my finger specifically on anything. I got to a point I didn't feel like she wanted me to help her do anything. Maybe just a lack of emotional support when I really needed it, and she just wasn't there. Or, I'd be feeling really troubled, and, uh, I'd go to her to sit down and talk, and it would be like a 10-minute deal. She'd say, "Oh, well, look, you'll feel better after we go to a movie, or after we do this or that." It just wasn't working. We seemed to have two different ideas of what we wanted when we went somewhere.

The client reveals his essentially dependent manner of relating to his wife, and her apparent willingness to accept his passivity. He describes as well his growing resentment. But, rather than recognize his own contribution to this relationship pattern, he blames his wife. What they appear to have had going is a kind of war between them. If it was his idea, it was a good one; if it was hers, it wasn't; and *vice versa*. During the exchange above, the counselor attempted to intervene with a cognitive appeal to help the client begin thinking by providing examples rather than continue complaining. The counselor sensed that the client was feeling in better control at the moment and wanted to determine how he might respond to this attempt at helping him split the ego. The intervention was only partially successful. While the client was not able to recall a specific example of their contentious interaction, he nonetheless, described the pattern in general terms, so that the counselor was able to infer its broad outlines from the client's perspective. The counselor tries once again to intervene with a cognitive appeal, as follows below.

CO.   How is it you got yourself into such a painful relationship?

The client is still unable to be reflective in response to this intervention. Instead, he recounts some of the historical events at the time of his marriage and in doing so provides important information.

CL.   (*Sighs, long pause*). I got married right after I finished my 4-year work commitment with the church group. I relate that, at the time . . .it's like you come back, you're expected to get married. Nancy, my wife. . .I have an older sister, Nancy, and my wife's name is Nancy, so it gets a little confusing. . .they became very. . .well . . .close friends, not very close friends. And when my parents moved to the coast from here, my wife, Nancy, was always there to meet me when I came home on vacation and she had gotten very close to my parents. I'd come back and she'd be in the house, and it was expected, certainly by her family, she's Greek, and later by mine, that we'd just get married. There was really never any doubt. The mistake I think I made, a long time ago, was just falling into that and not saying, "No, I need to live by myself for a while to make up my own mind." I went with the church group at 17, right out of high school, spent 4 years working on different Indian reservations, came right back and got married.

The client continues with a recital of his history by describing how often the family moved, how he never had a great deal of security as a youngster, did not make any close friends because of the frequent moves, and how, to this day, he does not have "one close friend." He provides useful information about the possible way in which his wife Nancy and his older sister Nancy are confused in his mind. He concludes this by saying:

CL.   I don't know what happened. I don't know when Nancy and I stopped growing together and started going in entirely different directions, but I feel now that we have.

CO.   Do you have any children?

CL.   No, no. . .(*long pause*). . .that was a point of contention earlier in the marriage.

CO.   On whose part?

CL.   Well mine. I wasn't. . .all I can remember of my childhood growing up is my parents arguing. It's funny, I never really thought it would bother me, but maybe it did, because she wanted to be married and have a family and I really didn't want to have any children, and I don't know whether she acquiesced to that or what. The decision was just made that we didn't care to have any children. Ah, I guess there's something else that really bothers me while we're on the subject. I mean, uh, I don't know if it's due to my age, and realizing that I'm not going to be around forever, wanting to perpetuate the species. . . Sandy and I were talking somewhere along these lines the other night. All of a sudden I realized that if I was going to have children, this is the woman I'd like to have them with. And that affected me quite deeply, because I never had a stirring for years and years. . .like that, and, uh, that upset me quite emotionally.

CO.   My sense is that you're able to share more intimacy with Sandy than you were able to with Nancy, is that true?

CL.   It doesn't make any sense, but that's right. I never felt this comfortable with anybody, and were at a point where things are coming up that you talk about that you. . .(*hesitates, struggles with sad feelings*). . .I never really talked about with anybody else, because I know that she'll understand. Where, if a lot of them came up with Nancy that she'd, I mean, I tried before and it didn't work and I guess I just stopped trying, because it hurts when somebody laughs at your dreams. I think that. . .that leaves a scar that you forget about and then it starts coming back. And the way I felt was. . .it's due primarily to the first week of this month and my night with Sandy, and all the things I closed away. All the gremlins, and the problems, like, uh, the doors in your mind, they just all opened up. . .(*cries*).

CO.   I understand.

The end of the hour was drawing near, so when the client composed himself, the counselor inquired what he knew about counseling and the counselor. These queries were posed to determine the client's pre-formed expectations about counseling and the counselor.

CO. What do you know about counseling?

CL. Not much more than you learn in a few psychology classes. Unfortunately when it comes to you, I don't know how much good that does, 'cause you try to rationalize, and. . .

CO. Well, let's start with that. What do you know about me?

CL. All I really know about you (*slight laugh*) is that, uh, I needed to find somebody to talk to, and when Al found out I was having problems, he recommended you as somebody I could come and talk to, somebody that had really helped him. Uh. . .(*pause*) and I just realized that I needed some help to try and, uh, straighten things out for me.

CO. You've not had any counseling before?

CL. No, I considered it a couple of years ago. I think that might have been another mistake if I didn't do it, because even then I realized things were just not going along the way I really thought they should.

CO. Sometimes we have to hurt an awful lot before a decision is made to ask for help. My recommendation would be, with the kind of problems you're describing, that you try counseling on a once-a-week basis. Do you know anything about your circumstances right now that would prevent you from keeping once-a-week appointments?

CL. No. I know I need to get some things straightened out.

CO. Well, the most important, immediate kind of thing is to help you reduce that tension level.

CL. I mean, it's a matter of, you know, I have all the classic symptoms. I've lost weight (*laughs*), I'm not sleeping, I'm irritable.

CO. Do you know what those are symptoms of?

CL. Mmm, what? Symptoms of, I don't know, being under stress or anxiety or indecision.

CO. Those are symptoms of depression.

CL. I guess I've never thought of it as being really depressed, but I (*laughs*) am.

CO. You're pretty blue, I think.

The remainder of the session is taken up with making arrangements for the client's next appointment, and of encouraging the client to call the counselor in the intervening week if his feelings become urgent.

CO. If those feelings get too intense, why not give me a call?

CL. I'll be okay till next week. I guess the biggest problem is, I mean, that I would give in to the urge, to, uh, just to call Sandy, to meet her.

CO. Um, hmm.

CL. As strong as that urge is there's another one saying that, "You can't do that."

(*Session ends.*)

Given these observations from the initial interview and those gathered over the next 2–3 months, the counselor developed the case formulation that can be found in Table 10.1.

The flow of insight: the working-through phase

Toward the end of the third month of counseling, the client was feeling better about himself. His depression had lifted considerably and he was less anxious. With his affect under better control, he was much more responsive to the counselor's attempts to help him become curious about himself and to provide specific details about his concerns. For example, considerable time was spent in helping the client deal with both his fears and his anger in dealing with his wife regarding a divorce. As it turned out, he and his wife were able to cooperate, albeit reluctantly, in moving toward a divorce settlement that would be fair to both of them. Moreover, he was weathering the ordeal of working with the lawyers and his wife over the lengthy waiting period without the crippling guilt and depression he had experienced earlier. He felt better because they were both behaving reasonably with each other. At this juncture, then, his presenting complaints had lessened due to his acceptance of the working alliance the counselor offered him.

He resumed a relationship with the young woman, Sandy, with whom he had been sexually intimate while on the out-of-town business trip a month before he entered counseling. He was strongly attracted to her, yet fearful of his own wishes and feelings in this regard. The couple spent a few weekends together away from the city in which they lived. Most of their time on these weekends was spent in love-making, intimate conversation, and long walks. During these encounters, the young woman introduced the client to new methods of sexual foreplay which exhilarated this heretofore sexually inhibited man, but which also left him feeling depressed and guilty for most of the following week. After their fourth and final weekend together, the client reported that he had learned his companion was a long-term drug addict and that she had been using drugs regularly while she was with him. She had also urged him to try some drugs at this time. This greatly angered and disappointed the client. Her response was to get angry

Table 10.1 Case formulation of the initial phase of counseling

Presenting complaints
Not able to feel close to his wife.
Some initial suicidal thoughts accompanied by thoughts that he was not in control of what was going on.
Complained that he was indecisive.
Unable to complete the final requirements for his degree.
Difficulty concentrating.
Flare up of urinary tract problem accompanied by frequent mild-to-moderate pain and urge to urinate.
Complained that he was confused.

Precipitating stress events and dates of onset
Had moved out and separated from his wife the weekend before his first appointment with the counselor.
Had sexual intercourse with another woman while on an out-of-town business trip 3 weeks prior to first session.
Left a previous well-paying job in the private sector to work in the public sector over a year ago.
Father died 3 years ago.

Defenses
Regression (e.g. often cried when feeling remorseful during early sessions).
Repression (e.g. "I'm quite confused"; forgotten aggressive and loving wishes and experiences inhibit assertiveness which shows up as, among other things, moral anxiety accompanied by indecisiveness).
Turning against the self (e.g. depression; self-reproach; suicidal ideation).
Splitting the affect (e.g. often generalizes rather than provides detail; provides conclusions without saying how he arrived at them; summarizes by glossing sequential details).
Active into passive (e.g. "Rather than fighting with my wife, it's easier to let her make the decisions"; rather than initiating sex with a woman, waits for her to make the first move).
Somatization and Displacement (e.g. urinary tract flares up during stressful times with wife and father).
Reaction formation (e.g. overcompliance, conscientiousness, and concern about following the rules, yet longing to do as he pleases).

Predisposing influences
The client was raised in a conservative, middle-class family, the second oldest of four children and the oldest of two sons. He had one older and one younger sister and one younger brother. He remains closest to the oldest sister. The family moved a great deal during the client's childhood and adolescence due to the father's work, which also kept the father away from home for extended periods. The client reports being particularly angry and depressed about one of these moves that occurred when he was in junior high school. He described himself as feeling lost and unable to get his parents to respond to his needs at this time. He reported that his father was a stern disciplinarian with his children and that he was also emotionally distant from the client. During latency, the client recounted that he was made to move his bedroom to the basement so that his sisters and brother might have more room upstairs. He remembers feeling

Table 10.1 (*continued*)

---

rejected and isolated from the family during this time, and believes he was being punished for something.

The father died 3 years prior to the client's entering counseling, and the client reported a sense of relief at his father's death. He had many memories of his father's disapproval of his friends and of his interest in girls. He longed for a closer relationship with his father, and felt rejected by him. He described his mother as domineering, critical, and in league with his father's intentions for him. Reports that none of the children felt close to mother. Mother apparently acquiesced to the husband in most matters pertaining to the family. He reported never speaking back to his father in anger, but having had frequent arguments with his mother.

The older sister married soon after she finished college, but the marriage ended in divorce shortly thereafter. She and the client would occasionally console each other about their parents' perceived mistreatment of them when they were children, and the client reported that he now turns to his older sister for solace. This sister is again having difficulty maintaining her second marriage. The youngest sister was also reported to be having serious marital difficulties at the time of the client's entry into counseling. The younger brother, the youngest of the four siblings, has recently married against his mother's wishes. The client believes the brother married because his wife was pregnant. Contact between the two brothers has been minimal, partly because of a 12-year difference in their ages, and partly because they were never close.

The client dated infrequently in high school, had a few close male friends, and became active in a rock band for a brief time. The group would rehearse in the client's home, but this displeased his father so he gave it up. Toward the end of his high school career, he began dating a girl of whom the parents approved. They expressed the wish that he marry her after graduation. Instead of complying with their request, he joined a church group that did altruistic work with migrant workers and native Americans and moved to another part of the country immediately upon graduation. He had made a commitment to work with this group for 4 years. During the course of his work, he and the young woman corresponded and, at the same time, she kept in close contact with his family. As his time for his release from the religious group drew near, the client decided rather impulsively to ask the young woman to marry him when he came home. The couple did so, and the client's parents were very pleased with his decision. Soon after the marriage, the young couple decided, at the client's behest, that they should not have any children. To ensure his part of this agreement, and with his wife's encouragement, the client took unusually strict measures to impede his fertility.

Unanswered questions
During the first phase of the counseling, specific information about the following items was not yet available:

What were the leading personality characteristics of the parents and siblings?
What were the predominant patterns of interaction with the client and among themselves?
How did the client react to the frequent moves?

Table 10.1 (*continued*)

What were the circumstances surrounding the client's joining the religious group upon high school graduation and his marraige immediately following his return home?
What is his former wife like?

Conditions for which the client needs help
In stating the conditions for which help is needed, the counselor drew upon the material provided by the client during the first few months of the work. This formulation was subject to change in light of new information as the case unfolded.

The pattern of the client's defenses and elements of his history, both of which indicated a generally obsessive style of thinking, acting, and handling feelings, and interacting with significant others, suggested that a portion of his emotional development had been fixated to the anal-aggressive and phallic-oedipal stages. Rather than cooperate with his wife or his parents, he would become passive and obstinate. He had strong defenses against regression to angry wishes and fantasies in his relationships out of his fear of his father's retaliation. At the same time, he had rather strong needs to re-enact the oedipal situation in his fantasies, and in some of the romantic relationships he became involved in following his subsequent separation and divorce. A major motive for a few of the relationships he engaged in was the satisfaction he received from trying to take away another man's wife or girlfriend; or when he simply enjoyed frustrating other males who had some authority over him. Satisfaction was to be paid for with guilt and depression, however.

Thus, his conflicts reveal his ambivalence and the severity of his superego. His decision-making is anguished, as when he wanted to finish the final requirements for his graduate degree to please himself and his dead father, but thought doing so would mean giving in to his faculty supervisors and his father; or when he wanted to enjoy an intimate sexual encounter with a woman and thereby please her too, but felt doing so would incur his father's wrath. In sum, the client had accommodated his oedipal fears by greatly restricting both his masculinity and his pleasure. On the one hand, he married the woman his father approved of in order to placate the latter, but, to spite both his father and his new wife, he would not permit himself to love and cooperate with her or have children with her.

Treatment goals and criteria for progress

Intermediate

Establishment of a firm working alliance will function to temporarily mitigate some of the strong negative affects that arise in consequence of his emotional conflicts.
Achieving relief from guilt-related problems due to separation from wife will help further reduce anxiety and depression.
Improvement in capacity for intimacy and mutuality will be reflected in choice of more mature romantic partners.
Finishing requirements for graduate degree will reflect improvement in capacity for collaboration with other males.

Table 10.1 (*continued*)

Longer-term

Understanding some of the developmentally-based factors within him that have contributed to his emotional problems will promote insight and further behavior change.

Plan of action
Weekly, insight-oriented counseling.
Offering the client a working alliance in which he will be encouraged to report freely and work collaboratively in understanding the significance of the material.
The focus of the counselor's interventions will likely proceed in this order:

1. Promote understanding of the relationship between recent precipitating stresses, such as the out-of-town affair, asking his wife for a divorce, moving out, and his depression and guilt.
2. His relationship with his wife.
3. His current romantic relationships, and those with his co-workers and faculty.
4. His family and the past.

Resistances will be confronted and clarified (e.g. his tendency to resist open communication in providing specifics, self-reproaches, rationalization, and the like) when they become available.

---

in return and to inform the client that she had no intention of stopping her drug usage. The client terminated the relationship at this juncture.

The client's reporting of this episode and his attempt to understand it marked the beginning of the middle phase of counseling. Rather than sink into a bottomless depression because of the guilt he felt about his behavior with the woman, and the disappointment over the break-up, the client was now able to manage these affects better and, importantly, to wonder what led him to take up this relationship in the first place.

The key material that led, over time, to the surfacing of some of his underlying conflicts was his problematic stance toward women in whom he was romantically interested. For a considerable amount of time during the middle phase of counseling, his abiding manifest concerns had become: (a) dealing with the ambivalence of deciding whether or not to date a woman, and if he did, whether or not to become sexually intimate with her; and (b) struggling again with indecision about finishing his graduate study and its increasingly clear tie to his perception of his late father's wishes for him. These concerns surfaced in the context of his transference relationship with the counselor. The resistances against exploring the transference components of these issues were motivated by: (a) fear of his conscience, which was related to his wishes to violate his father's/counselor's prohibitions; and (b) fear of his father's/councelor's disapproval and rejection for having done so. These resistances often made it difficult for him to tell the counselor what he was thinking in this regard, or to provide the details about the actual experiences he was having with women or what he was doing about his academic work. To do so risked a return of the guilt and depression and the fear of the counselor's disapproval.

Initially, gentle confrontations of the resistances, and the counselor's willingness to accommodate them when appropriate, led to the client's tolerance for experiencing these affects and examining their associated ideas and memories in the session. Quite naturally, much of the content had to do with his thoughts about and memories of his father, mother and male authority figures in his life.

A considerable amount of progress was made during the remainder of the first year and the first half of the second year in helping the client acquire an intellectual understanding of his central emotional difficulties. Gradually, he began to report in greater detail his wishes and some of his current experiences with women. He became adept at recognizing when some of his fears were about to surface when on a date or when simply interacting with a woman, and he was able to pinpoint what was troubling him. During this time, he began to recognize that he wanted the counselor's approval of him and his permission to pursue his sexual interests in a woman. But, at the same time, he also adopted an aggressive stance in reporting these matters to the counselor. On occasion, he became defiant with the counselor and said he "was going to do what he wanted to," even though he was convinced the counselor would disapprove of it. Just as often, he would undo his defiant stand by reassuring the counselor he was not going to jump in and out of bed with every woman he met. The client's transference reactions had now become problematic for him, and for the counselor, too.

The transcript material presented below contains material relevant to the client's transference reaction. It is included here to help illustrate several principles of psychoanalytic counseling that we have presented in previous chapters. We hope to show how the client's transference reactions to the counselor at this point in the work facilitated his achievement of additional insight. Our discussion of this matter will be framed in terms of the model of the path of client understanding presented in Chapter 4. In this way, we will call attention to relevant client and counselor events and their interactive sequence in the session.

In the interview prior to the one to be presented below, the client was defiant in his reporting about a young married woman to whom he was attracted and who he was now dating. At one point the counselor confronted the client about his motives for intruding himself into an intact marriage. This helped him see both the pleasure he took in going against his father's proscriptions and the fear he felt in reporting the details to the counselor.

He had, thus, become aware of his transference reactions to the counselor. This material served as a precipitant for some of his thoughts and actions during the ensuing week, and was still on his mind when he returned for his next appointment.

CL. Well, let's see. I talked to Nancy earlier this week on the phone and changed the stipulation on which our condo would be sold. We will split all the assets and everything else.

CO. Um, hmm.

CL. I don't think we talked for about 5 minutes before we were arguing with one another. Actually, what was happening was that she said, "Well, don't get so snippy with me" (*mimics wife's voice*), or something like that.

CO. Yes?

CL. It's funny because I wonder if she noticed I was being a little firmer, because I wasn't really aware of being snippy, whatever snippy is. It upset me for some reason.

CO. You had an argument?

CL. Yeah.

CO. What was that about?

CL. She, Nancy, can still upset me, and my current frame of thought seems to extend to all women. I think I equate that with some kind of control that they can still make me mad. They really can't; it's something I know I'm doing to myself; but still that upsets me for a couple of days. . . . .

CO. Why don't you go back and let's detail that conversation. What was said?

CL. Well, really, I just called her up and, uh. . .I had gone over to see her to take back a few things I had, and I had put in a switch for her and done some other things. It's like we still don't talk (*sighs*). I don't really know what it is, uh, I think part of it was just discussing the stipulation. I have trouble talking to her about the divorce, far less trouble that she has talking to me about it, but that might be a misconception. Um, but all I told her was, "Well, you'll have to make arrangements with my attorney to go down and sign the stipulation." To me that's about the tone of voice I seemed to be using, but all of a sudden she seemed to take it, "Well. Can't you just have it mailed out?" Of course I could have, and jeeze, I think I over-reacted, so I said "Well what!?" and "Come on! If you want me to mail it, just ask me to mail it, don't. . ." As I say, it might have been a misinterpretation, especially on a very sensitive subject. But what I really had trouble understanding is why I let it bother me for as long as I did, and maybe it still is bothering me, somewhat, um. . .

CO.   How did it bother you?

CL.   Well, I was angry. I think I felt again like, jeeze, look what she can still do to me. I think the feeling that upset me more than anything was "Why am I upset? Why am I letting her. . ."

CO.   The feeling was one of being controlled by her?

CL.   Yeah. "Why am I letting her upset me?" was my reaction at the end of the conversation. Uh, I think that kind of set the tone for the rest of the week. It was a lousy week.

CO.   Um, hmm.

CL.   Uh, for the most part, uh, it bothers me. I don't know if. . .I'm not beyond that, but I thought I could handle that a little better, maybe. I mean, there is some progress in at least I recognized it, and I was wrestling with that during the week. Uh, and I managed finally last night. . .that is, I don't know if it's the coming here every week. . .I'm not going to let it bother my weekend and just resolve it as best I could. I just decided to move on because there was, "Why let it bother me any longer? My God, I've already worried about this for 3 days," or something. It's more than enough. Uh, but that wouldn't have bothered me at all, I mean it's still the word "divorce" that carries a lot of connotations for me. I find that difficult and all of a sudden, a lot of these things I started looking at and I wondered how much of this is tied together, in that the only thing my Dad ever approved of for me was working for the church group and marrying Nancy. We talked about some transference and that sort of thing last week, and I think that's true.

CO.   Um, hmm.

CL.   Uh, because I was very apprehensive about coming in here and talking to you today. But now I've got to go in and say, you know. . .The only parental approval I ever really remember was working for the church group and marrying Nancy; and now that I've dissolved the thing with Nancy, I just, you know, I'm without the parental approval of my father. There's no way he can give it to me, obviously, even if he could. Or, even if he would have, it wouldn't have changed the ultimate outcome. I wouldn't have stayed married to Nancy whether he approved or disapproved. But, it hasn't made any difference whether he was living or dead right now. . .

CO.   So it seems.

CL.   There's still the feeling that one of the few things I've gotten his approval on I've undone, and I doubt seriously whether he would approve of my behavior—what behavior?—that is going on now. A lot of that is governing my relations with women because he wouldn't approve of me going out and carousing around, which I'm not doing, uh. . .

CO.   You're doing exactly what he wants you to do.

CL.   I'm sitting here going, "OK. I'm staying home, and I'm being diligent working on my degree requirements. I've got to re-do my paper for the umpteenth time. Uh, I work on my papers, I don't go out and make contact with any of these women. I guess a lot of this might tie into something. At least I've been able to think about, uh. . .relationships with women some this week, and why I am putting up so many walls or drawing so many lines. I have trouble differentiating between what I see is chasing after a lady, and just wanting company; now there's a difference.

CO.   Right.

In this opening segment, three events in our model of the path of client understanding are evident: client complaints within the context of current events, counselor restraint, and counselor empathy. At the outset, the client identifies several complaints arising out of the current events he has experienced. He is angry at his wife and upset with himself for letting his wife "control" his feelings. This reminds him of his father and his need for the latter's approval, and that bothers him too. He is fearful about coming to the counseling session because he is now aware that some of his present thoughts and feelings are related somehow to the counselor. Finally, he is troubled because he has difficulty deciding whether to "chase after" women or just enjoy their company.

Through all of this, the counselor is restrained so that the client can report without undue interruption all the present concerns he has and the dates and circumstances that surround their occurrence. In this way, the counselor learns what is uppermost in the client's mind, what direction his thoughts seem to be taking at this time, and what resistances are beginning to surface. It also becomes clear that the previous session has been on his mind, because the client states that he has thought about some of these things and they seem to be related. But, it is not yet clear which of these complaints will be the chief complaint for the hour. However, the counselor suspects it is likely that the thread that will connect this hour will have to do with the conflict around his guilt and the need for his father's (counselor's) approval.

The counselor also tries to stay in tune with the client's thoughts and feelings and to communicate these to the client. As the client spoke about the angry phone conversation with his wife and his complaint that it upset him, the counselor intervened by asking if the feeling wasn't one of being controlled, and the client agreed. Later, the counselor remarked to the effect that since the client was not out carousing with women, he was doing exactly what his father wanted him to do. Both of these empathic interventions seem to have helped the client provide additional material in this realm.

The client begins the interview with current events, the counselor attempts to be helpful with restraint and with empathic interventions. These events mark the beginning of a sequence of events that lead to later client insight according to our model of the path of client understanding (see Chapter 4). The interview continues from where it left off, again illustrating the use of counselor restraint, along with two additional events in the model: the counselor's use of cognitive appeal to encourage the client to continue the work of thinking and talking, and the client's consequent deepening of the material he is reporting.

CL. And I am having trouble distinguishing that difference. That realization seems so simple; yet, it was such a monumental thing (*laughs*) to me to all of a sudden realize, "Wait! Wait! Wait! Come on. What's wrong if you want her company. I mean,there is a line here; you're not going to call her up every other night and chase after her." No, I'm not going to do that, but there's certainly nothing wrong calling her up on the telephone a couple of times to try and arrange something. I used to think that was cheating. Well, that's been some of the problem. I've never before made a differentiation, so there was no kind of contact. It was always, "Well, you call me." That's always the line I'd use.

CO. Sure.

CL. Uh, like we discussed last week about Darla, it's like I'd say to her, "If you want to do it, that's fine with me. Don't ask me to take any responsibility." I've been thinking about this a lot this past week.

CO. I can see you've done some good thinking. Go ahead.

CL. That's been the amazing problem. It's like I've been waiting to get laid and have that be the miracle cure. As if that would be the important thing. That's not going to make any difference at all. It's going to be nice, but it's not going to make any difference in any real lasting way. Everything's not going to be better that way. That's something that, hopefully, will come. . .

CO. It seems that one meaning this has for you is that you can't enjoy yourself when you are with a woman because of fear of father's disapproval.

CL. Yeah, sure, certainly. Uh, it's like Darla. . .I. . .she. . .(*sigh*). . .I thought this was over and it's not. Uh, she. . .I've met her after class a couple of times to exchange information with her on the paper she was doing. I came out of class the other day and there she was. I could be ignorant and just say, "Hello. How are you? I thought we weren't going to see each other any longer?" But, I think there's a little problem there. No, I don't think there's a problem, there is a problem. It just personifies a lot of other things. I'm not just being chased around by a woman, I. . .I don't know if I'd call it chased, but she's called once since then.

The client continues in this vein and says:

CL. That's a new thing I'm trying to deal with, Uh, I mean, it's (*laughs*) coming here talking about myself. My word, I mean, it's very difficult anyway. I still haven't been able to really reach that, not with any degree of comfort. The thing is that it's hard for me to say to Darla, "Look, I like you. It's nice to see you, but you're married and you've got a family, so leave me alone." Uh. . .it's hard for me to say that because she is giving me something I haven't had for a while and that's, you know, your ego strokes. I think I'm having trouble especially now because everything seems to be in relation to women. It seems to be in such a state of flux, so it's nice to have someone I feel comfortable with. But since she's married, I don't honestly know if I want to do that. I don't know if we can be friends because of that strong physical attraction.

CO. And you are asking me for permission to proceed?

CL. I am. Sure. And in asking you, I'm saying, "Dad. . .", you know, that's why I wanted to talk about it. I wasn't going to talk about it today, but that's exactly it. I mean here's somebody to give me permission to go ahead. But that's impossible, nobody can do that for me.

CO. Just talk about the urge to get my approval for that.

In the sequence above, the counselor intervenes with a technical manipulation in telling the client that he has already done some good thinking about the understanding he has achieved *vis-à-vis* his conflictual relationship with the married woman, Darla. This portion of the intervention is intended to help further mobilize the forces within the client that are on the side of curiosity and reflection. In the second half of the counselor's intervention, the counselor simply urges the client to continue in the interview with the thinking he has begun during the week. The client does so by deepening the significance of the material. First, he describes his hesitancy in meeting Darla after class. Then he shares how his attraction to her and his relationship with her help him see how the problem is general to his relationships with other women, and how it is difficult to talk about this with the counselor.

In the next sequence, we will note the occurrence of resistance to proceeding with the material and the counselor's attempts to highlight the resistance. Initially, the client does not respond to the counselor's request to talk about the client's wish for the counselor's approval. Instead, he continues with how he is of two minds about the relationship with Darla. Once again, the counselor tries to bring him back to the topic of wanting the counselor's approval.

CO. Please talk about what it feels like to want me to approve of that.

CL. I think what it is. . .is, I don't know, dependency on. . .what? I guess as a child, I so much wanted my father around, and he never was. Uh, that I still seek his approval even now, uh, on some things, and I. . .it really hurts not to have it.

The client finds it easier to talk about the remot past and his father at this point rather than about his feelings about the counselor in the present. Once again, he returns to the topic of Darla and his ambivalence. The counselor now intervenes with a confrontation in the hope of further highlighting the client's resistance. This is only partially successful, but the ongoing material presents further opportunities to help the client deal with the avoidance of talking about his rebellious feelings toward the counselor.

CO. You're having some trouble centering your thoughts on me right now, aren't you?

CL. Yeah. Face it, I mean, I'm seeing a married lady and you're right (calls counselor by name), if I wanted to, I could take her to bed. I thought about that this week. I mean, I reached the line with her and that was it, and I started thinking about it. I could do it, it wouldn't take much persuasion on my part to do that.

CO. I can't help notice the defiance in your eyes as you say that.

CL. Um, hmm, sure there is. I think what I see is, "All right, I'm going to do it anyway." There is so much of this tied up, it. . .it just seems to be related; I (*pause, sighs*). . .but, I, I don't understand why. I think knowing that I can take Darla to bed is. . .is rebellion against something; against somebody telling me, "No. You can't do this."

CO. And what does that feel like, that rebellious feeling?

CL. I think it feels a little juvenile actually (*laughs*). It's there. It isn't all that bad. I was never a rebellious teenager. I just went along and did pretty much everything that was expected. And now, I want to be rebellious. I want to do something rebellious. I want to do something that is not socially acceptable. Unfortunately, it's not acceptable to me either, taking Darla to bed. It would be really nice, but I, honestly, you know, it's a ridiculous situation. It's not going to do either one of us any good. But we have something out of it; she's getting something from me, and I'm getting something from her, you know. . .uh, I seemed to have slipped away from the point (*sigh*). . .

The counselor tries to help the client pick up his prior train of thought about his rebellious wishes, and says:

CO. The urge is to want my approval, but at the same time to argue with me.

CL. Yes, that's right. . .(*sighs*)

CO. Feels like I'm controlling you. . .

CL. I think that's it. It was the same thing with my faculty committee.

The client then goes on to describe how his committee wanted changes in his program and some of his written work. He reports feeling angry and rebellious with them and wants to tell them off. Yet, he takes back this anger by saying the decision to finish his degree is actually his own. The counselor again points out the client's resistance:

CO. I think you're avoiding your feelings of confrontation with me.

CL. Yes, I am. I'm working around that in every way I can, because if I do that, if I come up here and have a confrontation with you, I mean it's going to be like having a confrontation with my father, and wanting to say, "Enough is enough! You've controlled me. You've had your life; however you lived it was your business. Just let me live mine, whether you approve or disapprove. Yes, I want your approval, that means a lot; but I can live without it if I have to." And it's that statement that I don't really believe. I have trouble making that break, thinking I want your approval but I don't have to have it. That's not true. What I want is your approval on anything that I'm unsure of.

CO. Um, hmm.

CL. Okay. I'm beating my head against the wall to finish my degree to the exclusion of other things. That's acceptable. Going out and playing around with women is not acceptable. So what I look for is approval that it's okay to go out and see these women. I still have to laugh at myself because I come in here and I'm so damned uncomfortable about talking about seeing these ladies. I feel like I'm jumping in and out of bed with every woman I see, and that's far from the case. I'm still really uncomfortable and that stems from my saying to myself, "Jesus, what would Dad think. Oh, God!" That is still governing a lot of my behavior. Maybe the best thing my father ever did for me is die. That is really a powerful statement, but his control still goes on. It's funny because he was never around. It's something I've constructed. Here you are (*speaking to counselor*), you know, a lot of it is transferred so, "If (*uses counselor's name*) says it's OK, then it's probably OK."

CO. Let's just try to continue following your thoughts about this feeling of being approved or disapproved of and of being controlled.

The client continues to talk about the trouble he has distinguishing between taking advice from someone, like his faculty committee, and being defiant. The counselor then offers the following interpretation:

CO.   I believe the wish here is that I would say, "No, you may not go to bed with Darla," so then you would have a real excuse to be angry and defiant with me.

CL.   Sure, it would be wonderful, but how can I. . .? I could sit here and be angry and defiant, but I still wouldn't do it (go to bed with Darla) anyway; she's a married lady. Like we talked about last week, if she makes the decision, then the responsibility's not mine. Well, that's crap. I can't live with that, it's that simple. I don't know how I'm going to deal with that problem, but I know it won't be in bed. I think that comes from the realization that going to bed with a lady is not going to make everything better; that's not the cure.

The client seems to agree with the counselor, but only with the part about how nice it would be to go to bed with Darla. He continues to avoid exploring his angry and defiant feelings with the counselor. The counselor then intervenes with another confrontation.

CO.   I think you're rationalizing right now and that helps you avoid the feelings of conflict you have with me.

CL.   Uh, well, the honest to God's truth is, yeh, I wouldn't mind taking her to bed at all, and then I'd be getting it from two sides. One, she is married and there's a certain social stigma of my own that I have trouble dealing with, let alone trying to deal with your approval or disapproval. Having to tell you I've gone to bed with a lady is part of the reason I won't do it. I would feel terribly uncomfortable walking in here and sitting down on this couch and telling you, "Well (*uses counselor's name*), I went to bed with a married woman." I don't know exactly what I expect you to do, chastise me, like, "Well, you shouldn't have done that. Shame, shame."

CO.   What else do you imagine?

CL.   Oh, I think what it is is that it's just Dad sitting there and going, "You did what?" and I'm really being chastised for that.

CO.   So, the fear would be that I'd sit here and I'd be somehow dismayed and say, "You did what?!"

CL.   It would be immense disapproval from someone who's approval I really desire. I really want that approval.

CO.   So, right now, you're feeling disapproved of.

CL.   Um, sure, but I think what I feel is I should have said no when I saw her and when she called me. I should have said, "Get lost. You're married; I don't want to have anything to do with you." But that's not really the way I feel. So, I'm at odds with myself. I like her, she's a nice lady, but I think I have enough control of myself to keep her, you know, to keep it out of the bedroom; to stop, to not have sex.

CO. It sounds like you're trying to reassure me that that isn't going to happen.

CL. Sure, I think I am, and I'm trying to reassure myself, too. She calls up and wanted to stop by the apartment, and I said no, because I'm not sure I can do that; I think I can, but I don't know if I. . .I feel that it would be damaging to me to take her to bed.

CO. The bottom line is that you don't want to come in here and tell me you've taken her to bed.

CL. Sure, that's the bottom line, uh. . .and that bothers me. I mean that I am now doing some things, not doing some things, because I have to come in here and tell you about them. That's a problem?

CO. You mean the conflict with me?

CL. Uh, huh, but I also realize it can't just be you. It's what you represent to me, which, in a lot of cases, is a father figure and authority. Someone who can approve or disapprove of what I do. Then I realize that, still, the bottom line is I never have to walk through that door again.

CO. As if you'd be saying, "Screw you Dad!"

Following this intervention, the client finally begins to recall in broad outline some memories. He has begun to proceed from his transferential reactions to the counselor to their antecedents in his thoughts and feelings about his father.

CL. Yes, exactly. "Take that, Dad!" A lot of that emotion is tied up between wanting to love him and really not. . .uh. . . . . .uh. . .it's almost a feeling of hate, you know, because he was never around; wanting so much to have a father like the other kids and he was just never there. If I look back, there were a lot of nights I hated him for not being there. And it didn't get much better when the only thing he approved of was my joining the church group and going away to work with them. Because I knocked my brains out to get good grades in school, uh. . .I worked almost every night. I did play in a rock and roll band but he didn't like that. Maybe that was my teenage rebellion, I don't know, but it hurt, and it still hurts to look back and know that now I can sit here and say I really hated my father. He's a man I really didn't know the last few years of his life. Others can look back and see a picture perfect relationship; father and son playing baseball in the front yard and that sort of thing. That just never happened, and I think I missed that. I really dislike him for not being there when I needed him and for leaving me with my mother. I mean, he was out doing what he had to do to make a living. I'll rationalize it a little bit.

CO. You mean you are going to take back your anger?

CL. Yeh, sure. I'm really mad to this day that he wasn't there, and he isn't here now. I think, in a lot of ways, I still want to say, "Let me explain, especially about my marriage with Nancy. See, it just wasn't working. It was just stifling me." So, here I'm going to try to explain it to you, uh. . .I didn't realize how much of that was really there. Still, coming down here and letting our sessions uh. . .influence my behavior. Just the fact that I have to come here and talk to you, the influence, you know, what I do or won't do. . .um. . .it's not something I'm real comfortable with.

CO. I appreciate that and I understand how uncomfortable that makes you; but, if you can continue to pursue it, we'll learn a great deal.

The client returns to his ambivalence and in decisiveness regarding Darla. He mentions how the fact that she is a mother and is married is like "poison" and he should "head for the exit sign." The counselor responds:

CO. Part of the basis for the attraction is that she's married, and there is that silent member here again, her husband.

CL. I think I'm upset at myself because I can't say "Go away." I feel somehow that I want my Dad's approval again, or society's.

CO. There seems to be a part of you that wants to take this woman away from her husband.

CL. Yeh, and that's the problem, because if it is, then it's only for a little while, you know, I'm not looking for any kind of a long-term relationship. But, here's another man's wife. So, if you look at it on a sexual conquest basis, guess what? I win this time. I don't like that either.

CO. Darla represents such a fantastic set of possibilities for solving several problems at once.

CL. Yes.

CO. On the one hand, you can reverse the pain you felt with Sandy, and on the other, you can also tell me and your Dad, "Go to hell! Look what I've done."

CL. That is the appeal right there. What a terrific opportunity to do all these things.

CO. You wouldn't want to be defiant unless you felt that I had some stake in deciding how you should enjoy yourself.

CL. Um, hmm, yeh. It ties in so well with a lot of other things I'm doing right now. I'm exerting myself in a lot of different areas, and now I'm slowly moving into this sexual area, which is the hardest one of all. And I am still very uncomfortable coming down here again and again, because to me, I sound like a sex maniac, it's on my mind all the time. It's not on my mind all the time. So now I'm trying to explain to you that it's not.

With his typical ambivalence, the client continues to explore how his conflicts over the relationship with Darla manifest themselves and how they tie in to his guilty feelings about wanting his father's approval.

CL.   See, here it is again. I don't want you to think that all I think about is going to bed with women, and so, I'm not going to see anyone. One thing Darla has done for me is make me realize it's nice to have a lady around, and that's something I think I just pushed out all together.

CO.   One of the reasons you married Nancy was that there was no conflict in that because it was sanctioned by your father.

CL.   Yes, that's right.

CO.   Any woman that you went out with on your own, out of your own initiative and interest would bring you into conflict with your father.

CL.   Truly. And now I think I'm ready to at least face some of the conflict, not only with him, but within myself.

The session ends shortly thereafter. In this session, the client has learned more clearly how he has been living out, in his relationships with women, the counselor, and the male members of his faculty supervisory committee his conflicts involving dominance and submission, guilt and defiance. He has also begun to recognize how he uses avoidance and indecision to cope with the strain the conflicts engender. He is still not at peace with himself about these matters, but he is beginning to recognize that he has more choices about what to think, feel, and do than he previously realized. The counselor's plan of action in this hour included helping him deepen the material with cognitive appeals, confronting his avoidance of his feelings about the counselor, and interpreting some of the more manifest meanings of his feelings for the counselor in terms of their history in his feelings about his father. For his part, the client was able to overcome considerable resistance in talking, however cautiously, about the defiance he felt toward the counselor. He did what he could in recalling similar feelings and attitudes he had experienced with his father during adolescence. Then, he was able to begin the process of examining how these conflicts had been reinstated in several of his present relationships. Through all of this, the working alliance remained firm. Because of the alliance, the counselor was able to confront the client consistently and firmly with the expectation that he would be able to split the ego and reflect on his actions. The client's gain of insight in this hour was not extensive, but it marked the beginning of an increasingly productive phase of working through.

The client continued to make gains in understanding his feelings and his motives. This was in large part due to his increasing ability to notice his own resistances and to work on clarifying them with the counselor's help. For example, he began to suspect that his long-standing aloofness from his mother, and his reluctance to visit her, were related to how he felt about his late father. After a period of time in which his relationship with his mother was focal in the interview material, he began to surface affectionate feelings for her, as well as concern for her well-being. He also became concerned about his younger brother's welfare. He reported many memories in which he longed to be closer to his mother, but was afraid his father would disapprove. He recognized that, in consequence, he had withdrawn from her emotionally and, moreover, had arranged to stay physically distant from both his parents when he and his former wife moved to his present location many miles away. He began to regret that he had not been closer to his younger brother and of more help to him.

He took the opportunity afforded by a vacation period to travel to his mother's home and made elaborate plans about what he was going to do for her around her house and how he was going to entertain her while on his visit. These plans even included taking her to a tea dance, something she had always enjoyed. Since the younger brother also lived in the same city, his plans included spending time with him, as well. On his return, the client reported that the visit had gone well, and while he experienced some of the old strain he used to feel in his relationship with his mother, he was satisfied that he could now enjoy her company as her adult son. He also reported that his younger brother had appreciated seeing the client and seemed willing to get to know him better.

He also began to recognize the rather serious emotional problems that had long plagued his older sister, and how the two of them had reinforced each others' fears and avoidant behaviors in dealing with their parents and each other. He explored the ways in which he had identified his wife with his sister, and how this had been a factor in his decision to marry his wife. He felt badly for his sister and her present marital difficulties, but was able to pinpoint several ways in which she was contributing to this difficulty. He began to listen to her more carefully in their frequent phone conversations. She remarked how much more confident he seemed. His attempts to understand her were both gratifying to her and made it possible for her to accept his suggestion that she seek professional help.

At the same time the client's relations with his family members were improving, he also began to make progress on finishing his degree. He recognized that his avoidance of this task was fear-governed. It frightened him to have to submit his work to his faculty supervisory committee. He feared they would laugh at his efforts and find him lacking in sufficient intelligence to complete his program. He just didn't feel prepared to be evaluated on his work. Again, in this area, he felt like a little boy whose body was being compared to those of the grown men on his committee. He had chosen to handle these fears of masculine competition by avoidance and defiance. These oedipal themes began to dominate the material in this portion of the middle phase of counseling.

Progress was achieved in this area when the client began to understand that he had been treating a faculty evaluation of his work in finishing the degree requirements as if it were a character and fitness test administered by his father. He just knew he could never match his father's mental and physical equipment, so why try? He would be hurt if he competed in this way. He began to see that behind his conscious attitude of defiance of what he perceived his father's wishes to be was his fear that he would be judged as inadequate. Once again, his father would have won and he would have lost. Surfacing these fears and their associated ideas put them into perspective and gave his healthy ego the opportunity to weigh them against reality. He was able to accept the fact that his faculty were on his side and eager to help him succeed. He began to actively seek the assistance of his major advisor and to cooperate with the latter's suggestions for improvements in his written work. While these experiences were still somewhat frightening for him, the client moved ahead by presenting even more of his work to his academic supervisors. His confidence in his own ability to think, write, and critically evaluate his work grew steadily, as did his capacity to enjoy and take realistic pride in what he was doing in this area.

Concerns about his romantic life were never far removed from his interview material during the middle phase of the work. His sexuality was a sensitive barometer to both his long-standing emotional problems and to his current state of well-being. His relationships with women were the arena in which his ambivalence was the greatest and his resistances the strongest. During the middle phase, he began several other dating relationships and they can be placed on a continuum, beginning with maladaptive and ending with adaptive. Following his brief re-encounter with the drug-addicted woman, Sandy, he did not date for several months. Although the counselor attempted to confront this avoidant behavior early on, it was not successful. During a period of time when his conflicts were particularly evident, and he was also very lonely, he decided to date an old friend. Although he was attracted to this particular woman, he felt it was better to keep the relationship platonic and not try to become intimate with her. The couple had several dinner dates followed by long conversations at her apartment. She soon tired of this and invited him to get closer to her. He was not ready to handle intimacy with her, and broke off the relationship. His fears about guilt were still strong and he continued to complain that he could not rid himself of his father's admonitions in regard to sexuality.

This experience was again followed by a period of withdrawal from contact with women. But this time, the client was a bit more curious about his reactions and a little more willing to look at his resistance to exploring these matters. His desires to be with a woman sexually became much more conscious and tolerable during this period, and he began to fantasize about meeting and dating some of the women he saw in his classes and at work. He still had difficulty talking with the counselor about these things, but he was able to provide considerably more material, in any case.

During one rather maladaptive relationship with yet another married woman, the counselor confronted the client about his oedipal motives for the affair. This confrontation had the apparent effect of engaging his reasonable ego because he then surfaced aggressive wishes and feelings he had for both the woman and her husband. He went on to connect this to his recognition of how the affair was another thinly disguised displacement of his anger towards his father and his defiance of him. The counselor and the client continued to work on clarifying this matter for several more sessions, during which he surfaced many memories from his childhood and adolescence related to it. Then, during a subsequent session, he suddenly stopped. When asked what was keeping him from continuing, he struggled against strong affect to speak. Finally, he revealed that he had just realized why he had taken medical action to restrict his fertility. With great sadness and tears, he now understood that he had acted, on the one hand, to defy his father by not producing any grandchildren, and, on the other, to punish himself for his guilty thoughts and actions. The price had been very high. He broke off the relationship with the woman shortly following the insight he had achieved.

Toward the end of the middle phase of counseling, the client met and fell in love with a divorced woman with two children who lived in a distant city. He had been introduced to her by a mutual friend while they were both on vacation at a resort area. This relationship developed slowly and cautiously on the part of both members. During this time, the client reported freely on his thoughts and feelings about his new love. He noticed for the first time that he was also much freer from the ambivalence and guilt which had always accompanied his romantic wishes. The couple spent many weekends together, either with her traveling to his city, or by him driving to hers. She was particularly eager that he meet and know her children. He was somewhat fearful about doing this, but soon developed a genuine affection for them. As the relationship deepened and the client learned more about the woman and about himself in relation to her, he began to contemplate asking her to marry him. After several sessions in which he worked through some of his remaining fears about his capacity for intimacy and for maintaining a long-term relationship with her, the client asked her to marry him and she consented. As plans for the wedding were under way, the client also began to consider the possibility that he might like to have children with her. She was willing to have more children with him and this led him to investigate whether the earlier action that had blocked his capacity to procreate could be reversed.

Termination phase

As the client and his fiancé made their wedding plans, he also finished his final requirements for his graduate degree and went through commencement. Shortly after this, the termination phase was formally ushered in by the client's announcement that he thought the work was coming to an end, and did the counselor agree? The counselor stated that it seemed as though the client was feeling much better about the way his life was going at the present time. They had accomplished a great deal together and, thus, it did seem like a good time to consider ending the work. The remaining 2 months were taken up, not only with continuing to clarify and understand the problems that brought the client to counseling, but now, more importantly, with helping the client in dealing with ending the relationship with the counselor, planning for his marriage, and reviewing what had been accomplished in counseling.

It was expected that issues of separation and loss would become apparent in the client's material as he spoke about termination. Because the thought of termination was painful for the client, he would try to avoid dealing with it whenever his feelings were particularly strong. However, the issue of termination was kept surfaced by the counselor throughout the final phase, so that the client would have maximum opportunity to experience and work through his thoughts and feelings about it. Moreover, by doing this, it was possible for both of them to evaluate the client's readiness to terminate.

In responding to the termination phase, the client briefly experienced some of the complaints that had brought him to counseling in the first place, but in a milder form. He felt depressed, somewhat guilty, and his old ambivalence and indecisiveness returned when he said, at one point, "Maybe getting married isn't such a good idea." The counselor suggested that he might be trying to ask for more sessions by producing additional complaints for the two of them to work on. He laughed and had to agree. He was sad that he would no longer be seeing the counselor on a regular basis, and that all of his emotional problems had not been solved. Yet, he was eager to try things on his own. The client summarized for himself the gains he had made in self-understanding, improved relationships with others, and completing his education. The counselor reassured him that the door was open for him to return at some future time should he want to do so.

The final session was a time for saying goodbye, and not for work (Anderson, 1964). The counselor asked about and discussed with the client the latter's plans for the future. As well, the client inquired about the counselor's plans and the latter told him of them. The counselor thanked the client for the hard work he had done and told him that he, the counselor, had learned a great deal from him about counseling that would benefit future clients. The client expressed his appreciation for the counselor's help and then departed with a warmhearted handshake.

Therapeutic gains

The client's verbal reports and the counselor's observations indicated that the following progress had been achieved by the client over the course of counseling:

1. He had begun to experience intimacy and mutuality in his relationship with his fiancé.
2. His interactions with his fiancé, mother, and siblings were relatively freer from the guilt, depression, and indecisiveness that had dogged him for so long.
3. He had moved forward to finish his graduate education and took pride in his academic accomplishments.
4. He was much less indecisive in his daily life.
5. He had greater insight into both his strengths and vulnerabilities:
   a. He was aware of many of the ways in which his mind worked to protect him from unpleasant thoughts and feelings; e.g. his use of the defenses of denial, active into passive, indecision, reaction formation, and repression, in particular.
   b. He understood how many of his oedipally-based fears and wishes had been reinstated in his adult relationships with his former wife, lovers, mother, and, on occasion, the counselor.

In presenting this case, we are aware that not all of the client's problems were solved, neither could they necessarily be solved within the time that was available. He still has a lot to learn about himself *vis-à-vis* his wife and his new role as a father. We suspect that interactions with his stepchildren will surface some of his old competitive fears, anger, and guilt. It is also likely that when some of his conflicts are active, he will experience indecisiveness. Yet, we believe that the insights the client did achieve helped him begin the process of making structural changes that will result in more satisfaction with himself and others. He knows more about himself now, has choices in thinking and feeling that he did not previously have available, and is more able to move into relationships and monitor his reactions to them. At the same time he is considerably less vulnerable to becoming overwhelmed by his guilt or depression and has, thereby, more access to his good mind. Because the client and his new wife moved to a distant state immediately following termination, we do not know how well the client fared in the months after counseling. We are reasonably certain, however, that, given the client's positive experience with counseling, he will be able to ask for further professional assistance if necessary.

Part III

SPECIAL TOPICS:
COUNSELING WOMEN,
ETHICS AND RESEARCH

11 Psychoanalytic perspectives on counseling women

This chapter has two major aims. First, we present our perspectives on some significant issues raised by feminists and others concerning the appropriateness of applying psychoanalytic counseling approaches and self psychology theory to women. Second, we hope to encourage readers who have serious reservations about rapprochements between psychoanalysis and feminism to think about our perspectives, so that they may apply or adapt what we have suggested in earlier chapters to their work with female as well as male clients. There are various connotations or perspectives on what is meant by feminism. The term can communicate very different ideas for different individuals. What we mean by feminism or a feminist perspective has been succinctly stated by Matlin (1987):

> A feminist is a person whose beliefs, values and attitudes reflect a high regard for women as human beings. A feminist, therefore, is someone who believes that women and men should be socially and economically equal (p. 4).

We are by no means unique in seeking to create dialogue between psychoanalysis and feminism (see for example, Sayers, 1986; Baruch & Serrano, 1988), and our motives in attempting to do so are similar to those of other commentators. As Baruch and Serrano (1988) note:

> Feminism has come to the realization that the oppression of women does not lie solely in the institutions of the society, the social and economic structure. It now recognizes that something hidden fuels this structure, the unseen and often unspoken but powerful feelings of the unconscious, the entire apparatus of what is called the symbolic order, that is, the language, values, myths, images, and stereotypes that influence and are influenced by our psychological life (p. 11).

Understandings of both intrapsychic life and the social constructions of reality are needed to inform our work with clients, particularly in a period of changing views related to gender roles.

There are multiple difficulties in achieving these aims. There is a cluster of concerns related to presenting material directed toward a specific segment of the client population in a book such as this, whose major focus is description of theory and technique. There are givens that a trained counselor can take for granted and therefore do not need elaboration in a text such as this. For example, any theory of personality and its applications to counseling are subject to criticism, so it may seem incomplete to deal with only one class of criticisms. Well-trained counselors know, and certainly Kohut realized, that cultural experiences are significant factors in shaping personality and psychological health; so it may seem superfluous to re-emphasize the point with women. Counseling of whatever orientation or technique has to be individualized, so perhaps no group should be singled out, but if we are going to discuss one, why not talk about others, such as minorities or the elderly? Lastly, as important as they might be, special considerations such as we present here are beyond the major intent of this book, which, as we have stated in the Preface, is to help the counselor use psychoanalytic schemata as a means of understanding the client's interview behavior, intervening in that behavior, and judging the efficacy of that intervention.

Another cluster of concerns relates to the legacy of Freud, perpetuated by his disciples and other neo-analysts, which stresses the inherent inferiority of women. As Sayers (1986) notes, Freud "remained convinced to the end of his life that women should be subordinate to men" (p. 101). This assertion provides the cornerstone for feminist resistance to anything psychoanalytic, and the implementation of this assertion has been harmful to the autonomy and self-esteem of many women. It has also influenced perspectives regarding the development and psychological health of women in general and women clients in particular.

The existence of this second set of difficulties lessens our concern about the first set. Where psychoanalytic approaches are concerned, women *are* a special case as they have suffered significantly from both correct and incorrect interpretations of the work of various theorists and counselors. It is this second set of difficulties in the legacy of psychoanalysis with respect to women that provides a major focus of the chapter.

There is another set of difficulties that seems worth noting here. When psychoanalysts talk about women and women clients, or feminists talk about the influence of psychoanalysis in our culture, strong emotions often accompany these discussions. However justified such emotions might be, when emotionality is salient it is difficult to present a dispassionate discussion or a definite point of view without an accompanying tone that might be more like partisanship than scholarship. The realization of this set of difficulties is not new with us either. Emotionality often runs high between these two groups. For example, there are many scholars and professional counselors or therapists who adopt psychoanalytic viewpoints and who write about women's issues or work with women clients. In interviewing 19 such women scholars and practitioners from Britain, France and the United States, Baruch and Serrano (1988) discovered that many of them did not wish to call themselves feminists. This was more the case for the women from Europe than those from the United States. As these authors note, the reasons vary:

> For some writers . . . feminism is simply another "ism," a term molded on "the other great words of the culture that oppress us." . . . For others, the word carries an anti-male connotation, even a hatred of men, and always a rejection of them . . . Some analysts . . . worry about the capacity of feminism to oppress men . . . A view less directed toward men . . . holds that feminism is sometimes objectionable because it is an ideology and like all ideology sacrifices truth to a cause (p. 9).

For much the same set of reasons, of course, many feminists have great reluctance to have their work associated with psychoanalytic thought. They see psychoanalysis as opposing women, anti-female, and an ideology that provides a "rationale" for the continued subordination of women.

We are probably not immune from errors of emotion or ideology, but it is our intention to present a perspective on these issues rather than a defense of a rigid position. Contemporary knowlege of personality development and therapeutic processes is such that theoretical coherence and universal application to every case is impossible to achieve. In addition, all psychological viewpoints regarding treatment are influenced by current social and political climates and ideologies, as well as by the science, theories, and practices of counseling. Our viewpoints are no different.

We believe that psychoanalytic approaches are not without flaw with respect to women, but they do have something to offer in the counseling of women. We further believe that the voices of feminism are not without flaw either, but they have made significant positive contributions in the understanding and counseling of both men and women. Sayers (1986) has articulated how each has important contributions, and we hope that discussions such as hers and ours would encourage counselors to look anew at how insights from both traditions can inform and improve our treatment policies.

Criticisms and confounds of psychoanalytic approaches

As we noted in Chapter 1, psychoanalysis is "a complicated doctrine consisting of a mixture of ideas" [p. 6] and attendant contradictions. Its origins, being Continental European philosophy, science, and medicine of the late 1800s, are in sharp theoretical contrast to the institutional development of the counseling profession in the United States, which occurred through public and higher education. Since there is such a contrast in these cultures, it is easy to understand how Freud's theory of personality has attracted many adherents, yet has provoked extensive controversy with respect to his opinions regarding women. His views have been attacked from every perspective—scientific, experiential, and ideological—and yet remain embedded in most Westerners' thinking about everyday life.

Lerman (1986) has suggested that psychoanalysis is fundamentally flawed, particularly unsuited to provide explanations about women's behavior and development, but that nonetheless it holds tremendous influence in both the professional and lay communities. She suggests that psychoanalysis possesses such influence because of its longevity, and because it:

> . . . has always existed as a separate entity apart from all other scientific pursuits within the social sciences and accountable to no external academic or other system of checks (p. 3).

Psychoanalysis is the standard against which other theories of personality or strategies of counseling are measured, and many of its assumptions are implicit in various products of our culture. As Brown (1984) articulates:

> The art, literature and criticism of this century assume that there *is* an unconscious mind, that behavior *is* motivated and determined by early experience, that there *is* an oedipal struggle between father and son, that women *do* lack the objectivity bestowed by a successful resolution of the oedipal conflict.

Whatever one thinks of their perspectives, Brown (1984) and Lerman (1986) direct us toward important issues which arise from the content of the theory itself, as well as significant problems apart from its content. A major question outside of the content proper is how to minimize the confounding of psychological theory and political ideology, and how to resolve the difficulties such confounding can pose for the advancement of science and its applications (see Sampson, 1977, 1988).

The reasons for confounds are many. The fact that the culture does inform both psychological theory and politics is one, but it may not be the most important. The culture also shapes the psychological development of persons, and theories about that development are based on observations of persons who are a product of their culture. In addition, no matter how "objective" scientists and clinicians try to be, they bring their personal lives to every observation. Personal lives are influenced not only by formal training and the ambience of the historical period in which one lives, but also by one's gender, and how one's gender is treated by significant others and experienced by the self. As noted elsewhere, (e.g. Meara, 1990a) it is difficult to separate careful science and expert application from personal or currently accepted ideology. Such separation may be impossible when dealing with appropriate approaches to counseling.

Freudian views of women's psychological development have long been controversial (see Horney, 1926/1967b; Thompson, 1964) and more recently a topic of criticism and reappraisal by contemporary feminist scholars (Chodrow, 1978; Lerman, 1985; Lewis, 1986; Mitchell, 1974; Sayers, 1986). Although her critique is not without its problems, Horney is considered by many to have articulated the first direct challenge to Freud's views of male superiority and female penis envy as a central construct in women's personality development (see for example Walsh, 1987; Westkott, 1986). As Westkott notes, Horney was attempting to extricate an understanding of female sexuality and psychology from an explanation that assumed "primary phallic sexuality" (Horney, 1933/1967a, p. 161).

> . . To stay within the terms of the discourse that Freud had established . . . Horney had to accept the validity of instinct theory. Her assumption of primary female instincts led her to others that she pitted against Freud's: a biological envy for a biological envy, a female sexual instinct for a male one, a female superiority for a male superiority, a vaginal symbol for a phallic one (Westkott, 1986, pp. 55–56).

According to at least one commentator (Danielian, 1988) not only did Horney's (1939) critique of psychoanalysis ostracize her from the Freudian inner circle, but her later work, *Neurosis and Human Growth: the Struggle Toward Self-realization* (Horney, 1950), was a "major contribution to self-theory" (Danielian, 1988, p. 6) and it also was ignored even to the point of "Kohut and the Kohutians dating the history of self-psychology as not more than fifteen years old!" (Danielian, 1988, p. 7). Danielian presents us with an example of the complexities of trying to untangle psychological theories and ideologies as he speculates on the reasons for the differential receptions accorded to the ideas of Horney and Kohut, which he believes to be very similar:

> Did Kohut "treat" the self-object needs of the analytic establishment better than Horney did? If so, was this because of their differing personalities and character structure, because of sexism within the field (Paul, 1985) or because of the vastly changed times? Did the tributaries of Horneyan and Sullivanian thought arrive too early on the analytic scene to allow serious consideration?

Were they "mistimed" and "overstimulating" to the existing system? (Danielian, 1988, p. 22)

Danielian closes his paper by asking for the Horneyan and Kohutian theorists to each understand the vulnerabilities of the other. We concur that it is the concepts and their applications which are more worthy of our attention than the politics of their acceptance, and we believe that counseling can be improved by learning from and respecting the strengths of various theoretical orientations.

In the 1970s feminist scholars began to join their voices to refute the classical Freudian interpretation of development, particularly the development of women. This work received a better hearing than did Horney's. Freud's depiction of all development as phallic-centered, his notion of masculinity in both sexes, and in particular his idea of penis envy as a central component of feminine development, were severely questioned (see Donovan, 1985). Feminist scholarship, the popularity of non-psychoanalytic approaches to counseling, and the heightened attention to gender issues in social psychology have sharpened the focus upon psychosocial as well as psychodynamic factors in personality development and counseling approaches. While biology may be critical, commentators, social psychological researchers, and counselors believe environmental factors can moderate its influence. This changing ideology, along with recent research, observations during counseling, and historical circumstances seem to have created a receptive environment for re-evaluating Freud's conceptualizations of female development.

To reconcile the differences between psychoanalytic theory and later scholarship, and to accommodate their experiences with women clients, psychological counselors searched for paradigms more compatible with their views of human development and counseling processes. Interest in self psychology began to emerge and techniques based on tenets of humanism and behaviorism became popular in counseling. Other more social psychological interpretations of psychoanalytic thought became increasingly influential, particularly in regard to understanding women (cf. for example Westkott, 1986).

Parts of the psychoanalytic community have maintained allegiance to the accepted Freudian view or altered it in such a way that appears to support the inferiority of women (see for example Chehrazi, 1986). This has angered feminists and others, caused sharp debate and provided a general ambience of distrust with respect to the effectiveness, relevance, and fairness of psychoanalytic counseling for women. Psychoanalytic counseling has been seen as a way to keep a woman "in her place" or as a "hazardous cure" (Tennov, 1976). It has also been seen as a reflection of, and an aid to, maintaining a general cultural ambience that devalues the worth of women and their accomplishments.

Challenges to the psychological accuracy and political fairness of this ambience have become more accepted; definitions of mental health have become more informed and elaborated, and the culture and the psychological community have changed their views about women's roles. We, along with other contemporary counselors, realize that self psychology and all other approaches to counseling are not without their problems and that theories continue to evolve in the context of contemporary ideology. In addition to understanding how theory and context inform each other, there are always new issues that need attention through research and careful observation of the counseling experience. For example, as role demands or economic opportunities change, different conflicts become apparent and different themes (or "prevailing problems") emerge in the work.

Theory needs to be able to accommodate contemporary context, but cannot be completely embedded in current ideology. As Chehrazi (1986) noted, ultimately these are clinical not political issues, and in our judgment informed discussions based on counseling experiences and scientific inquiry need to continue. We need to remind ourselves also that bias towaa class of clients is ethically inappropriate, and that personal respect for each client is always warranted (cf. Principles, Concerning the Counseling and Theory of Women, 1979).

In what follows we concentrate on two major areas of disagreement between feminist and psychoanalytic theorists, development of gender identity and the subsequent assumption of male superiority. We divide our comments as follows: (a) feminist formulation of gender identity within the psychoanalytic context; (b) integration of Kohutian self psychology and a feminist viewpoint; and (c) relevance of this formulation and viewpoint to our theory of the client, and its applications to the psychoanalytic counseling of women. In our analysis we borrow from the psychoanalytic theorizing of Fast (1984, 1990), Horney (1926/1967b), (1927/1967c), (1933/1967a, 1939, 1950), and Sayers (1986), and the commentary of Gardiner (1987) and others.

Gender identity

Science has not yet been able to inform us about emotional and personal development as much as we would like. This is certainly true in the area of gender identity. For example, we simply do not know how much or what kind of parental behavior may influence the gender-related behavior of children (see Maccoby, 1990). We cannot refute or affirm the accuracy of many theories of personality development. Yet practicing counselors need such theories to guide their work, lest therapeutic contradictions, if not confusion and chaos, ensue for the client.

Classical psychoanalytic theory (in its orthodox interpretations) and feminist thought have very different perspectives about gender identity, i.e. how males and females come to understand and to identify with their own gender and how, based on that identification, they interact with those of the other gender. Development of appropriate gender identity is considered central to the development of the self and the establishment of intimacy with another. Areas of disagreement between psychoanalysis and feminism about gender identity are both general and particular. In general, many psychoanalytic writers have emphasized invariant biological stages, while feminist theories rely heavily on psychosocial factors. In particular, much early and some contemporary psychoanalytic theory views men as superior and as masculine at birth. Women are seen as more bisexual at birth and need to work through (during the oedipal period) their anger, envy, disappointment, and loss at not being masculine, in particular not having a penis. There are other ways to conceptualize gender identity which accommodate psychoanalytic perspectives and do not view women as inferior. Such has been our intention throughout the chapters of this book. We present another such view based on the work of Fast (1984, 1990).

Fast (1984, 1990), while keeping with psychoanalytic thought, has provided an alternative to the conceptualization of women as inferior beings who suffer from penis envy. She terms her views of gender identity as a differentiation model. Her work takes into account both psychodynamic development and environmental events. She rejects the idea that either males or females are masculine at birth, but rather describes the gender identity of both as undifferentiated and overinclusive. As each gender becomes aware of its identity (as either masculine or feminine) each becomes aware of limits. For example, as one aspect of this recognition of limits, little boys become aware that they cannot give birth, and little girls become aware that they do not have a penis. Children also come to realize that their maleness or femaleness provides other limits as well. They become aware of their own limits before they become aware that those same limits apply to all others of their gender. For instance, a boy may realize he cannot give birth, but still may believe his very powerful father can.

In terms of gender differentiation, children receive substantial help from those around them who, in turn, treat them differentially from the time they are born. Early on, children begin to identify with the appropriate gender. Since, in Fast's views, gender identity is undifferentiated and overinclusive at birth, neither gender is at an inherent disadvantage in achieving developmental maturity. Fast also stresses the importance of environment, particularly the role of both parents, in gender development.

Fast (1984, 1990) traces her views of gender development through three important Freudian stages: "the period before children become aware of sex differences, the events surrounding their recognition of those differences . . . (around 18–24 months) . . . and subsequent oedipal period, in which they consolidate their gender-differentiated identities" (Fast, 1990 p. 116). She supports her views with therapy experiences, research data and re-interpretation of classic Freudian cases, (e.g. Fast (1984) *The Wolf Man*, pp. 160–183).

While she sees the processes for boys and girls as similar, and sees these processes for each gender from a beginning point of undifferentiation and overinclusion, she also recognizes specific content differences. For example in the oedipal period (Fast, 1984) she sees the typical developmental problems and outcomes for boys and girls as different. However, she bases the difference not upon penis envy, but rather on a typical family constellation where females are the primary care-givers for children of both sexes. In order to be male, boys must accomplish the difficult task of separating from their primary caretaker. In our view, if such separation occurs at the expense of maintaining the potential for adult intimacy, serious psychological problems for the male can result. Girls are not required to accomplish this clear separation in order to be female, but they do need to separate to become an independent female. In our judgment, failure to separate can result in enmeshment with the family of origin, which makes adult intimacy difficult and makes psychological problems from lack of intimacy more likely. So while the boys must accomplish a rather sharp and definite separation, the girls must be "both like their mothers in gender and distinct from them as individuals" (Fast, 1984, p. 106). The patterns would be different, of course, if parental duties were shared more equitably or the primary caretaker were male. While such care-giver activities are not the rule, they are occurring more frequently.

The reader is referred to Fast (1984, 1990) for further elaboration of these ideas. Our purpose in outlining some of her major points is to provide a context which is more gender-neutral in that it does not maintain that either gender is superior, or that the development of gender identity has its roots in envy for the biological endowments of the "superior" gender. Fast's view does not imply that the intellectual or competitive striving of women should be interpreted as penis envy or as a compensation for the narcissistic injury of not being male. It rejects the notion of male superiority, or any superiority on the basis of gender, and provides an opportunity to view with more equanimity and "objectivity" the similarities and differences between the genders as they accomplish their developmental tasks. It allows us to bring to psychoanalytic counseling (of both women and men) and to the working alliance, conceptual perspectives of psychoanalytic developmental thought, and to combine those perspectives with feminist viewpoints about the significance of environmental events in the client's past and present.

This kind of reformulation can have significant implications for counseling both women and men. The psychoanalytic views expressed by Fast and others present a compatible but less phallocentric perspective on the observations of Freud and many neo-analysts. If psychoanalytic counselors believe and communicate the attitude that neither gender is superior, this could make the working alliance an atypical experience for most clients, regardless of their gender. Such beliefs and actions regarding equality on the part of the counselor can be beneficial for the client, and might assist in achieving one of the goals of feminism: changing the general societal view of male superiority. We believe an attitude of male (or female) superiority on the part of society, the counseling community, or others is ultimately destructive to the psychological development of both genders and the subsequent formation of intimate relationships.

Self psychology and feminist thought

With Fast's (1984, 1990) conceptualization of the development of masculinity and femininity as a base, our discussion now focuses upon linkages between self psychology and feminist thought. Although Kohut worked primarily with male clients and his thinking demonstrates some uncertainty about female development, his conceptualizations of the development of the self are compatible with gender neutrality and particular feminist viewpoints which we favor. We believe that the use of self psychology is a more appropriate theoretical context for counseling women than either those versions of the classical Freudian theory that espouse male superiority or certain versions of feminist object relations theory, for example Chodrow (1978).

Our concerns with Freud's assumptions about male superiority have been reported above; our concerns with Chodrow's and other feminist object relations views relate to their narrowness, in particular their "neglect of cultural and historical contexts" (Gardiner, 1987, p. 768). We realize that in the object relations school there are exceptions; for example, Benjamin (1988) includes cultural perspectives in her work. As Showalter (1982) explains, however, many "psychoanalytic models of feminist-based criticism . . . cannot explain historical change, ethnic difference, or the shaping force of generic or economic factors" (p. 27).

In addition, Gardiner (1987) points out a series of other concerns with this work, which we share. These include placing significant emphasis on the oedipal period, tending to over-emphasize infantile experiences as determinants of adult personality, viewing femininity and wanting children as compensatory activities, and positing a symbiotic mother–child relationship to which the "mother regresses in order to care for her child" (p. 770).

We also find difficulties in some of the feminist object relations work that stereotypes the genders (e.g. women are empathic, men are competitive) and values the characteristics of women over those of men. Since psychoanalytic thought and its applications have contributed to the devaluing of women, for the time being it could be necessary and valuable for feminist viewpoints to infuse some balance in the situation and to over-value women. While some psychodynamic and other theoretical approaches assert gender neutrality, the worlds where clients and counselors live are typically not gender-neutral and often are not gender-fair. Rather than assign and esteem characteristics by gender, it seems more productive to value, and to be able to attest to the psychological health of, certain characteristics in particular contexts and roles regardless of the gender.

The myth of male superiority, which is so ingrained by Freudian thought and the milieu of Western thought, needed to be and probably still needs to be challenged directly and forcibly. Feminist criticism, in particular object relations theorists, have made pioneeering and significant contributions in formulating this challenge. Now that the challenge has been articulated, we believe the implementation of self psychology in the work of counseling has the potential for lessening some of the problems we have mentioned here, and provides a coherent foundation for including intrapsychic and cultural influences in studying feminine development and counseling women.

While there are several commentators whose work attempts to bridge self psychology and feminist theory, in what follows we rely heavily on the work of Gardiner (1987) as she makes a compelling case for the congruence of self psychology and feminist thought. For a more complete treatment of the topic we refer you to this work and others.

For the most part, Kohut's theorizing did not deal directly with the issue of gender; so, while he may not have devoted the attention more contemporary scholarship demands to the psychological development of and counseling with women, we believe he should not be faulted out of hand of being biased against them. To begin with, and noted in his work and in prior chapters of this book, although caretakers of infants are primarily women, there is nothing in the theory to preclude male caretakers. Caretaking is neither seen as a symbiotic regression or as a compensatory activity, nor as gender-exclusive. Empathy is valued as an analytic tool, and a pivotal process in parents' suitable rearing of children. The development of empathy is viewed as a major aspect of psychological maturity for all persons throughout their lives, not simply for women or as a trait of "selfless" child care.

In two specific instances where Kohut (1974/1978a, 1974/1978b) addresses issues related to women's position in society and female sexuality, he does not endorse the classic psychoanalytic perspectives of women's inferiority or of penis envy or some other "biological attribute or deficit" as providing the basis for women's psychological development or psychopathology. The dynamics for the development of narcissistic personality disorder or the maintenance of narcissistic equilibrium are the same for men and women: "the self is poorly coherent [when it is deprived] of the mirroring acceptance of its totality and of the opportunity to merge with an accepting idealized selfother" (1974/1978a, p. 791). When asked (1974/1978b) why so few women have been idealized figures in society, Kohut answered in part:

> . . . I do not see, at least from my own clinical experience, that the narcissistic injury that undoubtedly is connected with the absence of the visible genitals in little girls is, in essence, different from the narcissistic injury to the little boy who discovers that his penis is very small as compared with the penis of a grown man. I believe, however, that a child is much more significantly influenced by the empathic attitudes of the grown-ups around him or her than by the givens of organic equipment (pp. 776–777).

Kohut does recognize that young girls experience the world differently from young boys and that there are differences in the ways adults react to them. While each has the need for the expression of grandiosity (and idealization), the biological differences do not determine this potential, they only lend specific content to it. He believes that little girls' experiences of not having a visible genital is a narcissistic injury, but psychological, not a biological one, and that both boys and girls suffer narcissistic injuries and it is appropriate empathic mirroring that keeps such injuries from developing into narcissistic personality disorders. As he states:

> What I am questioning is that it [this specific narcissistic injury] . . . accounts *per se* for the major disturbances of self-esteem encountered in women . . . or . . . that it is the essential motivating force that propels every girl, via reaction formations, substitutions, displacements and other primary processes, toward womanhood, in particular that it underlies a woman's wish for a child (p. 786).

That is not to assert, however that Kohut's applications of his theory to counseling were always non-sexist, or that he was not a product of and a participant in the sexism of his era and profession. There is nothing inherently sexist, however, in his conceptualizations of self psychology, and his ideas can be appropriately and productively applied to the counseling of both men and women.

Gardiner (1987) stresses a number of major links between self psychology and contemporary feminist approaches to development, particularly the development of women. We mention four that we believe to be particularly salient for psychoanalytic counseling: (a) valuing of empathy; (b) emphasis on pre-oedipal development; (c) model of maturity; and (d) treatment of the concept of selfobjects.

The correspondence of Kohut's views of empathy and feminist thought have been mentioned immediately above in this chapter. The significance of empathy and empathic mirroring for psychological health and the work of psychoanalytic counseling have been stressed throughout the book (see especially Chapters 2 & 3). Further elaborations of empathy will not be pursued here. It seems important to reiterate, however, that the topic is central to our views of psychological development and psychoanalytic counseling, and represents a clear bond between self psychology and feminist theory. Empathy, of course, has long been seen as an essential tool for counselors (see Rogers, 1957) and an important concept in the development of pro-social behavior by Bateson (1987) and his colleagues (Bateson, Fultz & Schoenrade, 1987).

Self-psychology emphasizes the importance of care-giver (typically female) influence in the pre-oedipal period, when bonds are formed and empathic mirroring of the child's grandiosities and idealizations is critical. The theory does not depict this phase as over-deterministic, but rather sees development and change possible and necessary throughout the life span. Women's historic role as primary care-givers is valued, but care-giving is not confined to one gender and counselors of either gender can be treated by the client as (and are indeed able to "stand-in" for) a selfobject of either parent. By emphasizing the importance of the pre-oedipal period for both genders, self psychology de-emphasizes phallic-centered development and the notion that penis envy is a cornerstone of female development. Feminist scholars (e.g. Dinnerstein, 1976) who study women's development believe that events in the pre-oedipal period are influential in the development of the mother–daughter relationship.

As Gardiner (1987) and others have indicated, Kohut's (1977) characteristics of psychological maturity are not related to cultural expectations of masculinity. Achievement of maturity is not seen as linear progression from symbiosis to individuation, nor is autonomy viewed as the major goal of psychological development. To the contrary, mature psychological development for the self psychologist includes interdependence, empathy, creativity, and love of others.

> Self psychologists see all people embedded for life in a network of human relations, and they posit mature interdependence and altruism as among adult developmental goals for both sexes . . . (Gardiner, 1987, p. 772).

Such a view of psychological health, while compatible with the values of many feminists, is in conflict with the pressures for individualistic competitive success which are dominant values in the United States and other industrialized countries. What should be done about this conflict illustrates a major difference between most psychoanalytic approaches and most feminist approaches to counseling. The psychoanalytic approaches stop with the client; for many feminists this is only the beginning—they want to change the societal structures that put their clients in conflict and/or disadvantage them. As Sayers (1986) notes:

> Feminists . . . are . . . agreed in recognizing the current injustice . . . whereby our society both promises freedom to all its members, men and women alike, yet systematically discriminates against women . . . I have been arguing that a central object of psychoanalytic therapy is to bring about full recognition of such conflicts and contradictions, and of the frustration to which they give rise in the personal lives of clients . . .
>
> The starting point of psychoanalysis, however, is not society but individual suffering . . . It regards its object as achieved once it has enabled its patients to become fully conscious of the gap that exists between illusory and actual fulfillment of their needs. Once it has enabled its clients to recognize this gap . . . psychoanalysis regards its therapeutic project as complete. It believes that its clients are then in the position to begin effectively to change reality so that their needs might actually be met. By contrast, feminism [believes that] there is a need to go beyond such consciousness and individual action based on it . . . to bring about the changes in society necessary to the needs of women being fully met. It recognizes that this depends on social as well as individual change, and on collective as well as individual struggle. . . Psychoanalysis stops short of this recognition. For feminism it is only the beginning (pp. 167–168; 180–181).

Seeing healthy individuals of both genders embedded in a network of human relationships, and including creativity and altruism as attributes of psychological maturity makes less likely the acceptance of deficit status for either gender, with its attendant obligatory compensatory behavior based on biology. Men and women may or may not display these characteristics differentially, but there are bound to be within-gender differences as well, since the characteristics are believed to be psychologically based and subject to change.

Self–selfobject relationships, as delineated by self psychologists, integrate the importance of intrapsychic, interpersonal, and historical context. Such a view accommodates the many critics who believe the impact of psychosocial factors upon the development of gender identity and personality structure is under-represented in a Freudian biological determinism. As noted in the introductory comments to this chapter, we believe that cultural pressures influence psychosocial development. Historical eras espouse different views of child-rearing and of appropriate behavior, and thus contribute to the differing frequency of certain personality structures (e.g. narcissistic or borderline) over time. Kohut (1974/1978b) states:

> . . . that it is up to the historian to undertake a comparative study of the attitude of adults toward children at different periods in history in order to

throw some further light on the conditions Freud tried to explain biologically (p. 777).

We end this section by noting the significant discrimination that women have suffered at the hands of orthodox Freudian thinking. We believe the conceptualizations and critiques of such Feminist scholars as Fast (1984, 1990), Gardiner (1987), and Sayers (1986) have enhanced psychoanalytic thought and focused needed attention on the influence of psychosocial factors in the client's life. We believe further that self psychology as espoused by Kohut does offer a coherent theoretical framework for looking at personality and development and for doing the work of psychoanalytic counseling that does not demean either gender.

Applications of self psychology theory to counseling women

In Chapter 3 we presented a counselor's theory of the client from a Kohutian self psychology perspective. Although experiences are different for men and women, we believe this theoretical perspective is relevant for counseling with both genders. Difference does not imply dominance by, or subordination of, either gender. So in one sense what we developed in Chapter 3 needs no elaboration here; yet in keeping with th special emphasis of this chapter, we believe it is helpful to reflect specifically upon the applicability of the theory for the woman client. In Chapter 3 we recapitulated Kohut's view that it is critical for the child's development of a healthy mature self for the parents to provide a suitable target for the child's idealizations, and phase-appropriate empathic mirroring of the child's grandiosities. For a succinct comprehensive review of the major points in Chapter 3 the reader is referred to Figure 3.1 (p. 53) and Table 3.1 (pp. 62–63).

We believe that at this particular time in the history of the world it is extremely important for the woman client that the counselor be able to integrate the theoretical perspectives of self psychology with the contemporary psychosocial ambience that pervades the lives of many women. In particular, that ambience often communicates to many middle-class, college-educated (or college-bound) women ambiguous messages in terms of ambitions and goals for self-fulfillment of their talents and abilities. Some families may stress that such fulfillment must not come "at the expense of" women's roles as wives, mothers, care-givers to aged parents, and other types of expected supporting roles. Other families may stress that to achieve such fulfillment one must *give up* marriage and/or children or other intimate relationships. From birth, the messages to boys and girls are different in terms of assertiveness, appropriate ambitions, "noble ideals," and desired personality traits. For example, although there are exceptions and no

generalization applies to all, females typically receive less direct encouragement (and thus possibly less appropriate empathic mirroring of their
exhibitionism and grandiosities) for intellectual and competitive striving than
males. Such striving and ambitions are typically (or stereotypically) considered
to be "masculine" and thus for a little girl to embrace them or to follow
her intellectual interests might mean risking her identity as "feminine" or
the disapproval of one or both parents; not that such inappropriate empathic
mirroring does not happen to men.

More often, however, male grandiosity is mirrored appropriately, but a
(middle-class, college-bound) little boy, who professed his goal was to help
people and so wanted to become a nurse, might have similar difficulties.
Such a goal may be considered feminine (thus the target of less appropriate
empathic mirroring); thus the boy who pursues such an objective might
have to risk his "masculine" identity or the disapproval of one or more
parents. Either case can present a narcissistic injury to the child; and the
child may feel devalued. As Horney (1926/1967b) points out, persons who
are devalued have difficulty in personality formation. Westkott (1986)
maintains that women are typically more often devalued than men, and that
to gain status or security women play the supporting, help-giving, or care-
giving role that society has assigned them. Westkott further argues that
under this mask of being a self-sacrificing and supportive person, many
women are angry and rage against their inferior status. That is not to say
that many men may not rage against their role as "the provider who must
support and protect" their families.

Women clients who present as dependent or depressed may be reflecting
the result of lack of phase-appropriate empathic mirroring. When they were
toddlers and pre-schoolers, their parents may have (perhaps unwittingly)
enforced the cultural stereotypes about women's role. So often it may not
be the woman herself who has chosen such a role, but she has compensated
the best she could in trying to develop the "ambitious" aspects of her self
and to meet the demands of her culture. It is important in such a situation
that the counselor maintain appropriate empathic mirroring of the client's
grandiosities and idealizations. The counselor also needs to understand the
client's desires to explore what her choices are and what experiences may
be responsible for "the current complaints" that brought her to counseling.

Power struggles can emerge when parents do not provide an adequate
target for the young child's idealizations. As noted in Table 3.1, severe
disruption in this process may result in a client engaging in "crude bouts of
center-staging to demonstrate a sense of power which isn't there." Typically,
our culture is less judgmental when men rather than women engage in such
demonstrations of power. Whether the attempts to gain power (for example,
by idealized merging with the counselor) take the form of ingratiation or
dominance, a counselor could be tempted to be less tolerant of a woman

client. A stereotype in our culture is that it is not appropriate for women to seek power, to be powerful, or in particular to have any power (save sexual seductive power) over men.

As Scher and his colleagues (1987) have amply demonstrated, men and male clients suffer from bias also; but typically the psychoanalytic perspective and Western culture have championed masculine superiority, and often it is difficult for either a male or a female counselor to break loose from implicit beliefs and expectations that a woman is inferior. Our cultural ambience finds it much more acceptable to fault women for being too exhibitionist, assertive, ambitious, or self-seeking than it is to criticize men for these same traits and behaviors. Men, however, are not immune from the criticisms of our culture; they are faulted for being passive, non-aggressive, "soft," and the like. Both genders risk their very fragile psychological selves as they make their way in a world of stereotypical expectations.

As explained by Kohut's theory of the development of self, appropriate parenting and prizing of the exhibitionism and assertive qualities, as well as understanding of the child's idealizing needs, is essential to a cohesive, bi-polar, adult self. In our current times, the psychosocial factors of a woman's life could make these developmental processes even more problematic for women, and we encourage the counselor to be attuned to this situation.

Another significant feature of Kohut's self-psychology is the tension posited in the development of the two poles of the self: ambitions and goals. The tension between being energized by ambition and pulled by ideals or goals can be productive, but not always. Again, the psychosocial factors in the lives of many women can come into play here, as there can be more disharmony between ideals (or idealized persons) and ambitions in the messages given to women in contrast to those given to men. The cultural idealizations of woman (mother earth, fertility, religious symbol of goodness and purity) and men (king, lord, warrior) are quite different. The culture rewards with status and money ambitions that are more in line with male idealizations, so at this point in history in the middle and upper classes of Western civilization, it seems easier for men to integrate ideals and ambitions (beyond relationship and family) than for women.

Self psychology can assist us in understanding the communications of and providing interventions for a woman client who comes to psychoanalytic counseling with conflicts and confusions on these issues. A needed adjunct in this work, with every client, is consideration of how contemporary psychosocial factors influenced the client's development. As indicated above, self psychology as articulated by Kohut allows for this needed adjunct, as it sees as significant in the life of the client the role of current historical context.

It is reasonable to assume that many clients (men and women) have suffered significant devaluing and narcissistic injury during the pre-oedipal period (and after). Pre-oedipal devaluing can be recognized (if not articulated) by the child when the parent engages in continued phase-inappropriate lack of empathic mirroring and chronically fails to understand the child's need to idealize and merge with the powerful parental selfobject.

Psychoanalytic counseling of a woman client who presents with disturbances in self-development can be facilitated if the client is not viewed as inferior on the basis of gender, and if the perspectives of self psychology are integrated with the client's perspective about how she has experienced the contemporary ambience for women in Western culture. Appropriate counselor empathy for the difficulties of women's personality development and everyday coping in this ambience is also necessary. Such an integrative approach seems more efficacious than locating the problem within the woman client ("blaming the victim"); and in particular placing blame upon her for not resolving her sense of loss over not being male.

The counselor needs to be an unbiased "vicarious observer" who can mirror the ambitions of the woman client and understand current psychosocial realities of her life. Such current realities make it much more likely that the contemporary woman client is much more likely to experience envy of "privilege" rather than envy of anatomy. A skilled empathic psychoanalytic counselor can be uniquely qualified to assist the woman client to understand the narcissistic injuries that led to such envy and/or other difficulties in her daily life.

Summary

In light of extensive feminist criticism, we have reviewed the appropriateness of psychoanalytic counseling for women, and discussed the complexities of separating political ideology from psychological theory. We have presented a differentiation model of gender identity (Fast, 1984, 1990), which views neither gender as superior. In this model, both genders begin life as psychologically undifferentiated and overinclusive; the structures and processes of differentiation are similar for both genders, but the content-specific tasks of developing a gender identity are different.

We have proposed that self psychology accommodates both the psychoanalytic perspective and much of the feminist criticism leveled at that perspective. This accommodation is based on self psychology's views with respect to empathy, its emphasis on pre-oedipal development, model of maturity, and treatment of the concept of selfobjects (Gardiner, 1987). In addition, the process of developing a mature self, as articulated by Kohut, is gender-neutral and recognizes the importance of historical and psychosocial factors in the development of personality. Understanding issues related to development of the self (particularly phase-appropriate empathic mirroring of the child's grandiosities, and willingness to serve as the target for the child's idealizations), and Western culture's ambience, which is ambivalent about women's achievement (apart from traditional roles), are important perspectives in counseling the woman client and in building the working alliance with her.

We caution against implicit bias against either gender, and encourage the counselor to be vigilant against "taken for granted" sentiments in our culture related to women's inferiority (either psychological or intellectual) or their inherent envy of masculinity. We note how women may receive ambiguous messages about the appropriateness of their exhibitionism, assertiveness, and ambitions in light of their societal assigned role as care-givers. We believe the skilled and empathic psychoanalytic counselor can provide competent, fruitful counseling for the woman client.

12 Ethical considerations in psychoanalytic counseling

Presenting a discussion of ethics in a manner that is helpful in a book such as this is fraught with difficulties. On the one hand those who read this book are probably well versed in the professional standards and ethical guidelines appropriate for their work (e.g. American Psychological Association, 1990; American Association of Counseling and Development, 1987; American Association for Marriage and Family Therapy, 1988; Principles Concerning the Counseling of Women, 1979). In addition, most help-givers strive to lead proper personal and professional lives, and to exhibit correct behavior in the professional role of counselor. So, much of what we say is already known to many.

On the other hand the enormity of the literature and the significance of the topic call for a much more ambitious chapter than is possible in a text of this sort. In addition, it is natural for readers to hope for specific information about exactly what to do in a variety of perplexing circumstances that confront the counselor in the daily work with clients. There are an increasing number of excellent texts which treat specific ethical dilemmas in detail and/or discuss complex ethical issues in depth (e.g. Callan, 1988; Keith-Speigel & Koocher, 1985; Pope & Vasquez, 1991; Rosenbaum, 1982). Our purpose here is not to duplicate this work; our discussion is focused less on "how to do" and more on "how to think about" ethical decision-making in psychoanalytic counseling.

We believe that appropriate professional and ethical behavior is much more than a matter of what to do. It transcends sets of guidelines or acquired personal intuitions, as the literature about ethics is often characterized more by debate than consensus. Since ethical reasoning is blended with theoretical and practical features of psychoanalytic counseling, it is important for the counselor to evaluate continually how ethical decisions relate to therapeutic processes such as understanding the client, building a working alliance, working with resistance, and other phenomena. It is helpful to have a framework for thinking about ethical matters.

Ethical considerations are neither value- nor context-free; the ethicality of a certain action is judged, in part at least, by the values of the culture that encompass it and the specific context of its occurrence. The context of counseling, for example, influences our judgment about what is appropriate. In psychoanalytic counseling, client transference reactions are seen as a necessary part of the process and managing them appropriately is seen as an important aspect of the work. The "standard of care," therefore, is different for a psychoanalytic counselor than for a client-centered counselor who might value support over "working through," or a rational-emotive counselor who might value reason over affect. While to be sure these are matters of technique, they go far beyond technique to beliefs about the human condition (e.g. personality development, motivation, treatment) and values with respect to what is appropriate and ethical. The three theoretical orientations mentioned here are all ethically appropriate, but there are some modes of treatment that would be considered unethical. In addition, if a client were led to believe that he or she would experience one form of treatment, and the counselor abruptly changed the style or orientation to another, the consequences could not only be therapeutically damaging, but could have ethical implications as well.

Our culture is pluralistic and its values diverse. The same can be said of communities of psychological scholars, counselors, and others in the human development or help-giving professions. This is clearly the case in the counseling communities. We cannot learn what is ethically appropriate for all time and in all situations. Counselors and other professionals can, however, learn about and refine frameworks for ethical decision-making, apply these frameworks to their professional work, and hope that through this study and experience they make mature and appropriate ethical decisions.

Ethical decision-making is both a matter of "what we do" and "who we are." Through study and experience we develop into morally mature persons who can be trusted to be, and are, motivated to achieve appropriate decisions and who are expert enough to critically evaluate ethical dilemmas. Understanding and working out "what to do" when confronted by an ethical dilemma resides mainly in the realm of what is termed Principle Ethics, while questions of "who we are" are the primary focus of so-called Virtue Ethics (Jordan & Meara, 1990). These concepts and their relevance to the ethics of psychoanalytic counseling are a major focus of this chapter and are more thoroughly discussed below.

Our major purposes in this chapter are twofold: (a) to suggest a framework for the application of Principle Ethics, and how it might be applied to the ethical conflicts and dilemmas that arise in the science and practice of psychoanalytic counseling; and (b) to argue the relevance of Virtue Ethics as a necessary complement to Principle Ethics, in order to ensure the highest standard of ethical behavior that is possible on the part of professionals, in particular psychoanalytic counselors. We begin with some thoughts about definitions and theoretical matters.

Definitions and theoretical considerations

As Meara & Schmidt (1991) note, in both the everyday and the professional worlds the word "ethics" is often used to convey different ideas (e.g. ranging from personal morals to written codes of professional conduct). It is a term whose definition itself could occupy this chapter; but which we delimit to issues related to psychoanalytic counseling. When we speak of ethics here, we are talking about applied normative ethics; i.e. looking at questions of what is ethically acceptable or not acceptable (and why that is so) in our professional activities, and in other aspects of our lives that impinge upon our professional work. The intimate nature of psychoanalytic counseling, the expanding diversity of both professionals and clients, combined with the increasing professionalization of the United States culture (cf. for example, Napoli, 1981; Hatch, 1988; Meara, 1990a) make ethical awareness and decision-making a constant responsibility for counselors and therapists. The diverse values of our culture and of our professional and personal lives combine to make ethical consensus impossible.

Our task in this section, then, is not to proscribe what one should do, although we have strong biases about that, but rather to talk about approaches to making decisions with respect to the ethical acceptability of certain behaviors and actions. Although we cannot expect counselors and therapists to be experts in ethical theory, a discussion of theory seems a place to start.

We begin our theoretical excursion with a review of Beauchamp & Childress's (1979, 1983, 1989) model for moral justification, which has been suggested by Kitchener (1984) as a guide for ethical decision-making in counseling psychology and other helping professions. The model consists of two levels of ethical reasoning: the intuitive level and the critical-evaluative level (cf. Kitchener, 1984; Beauchamp & Childress, 1989; Meara & Schmidt, 1991). The first refers to the ordinary moral sense of individuals; it is the second that is the focus of our attention here.

The critical-evaluative level consists of three sub-parts, which are considered to be hierarchical and are (from low to high): (a) rules; (b) principles; and (c) theories. Rules can be laws or codes of conduct which are enunciated by professional organizations; rules can lose their significance if they violate a higher principle. Drane (1982) states that principles are:

> . . . ethical values in verbal or propositional form which either have or presume to have universal applicability (p. 31).

At the top of the hierarchy is theory, which addresses the questions of why (e.g. is fidelity in professional relationships important? And if so, why?). Beauchamp & Childress (1989) note:

> A well developed ethical theory provides a framework of principles within which an agent can determine morally appropriate actions (p. 25).

There is no completely satisfactory ethical theory; and individuals can arrive at the same conclusions from different theoretical perspectives. Two theories which permeate the literature and are used by Beauchamp & Childress (1989) in developing their discussions of ethical principles are rule utilitarianism and deontological theory. As Meara & Schmidt (1991) explain:

> Utilitarian theories generally judge actions as right and/or good with respect to the consequences they produce. Rule utilitarians do not judge each act in isolation, but rather in a context with an integrated system of rules or principles, where the standard of rightness or goodness is ultimate or cumulative effects of the action performed by many persons. They allow exceptions to or the disregarding of a rule only when another moral rule is more binding (pp. 242–243).

According to Beauchamp & Childress (1989), deontological theories:

> . . . hold that some features of acts other than, or in addition to, their consequences make them right or wrong and that the grounds of right or obligation are not wholly dependent on the production of good consequences (p. 36).

From these basic differences, (emphasis on cumulative effects of the consequences vs. emphasis on some duties or obligations "no matter what"), follow both similarities and differences in ethical judgments. For example, a counselor might not exploit a client financially because of the cumulative effect such actions may have on the credibility of the profession; while another may not exploit a client financially because such activity is simply wrong "no matter what." On the other hand, one counselor in some circumstances may facilitate or support an autonomous decision of a terminally ill client (whom the counselor judges to be competent) to choose suicide because that counselor believes that the suicide is in the client's best interest; while another believes that the fiduciary relationship between counselor and client does not extend so far that it violates a principle of sustaining life whatever the circumstances.

The three levels, (a) rules, (b) principles and (c) theory are considered hierarchical, since if one cannot resolve an issue at one level, one has recourse to a higher level of reasoning. The levels are related and any decision could be made because all three levels are in concert with one another. To follow through on our first example above: financial exploitation may be seen as a violation of the *rule* of prohibition of dual relationships found in most professional codes of ethics; or a violation of the *principles* of fidelity and autonomy (which will be discussed below); as well as a violation of one's ethical *theoretical* perspective or prescriptive.

Often the levels of decision-making are not in concert, and then recourse to a higher level and other deliberations are necessary to resolve an ethical dilemma and take action. For example, to support suicide can be seen as a violation of many professional codes or rules which specify the counselor's responsibility to act in the face of "clear and present danger" to a client or others. It can also be seen as a violation of the principle of non-maleficence ("do no harm," to be discussed below). But to a rule utilitarian these guidelines might be transcended by the notion that this instance provides an exception to the normally accepted rules and principles. In the judgment of the counselor the consequences of supporting this specific decision for suicide may be less severe and less damaging to the client or to the counselor's philosophy of life (or theoretical purview), and justified by a particular integrated ethical system of rule utilitarianism.

Psychological theory and ethical theory

Whatever one's ethical theoretical orientation (and for most professionals it is probably more implicit than explicit) psychoanalytic counselors and other counselors have to consider the correspondence between their ethical theory and the personality theory which guides their therapeutic practice.

Our brief excursion into theory makes one thing obvious. The ethical theories we mention indicate the importance of choice, and seem far from the biological determinism of Freud and other neoanalysts. Both client and counselor have ethical choices to make, and our views about ethical choice are similar to our views about other choices in counseling. We, like others who take a psychoanalytic perspective on personality development, treatment, and change, believe that the past is influencing the present, and what is psychologically unresolved in the past is being re-enacted and acted upon in the present. However, as our previous chapters have attempted to make clear, we also see both client and counselor as agents, and our philosophy of personality also borrows heavily from the work of Brentano (1955) and the act psychologists.

The traditions of act psychology, the importance of mental processes (rather than simply content) are apparent in the traditions of counseling psychology and specific forms of non-medical counseling or therapy, and are central to our development of psychoanalytic counseling. As Meara (1990b) notes:

> Our view of human action sees persons as agents capable of managing and enhancing their inner selves, important commitments, interpersonal relationships, and their world of work. This view doesn't prevail because we are segregated from or are unaware of the biological determinism of Freud or the environmental determinism of Skinner and other behaviorists. Our tradition has been to entrust to others their own welfare while offering a context that emphasizes prevention, development, and, when needed, remediation (p. 48).

The goals of psychoanalytic counseling are to enable the client to understand the multiplicity of influences that motivates feelings, thoughts, and actions, so the client can experience more control and exercise more direction in life.

This is not to say that the client is not vulnerable; but rather that the vulnerability of the client makes the ethical obligations of the counselor more stringent. Such vulnerability on the part of the client can mean that the client is currently less able than usual to exercise sound judgment. At such times the counselor is extremely influential and needs to be aware of that influence from an ethical as well as a technical perspective. The ethical perspective of the counselor then weighs heavily in the conduct of psychoanalytic counseling, and road maps are needed to facilitate individual ethical decisions, as well as patterns of appropriate ethical behavior toward the client.

Our ethical perspective borrows from both the rule utilitarian position and the deontological one, which is not uncommon. We see the combining of these perspectives, especially when balanced with principled reasoning and developing moral sensitivities, as complementary to and a necessary part of our views of psychoanalytic counseling. Specifically, we are not strict determinists (we borrow from both the Freudian and Brentano traditions); we do believe some behaviors are unethical for the counselor, regardless of the circumstance; and we believe that at times it is permissible (occasionally even obligatory) to make exceptions to *prima facie* principles or rules. We believe psychoanalytic counselors need to develop a conceptual scheme to guide ethical decision-making in both the unique and the routine ethical circumstances that occur in the day-to-day activities of psychoanalytic counseling. Although there are many ethical, professional, and technical challenges, as well as many conflicts in the life of a psychoanalytic counselor, there need not be an inherent conflict in one's view of ethics and one's view of psychological treatment.

At the heart of our conceptual scheme is the second level of the Beauchamp & Childress (1989) and Kitchener (1984) framework for moral justification; that of principles. It is at this level that the bulk of the ethical reasoning which is based on Principle Ethics occurs for the professional psychoanalytic counselor.

Principles for ethical decision-making

As noted above, principles can be viewed as values which are thought to have some universal applicability. In applied professional ethics, Principle Ethics are often used to solve ethical dilemmas or quandaries. Jordan & Meara (1990) characterize Principle Ethics:

> . . . as approaches that emphasize the use of rational, objective, universal, and impartial principles in the ethical analysis of dilemmas (p. 107).

A helpful conceptualization of Principle Ethics is that which is proposed by Beauchamp & Childress (1979, 1983, 1989), which is believed to be applicable to psychology, counseling, and other such endeavors (see Drane, 1982; Kitchener, 1984). The principles are at the middle of the critical evaluative model of moral justification which we have reviewed above. While we believe that in and of itself Principle Ethics is not sufficient, especially for counselors (see Jordan & Meara, 1990), it does provide a means of conceptualizing dilemmas and a guide to reasoning what to do to resolve them. Beauchamp & Childress (1989) develop "four moral principles applicable to scientific research, medicine, and health care" (p. 307). We think they are also particularly applicable to psychoanalytic counseling. These are so-called *prima facie* binding; that is, on the face of it these principles are ethically binding unless superseded by a competing principle or higher order theory.

We will define each of these principles as we discuss them; as proposed by Beauchamp and Childress they are: (a) respect for autonomy; (b) non-maleficence; (c) beneficence; and (d) justice. From these four obtain other derived ethical rules, such as veracity, privacy, confidentiality, and fidelity. Kitchener (1984) basing her reasoning on the work of Beauchamp & Childress (1979, 1983, 1989) and the work of Hare (1981) presents the four principles and the obtained concept of fidelity as significant in ethical decision-making processes for counseling psychologists. We believe the principles and the obtained concept of fidelity provide a useful heuristic in helping the psychoanalytic counselor to develop as an ethical professional and to solve specific ethical dilemmas.

Respect for autonomy

The culture of the United States and the ambience of psychoanalytic counseling values individual autonomy. It is essential for the psychoanalytic counselor not only to value autonomy, but also to respect the autonomy of the client. This principle is based on the belief that each individual is a person of intrinsic worth. At times it can be difficult to respect someone's autonomy if the counselor believes, for example, that the client is not acting in his or her own best interest. Informed consent, an essential ingredient of psychoanalytic counseling, is rooted in the principle of autonomy. Other related issues include client decision-making with respect to the duration and tenor of the work, respecting confidentiality, and the counselor's belief and regard for the client as a force for good in the resolution of personal difficulties that brought the client to the work of counseling.

Non-maleficence

Those who have a fiduciary responsibility to others have long been enjoined to "do no harm"; this sentiment is embedded in the Hippocratic Oath taken by all physicians. Wanting to "do no harm" is surely not the same thing as being clear on how to achieve that goal. It goes without saying that the counselor must be competent, with respect to both human dynamics and the theoretical orientation that is being used, but clearly this is not enough. One needs to be aware of the client's understanding of the working alliance and the limits of therapy. Psychoanalytic counseling, like all therapy, takes unexpected twists and turns and harm is not always foreseeable. Judgment is always involved, particularly in potential emergency situations: when to intervene and when to not. Accurate prediction with respect to the future effects of an action, as well as thoughtful retrospection, are needed to determine if certain policies or strategies are harmful. For some activities the result may not be known for many years, if at all.

Beneficence

The principle of beneficence requires that one "do good" for others. If psychoanalytic counseling or any similar form of treatment is not beneficial, it is not considered ethical to continue it. Having a positive influence in the life of another is a more demanding requirement than no "doing no harm." Exercising beneficence as a psychoanalytic counselor means that research, as well as clinical experience and judgment, is important in determining the benefits of counseling and the efficacy of a particular counselor. The goals of psychological research and psychoanalytic counseling can be in conflict. Some research activities that are themselves quite ethical could be quite problematic when applied to actual psychoanalytic counseling. For example, if a counselor is the researcher, issues of dual relationship arise; if the researcher is not the counselor, there could still be concerns with respect to how the research might affect the therapeutic alliance or other aspects of the work. For a full discussion of these issues, see Meara & Schmidt (1991).

Justice

One conceptualizatiom of justice is the equitable distribution of burdens and benefits. For the psychoanalytic counselor, issues of justice arise from both within and outside the work. Each private counselor is limited in the number of clients seen and in the amount of *pro bono* or reduced fee work offered. Agency counselors have additional limitations, and in general cannot work with everyone who could benefit. There becomes an immediate justice issue as to who to select, and who, if anyone, should be seen for free or at a greatly reduced fee. Many counselors have more requests from those who can pay than they can possibly meet. How to distribute one's time in a just fashion is not always intuitively obvious.

Fidelity

Fidelity is a principle that is derived from the other four and focuses on relationships and the fiduciary responsibilities that are part of a professional relationship, such as that between psychoanalytic counselor and client (Kitchener, 1984; Beauchamp & Childress, 1989; Meara & Schmidt, 1991). The ethical role of a psychoanalytic counselor goes well beyond the role of that person as a private citizen, spouse, or other family member. A counselor is in a position of power with a client, who is usually quite vulnerable. It is easy for a counselor to inadvertently use that power to create a dual relationship. The concept of dual relationships is explored more fully below. The importance of the working alliance and transference to the work exacerbate this potential for abuse. The abuses are often more subtle than flagrant. It is easy to inappropriately manipulate or be inappropriately manipulated by a client with respect to matters that are not directly related to the work.

Summary of Principle Ethics

It is easy to see how these principles can be in conflict with one another, and thus it can often be difficult to determine which takes precedence. For example, the counselor may determine that a client is dangerous to self or others and therefore may decide that the principle of non-maleficence takes precedence over respect for autonomy and the fiduciary responsibility of confidentiality (a component of fidelity and trust) that has been established during the development of the working alliance. Although the potential for such a decision may be part of the "ground rules" stated by the counselor at the beginning of the work, steps to break confidentiality or to restrict the client's autonomy are not taken lightly or without reflection on their ethical and therapeutic consequences. The counselor cannot always depend on the client to understand this supposed "breach" in their relationship.

The principles, however, do assist in clarifying what ethical issues are involved in a specific decision, and provide a framework for sorting out proper actions. In addition, a counselor skilled in the application of these principles can have some assurance that a particular judgment (or series of judgments) has some ethical rationale, rather than depending upon an intuitive (although often unerring) sense of what to do. Consistent use and application of the principles can also assist the counselor in the development of ethical judgment.

Relating the principles to practice

Although this is not a "how to do" chapter, it seems appropriate to present at least one example of how to relate the principles we have discussed to common occurrences in psychoanalytic counseling. Ethical decision-making is both complex and coherent. As noted above, the principles are not isolated from one another, from the character of the counselor, or from the codes endorsed by the counseling professions. One weighs all these factors when deciding on professional courses of action or contemplating ethical dilemmas. Of the myriad of possible examples, we have chosen to explore the topic of dual relationships. To set the stage for this discussion we present a few thoughts on the counselor's emotional reactions to the work and the client.

Counselor reactions   Braun (1982) notes:

> Patients create feelings in therapists no matter what their clinical or theoretical stance (p. 140).

The reality of these feelings and reactions is not disputed in the counseling community whether one chooses to label them as countertransference, inappropriate affect, or one of the inherent risks involved in building a working alliance. It is as important that the counselor be aware of and monitor these reactions as it is for the counselor to be a person of integrity and to have developed a rationale for ethical decision-making. In exploring ethical issues in treating persons with religious beliefs, Braun makes this point in eloquent fashion:

> Presuming that the therapist already possesses a genuine ethical core, the integrated personality needed to follow his or her ethical sensitivities, and a commitment to uphold the ethical code of his or her profession, then the foundation for working ethically with religious persons rests in the exploration and monitoring of the therapist's emotional reactions (p. 140).

We would argue that his point generalizes to work with all clients. Whatever the ethical question, the nature of the work is so intimate that the counselor needs to be vigilant with respect to his or her own emotions before ethical decisions can be made, or before deciding what issues (e.g. autonomy, fidelity, etc.) are most relevant to a course of action or a decision. The counselor needs to be aware of feeling not only toward the client, but also toward the topic.

In describing potential sources for the counselor's emotional reactions, Braun (1982) uses the term countertransference and elaborates on three kinds: (a) cultural, i.e. general background and affect-laden memories of specific cultural influences; (b) sub-cultural, meaning in this case the mental health field; and (c) individual, referring to the counselor's personality and hidden conflicts. For a thorough treatment of these constructs the reader is referred to Braun (1982). For our purposes, suffice to say that all these factors influence the counselor's judgment, even to the point of defining ethical principles (e.g. what is justice?), let alone applying them to specific situations. One cannot escape influence; it is critical that the influence not be undue, since the intrinsic vulnerability of being a client makes it virtually impossible for the client to overcome untoward, interfering, emotional reactions on the part of the counselor.

Dual relationships The counselor has more power than the client and, despite all strategies to equalize power, that fact remains. The idea that the counselor could equalize power implies, and correctly so, that the counselor does indeed have the greater power, including the power to decide whether efforts should be made to equalize it. In building the working alliance, in deciding about "tact timing and dosage," and in all other phases of the treatment, the power of the counselor is evident to all who are engaged in the research and the practice of counseling. Power can be seductive and it becomes easy to luxuriate in it and deceive oneself about one's importance. Indeed, a significant vocational hazard for counselors is a feeling of omnipotence (see Marmor, 1974; Robertiello, 1978). If such feelings are allowed to develop, they can lead a counselor into a dual relationship with the client. Issues related to dual relationships are one of the most frequent complaints received by ethics boards (see, for example, Ethics Committee, 1987). Dual relationships can take many forms; common ones are social, financial, and sexual.

A dual relationship with a client is to be avoided; it is a serious ethical matter because it violates at least two principles: respect for the client's autonomy, and the fiduciary responsibilities of the counselor. When tempted to develop a dual relationship, or when the counselor inadvertently finds him or herself in one with the client, it is not sufficient to make a global judgment about the merit of the relationship. Such global judgments are easily clouded by counselors believing that they know what is best for clients. It seems more helpful to have a clear grasp of the principles of respect for autonomy and fidelity, and to examine the possible or actual relationship against the requirements of these principles. The client comes to counseling with a set of expectations about the relationship, and vulnerabilities that preclude the client being able to choose freely an additional kind of alliance with the counselor. The counselor has a set of obligations to be counselor and counselor only to that client. If the counselor is deluded by power into creating a dual relationship, the client's autonomy is abused, the working alliance is damaged, and the professional contract (i.e. the counselor's implicit if not explicit promises) is broken.

Virtue ethics

A knowledge of Principle Ethics and practice with applying them can assist the psychoanalytic counselor in deciding what to do, and provide direction for the development of ethical judgment. Many ethicists and other scholars, however, believe that relying on Principle Ethics alone is not sufficient to insure sound ethical decision-making, and that training in Principle Ethics does not guarantee that professionals will be ethical persons in their everyday dealings with clients and colleagues (MacIntyre, 1966; May, 1984; Beauchamp & Childress, 1989; Jordan & Meara, 1990). These writers and others believe that training in Virtue Ethics is needed to complement the quality of ethical judgment that is developed through the understanding of Principle Ethics. While Principle Ethics focuses on the question of action (What shall I do?), Virtue Ethics focuses on the question of character (What shall I be?). An understanding of Virtue Ethics, as well as the development of moral virtues, seems particularly salient for psychoanalytic counselors whose work places them in working alliances with those who are often struggling with their own character development (e.g. those with borderline, obsessive, and narcissistic personality traits).

The kind of person the counselor is is as important to the work as what the counselor does. As Beauchamp & Childress (1989) note: "We evaluate the moral worth of agents no less than their actions" (p. 374). For many individuals in our contemporary culture, the counselor often fulfills the roles of mentor or confident, priest or healer, which in earlier times were reserved for members of the church or the academy. The client thus expects that the counselor is a person of high character who can be trusted; and implicitly, if not explicitly, judges the counselor's values and moral worth. All clients want their counselor to be a "good" person, in their own terms of what that means.

Virtue, particularly moral virtue, is not a popular word in our contemporary culture, and it is surely not popular in circles that are traditionally populated by psychologists and counselors. Issues that seem to be religious or morally philosophical are often viewed as inappropriate by psychology's therapeutic and scientific communities. In addition to the problems with the word "virtue", Virtue Ethics itself is difficult to explain and to distinguish definitely from Principle Ethics. For example, often the same word (e.g. fidelity) is used to describe both an ethical principle and a moral virtue. As Jordan & Meara (1990) point out, approaches to ethical decision-making that incorporate Virtue or Principle Ethics are not necessarily mutually exclusive. While there are differences between these points of view, these are not two coherent unambiguous competing philosophical systems; and indeed we see the competent ethical psychoanalytic counselor as relying on both principles and virtues. However, in order to enrich our discussion we define Virtue Ethics, discuss its application to psychoanalytic counseling and make some distinctions between virtue and principles as best we can.

As Jordan & Meara (1990) explain:

> . . . virtues historically have been viewed neither as situation specific nor as universal maxims but rather as character and community specific. They are nurtured habits grown mature in the context of a formative community and a shared set of purposes and assumptions. This process begins in the community of one's childhood and continues throughout life. Professional training and practice introduce new contexts and communities wherein professional virtues can be articulated and nurtured by students and professionals. People socialize one another into a professional culture that they continually construct and shape and from which they seek inspiration. As time passes certain shared assumptions and values are "taken for granted" and form the character of the profession and are part of the individual characters of the professionals (p. 110).

From this description one can grasp the elusiveness of this concept, and conceptual difficulties inherent in applying it to professional ethics. Beauchamp & Childress (1989) offer some helpful clarifications. They state that:

> We understand the term virtue in general to refer to a trait of character that is valued as a human quality. A moral virtue is a trait of character that is morally valued (p. 375).

Earlier, in regard to Virtue Ethics, they assert:

> . . . morality is viewed principally as the expression of a person's virtuous character, rather than as action in accordance with principles or rules (p. 374).

The categories of Principle and Virtue Ethics are complementary. Often it is the morally virtuous person who is the first to realize that it is difficult to discern a correct action (i.e. that an ethical dilemma exists) and that one must have recourse to principles, and the careful weighing of principles, before taking action. By the same token, a person who learns about weighing competing principles in making judgments in the context of a community of shared beliefs about the human person is participating in his or her own character development. A beginning professional may start by simply learning the rules of "what is right," progress to understanding the principles that support (and in some cases contradict) that rule, gradually develop powers of discernment and conscientiousness in considering ethical issues, and finally realize that what kind of person one is greatly affects how one accomplishes both the moral and skillful aspects of professional life. The professional acquires appropriate traits or dispositions to act in morally virtuous ways. Standards for counselors and others in training to be professionals often imply the importance of Virtue Ethics; e.g. the criterion may be stated in terms like "the student is to 'inculcate' the ethical expectations of the profession" (cf. American Psychological Association, 1986).

Which virtues are important in professional life, of course, depends on one's view of the profession in question and its obligations to its clients. Several authors (see Beauchamp & Childress, 1989; Jordan & Meara, 1990) have prepared prototypic lists which compare virtues and principles. While not exhaustive, these general lists make the point that principles and virtues are complementary aspects of professional moral life. Table 12.1 illustrates the Beauchamp & Childress scheme, which demonstrates the primary virtues and the secondary virtues that correspond to the fundamental and derivative principles that we have discussed in the first part of this chapter. We believe that this list represents a solid basis for the ethical practice of psychoanalytic counseling. It is easy to see the correspondence between the principle or obligation (e.g. respect for autonomy) and the virtue or character trait (respectfulness). As the labels imply and as noted above, the principles or obligations are action guides (i.e. things one does), and the virtues or character traits portray a mode of being (i.e. the kind of person one is).

Since virtues typically go beyond the minimum that is required by the codes of the profession, there can often be disagreement about whether any virtue is required. We would argue that an important component of a profession is its contribution to the common good (see Hatch, 1988; Jennings, Callahan & Wolf, 1987), and that an essential component of psychoanalytic counseling is the intimacy of the working alliance. These two factors make it seem to us that it is appropriate for psychoanalytic counselors continually to develop their knowledge and awareness in the domains of both Principle and Virtue Ethics. Such development seems important to the counselor, the client, and the profession.

We provide below an example of this importance, and the pairing of Virtue and Principle Ethics. Although any pairing from Table 12.1 would be relevant, we chose the derivative obligation of veracity and the secondary virtue of truthfulness. One need only look to the dramatic increase of lawsuits in the United States, where patients and clients are suing professionals, to see that the trust between professional and client is not high. Often these lawsuits are for malpractice, negligence, or forms of unethical conduct. Insurance rates have soared and professionals are advised to have specific written contracts with clients (cf. Everstine et al., 1980). As professional care becomes more depersonalized, trust erodes and clients may not be able to rely upon the character of a professional or a profession they do not know. In many instances, e.g. in highly specialized fields of medicine, physicians and patients simply do not know each other. A lack of trust is often mutual: the professional does not trust the patient not to

Table 12.1 Correspondence between ethical principles and virtues

Primary principles (obligations)	*Primary virtues*
Respect for autonomy	Respectfulness
Non-maleficence	Non-malevolence
Beneficence	Benevolence
Justice	Justice or fairness
Derivative principles (obligations)	*Secondary virtues*
Veracity	Truthfulness
Confidentiality	Confidentialness
Privacy	Respect for privacy
Fidelity	Faithfulness

(Adapted from Beauchamp & Childress, 1983; 1989)

sue for failure to achieve a perfect result, and the client does not know the character of the professional well enough to make a judgment about his or her trustworthiness. As Beauchamp & Childress (1989) note:

> . . . when strangers interact in health care, character will generally play a less significant role than principles and rules that are backed by sanctions (p. 383).

Psychoanalytic counseling depends on trust; the working alliance is a special bond and progress in the work cannot occur without belief in the other's veracity and truthfulness. A psychoanalytic counselor needs more than rules to guide actions, and sanctions from the community to enforce those rules if the client is to have a productive therapeutic experience. The counselor needs to be both a trustworthy person and a person of trust, who goes beyond the minimum ethical obligation. A counselor shares part of him or herself with the client, and part of what is shared are ethical character traits or virtues. While truthfulness is our example, the other virtues (as displayed in Table 12.1) of respectfulness, fairness, faithfulness, and the like are no less important.

An important aspect of professional life is its character and its reputation for fairness and honesty, as well as competence. If counselors become simply rule interpreters, pushing the limits of what the culture or the law will allow, we will lose our special status and the public will revoke our right to set our ethical standards and otherwise regulate ourselves. We will lose this right because we will no longer be seen so much as advocates for the common good, but rather more like a business or trade, where the watchword is often "buyer beware." There are already signs of this happening in the United States. For instance, in the 1976 Tarasoff decision, the State Supreme Court of California ruled that therapists not only have a general duty to intervene in the case of "clear and present danger," but also had a specific duty to warn an intended victim of the potential violence of a client. In most cases, such an action would almost surely severely damage the working alliance. Recently, the American Psychological Association changed its *Ethical Principles* regarding public statements to avoid being considered guilty of "restraint of trade" by the United States Federal Trade Commission (American Psychological Association, 1990). Professions must exist in the context of the culture which supports them, and the principles and character they develop to guide their work cannot be understood apart from that context. Their character (i.e. their virtues) must be known and valued by the culture for them to enjoy self-determination and autonomy in regulating their own standards.

Summary

For the psychoanalytic counselor, developing a sense of ethics is much like developing counseling competence. Both require a certain type of judgment and character. Both depend on theories and principles for their coherence and context; and both rely on experience in applying theory and principle to develop character traits, habits, and techniques which are sophisticated and effective and become a routine part of the counseling process.

There are parallels in developing both therapeutic expertise and ethical judgment. For example, the working alliance is based on the ethical obligation of fidelity; and while counselor restraint is based on the non-moral virtue of patience, chronic failure to exercise restraint can easily become an abuse of power, a significant ethical issue. Habitual abuses of power can be considered a character flaw, a serious defect in virtue, that would seriously limit one's qualifications to be a psychoanalytic counselor.

Our purpose in this chapter, therefore, has been to raise consciousness with respect to how Principle Ethics and Virtue Ethics are an integral part of psychoanalytic counseling and the development of psychoanalytic counselors. We trust this consciousness-raising activity with respect to how lprinciple and Virtue Ethics relate to psychoanalytic counseling will provide the reader with initial ideas for integrating therapeutic and ethical competence in a more deliberate and self-reflective fashion. We have tried to make evident that we do not see therapeutic and ethical competence as disparate, neither do we view ethics as something that is simply applied to the psychoanalytic counseling process. But the counselor cannot learn this integration from an individualized ethical or therapeutic character or develop judgment solely from reading about these ideas. Experience, i.e. experiencing significant ethical questions as part of experiencing the role of the counselor and the ambience of the counseling interaction, is necessary.

In integrating ethics and psychoanalytic counseling the questions of (a) "What shall I do?" as addressed by Principle Ethics and (b) "Who shall I be?" as addressed by Virtue Ethics are significant and enduring. They form part of our training as psychoanalytic counselors and are constantly being reassessed as we engage in the process of counseling a client. These questions, joined with our philosophical beliefs about and attitudes toward the human person, the research knowledge, clinical experience, and technical skill we bring to each interview combine to form the basis of the most important question of all: "How is this client to be best served?" That question can only be adequately answered after these prior questions have been considered.

13   Research

In this book, we have offered a psychoanalytic approach to the understanding of client behavior and the counseling process. We have attempted to show that the practice of psychoanalytic counseling is a deliberate and planful process. We believe it is a process that is facilitated when the psychoanalytic counselor combines the dual roles of scientist and practitioner (Pepinsky & Pepinsky, 1954). In both of these roles, the deliberate and informed use of the scientific tasks of observation and inference are important aspects of the counselor's responsibilities. Therefore, to help the counselor become oriented to scientific method in her or his practice, we have stressed the important role of observation in listening to and otherwise learning about the client. As well, we have introduced our evolving theoretical formulations of the client (Chapters 2 and 3) and our tentative models of the counseling process (Chapter 4) to enable the counselor to use his or her observations to draw inferences about the client's behavior. In this way, we have attempted to help the counselor link theory with practice. For the same reason, we have also provided rating scales for the informal assessment of the client before, during, and after counseling (Chapter 6), and guidelines for organizing client communications (Chapter 7) in the interview.

In the practice of counseling, all of this requires that the counselor also be curious, as well as compassionate; objective, as well as empathic. What remains is for us to consider ways of helping the counselor submit our theoretical formulations to ongoing revision based upon empirical research on the process and outcomes of psychoanalytic counseling. It is here that, in the work of the counselor as scientist–practitioner, psychoanalytic theory in its many forms offers heuristic access to developing refutable knowledge about clients and counseling.

To begin the actual research endeavor, the counselor can ask questions like these: apart from our intuition that things have gone well, how do we otherwise know when psychoanalytic counseling is effective? What events that occur during counseling are related to such desired outcomes as decreased symptoms, increased interpersonal effectiveness, or insight, and how should we go about investigating such events and their connection to outcome? To a considerable extent, our psychoanalytic orientation will guide us in raising many of the questions that need to be asked. As Pepinsky and Pepinsky (1954) noted many years ago, theoretical orientation does affect the counselor's research and practice; however, they also argued that there are general questions about counseling that transcend theoretical orientation. These questions, too, need to be addressed by the counselor as a scientist–practitioner if counseling is to be helpful, and if new data-based knowledge of the counseling process is to be generated. The Pepinskys' questions bear repeating here:

1. What is the client like?
2. How did the client get that way?
3. What is the counselor doing during counseling?
4. What is the client doing during counseling?
5. How do the counselor and client interact during counseling? (Pepinsky & Pepinsky, 1954, p. 276).

These questions are a prologue to subsequent questions that need to be asked about counseling outcomes:

6. How has the client changed?
7. What is the relationship between (a) the client's behavior subsequent to counseling and (b) the previous behavior of counselor and client during and prior to counseling? (Pepinsky & Pepinsky, 1954, p. 277).

Since the Pepinskys raised these questions and pointed out the difficulties inherent in assessing the efficacy of counseling, many new methods for designing counseling studies have been developed, and new quantitative and qualitative techniques for the collection and analysis of data have been derived (Gelso, 1985; Hoshmond, 1989; Howard, 1985, 1986). Then, as now, we need to increase our scientific knowledge of the counseling process through empirical investigations. Our general task in this chapter is to explore how these important questions might be addressed in research on psychoanalytic counseling and to present some research evidence that has accumulated to date. To this end, we first present an overview of some current methodological approaches to research on counseling and some of the problems associated with them. Then, we consider some of the recently developed psychological measures that are particularly relevant for use in research on psychoanalytic counseling, and present evidence of their psychometric qualities. In our discussion of instruments, we also review selected empirical studies in which these instruments have been used.

Methodological approaches to research on counseling

How research should be conducted on counseling remains an open question at the present time. Unlike the road to the unconscious (Freud, 1957b), there is no "royal road" to the discovery of knowledge about the counseling process. This state of affairs, which has long been recognized by psychologists, was again recently acknowledged by the members of the research group at Counseling Psychology's Georgia Conference (Gelso *et al.*, 1988). The members of the group explicitly called for a diversity of methods because of the complexities that face researchers as they try to understand the many events that comprise psychological treatment. Researchers, as well as researchers-in-training such as students, are called upon to have an appreciation of the range of current methods and of the important methodological assumptions that inform them (Hoshmond, 1989; Howard, 1984; Polkinghorne, 1984; Patton, 1982a, 1984; Strong, 1991). Accordingly, we will not review in this section the content of current research in as much as that has been comprehensively reviewed elsewhere (cf. Gelso & Fassinger, 1990). Rather, we shall briefly consider some of the assumptive foundations of scientific methods for conducting research on counseling.

A conceptual framework

There are many ways for the researcher to describe and then analyze events in psychoanalytic counseling. The researcher's choice of method rests in part on assumptions about human behavior and the conduct of inquiry and, of course, on the purposes for doing the research. A researcher's scientific interest in psychoanalytic counseling interview events may be conceptualized in terms of two dimensions of data collection and analysis: (a) goals; and (b) methods. By goals, we have in mind the researcher's basic purposes in doing the research. As M.Q. Patton (1990) points out, the researcher's purpose controls other features of the research endeavor. From purpose follow decisions about design, measurement, data analysis, and reporting. We conceive of the majority of counseling research as consisting of one or the other of two broad and contrasting goals, or their combination.

The first goal is the derivation of explanations of the antecedents, if not the causes, of the counselor's and client's behavior during and following counseling. The second goal is to gain understanding about what events in counseling mean for the client and counselor. As shown in Figure 13.1, Dimension I presents a continuum of goals that range from: (a) an explanation of counseling events in terms of their accord with the researcher's *a priori* scientific conceptions; to those that call for (b) a description and analysis of naturally occurring counseling events in terms of the meaning they have for the client and counselor. At either end of the goals dimension, the research operates with certain meta-scientific assumptions or principles (see Chapter 1) which inform the researcher's *a priori* conceptions of human behavior and scientific inquiry.

In the first case, the research is informed by the following methodological assumptions or principles:

1. *Reductionism*: in the last analysis, the counselor's and client's behavior can be explained by recourse to the operation of underlying cognitive or physical processes and structures.
2. *Determinism*: the counselor's and client's behavior which the investigator is interested in studying has specifiable antecedents that cause, or at least influence, it.
3. *Motivation*: the source of the client's or counselor's behavior (i.e. the reason they behave as they do) is found in their physical make-up and/or in environmental stimuli.
4. *Historico-genetic explanation*: the client's and counselor's behavior has its antecedents in their remote, as well as in their recent, biographies.
5. *Need for theoretical explanation*: except for a "radical" behaviorist's account, results of counseling research that square with theoretical accounts advance science by providing the most coherent scientific explanation.

In the second case, the researcher operates with a set of meta-scientific principles that are logically incompatible with those above. These principles are:

1. *Holism*: the perspective that events in counseling are to be understood in terms of their embeddedness in a locally managed and totally situated context.
2. *Empathic introspectionism*: much like the practicing counselor, the researcher assumes that the counselor's and client's subjective understanding of events is both knowable and acceptable as data.
3. *Motivation*: in this case, the researcher assumes that the origins of the client's and counselor's behavior are to be found in their intentional actions.

By methods of data collection and analysis (dimension II in Figure 13.1) we mean the techniques and strategies the researcher uses to observe and analyze events that are of scientific interest. Methods of data collection and analysis vary with the researcher's goals or purposes which, in turn, are influenced by the methodological assumptions listed above. On the dimension of methods of data collection and analysis, there are, at one end, those that call for the analysis of quantified data collected through pre-structured methods of experimentation, interviews, tests, or coding schemes. The use of such methods permits the researcher to make claims about the statistical or causal relations among observed events, and/or their accord with *a priori* conceptions of what the data mean. At the other end of this dimension are methods that entail the use of direct observation and content analysis of naturally occurring counseling events. The methods at this end of the continuum are intended to permit the researcher to provide close description of actual interview events, their pattern or structure, how client and counselor managed them, and what they mean to them.

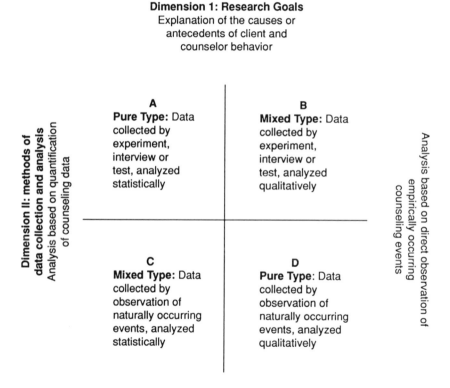

Figure 13.1 A scheme for classifying the methodology of counseling inquiry

The experimental/quantitative approach At the explanatory or causal end of the goals dimension, the researcher might construe events in counseling and in the life of the client and counselor as "caused," in this case, either by dynamic underlying physical processes, and/or by environmental events. Thus, the observable events of the client and counselor in which the investigator is interested are assumed to be the manifestations of underlying physical processes, and/or the consequences of specific antecedent environmental contingencies. The work of the researcher is either to test hypothetical propositions about these variables under experimentally or statistically controlled conditions, or otherwise to collect data on them with the use of previously developed analytic schemes, into which observable events, as manifestations of these variables, are coded by raters or by the research participants themselves. The researcher's ultimate aim in this paradigm is to develop theoretical accounts or to provide statistical estimates which explain variations in the controlled observations. The advancement of knowledge of counseling through theory-driven research is, thus, a major goal of many researchers who approach inquiry from this perspective (Strong, 1991).

The above is a characterization of the post-positivistic or "received" view of scientific method in the social and behavioral sciences (Polkinghorne, 1984). It is also referred to as the "quantitative" or "experimental/quantitative" approach. When combined with the quantitative end of the method of data collection dimension, quadrant A, Figure 13.1, forms a pure type of this approach. We have borrowed the idea of combining the two ends of our continuum to create a "pure type" from M.Q. Patton (1990). There are many variations of this pure type in counseling research, but we will mention here only three: the formal laboratory or analogue experiment; the statistical study; and content analysis.

1. The first example of such a pure type is the classical psychological *laboratory or analogue experiment* (see Pepinsky & Patton, 1971). This procedure of data collection is directly derived from the reductive, experimental tradition in the natural sciences. In counseling research, the experiment consists of a set of procedures designed to produce events that appear more or less like those in a naturally occurring counseling encounter (Pepinsky & Patton, 1971). That is, the experimental conditions are an "analogue" of events in counseling. The subject is then invited to participate in the experiment by complying with the experimenter's procedures. In setting up the design, and in making it operational, the experimenter retains strict control over the variation in one or more antecedent (independent) variables, here conceived of as intervention or treatment conditions to which the subjects are exposed, and presumably influenced. Such variations in these treatment conditions usually create two or more groupings of subjects. Following exposure

to these treatment conditions, the experimenter then observes the resulting variation in one or more dependent variables on which the subjects' performance has been measured. In this way, the experimenter can examine the data for predicted differences between and among the groups that have been created by the design. Much of the early research on social influence in counseling, for example, has used the laboratory or analogue approach (see Strong, 1968, 1991; Pepinsky & Patton, 1971).

2. Another frequent type of quantitative study in counseling is the *statistical* design. Usually, these designs employ some variation of associational statistics to analyze the data. In this variation, the researcher first asks his or her research participants to respond to the items in two or more psychological measures. In this way, the researcher obtains the scores of a sample of counselors and/or clients on these formally constructed scales, and then examines statistically the relations among the scores on these variables. The purpose of the statistical analysis of the data is either to test an hypothesis about the significance of and direction of these relations, or simply to describe, again statistically, and perhaps for the first time, the resulting network of relations among them. Much so-called "descriptive" research on counseling uses this variation. Deriving knowledge of the network of statistical relations among variables is said to be a necessary pre-condition to later, more precise experimental inquiry on these variables. Increasingly sophisticated statistical procedures are being used to analyze counseling data in the statistical approach (see Gelso, 1987).

3. Finally, *content analysis* of events in counseling via a pre-structured coding scheme is another frequent quantitative method used by researchers. In fact, at this time, the use of coding schemes to investigate counseling process and outcome is the most frequent or modal method of data collection. In this variation, the researcher develops or uses an already developed analytic device for observing events in the interview by translating them to the terms of the coding scheme (Patton, 1989). In other words, the content of the counseling interview is analyzed by somehow classifying it according to the categories of the coding scheme. Ordinarily, raters are first trained to use the coding scheme with sample data, and then are given the task of coding actual instances of counseling events from either direct observation or transcripts. When the raters are finished, the frequencies of events that have been coded into each of the categories in the coding scheme are subjected to various kinds of statistical analysis so that statements about the content of counseling process and/or outcome can be made.

Questions that can be addressed in Quadrant A of Figure 13.1, the pure experimental/quantitative approach, might be something like these: how are variations in certain measurable client attributes, such as severity of presenting complaints, related to variations in other specific and measurable client interview events, such as strength of the working alliance? How is the frequency of a certain class of counselor intervention, such as confrontation, related to the frequency of a certain class of client response, such as disclosure of significant material, and how are both of these related to degree of client insight? Counseling research in this tradition has generally focused on either the counseling process, on counseling outcomes, or on linking specific process variables to specific outcome variables. As Pepinsky & Pepinsky (1954) have noted, ". . . process–outcome research has the advantage over other methods of telling us how what happens during counseling is related to what happens outside of the situation" (p. 272).

The qualitative/descriptive approach At the other end of the goals continuum, the researcher may construe observable events in counseling as the more or less orderly and intentional productions of a client and counselor who are otherwise assumed to be active interpreters and managers of those observable productions (Howard, 1984; Patton, 1984). The researcher's task in this paradigm is to provide a detailed description and analysis of some sequence of the ongoing events in counseling as they occur naturally. Thus, the purpose of the researcher is to determine what those events mean to the counseling participants, how they interactively make ongoing events meaningful, or how this socially constructed meaning is used to further their interactive purposes. This paradigm with its many variations (Patton, 1991) is an alternative (Hoshmond, 1989) to the received view and is sometimes referred to as the "qualitative" approach. Other labels for this approach include the phenomenological, ethnomethodological, interpretive, or hermeneutic approaches.

Questions that can be asked in the naturalistic/descriptive approach include: what effect on the structure of the ongoing discourse does the counselor's use of confrontation or cognitive appeal have? Of what does client insight consist as the client's and counselor's work in the interview? What are the characteristics of the sequences of counselor and client talk in which client resistance (or any other phenomenon) is manifest? Because research in this tradition is more descriptive at the present time, researchers are apt to focus more on events during counseling and on their analysis, than on their relation to outcomes *per se*.

Methods of data collection in the qualitative tradition focus on the observation of naturally occurring events, often *in situ*. That is, the researcher may be a participant with the subjects who are the focus of the investigation, or he or she may record whole interviews, or selected sequences of client and counselor utterances, via audio- or video-tape for later analysis. Thus, analysis emerges from events that are directly observable in the counseling interaction. The pure case of the qualitative paradigm is found in Quadrant D of Figure 13.1.

Mixed approaches   Quadrants B and C of Figure 13.1 consist of mixed variations of the two approaches (see M.Q. Patton, 1990). These two quadrants combine either explanatory or descriptive goals with either qualitative or quantitative methods of data collection and analysis. For example, in Quadrant B of Figure 13.1 it would be possible to use a strictly experimental design and randomly select clients on one or more pre-defined grouping variables. Such variables might be things like severity of the client's presenting complaint and client readiness to accept a working alliance. When clients had been measured on these variables they would then be assigned a corresponding condition in the design. Yet, the source of the data could well be actual counseling discourse analyzed for its recurring features before, during, and following counseling. Thus, the researcher proceeds to produce a description of the discourse in each experimental group in the design, analyzes that discourse in terms of the themes that emerge, and then compares and contrasts the thematic patterns or other phenomena that have arisen from the analysis.

By contrast, Quadrant C of Figure 13.1 would consist of a study that begins with a very open-ended qualitative description of counseling interview data, but ends by analyzing the data thus described with statistical procedures. In this mixed case, the researcher begins to look at the counseling interview data without any preconceived notions about the attributes of the clients or about what else might be important as they interact with their counselors. As the researcher proceeds to inspect the interaction, he or she may begin to identify recurring themes or other events in the interviews. Each time such an identification is made, the researcher creates a category and codes similar events into it, at the same time noting the topic under discussion. The researcher then goes on to analyze statistically the frequencies of occurrence of these events and relate them to other variables, such as client gender, counselor gender, client problem type, and the like.

Some methodological caveats

In all four quadrants of our conceptual scheme the researcher is concerned with the observation of events in counseling. In the experimental/quantitative approach, the researcher is guided by the use of various *a priori* analytic schemes that may include explicitly stated hypotheses and their accompanying experimental designs, and/or rating scales or coding schemes. In the descriptive/qualitative approach, the researcher observes the ongoing interaction, either as it naturally occurs or via recordings of it, and does so without recourse to an explicit, formal set of ideas about which observations to select or de-select. In the pure experimental/quantitative approach, conceptual analysis precedes the collection of data. In the pure descriptive/qualitative approach, conceptual analysis follows data collection. In the mixed types, these distinctions do not hold, as the analysis may occur before, during, and after in each case.

As can be seen, the methods of data collection and the researcher's analytic tasks vary considerably, depending on the goals of the research. Essentially, in the pure case of an experimental/quantitative study, the researcher's problem is to reconcile the results of the research with his or her prior conception of what those results are supposed to mean. It is often very difficult to bring about an exact correspondence of meaning between the researcher's *a priori* conception of results and the actual appearance of the results themselves. By the same token, the descriptive/qualitative researcher's problem is to determine what the data mean during and after they have been collected. This is often difficult to do in ways that show coherence and which explicate for others how the researcher reached his or her conclusions. Because of these analytic problems in both of the pure types, many methodologists (see M.Q. Patton, 1990) recommend that researchers deliberately select a variety of approaches to any study.

The majority of counseling studies up to the present time, however, have been conducted and the results interpreted within the experimental/quantitative paradigm. This is in large measure due to the fact that the scientific training of graduate students in psychology is almost exclusively in the post-positivistic, quantitative approaches. Only recently have researchers begun to use some of the qualitative methods to investigate the events in counseling (cf. Hoshmond, 1989). There are merits to both scientific approaches and their admixtures in the generation of knowledge about counseling. We would do well to let such factors as our research purposes, the breadth or depth of the study, what kind of data will be analyzed, and problems of reliability and validity help us make choices among research methods to employ. A recent book by Heppner, Kivlighan and Wampold (1991), entitled *Research Design in Counseling*, is recommended as an excellent introduction to the experimental/quantitative approach. M.Q. Patton's (1990) book, entitled *Qualitative Evaluation and Research Methods*, is recommended as a comprehensive treatment of various approaches in the naturalistic tradition.

Some instruments relevant to research on psychoanalytic counseling

In the experimental/quantitative tradition, the counseling researcher's task of observation is very often carried out with the use of formally constructed psychological measures. The observed scores on such measures become, then, the data which the researcher analyzes to carry out her or his research purposes. Typically, these instruments take the form of measures of client and counselor attributes and/or the perceptions of these persons of counseling process and outcome events. The instruments are usually designed to be answered by clients and counselors themselves or by trained raters who have otherwise observed the counseling participants and their interaction. To stand as adequate to the task of accurate observation, such measures are only as good as their psychometric properties. Scale construction or measurement is one of the most technical fields in the discipline of psychology. An extensive literature has evolved on standards and methods of constructing psychometrically sound measures. For an introduction to this field, the reader is referred to Nunnally (1978), *Psychometric Theory*.

In this section we will describe several quantitative measures that we and others have constructed for use in research on psychoanalytically oriented counseling. We will also include reports of several studies in which these instruments have been used. So that the reader will be able to understand the measures themselves, we will pay particular attention to following their psychometric properties: the methods of scale construction used in developing them; and, where available, their estimates of scale reliability, inter-rater reliability, and construct, concurrent, and predictive validity.

The Working Alliance Inventory (WAI)

As we have seen throughout this book, and particularly in Chapter 5, the working alliance between the client and counselor is regarded as a very important part of the process in psychoanalytic counseling. Until Greenson (1967), Bordin (1979) and Gelso and Carter (1985) conceptualized the elements of this aspect of the client and counselor relationship, there was no model of it that had both scientific coherence, based on an explicitly defined relation to psychoanalytic theory, *and* clinical relevance. We believe that empirical inquiry on the working alliance is one of the most important fields of counseling research at the present time. Research on the working alliance is relevant to not only the practice of counseling, but to counselor training and supervision as well.

Horvath & Greenberg (1989) developed the items for the WAI by drawing mainly upon Bordin's (1979) extensions of Greenson's (1967) earlier formulations. Bordin went beyond Greenson by rejecting the latter's notion that the working alliance works in partnership with the transference relationship. What Greenson means in this instance is that the positive transference makes possible the working alliance. Instead, Bordin's concept of the alliance is that the counseling participants are conscious of its elements. For this reason, Bordin (1979) claims his model is appropriate for use in research on a variety of theoretical approaches to counseling. We are in agreement with Greenson's (1967) assumption about the role of the transference in the formation of the working alliance. However, this does not reduce the utility of the use of the WAI in research on psychoanalytic counseling.

Briefly, Bordin (1979) proposed that the working alliance consists of three elements: tasks, bonds, and goals. In Bordin's (1979) terms, tasks refer to all of the behaviors and thoughts of the counseling participants that make up the important ingredients of what we ordinarily refer to as the counseling process. The counselor's interventions and use of theory, and the client's responses and reasoning, comprise this element. For the relationship to function smoothly, both participants must perceive the tasks as relevant and be willing to perform them. Bonds refer to the affective component of the relationship. Specifically, for the working alliance to be effective, there must be a positive attachment between the pair based on mutuality, trust, acceptance, and confidence. Goals refer to the mutual endorsement by the client and counselor of the outcomes they are seeking by the tasks they perform.

Performing a content analysis of Bordin's (1979) three dimensions, Horvath and Greenberg (1989) developed sets of items for each dimension for both a client's and a counselor's version. Items were first written in a Likert-style five-point scale response format "to capture a feeling, sensation, or attitude in the client's field of awareness that may be present or absent, depending on the strength of one of the components . . ." (Horvath & Greenberg, 1989, p. 225). The wording and content of some of the initial items were later refined by giving them to experts and professionals. After pilot testing on 29 graduate students in counseling psychology (Horvath, 1981) to obtain initial estimates of reliability (e.g. overall scale item homogeneity, = 0.93 for the client version and 0.87 for the counselor's version), the initial item pool was reduced to 36 items (12 in each scale), now placed in a seven-item Likert response format. An example of an item from each scale in the WAI is as follows:

1. Tasks: "_____ and I agree about the things I will need to do in therapy to help improve my situation."
2. Bonds: "I feel uncomfortable with _____."
3. Goals: "We agree on what is important for me to work on."

Research using the WAI The WAI has since been used in a series of studies that have added to its psychometric qualities. Several of these studies test the proposition that higher scores on the WAI, indicative of a stronger working alliance, will be positively related to measures of counseling outcome. We will mention two of these studies here as illustrative examples. First, in a study of 29 counselor–client dyads engaged in a variety of theoretical types of short-term counseling (Horvath & Greenberg, 1989), the total WAI score (recorded after the third session) was found to be significantly related to client- and counselor-rated outcome measures of satisfaction and change in counseling.

In another study of the predictive validity of the WAI, Moseley (1983) used 25 client–counselor dyads representing a broad range of theoretical orientations and employed the same outcome measures as used earlier. In addition, Moseley also included measures of state and trait anxiety, self concept, and target complaint. A composite alpha (overall scale reliability) for the WAI on this data set was 0.93. The measures of state and trait anxiety and self concept were not found to be significantly correlated with WAI scores. However, as in the earlier study, WAI scale scores were significantly correlated with the composite outcome score (bond = 0.46; task = 0.50; goals = 0.37), and to the satisfaction outcome score (bond = 0.71; task = 0.63; goals = 0.50). Moreover, the bond ($r = 0.51$) and task ($r = 0.53$) scores were also significantly correlated with reduction in the client's target complaints.

Many counseling researchers are now using the WAI to investigate relationships between the client and counselor working alliance and various other measures of process and outcome. The WAI has thus far held up quite well in demonstrating its worth as a measure of the counseling process.

The Supervisory Working Alliance Inventory (SWAI)

A task that faces many counseling practitioners is that of teaching and supervising less experienced persons in the work of counseling. Moreover, we believe that all professional counselors have a responsibility for training, regardless of the setting in which the work is done. In this regard, the relationship between the trainee and the supervisor in counselor supervision is no less salient in this situation than it is in counseling. In developing the SWAI, Efstation, Patton & Kardash (1990) adapted the ideas of Greenson (1967) and several other authors, including Patton (1984) and Pepinsky & Patton (1971). Efstation, Patton & Kardash (1990) define the relationship in supervision as ". . .a working alliance in which social influence occurs . . .through activities performed by the participants" (p. 323). Their scale construction task consisted of extrapolating from Greenson (1967) and others in the writing of items to represent the set of actions in which each participant in supervision engages. Sets of 30 trainee and supervisor items were written as mirror adaptations of each other and then placed on a seven-point Likert response format. An example of an item from the supervisor's version is as follows: "I facilitate my trainee's talking in our sessions." Its counterpart in the trainee's version is: "My supervisor helps me talk freely in our sessions."

Six hundred and fourteen directors of internship programs in professional psychology and directors of graduate training programs in counseling and clinical psychology were asked to give the appropriate set of SWAI items to a supervisor and his or her trainee. Both supervisors and trainees also responded to the Supervisory Styles Inventory (SSI; Friedlander & Ward, 1984), a measure of the degree to which a supervisor or trainee endorses behaviors representative of each of three factorially derived dimensions of supervisory style: Attractive, Interpersonally Sensitive and Task-oriented. The SSI scales were administered to obtain estimates of convergent and divergent validity for the SWAI. In addition, the trainees also filled out a measure of supervision outcome, the Self-efficacy Inventory (SEI; Friedlander & Snyder, 1983). The SEI was included as a criterion variable to determine the predictive validity of the SWAI. Usable data were returned for 185 supervisors and 178 trainees.

When the data were returned, the authors then set about trying to determine whether there were interpretable dimensions underlying each set of 30 items. Following a principle components extraction followed by an orthogonal (varimax) rotation, three factors, accounting for 35% of the variance, emerged for the supervisor's set of items, and two factors, accounting for 38% of the variance, emerged for the trainee's item set. The three supervisor factors were labeled: Client Focus (nine items that represent the emphasis the supervisor places on helping the trainee understand the client); Rapport (seven items that represent the supervisor's effort to build rapport with the trainee); and Identification (seven items that represent the supervisor's perception of the trainee's identification with him or her). The two trainee factors were labeled as follows: Rapport (12 items that represent the trainee's perception of support from the supervisor); and Client Focus (seven items that represent the emphasis placed by the supervisor on the work of understanding the client). The items for the supervisor and trainee SWAI scales are presented in Table 13.1.

In this study, the alpha (scale reliability) coefficients for the three SWAI supervisor's scales were 0.71 for Client Focus, 0.73 for Rapport and 0.77 for Identification; and for the two trainee scales, they were 0.90 for Rapport and 0.77 for Client Focus ($n = 178$). Estimates of convergent validity for the SWAI were obtained by correlating it with the scales of the Supervisory Styles Inventory (SSI) for $n = 178$ supervisor–trainee dyads. As might be expected, both versions of the SWAI Client Focus scale correlated moderately (0.50 and 0.52) with the SSI supervisor and trainee Task-Orientation scales. To obtain estimates of divergent validity, the authors correlated both SWAI Client Focus scales with the SSI supervisor's (0.20 and 0.30) and trainee's

Table 13.1 Supervisor's and trainee's versions of the Supervisory Working Alliance Inventory (SWAI)

SUPERVISOR'S VERSION

Client Focus
1. I help my trainee work within a specific treatment plan with his/her client.
2. I help my trainee stay on track during our meetings.
3. My style is to consider carefully and systematically the material that my trainee brings to supervision.
4. My trainee works with me on specific goals in the supervisory session.
5. In supervision, I expect my trainee to think about or reflect on my comments to him/her.
6. I teach my trainee through direct suggestion.
7. In supervision, I place a high priority on our understanding the client's perspective.
8. I encourage my trainee to take time to understand what the client is saying and doing.
9. When correcting my trainee's errors with a client, I offer alternative ways of intervening with that client.

Rapport
1. I encourage my trainee to formulate his/her own interventions with his/her clients.
2. I encourage my trainee to talk about the work in ways that are comfortable for him/her.
3. I welcome my trainee's explanations about his/her client's behavior.
4. During supervision, my trainee talks more than I do.
5. I make an effort to understand my trainee.
6. I am tactful when commenting about my trainee's performance.
7. I facilitate my trainee's talking in our sessions.

Identification
1. In supervision, my trainee is more curious than anxious when discussing his/her difficulties with clients.
2. My trainee appears to be comfortable working with me.
3. My trainee understands client behavior and treatment technique similar to the way I do.
4. During supervision, my trainee seems able to stand back and reflect on what I am saying to him/her.
5. I stay in tune with my trainee during supervision.
6. My trainee identifies with me in the way he/she thinks and talks about his/her clients.
7. My trainee consistently implements suggestions made in supervision.

Adapted from Efstation *et al.* (1990). Copyright 1990 by the American Psychological Association. Adapted by permission of the publisher.

(0.04 and 0.21) versions of the Attractive and Interpersonally Sensitive scales. Moreover, both versions of the SWAI Rapport scale had low correlations (-0.06 and <0.00) with the SSI Task-oriented scales.

Table 13.1 (*continued*)

<hr>

TRAINEE'S VERSION

Rapport
1. I feel comfortable with my supervisor.
2. My supervisor welcomes my explanations about the client's behavior.
3. My supervisor makes the effort to understand me.
4. My supervisor encourages me to talk about my work with clients in ways that are comfortable for me.
5. My supervisor is tactful when commenting about my performance.
6. My supervisor encourages me to formulate my own interventions with the client.
7. My supervisor helps me talk freely in our sessions.
8. My supervisor stays in tune with me during supervision.
9. I understand client behavior and treatment technique similar to the way my supervisor does.
10. I feel free to mention to my supervisor any troublesome feelings I might have about him/her.
11. My supervisor treats me like a colleague in our supervisory sessions.
12. In supervision, I am more curious than anxious when discussing my difficulties with clients.
13. In supervision, my supervisor places a high priority on our understanding the client's perspective.

Client Focus
1. My supervisor encourages me to take time to understand what the client is saying and doing.
2. My supervisor's style is to consider carefully and systematically the material I bring to supervision.
3. When correcting my errors with a client, my supervisor offers alternative ways of intervening with that client.
4. My supervisor helps me work within a specific treatment plan with my clients.
5. My supervisor helps me stay on track during our meetings.
6. I work with my supervisor on specific goals in the supervisory session.

<hr>

Research using the SWAI   In examining the predictive validity of the SWAI scales, Efstation, Patton & Kardash (1990) conducted a hierarchical regression analysis to predict scores on the Self-efficacy Inventory (SEI), using the data set above. After inspecting the correlations among all the scales in their study, these authors selected the following scales as predictors: SSI supervisor Interpersonal Sensitivity, SSI trainee Task-orientation and SWAI trainee Rapport and Client Focus. The multiple correlation among these four predictors and SEI scores was 0.37, $F(4, 171) = 6.83$, $p < 0.001$, accounting for 14% of the variance. The standardized beta weights for the SSI supervisor Interpersonal Sensitivity and SSI trainee Task-orientation scales were: −0.14, 0.27. The weights for the SWAI trainee Rapport and Client Focus scales were 0.19 and −0.12. Although the amount of variance accounted for in SEI scores was small, the two SWAI trainee scales were significant predictors. The authors believe the SWAI can be a very useful instrument for research on the training of psychoanalytically oriented and other counselors.

The Utah Counseling Outcomes Project (UCOP)

In the early 1980s, a multivariate scale construction project was undertaken by the first author and some of his graduate students at the University of Utah. Based on a multivariate model of counseling outcome dimensions, the authors developed 49 rating scales to measure attributes of the counseling process. Drawing upon the nexus of thought about the process of psychoanalytically oriented psychological treatment and its desired outcomes, the investigators in the UCOP project defined four client dimensions that represent desired outcomes, and then constructed the counselor dimension to reflect a range of intervention techniques counselors are observed to use with clients. In addition, they defined the concept of outcome as a variable that has a continuous status throughout the course of counseling. Thus, an "outcome" is present in some form during the "process" of counseling. Measuring the counseling process involves, therefore, the observation of the status of any of these variables at different points in time and then comparing the observed differences (if any) from one time to the next (see Patton, 1982b).

The UCOP model consists, then, of four client dimensions and one counselor dimension, each with multiple attributes. The client dimensions were labeled as follows: (a) Client Improvement in Social Relations; (b) Client Reduction of Unsuccessful Adaptive Response Patterns; (c) Client Coherence of Schemata of Self and Others; and (d) Client Change in Cognitive Operations. The counselor dimension was called: (e) Counselor Intervention Modes. Figure 13.2 is a representation of the entire UCOP model.

To scale the attributes in each dimension, sets of 16 anchor statements were then written for each of them, using Thurstonian techniques for developing empirically derived rating scales with known interval values (Patton, 1981b; Robbins & Patton, 1986). The UCOP investigators conducted a series of item-writing conferences in which these 16 anchor statements for each attribute were written to represent a continuum of severity or effectiveness. That is, each anchor represented a point on the continuum describing what client behavior or a counselor intervention might be like at that point on the continuum. The rater's task in filling out the scale would,

A. Multivariate outcome dimensions for the modeling of counseling processes

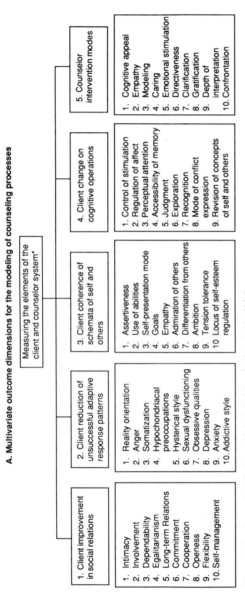

Measuring the elements of the client and counselor system*

1. Client improvement in social relations	2. Client reduction of unsuccessful adaptive response patterns	3. Client coherence of schemata of self and others	4. Client change on cognitive operations	5. Counselor intervention modes
1. Intimacy	1. Reality orientation	1. Assertiveness	1. Control of stimulation	1. Cognitive appeal
2. Involvement	2. Anger	2. Use of abilities	2. Regulation of affect	2. Empathy
3. Dependability	3. Somatization	3. Self-presentation mode	3. Perceptual attention	3. Modeling
4. Egalitarianism	4. Hypochondriacal preoccupations	4. Goals	4. Accessibility of memory	4. Caring
5. Long-term Relations	5. Hysterical style	5. Empathy	5. Judgment	5. Emotional stimulation
6. Commitment	6. Sexual dysfunctioning	6. Admiration of others	6. Exploration	6. Directiveness
7. Cooperation	7. Obsessive qualities	7. Differentiation from others	7. Recognition	7. Clarification
8. Openess	8. Depression	8. Ambition	8. Mode of conflict expression	8. Gratification
9. Flexibility	9. Anxiety	9. Tension tolerance	9. Revision of concepts of self and others	9. Depth of interpretation
10. Self-management	10. Addictive style	10. Locus of self-esteem regulation		10. Confrontation

* The evaluation of counseling "effectiveness" is the task of observing the extent to which the client's scores on the outcome measure's above move in the appropriate direction over time.

B. Deriving knowledge of processes within the counseling system

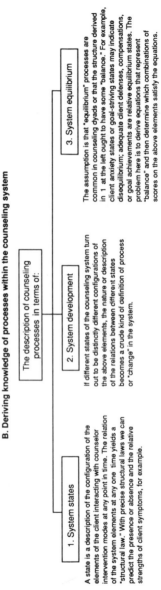

The description of counseling processes in terms of:

1. System states	2. System development	3. System equilibrium
A state is a description of the configuration of the elements of the client interacting with counselor intervention modes at any point in time. The relation of the system elements at any one time yields a "structural law." With precise structural laws we can predict the presence or absence and the relative strengths of client symptoms, for example.	If different states of the counseling system turn out to be distinctly different configurations of the above elements, the nature or description of the relations between different states becomes a crude kind of definition of process or "change" in the system.	The assumption is that "equilibrium" processes are common in counseling dyads or that the structure derived in 1 at the left ought to have some "balance." For example, client anxiety states or goal-striving states may indicate disequilibrium; adequate client defenses, compensations, or goal achievements are relative equilibrium states. The problem here is to derive equations that represent "balance" and then determine which combinations of scores on the above elements satisfy the equations.

Figure 13.2 A multivariate model of the counseling process and its outcomes

therefore, involve comparing the client's behavior during or after counseling to that anchor on the scale that best represented the client's current status.

When the anchors had been written, several sets of 16 were given to practicing doctoral level professionals in counseling and clinical psychology and social work, and to advanced graduate students in counseling psychology who served as judges for rank ordering the anchors in a set. That is, judges were given the sets of 16 anchors along with a definition of the scale attribute. Then, the judge would take the set of 16 anchor statements and place each statement in a rank from least to most severe. The judges' rankings were then analyzed to obtain initial estimates of scale reliability and consistency. These data are presented in Table 13.2. The measure of overall scale reliability used was Kendall's W. This statistic is an index of the extent to which the judges were consistent in their ranking of the anchor statements in each set. The χ^2 values associated with each estimate of W were all significant beyond $p < 0.0001$.

As can be seen in Table 13.2, the estimates of scale reliability were uniformly high, i.e. greater than 0.70. These data gave the researchers confidence in proceeding to the next step of their scale construction efforts.

The next task in this scale construction project involved obtaining estimates of inter-rater reliability and agreement for the scales. Only if the scales could be used reliably, and with adequate agreement by persons rating actual counseling sessions, would the scales be appropriate for research on counseling and for later clinical use. The raters used for this project were three advanced PhD students in counseling psychology at the University of Utah and three at the University of Tennessee. Raters were trained in several sessions, during which they were introduced to the scale definitions and were then given sample tapes of counseling sessions to practice on. When the raters reached an acceptable level of agreement in their ratings, training was terminated and the actual rating task began. The UCOP investigators used 18 tapes of actual counseling sessions as the data set on which to obtain rater reliability and agreement estimates. The tapes were each 50 minutes in duration and were obtained from counselors in two local mental health centers, a university counseling center, and a regional Veterans' Administration Hospital. Each of the three raters listened to each tape and then completed the scales.

Estimates of inter-rater reliability (intraclass correlation) for all the UCOP scales, and estimates of inter-rater agreement (T-index) for all the scales except those for Dimension 5, Counselor Intervention Modes, are presented in Table 13.3. The two cases of the intraclass correlation coefficient (R) reported here include the average r for a single rater and the r for the composite of the three raters. In both cases, the error term was included to account for the fact that the raters were not randomly selected. The T index (Tinsley & Weiss, 1975) is an estimate of the amount of agreement

Table 13.2 Scale reliabilities for UCOP rating scales

	Kendall's W	χ^2	p
Client Improvement in Social Relations			
1. Trust	0.91	491	0.0001
2. Altruism	0.89	467	0.0001
3. Role Flexibility	0.91	491	0.0001
4. Self-management	0.92	524	0.0001
5. Supportiveness	0.87	496	0.0001
6. Dependability	0.87	496	0.0001
7. Intimacy	0.86	490	0.0001
8. Acceptance	0.91	491	0.0001
9. Mutuality	0.97	491	0.0001
10. Maintenance of Long-term Relations	0.88	462	0.0001
Client Reduction of Unsuccessful Adaptive Response Patterns			
1. Somatization	0.73	480	0.0001
2. Hypochondriacal Preoccupation	0.86	581	0.0001
3. Hysterical Style	0.79	523	0.0001
4. Sexual Dysfunctioning	0.91	546	0.0001
5. Obsessive Qualities	0.86	529	0.0001
6. Anxiety	0.88	582	0.0001
7. Addictive Style	0.81	519	0.0001
8. Reality Orientation	0.74	484	0.0001
9. Anger	0.79	495	0.0001
10. Depression	0.94	603	0.0001
Client Coherence of Schemata of Self and Others			
1. Self-presentation Mode	0.83	560	0.0001
2. Assertiveness	0.79	472	0.0001
3. Ambitions	0.75	474	0.0001
4. Differentiation from Others	0.80	492	0.0001
5. Admiration of Others	0.57	351	0.001
6. Goals	0.85	558	0.0001
7. Empathy	0.86	565	0.0001
8. Locus of Self-esteem Regulation	0.75	491	0.0001
9. Tension Tolerance	0.88	557	0.0001
10. Use of Abilities	0.80	514	0.0001
Client Change in Cognitive Operations			
1. Control of Stimulation	0.64	422	0.001
2. Regulation of Affect	0.78	491	0.001
3. Perceptual Attention	0.83	510	0.001
4. Accessibility of Memory	0.77	474	0.001
5. Judgment	0.68	439	0.001
6. Exploration	0.79	450	0.001
7. Recognition	0.69	393	0.001
8. Mode of Conflict Resolution	0.70	399	0.001
9. Revision of Concepts of Self and Other	0.87	574	0.001

Table 13.22(*Continued*)

	Kendall's *W*	χ^2	*p*
Counselor Intervention Modes			
1. Cognitive Appeal	0.74	568	0.001
2. Empathy	0.83	626	0.001
3. Modeling	0.83	649	0.001
4. Caring	0.75	561	0.001
5. Emotional Stimulation	0.69	477	0.001
6. Directiveness	0.80	563	0.001
7. Clarification	0.75	572	0.001
8. Gratification	0.73	571	0.001
9. Depth of Interpretation	0.42	324	0.001
10. Confrontation	0.70	547	0.001

among raters. The estimate included here is where agreement is defined as no more than one scale point difference among the three raters.

As can be seen in Table 13.3, the estimates of inter-rater reliability are stronger (moderate to high) when a composite of three raters is used to obtain the estimate than when only one is used. The estimates of agreement are only moderate in most cases. This latter finding suggests that additional rater training would help the raters increase their level of agreement and that the scales should not yet be used formally to make official clinical judgments about clients. The scales have, however, adequate psychometric properties for research on counseling.

The reader has already become familiar with the scales in client dimensions 1, 2, and 4, since these were presented in Chapter 6 on Client Readiness. We will highlight here, however, dimension 3, Client Coherence of Schemata of Self and Others, and dimension 4, Counselor Intervention Modes. The 10 rating scales in dimension 3 (Patton, Connor & Scott, 1982) were formulated by using ideas from Kohut's (1971, 1977) psychoanalytic psychology of the self (see Figure 13.1). The Self-presentation Mode (3), Assertiveness (1) and Ambition (8) scales were derived from Kohut's (1977) concept of the grandiose line of development. Differentiation from Others (7), Admiration of Others (6) and Goals (4) were developed to reflect Kohut's idealizing line of development. Finally, the UCOP researchers developed four scales to represent functions that Kohut (1971, 1977) argued were performed by the self: Use of Abilities (2); Empathy (5); Tension Tolerance (9); and Locus of Self-esteem Regulation (10). These 10 scales are useful to the researcher who is interested not only in counseling that is deliberately conducted from a self psychology orientation, but also that from a more classical psychoanalytic orientation.

The fifth dimension of the UCOP model, Counselor Intervention Modes

Table 13.3 Inter-rater reliability and agreement estimates for the UCOP scales

	Reliability (ICC)		Agreement 1 scale point difference
	Individual	Composite	T index
Client Improvement in Social Relations			
1. Trust	0.47	0.73	0.69
2. Altruism	0.51	0.75	0.45
3. Role Flexibility	0.48	0.73	0.63
4. Self-management	0.34	0.61	0.57
5. Supportiveness	0.53	0.80	0.63
6. Dependability	0.41	0.67	0.69
7. Intimacy	0.33	0.60	0.63
8. Acceptance	0.25	0.49	0.57
9. Mutuality	0.36	0.63	0.51
10. Maintenance of Long-term Relations	0.47	0.73	0.51
Reduction of Unsuccessful Adaptive Response Patterns			
1. Somatization	0.57	0.80	0.32
2. Hypochondriacal Preoccupation	0.40	0.60	0.38
3. Reality Orientation	0.55	0.80	0.75
4. Anger	0.38	0.65	0.38
5. Addictive Style	0.50	0.79	0.38
6. Anxiety	0.20	0.20	0.63
7. Sexual Dysfunction	0.40	0.66	0.45
8. Obsessive Qualities	0.58	0.81	0.57
9. Depression	0.57	0.80	0.63
10. Hysterical Style	0.46	0.72	0.26
Client Coherence of Schemata of Self and Others			
1. Self-presentation Mode	0.51	0.76	0.38
2. Assertiveness	0.50	0.75	0.63
3. Ambitions	0.66	0.86	0.57
4. Differentiation from Others	0.34	0.62	0.32
5. Admiration of Others	0.27	0.53	0.51
6. Goals	0.46	0.77	0.63
7. Empathy	0.41	0.76	0.51
8. Locus of Self-esteem Regulation	0.43	0.70	0.63
9. Tension Tolerance	0.35	0.66	0.45
10. Use of Abilities	0.45	0.80	0.51

(see Figure 13.1; Wright, 1980), consists of scaled attributes that represent various intervention techniques used by counselors. The range of scales proceed from those that represent techniques used when the client is less able to use a working alliance and is in need of support and direction, to

Table 13.3 (*continued*)

	Reliability (ICC)		Agreement 1 scale point difference *T* index
	Individual	Composite	
Client Change in Cognitive Operations			
1. Control of Stimulation	0.45	0.49	0.63
2. Regulation of Affect	0.28	0.53	0.45
3. Perceptual Attention	0.45	0.71	0.63
4. Accessibility of Memory	0.23	0.47	0.57
5. Judgment	0.74	0.89	0.82
6. Exploration	0.40	0.67	0.51
7. Recognition	0.31	0.57	0.57
8. Mode of Conflict Expression	0.32	0.58	0.57
9. Revision of Concepts of Self and Others	0.44	0.71	0.69
Counselor Intervention Modes			
1. Cognitive Appeal	0.16	0.78	
2. Empathy	0.01	0.13	
3. Modeling	0.59	0.98	
4. Caring	−0.08	0.36	
5. Emotional Stimulation	−0.06	0.32	
6. Directiveness	0.43	0.94	
7. Clarification	0.60	0.81	
8. Gratification	0.60	0.98	
9. Confrontation	0.54	0.97	

Note: χ^2s associated with *T* index all greater than $p < 0.001$.

those that are used when the working alliance is in place and the client is doing the work of thinking and talking. Thus, Cognitive Appeal (1) is a scale to assess the counselor's use of interventions to establish and/or maintain the working alliance. Modeling (3), Caring (4), Emotional Stimulation (5), Directiveness (6), and Gratification (8) are scales that measure the presence of interventions aimed at helping the client with crisis coping. Clarification (7), Confrontation (10), and Depth of Interpretation (9) are scales to assess the counselor's use of more insight-orientated techniques likely to be present in counseling when the client is in an established and firm working alliance and doing the work of problem-solving.

All of the UCOP rating scales reflect where the client and the counselor are at a given point in counseling. With these scales, it becomes possible to learn more about counseling. For example, another way of saying this is to note that a profile of the client and counselor's scores on these scales at a given point in time is a comment on the state of the counseling "system." Each of the scaled attributes has a potential relation to all the other attributes. Determining how these attributes are related to each other at a point in time tells us about the state or the "structure" of the client–counselor system. If the researcher then goes on to determine how different states are related, such information tells us something about how counseling develops over time. That is, if the profile of attributes at one time is very different from the profile at another time, we have a kind of rough definition of change in the system over time. Potentially, we can also say something about whether or not the client–counselor dyad is in balance at a given point in time. If, for example, we note that the client is rated high on Anxiety (dimension 2) and low on Self-esteem Regulation (dimension 3) and the counselor is high on Confrontation (dimension 5), we might decide the dyad is imbalanced. If, however, the client is rated high on Regulation of Affect and Exploration (dimension 4) and the counselor is also rated high on Cognitive Appeal and Confrontation (dimension 5), we might infer that the counseling system is in equilibrium at this point in time. In this way, the UCOP model allows the researcher to make refutable statements about the state, development, and balance of the counseling system.

Research with the Client Reduction of Unsuccessful Adaptive Response Patterns scales   To obtain measures of concurrent validity for some of these scales, Robbins & Patton (1986) used a canonical correlation analysis. Concurrent measures used in this study were six self-report scales of clinical symptom syndromes from the Millon Clinical Multiaxial Inventory (MCMI: Millon, 1983). Four of the 10 rating scales from the Unsuccessful Adaptive Response Patterns dimension were selected to match the MCMI scales. The four UCOP dimension 1 scales were: Addictive Style; Anger; Hysterical Style; and Depression. The six MCMI scales were as follows: Anxiety; Somatoform; Hypomanic; Dysthymic; Alcohol Abuse; and Drug Abuse. Research participants were 84 clients (62% males; 61% Caucasian, the remainder were Black; Mean age = 36.16 years, S.D. = 12.03) from a variety of inpatient and outpatient human services agencies. The research participants were rated in the early phase of counseling (mean number of sessions = 5.8 at the time of data collection) on the four UCOP scales by the eight staff counselors who were working with them. The clients filled out the MCMI scales. The interesting feature of this study is its attempt not only to obtain estimates of concurrent validity for the UCOP scales, but also to make inferences about the convergence of counselor and client ratings of the clients.

Three significant canonical variates resulted from the analysis. The first variate, accounting for 42% of the variance, appeared to be a Substance Abuse dimension because it was dominated by the UCOP Addictive Style rating scale and the Alcohol Abuse and Drug Abuse scales from the MCMI. This suggests considerable convergence between the counselor and client ratings of the client in this domain. The second variate, accounting for 23% of the variance, was interpreted as a Depression/Anxiety dimension. On this variate, the UCOP Hysterical Style and Depressive Style scales were matched with the MCMI Anxiety and Dysthymic scales. While it is apparent that the counselors and clients converged in their ratings of the client, the meaning of the dimension itself is not so clear. What is problematic here is the combining of both Anxiety and Depression in one dimension, suggesting the presence of both conditions in the clients. While that may well have been the case, it was not verified independently of these results. The third variate, accounting for 22% of the variance, was labeled an Anger dimension. Here, only the UCOP Anger rating scale appeared to define the variate, suggesting both that the MCMI scales appear to lack Anger content and a lack of convergence between counselor and client ratings. That is, the counselors appear to rate the clients as angry, but the clients either are not, or do not have a way of indicating that on the MCMI. Thus, these authors conclude that to the extent the MCMI scales are measuring what they purport to measure, there is evidence for the validity of the UCOP Addictive Style rating scale, and for the Hysterical Style and Depressive Style scales if one assumes that anxiety and depression co-exist as symptom states in the client.

Client self-report measures based on psychoanalytic concepts

Several measures of client characteristics based on Kohut's (1971, 1977) theory of the self have been recently developed. In this section, we will describe some of these measures.

Goal Instability and Superiority   Kohut's central developmental constructs of grandiosity and idealization were used to write items for two self-report rating scales (Robbins & Patton, 1985). Twenty items were written in a six-point Likert response format (1 = strongly agree; 6 = strongly disagree) to correspond to a working definition of the concepts of grandiosity and idealization. Items were written so that endorsement of them would represent less mature forms of grandiosity and idealization. This decision was made because the authors were interested in the relation of the items to career indecisiveness and lack of career planning among college age students. An example of an item in the grandiose set is as follows: "I could show up my friends if I wanted to." An example from the idealization set is: "I don't seem to have the drive to get my work done."

The items were given to 453 college students in two universities and their responses submitted to a principle components analysis using a varimax orthogonal solution. Two factors emerged, accounting for 41.5% of the variance. The stability of this factor structure was tested in a cross-validation sample of 130 college students and was found to hold up very well. The correlation between the two scales was 0.12 indicating the statistical independence of the two scales. Given these results, the authors selected 10 items for each scale, and each scale has a score range of 10–60, in which a higher score means more disagreement with the item. Alpha reliabilities for the grandiosity and idealization items were 0.76 and 0.81, respectively. Test–retest reliabilities for the two sets were 0.80 and 0.76, respectively.

After examining the item content of the 10 items for each scale, the grandiosity items were labeled Superiority (items reflecting a variety of less mature forms of grandiose self-expression), and the idealization items, Goal Instability (items reflecting a lack of goal directedness and inhibition in work). Several estimates of concurrent validity indicated that the two scales correlated significantly, as would be expected, with measures of self-esteem, narcissism, social desirability, interest pattern maturity, personal competencies, introversion/extroversion, and career decidedness.

Research with the Goal Instability and Superiority scales   Studies that have involved one or both of these scales have been extensive in the past few years. With a different data set than the one in the scale construction phase reported above, Robbins and Patton (1985) went on to examine the utility of the two scales in predicting college students' ability to formulate and pursue career plans. Eighty-eight college students enrolled in career and life planning classes were used. The criterion measures were level of career decidedness (Osipow, 1980) and level of career pursuit (Robbins, 1983). In the first hierarchical regression analysis involving four predictors, both the Goal Instability scale ($B = -0.19$, $t = 2.93$, $p < 0.05$) and the Superiority scale ($B = 0.20$, $t = 3.64$, $p < 0.01$) along with the other two predictors, were significant predictors of change in career decidedness following enrollment in a career planning class. In the second analysis, again involving four predictors, to predict level of change in pursuing career plans, the Superiority scale ($B = -0.43$, $t = 11.45$, $p < 0.01$) proved to be the best predictor. The beta weight for the Goal Instability scale was not a significant predictor in this case.

Since this work, Robbins and his colleagues at Virginia Commonwealth University have done considerable research using these scales (see Scott & Robbins, 1985; Robbins & Tucker, 1986; Robbins, 1987a; Smith & Robbins, 1988; Robbins & Schwitzer, 1988; Robbins, 1989; Robbins, Payne & Chartrand, 1990). In addition to the work Robbins has done on the psychometric properties of the two scales, it has been determined that the

Goal Instability scale is significantly related to adjustment and career development for older and retirement-age adults, and women's adjustment to college life. Kerr *et al.* (1991) have also determined that Goal Instability and Superiority are significantly related to the interpersonal behavior strategies used by behavior- or learning-disordered adolescents during or after treatment. Table 13.4 contains the items for the Goal Instability and Superiority scales.

Pseudoautonomy and Peer-group Dependence Lapan and Patton (1986) have developed two forced-choice, self-report scales for adolescents based on Kohut's (1971, 1977) concepts of grandiosity and idealization. An original set of 47 grandiosity and 48 idealization items were administered to 114 psychiatrically hospitalized and 118 non-hospitalized adolescents. Tentative scale definitions of grandiosity and idealization were written to guide item writing. The respondent's task was to choose between two descriptive statements that were intended to be equally acceptable to an adolescent but

Table 13.4 Items for the Goal Instability and Superiority scales

Goal Instability
1. It's easier for me to start than to finish projects.
2. I wonder where my life is headed.
3. I don't seem to make decisions by myself.
4. I don't seem to have the drive to get my work done.
5. I lose my sense of direction.
6. I have more ideas than energy.
7. I don't seem to get going on anything important.
8. After a while, I lose sight of my goals.
9. I have confusion about who I am.
10. It's hard to find a reason for working.

Superiority
1. My friends follow my lead.
2. I deserve favors from others.
3. I'm witty and charming with others.
4. My looks are one of the things that attract others to me.
5. I could show up my friends if I wanted to.
6. Running the show means a lot to me.
7. Being admired by others helps me to feel fantastic.
8. Achieving out of the ordinary accomplishments would make me feel complete.
9. I catch myself wanting to be a hero.
10. I know that I have more natural talents than most.

Adapted from Robbins & Patton (1985). Copyright 1985 by the American Psychological Association. Adapted by permission of the publisher.

which differed in validity in that the non-keyed alternative was written to be neutral to the content of the keyed alternative. The adolescent was instructed to choose the alternative in an item pair that described how he or she felt most of the time. After the item pairs were written, two advanced counseling psychology graduate students familiar with Kohut's theory served as judges by assessing whether each scored alternative in a pair could be assigned to its theoretically appropriate construct. A kappa correction·for chance agreement of 0.87 was obtained to support the assumption that the keyed alternatives represented the intended theoretical constructs of either grandiosity or idealization.

To assess the scale reliability of each set of items and to reduce the number of items to meet the criteria for factor analysis, two item analyses were conducted on each item set. Following the first analysis, 39 grandiosity and 36 idealization items were carried forward to the second item analysis. In the second analysis, the KR 20 index of scale reliability was 0.88 for the grandiosity item set, and 0.86 for the idealization set. Items in either set that did not have a corrected item-to-total-scale-score correlation of 0.40 or better were then eliminated. This was done to ensure that (a) only the items that were making a strong contribution to the scale would be retained for further analysis, and (b) the total number of items represented an acceptable ratio of items to subjects for the factor analysis. This procedure left 11 items in the grandiosity set, and 12 in the idealization set.

The factor structure of the items was determined by a principal components analysis with a varimax orthogonal solution. Two factors were found which accounted for 57% and 20% of the variance, respectively. Because not all the items on both factors were weighted heavily enough to have confidence in their contribution to the meaning of the factors, the authors selected the best eight from both the grandiosity and idealization factors. They then conducted another item analysis of these two eight-item sets, and the reliabilities were 0.77 for grandiosity and 0.75 for idealization. The eight items from the first factor appeared to represent the adolescent's hypersensitivity and independence from others in a kind of rebellious non-conformity. This set of items was labeled Pseudoautonomy. The second set of eight items appeared to represent the adolescent's defensive attachment to others as a substitute for his or her own internal ideals. This factor was labeled Peer-group Dependence. The correlation between the scales was 0.31, supporting the relative independence of the two scales.

Research with the Pseudoautonomy and Peer-group Dependence scales　To examine the discriminant validity of the two scales, Lapan and Patton (1986) conducted a discriminant analysis on the hospitalized and non-hospitalized groups ($n = 230$). The discriminant analysis used in this study included a stepwise regression procedure to predict group membership (where each scale is used as a predictor), a canonical discriminant function also used in the prediction of group membership, and the correlation between the two scales. Both scales proved to be significant predictors of group membership and the overall hit rate (concurrent prediction) in this classification was 73%. As would be expected, the mean score on these scales was significantly higher for the hospitalized than for the non-hospitalized group. The correlation between the two scales was 0.31. While this coefficient was significant given the number of cases, it still is low enough to support the claim that the scales are sufficiently independent of each other. The original sets of eight items for both the Pseudoautonomy and Peer-group Dependence scales are presented in Table 13.5.

In a later study by Kerr *et al.* (1991), it was also found that scores on the two adolescent narcissism scales were significantly correlated with measures of interpersonal behavior in a sample of adolescents both during and after treatment for learning and behavior disorders, and for adolescents who had never been in treatment. Currently, work is continuing with the original set of 97 items, with a large sample of adolescents using techniques from item response theory. Here, the investigators are examining the factorial structure and stability of the scales and their relationship to adolescent career development.

Shame-proneness   In a study whose purpose was to investigate the extent to which shame, as construed in Kohut's (1977, 1974/1978b, 1984) psychoanalytic self psychology, is a troublesome accompaniment of persons who have been identified as suicidal, Shreve & Patton (1988) constructed the Shame-proneness scale. Kohut (1974/1978b) suggested that persons who are unusually prone to shame suffer from a serious defect in the self that prevents them from maintaining a firm sense of self-esteem. Shame is then said to be the consequent of a failure of defensive maneuvers in the otherwise discohesive self.

Shreve & Patton (1988) wrote an initial item pool of 30 items using a six-point Likert response format (1 = strongly disagree; 6 = strongly agree). Item content depicted, from the person's phenomenal perspective, moderate to severe experiences of shame or its derivatives in a target population of adult individuals. Endorsement of an item represented the tendency to experience shame. Two groups of participants were used in this study. In the first group, 143 persons were recruited from those who were currently hospitalized in the acute admissions unit of a large state mental hospital as a result of either expressed suicidal threats or overt suicidal behavior. The second group consisted of 90 non-suicidal, non-psychotic persons hospitalized in the same institution. Both groups consisted of twice as many women as men, and the majority of these participants were unmarried or divorced and had annual incomes below $10000. In addition to the Shame-proneness

Table 13.5 Items for the Pseudoautonomy and Peer-group Dependence scales

Pseudoautonomy
1. (a)   I don't have to cheat to get what I want.
   (b)   Many times, I have to cheat to get what I want.*
2. (a)   I do what I want.*
   (b)   Most always, I follow the law.
3. (a)   I don't have to use my anger to get what I want.
   (b)   I use my anger to get what I want.*
4. (a)   Sometimes, I ask advice from other people.
   (b)   I run my own life.*
5. (a)   I am usually careful about what I do.
   (b)   Many times I do things on a dare.*
6. (a)   I get respect by being tough.*
   (b)   People seem to like me.
7. (a)   Many times I like adults to offer me help.
   (b)   Adults stick their noses into what is my business.*
8. (a)   I can depend on others to treat me fairly.
   (b)   Many times I have to take what I need.*

Peer-group Dependence
1. (a)   I can still feel good about myself if important friends get angry with me.
   (b)   I feel good about myself when I please friends that I look up to.*
2. (a)   I tend to believe what others say about me.*
   (b)   I can accept or reject what others say about me.
3. (a)   When friends cut me down, I try to be more like what they want.*
   (b)   When friends cut me down, I'm not too hard on myself.
4. (a)   I believe that people I look up to will not let me down.
   (b)   I am worried that people I look up to might push me away.*
5. (a)   Others' thoughts about me can easily become my thoughts about myself.*
   (b)   Others' thoughts about me can't easily become my thoughts about myself.
6. (a)   Other people's judgments about me usually influence the way I feel about myself.*
   (b)   Other people's judgments about me aren't as important as my own.
7. (a)   I feel really crummy when I am away from good friends.*
   (b)   I can pretty easily make new friends when I lose old ones.
8. (a)   I seem to attach myself to stronger people.*
   (b)   Some people look to me for help.

---

* = keyed alternative.
Adapted from Lapan & Patton (1986). Copyright 1986 by the American Psychological Association. Adapted by permission of the publisher.

items, all participants were also administered measures of Self-consciousness, Self-esteem, Hopelessness, Apprehensiveness and Suicidal Ideation to obtain estimates of validity.

To reduce the number of items to reach an acceptable item-to-subject ratio of 10:1 for factor analysis, an item analysis was conducted on the original 30-item pool. Using a criterion of 0.45 for the item-to-total-scale score correlation for each item, 16 items were retained for the factor analysis. The overall scale alpha for the set of 30 items was 0.91. The 16 items were submitted to a principal components analysis followed by a varimax orthogonal rotation ($n = 143$). Five factors with eigenvalues greater than 1.0 were extracted, but only the first factor (eigenvalue = 7.46, percent of variance = 46.7) had more than two items that loaded 0.35. This factor had 10 items that loaded significantly and which did not show significant residual loadings on the other factors. To examine the factorial stability of the items, the original pool of participants was randomly divided in half and a factor analysis again conducted on the resulting half. Nearly identical findings resulted for this second analysis. The alpha estimate for the 10 Shame-proneness items was 0.93, and a 0.81 2-week test–retest reliability estimate was obtained. The Shame-proneness scale was significantly and positively correlated, as one would expect, with measures of Self-consciousness and Social Anxiety, and negatively correlated with Self-esteem. However, the Shame-proneness scale was correlated at 0.49 with a measure of Guilt-proneness, suggesting that the two concepts are related.

Research with the Shame-proneness scale   A discriminant analysis was performed to determine the ability of the Shame-proneness scale to discriminate between the hospitalized suicidal and non-suicidal participants. With only the Shame-proneness scores used as the predictor, participants were correctly classified 72% of the time. When other variables are included with Shame-proneness, the latter is still a significant predictor, but Self-esteem becomes the most reliable predictor.

Shreve & Patton (1988) also used the Shame-proneness scale with the above data set to determine its effectiveness in predicting treatment outcome, here defined as length of stay in the hospital. The research participants were 143 of the individuals who had been hospitalized for suicidal threats or suicidal behavior in the same institution mentioned above. Length of stay in the hospital was the criterion measure and the following were the three predictor variables used in the regression analysis to predict length of stay: Hopelessness at the time of admission, Shame-proneness and Hopelessness at the time of discharge (a measure of Self-esteem was eliminated from this equation when it was determined that it did not correlate significantly with the criterion of length of stay). All three predictors proved to be significant in predicting length of stay in the hospital, although only 10% of the variance was accounted for in this analysis: Hopelessness at the time of discharge ($p < 0.05$); Shame-proneness ($p < 0.01$); and Hopelessness at the time of admission ($p < 0.01$).

Finally, in a recent study of bulimia and narcissism (Street, 1990) using 60 women beginning treatment for bulimia, scores on the Shame-proneness measure, in combination with three other predictors, were found to be a significant predictor of scores on a measure of bulimia. The final items from the Shame-proneness scale are presented in Table 13.6.

Concluding remarks

The ongoing development and testing of new instruments and new designs for research make it possible to test the congruence between psychoanalytic theory and clinical observation. We have argued that the practicing counselor is at his or her best when operating from the dual perspective of the scientist *and* the practitioner. The counselor, performing the scientific tasks of observation and inference, is in an excellent position to constantly subject her or his theoretical hunches to continual revision. In collaboration with the researcher, the practicing psychoanalytic counselor can provide the experience needed to make the researcher's theory more clinically relevant and testable. For example, the preceding chapters present many hypotheses that might be tested.

Psychoanalytic theories of the client and the treatment process are, in our experience, amenable to testing both in the interview itself and through formal research. We advocate, therefore, a strong "working alliance" between the counselor's roles of scientist and practitioner. Only when such an alliance is in place can the counselor-as-practitioner become an abundant source of information about the psychoanalytic counseling process, and the

Table 13.6 Items for the Shame-proneness scale

1. When I fail at something I feel as if all eyes were on me.
2. I am afraid that if I fail at something others will reject me.
3. I often feel disgraced.
4. I think my nose (or some other part of my body) just doesn't look right.
5. I rarely express myself in groups for fear of others laughing at me.
6. I feel ashamed even when I make a minor mistake.
7. When I feel ashamed, I want to run and hide.
8. When I do or say something stupid, I wish the earth would open up and swallow me.
9. My parents often made me feel ashamed.
10. I'm always worried that others will think that I'm dumb.

From Shreve & Patton (1988), with permission.

counselor-as-scientist a thoughtful evaluator of the meaning of such information. It is our hope that in the years to come such efforts will reward us with increasingly useful knowledge of counseling that is both scientifically coherent and clinically beneficial for our clients.

References

Adler, A. (1959). *The Practice and Theory of Individual Psychology*. Totowa, NJ: Littlefield-Adams.

Allen, J., Newsom, G., Gabbard, G., & Coyne, L. (1984). Scales to assess the therapeutic alliance from a psychoanalytic perspective. *Bulletin of the Menninger Clinic*, **48**, 383–400.

American Association for Marriage and Family Therapy (1988). *AAMFT Code of Professional Ethics for Marriage and Family Therapists* (revised edn.). Washington, D.C.: American Association for Marriage and Family Therapy.

American Association of Counseling and Development (1987). *Ethical Standards* (revised edn.). Alexandria, VA: American Association of Counseling and Development.

American Psychiatric Association (1984). *Diagnostic and Statistical Manual—IIIR*. New York: American Psychiatric Association.

American Psychological Association, Division of Counseling and Guidance, Committee on Counselor Training (1952). Recommended standards for training psychologists at the doctorate level. *American Psychologist*, **7**, 175–181.

American Psychological Association, Division of Counseling Psychology, Committee on Definition (1956). Counseling psychology as a specialty. *American Psychologist*, **11**, 282–285.

American Psychological Association (1986). *Accreditation Handbook* (revised edn.). Washington, D.C.: American Psychological Association.

American Psychological Association (1990). Ethical principles of psychologists (Amended June 2, 1989). *American Psychologist*, **45**, 290–395.

Anderson, N.S. (1964). *Formulation Outline*. Paper presented at a meeting of the Granite Community Mental Health Center Training Committee, Salt Lake City, UT.

Anderson, N.S. (1966, June). *Termination: Separation*. Paper presented at a meeting of the Granite Community Mental Health Center Training Committee, Salt Lake City, UT.

Anderson, N.S. (1967, March). Psychological aspects of moral responsibility. In: *Great Issues in Ethical Theory and the Moral Life*. Forum presented by the University of Utah Department of Philosophy, Salt Lake City, UT.

Arlow, J.A., & Brenner, C. (1988). The future of psychoanalysis. *Psychoanalytic Quarterly*, **57**, 1–14.

Atkinson, J.M., & Heritage, J. (Eds.) (1984). *Structures of Social Action: Studies in Conversation Analysis.* Cambridge: Cambridge University Press.

Barrett-Lennard, G.T. (1981). The empathy cycle: Refinement of a nuclear concept. *Journal of Counseling Psychology*, **23**, 91–100.

Barth, K., Havik, O.E., Nielson, G., Haver, B., Molstad, E., Rogge, H., Skatun, M., Heiberg, A.N., & Ursin, H. (1988). Factor analysis of the evaluation form for selecting patients for short-term anxiety-provoking psychotherapy. *Psychotherapy and Psychosomatics*, **49**, 47–52.

Baruch, E.F., & Serrano, L.J. (1988). *Women Analyzing Women: In France, England and the United States.* New York: New York University Press.

Basch, M.F. (1980). *Doing Psychotherapy.* New York: Basic Books.

Basch, M.F. (1988). *Understanding Psychotherapy: The Science Behind the Art.* New York: Basic Books.

Bateson, C.D. (1987). Prosocial motivation: Is it ever truly altruistic? In: L. Berkowitz (Ed.), *Advances in Experimental Social Psychology*, **20**, (pp. 65–122). Orlando, FL: Academic Press.

Bateson, C.D., Fultz, J., & Schoenrade, P.A. (1987). Distress and empathy: Two qualitatively distinct vicarious emotions with different motivational consequences. *Journal of Personality*, **55**, 19–39.

Beauchamp, T.L., & Childress, J.F. (1979). *Principles of Biomedical Ethics.* New York: Oxford University Press.

Beauchamp, T.L., & Childress, J.F. (1983). *Principles of Biomedical Ethics* (2nd edn.). New York: Oxford University Press.

Beauchamp, T.L., & Childress, J.F. (1989). *Principles of Biomedical Ethics* (3rd edn.). New York: Oxford University Press.

Bellack, L., Hurvich, M., & Gediman, H. (1973). *Ego Functions in Schizophrenics, Neurotics, and Normals.* New York: John Wiley and Sons.

Benjamin, J. (1988). *The Bonds of Love: Psychoanalysis, Feminism and the Problem of Domination.* New York: Pantheon Books.

Berliner, B. (1941). Short psychoanalytic psychotherapy. *Bulletin of the Menninger Clinic*, **5**, 204–213.

Bibring, E. (1954). Psychoanalysis and the dynamic psychotherapies. *Journal of the American Psychoanalytic Association*, **2**, 745–770.

Blos, P. (1941). *The Adolescent Personality.* New York: Appleton-Century-Crofts.

Bordin, E.S. (1943). A theory of vocational interests as dynamic phenomena. *Educational and Psychological Measurement*, **3**, 49–65.

Bordin, E.S. (1948). Dimensions of the counseling process. *Journal of Clinical Psychology*, **4**, 240–244.

Bordin, E.S. (1955). Ambiguity as a therapeutic variable. *Journal of Consulting Psychology*, **19**, 9–15.

Bordin, E.S. (1964). Response to free association as a reflection of personality. *Acta Psychologica*, **23**, 120–121.

Bordin, E.S. (1965). The ambivalent quest for independence. *Journal of Counseling Psychology*, **12**, 339–345.

Bordin, E.S. (1968). *Psychological Counseling.* New York: Meredith Corporation.

Bordin, E.S. (1979). The generalizability of the psychoanalytic concept of the working alliance. *Psychotherapy: Theory, Research, and Practice*, **16**, 252–260.

Bordin, E.S. (1981). A psychodynamic view of counseling psychology. *The Counseling Psychologist*, **9**, 62–70.

Bordin, E.S., Nachmann, B., & Segal, S.J. (1963). An articulated framework for vocational development. *Journal of Counseling Psychology*, **10**, 107–116.

Boring, E.G. (1950). *A History of Experimental Psychology* (2nd edn.). New York: Appleton-Century-Crofts.

Bowlby, J. (1980). *Attachment and Loss: Vol. 3: Loss, Sadness, and Depression.* New York: Basic Books.

Braun, J.A. (1982). Ethical issues in the treatment of religious persons. In: M. Rosenbaum (Ed.), *Ethics and Values in Psychotherapy: A Guidebook*. New York: The Free Press.

Brenner, C. (1982). *The Mind in Conflict*. New York: International Universities Press.

Brentano, F. (1955). *Psychologie vom empirischen Standpunkt (Psychology from an Empirical Standpoint)* Vols. 1–2. Hamburg: Felix Meiner.

Breuer, J., & Freud, S. (1957). *Studies on Hysteria*. New York: Basic Books.

Brown, L.S. (1984). Finding a new language: Getting beyond analytic and verbal shorthand in feminist therapy. *Women and Therapy*, **3**, 73–80.

Callan, J.C. (Ed.) (1988). *Ethical Issues in Professional Life*. New York: Oxford University Press.

Charney, L.A. (1982). The construction of scales to measure Client Improvement in Social Relations. Unpublished master's thesis, University of Utah, Salt Lake City, UT.

Chehrazi, S. (1986). Female psychology. *Journal of the American Psychoanalytic Association*, **34**, 111–162.

Chodrow, N. (1978). *The Reproduction of Mothering*. Berkeley: University of California Press.

Corsini, R.J. (1989). *Current Psychotherapies* (4th edn.). Itasca, IL: Peacock.

Danielian, J. (1988). Karen Horney and Heinz Kohut: Theory and repeat of history. *The American Journal of Psychoanalysis*, **48**(1), 6–24.

Dinnerstien, D. (1976). *The Mermaid and the Minotaur: Sexual Arrangements and Human Malaise*. New York: Harper & Row.

Donovan, J. (1985). *Feminist Theory*. New York: Ungar.

Drane, J.F. (1982). Ethics and psychotherapy: A philosophical perspective. In: M. Rosenbaum (Ed.), *Ethics and Values in Psychotherapy: A Guidebook* (pp. 15–50). New York: The Free Press.

Efstation, J.F., & Patton, M. J. (1985, August). *Scales to Measure Client Improvement in Social Relations*. Poster session presented at the annual convention of the American Psychological Association, Los Angeles, California.

Efstation, J.F., Patton, M.J., & Kardash, C.A. (1990). Measuring the working alliance in counselor supervision. *Journal of Counseling Psychology*, **37**, 322–329.

Ellis, A. (1962). *Reason and Emotion in Psychotherapy*. New York: Stuart.

Elson, M. (1987). *The Kohut Seminars: On Self Psychology and Psychotherapy with Adolescents and Young Adults*. New York: Norton.

Epperson, D.L., Bushway, D.J., & Warman, R.E. (1983). Client self-termination after one counseling session: Effects of problem recognition, counselor gender, and counselor experience. *Journal of Counseling Psychology*, **30**, 307–315.

Erikson, E.H. (1950). *Childhood and Society*. New York: Norton.

Erikson, E.H. (1959). Growth and crises of the healthy personality. In: G.S. Klein (Ed.), *Psychological Issues*. New York. International Universities Press.

Ethics Committee, American Psychological Association (1987). Trends in ethics cases, common pitfalls, and published resources. *American Psychologist*, **43**, 564–572.

Everstine, L., Everstine, D.S., Heymann, G.M., True, R.M., Johnson, H.J., & Seiden, R.H. (1980). Privacy and confidentiality in psychotherapy. *American Psychologist*, **35**, 828–840.

Fairbairn, W.R.D. (1958). On the nature and aims of psychoanalytical treatment. *International Journal of Psychoanalysis*, **39**, 374–385.

Fancher, R. (1973). *Psychoanalytic Psychology*. New York: Norton.

Fast, I. (1984). *Gender Identity: A Differentiation Model*. Hillsdale, NJ: Lawrence Erlbaum Associates.

Fast, I. (1990). Aspects of early gender development: Toward a reformulation. *Psychoanalytic Psychology*, **7**(Suppl.), 105–117.

Feigl, H. (1966). Some remarks on the meaning of scientific explanation. In: H. Feigl & W. Sellars (Eds.), *Readings in Philosophical Analysis*. New York: International Universities Press.

Fenichel, O. (1941). *Problems of Psychoanalytic Technique*. Albany, NY: The Psychoanalytic Quarterly.

Fenichel, O. (1945). *The Psychoanalytic Theory of Neurosis*. New York: Norton.

Ferenczi, S. (1933). The passions of adults and their influence on the sexual character development of children. *International Journal of Psychoanalysis*, **19**, 5–15.

Fisher, H. (unpublished manuscript). Logic Transformations of Psychological Defenses.

Fitzgerald, L.F., & Osipow, S.H. (1988). We have seen the future, but is it us? The vocational aspirations of students in counseling psychology. *Professional Psychology: Research and Practice*, **19**, 575–583.

Freud, A. (1936a). *The Ego and Mechanisms of Defense*. New York: International Universities Press.

Freud, A. (1936b). *The Writings of Anna Freud. Vol. 2: The Ego and the Mechanisms of Defense*. New York: International Universities Press.

Freud, A. (1945). *The writings of Anna Freud. Vol. 4: Indications for Child Analysis*. New York: International Universities Press.

Freud, S. (1953a). The interpretation of dreams. In: J. Strachey (Ed. and Trans.), *The Standard Edition of the Complete Psychological Works of Sigmund Freud* (Vol. 4 and Vol. 5, pp. 1–630). London: Hogarth Press. (Original work published in 1900.)

Freud, S. (1953b). Three essays on the theory of sexuality. In: J. Strachey (Ed. and Trans.), *The Standard Edition of the Complete Psychological Works of Sigmund Freud* (Vol. 7, pp. 136–248). London: Hogarth Press. (Original work published in 1905.)

Freud, S. (1954). Project for a scientific psychology. In: M. Mosbacher and J. Strachey (Trans.), *Sigmund Freud's Letters*. New York: Basic Books.

Freud, S. (1955). Beyond the pleasure principle. In: J. Strachey (Ed. and Trans.), *The Standard Edition of the Complete Psychological Works of Sigmund Freud* (Vol. 18, pp. 3–67). London: Hogarth Press. (Original work published in 1920.)

Freud, S. (1957a). Five lectures on psycho-analysis. In: J. Strachey (Ed. and Trans.), *The Standard Edition of the Complete Psychological Works of Sigmund Freud* (Vol. 11, pp. 3–59). London: Hogarth Press. (Original work published in 1910.)

Freud, S. (1957b). The unconscious. In: J. Strachey (Ed. and Trans.), *The Standard Edition of the Complete Psychological Works of Sigmund Freud* (Vol. 14, pp. 161–219). London: Hogarth Press. (Original work published in 1915.)

Freud, S. (1958a). On beginning the treatment: Further recommendations on the beginning of treatment. In: J. Strachey (Ed. and Trans.), *The Standard Edition of the Complete Psychological Works of Sigmund Freud* (Vol. 19, pp. 121–144). London: Hogarth Press. (Original work published in 1913.)

Freud, S. (1958b). The dynamics of transference. In: J. Strachey (Ed. and Trans.), *The Standard Edition of the Complete Psychological Works of Sigmund Freud* (Vol. 12, pp. 98–110). London: Hogarth Press. (Original work published in 1912.)

Freud, S. (1958c). Remembering, repeating and working through. In: J. Strachey (Ed. and Trans.), *The Standard Edition of the Complete Psychological Works of Sigmund Freud* (Vol. 12, pp. 146–157). London: Hogarth Press. (Original work published in 1914.)

Freud, S. (1959a). The question of lay analysis. In: J. Strachey (Ed. and Trans.), *The Standard Edition of the Complete Psychological Works of Sigmund Freud* (Vol. 20, pp. 179–247). London: Hogarth Press. (Original work published in 1926.)

Freud, S. (1959b). Family romance. In: J. Strachey (Ed. and Trans.), *The Standard Edition of the Complete Psychological Works of Sigmund Freud* (Vol. 9, pp. 235–248). London: Hogarth Press. (Original work published in 1909.)

Freud, S. (1959c). Inhibitions, symptoms, and anxiety. In: J. Strachey (Ed. and Trans.), *The Standard Edition of the Complete Psychological Works of Sigmund Freud* (Vol. 20, pp. 77–179). London: Hogarth Press. (Original work published in 1926.)

Freud, S. (1960). The psychopathology of everyday life. In: J. Strachey (Ed. and Trans.), *The Standard Edition of the Complete Psychological Works of Sigmund Freud* (Vol. 6). London: Hogarth Press. (Original work published in 1901.)

Freud, S. (1961a). Introductory lectures on psychoanalysis. In: J. Strachey (Ed. and Trans.), *The Standard Edition of the Complete Psychological Works of Sigmund Freud* (Vol. 15 and Vol. 16). London: Hogarth Press. (Original work published in 1916.)

Freud, S. (1961b). The ego and the id. In: J. Strachey (Ed. and Trans.), *The Standard Edition of the Complete Psychological Works of Sigmund Freud* (Vol. 19, pp. 3–69). London: Hogarth Press. (Original work published in 1923.)

Freud, S. (1961c). Civilization and its discontents. In: J. Strachey (Ed. and Trans.), *The Standard Edition of the Complete Psychological Works of Sigmund Freud* (Vol. 21, pp. 59–149). London: Hogarth Press. (Original work published in 1930.)

Freud, S. (1961d). The dissolution of the Oedipus complex. In: J. Strachey (Ed. and Trans.), *The Standard Edition of the Complete Psychological Works of Sigmund Freud* (Vol. 19, pp. 172–182). London: Hogarth Press. (Original work published in 1924.)

Freud, S. (1961e). Some psychological consequences of the anatomical difference between the sexes. In: J. Strachey (Ed. and Trans.), *The Standard Edition of the Complete Psychological Works of Sigmund Freud* (Vol. 19, pp. 243–283). London: Hogarth Press. (Original work published in 1925.)

Freud, S. (1962a). On the psychical mechanism of hysterical phenomena. In: J. Strachey (Ed. and Trans.), *The Standard Edition of the Complete Psychological Works of Sigmund Freud* (Vol. 3, pp. 26–43). London: Hogarth Press. (Original work published in 1893.)

Freud, S. (1962b). The aetiology of hysteria. In: J. Strachey (Ed. and Trans.), *The Standard Edition of the Complete Psychological Works of Sigmund Freud* (Vol. 3, pp. 189–225). London: Hogarth Press. (Original work published in 1896.)

Freud, S. (1962c). The neuro-psychoses of defence. In: J. Strachey (Ed. and Trans.), *The Standard Edition of the Complete Psychological Works of Sigmund Freud* (Vol. 3, pp. 43–86). London: Hogarth Press. (Original work published in 1894.)

Freud, S. (1964a). Analysis terminable and interminable. In: J. Strachey (Ed. and Trans.), *The Standard Edition of the Complete Psychological Works of Sigmund Freud* (Vol. 23, pp. 211–256). London: Hogarth Press. (Original work published in 1937.)

Freud, S. (1964b). Splitting of the ego in the process of defense. In: J. Strachey

(Ed. and Trans.), *The Standard Edition of the Complete Psychological Works of Sigmund Freud* (Vol. 23, pp. 273–280). London: Hogarth Press. (Original work published in 1940.)

Friedlander, M.L. & Snyder, J. (1983). Trainees' expectations for the supervisory process: Testing a developmental model. *Counselor Education and Supervision*, **22**, 342–348.

Friedlander, M.L., & Ward, L.G. (1984). Development and validation of the supervisory styles inventory. *Journal of Counseling Psychology*, **31**, 541–547.

Frieswyk, S., Allen, J., Colson, D., & Coyne, L. (1986). Therapeutic alliance: Its place as a process and outcome variable in dynamic psychotherapy research. *Journal of Consulting and Clinical Psychology*, **54**, 32–38.

Gardiner, J.K. (1987). Self-psychology as feminist theory. *Signs: Journal of Women in Culture and Society*, **12**, 761–780.

Garfield, S., & Bergin, A. (1986). *Handbook of Psychotherapy and Behavior Change*. New York: John Wiley and Sons.

Garfinkel, H. (1967). *Studies in Ethnomethodology*. Englewood Cliffs, NJ: Prentice-Hall.

Gaston, L., Marmar, C.R., Thompson, L.W., & Gallagher, D. (1988). Relation of patient characteristics to the therapeutic alliance in diverse populations. *Journal of Consulting and Clinical Psychology*, **56**, 483–489.

Gelso, C.J. (1985). Rigor, relevance, and counseling research: On the need to maintain our course between Scylla and Charybdis. *Journal of Counseling and Development*, **63**, 551–553.

Gelso, C.J. (1987). Editor's introduction. *Journal of Counseling Psychology*, **34**, 363.

Gelso, C.J., Betz, N.E., Friedlander, M.L., Helms, J.E., Hill, C.E., Patton, M.J., Super, D.E., & Wampold, B.E. (1988). Research in counseling psychology: Prospects and recommendations. *The Counseling Psychologist*, **16**, 385–406.

Gelso, C.J., & Carter, J. (1985). The relationship in counseling and psychotherapy: Components, consequences, and theoretical antecedents. *The Counseling Psychologist*, **13**, 155–243.

Gelso, C.J., & Fassinger, R.E. (1990). Counseling psychology: Theory and research on interventions. *Annual Review of Psychology*, **41**, 355–386.

Gelso, C.J., & Johnson, D.H. (Eds.) (1983). *Explorations in Time-limited Counseling and Psychotherapy*. New York: Teachers College Press.

Gill, M.M. (1963). *Topography and Systems in Psychoanalytic Theory* [Psychological Issues, Monograph 10]. New York: International Universities Press.

Gitelson, M. (1962). The curative functions in psychotherapy. *International Journal of Psychoanalysis*, **43**, 194–205.

Goates, B.L. (1972). *Practical Principles of Interviewing*: Which are Sometimes Hard to Remember. Paper presented at a meeting of the Granite Community Mental Health Center Training Committee, Salt Lake City, UT.

Golden, B., & Robbins, S.B. (1990). The working alliance within time-limited therapy: A case analysis. *Professional Psychology: Theory and Research*, **21**, 476–481.

Goldstein, A.P., Heller, K., & Sechrist, L.B. (1966). *Psychotherapy and the Psychology of Behavior Change*. New York: John Wiley & Sons.

Gomes-Schwartz, B. (1978). Effective ingredients in psychotherapy: Prediction of outcome from process variables. *Journal of Consulting and Clinical Psychology*, **46**, 1023–1035.

Goodey, I.M. (1985). Developing Interval Rating Scales for Five Attributes of Client

Improvement in Social Relations. Unpublished master's thesis, University of Utah, Salt Lake City, UT.

Greenson, R.R. (1960). Empathy and its vicissitudes. *International Journal of Psychoanalysis*, **41**, 418–424.

Greenson, R.R. (1967). *The Technique and Practice of Psychoanalysis*. New York: International Universities Press.

Greenson, R.R. (1978). *Explorations in Psychoanalysis*. New York: International Universities Press.

Guntrip, H. (1961). *Personality Structure and Human Interaction*. New York: International Universities Press.

Hare, R. (1981). The philosophical basis of psychiatric ethics. In: S. Block & P. Chodoff (Eds.), *Psychiatric Ethics* (pp. 31–45). Oxford: Oxford University Press.

Harrower, M.R. (Ed.) (1947). *Training in Clinical Psychology*. New York: Josiah Macy Jr. Foundation.

Hartley, D., & Strupp, H. (1983). The therapeutic alliance: Its relationship to outcome in brief psychotherapy. In: J. Masling (Ed.), *Empirical Studies of Analytic Concepts* (Vol. 1). Hillsdale, NJ: Lawrence Erlbaum.

Hartmann, H. (1939). *Ego Psychology and the Problem of Adaptation*. New York: International Universities Press.

Hartmann, H. (1951). Technical implications of ego psychology. *Psychoanalytic Quarterly*, **20**, 31–43.

Hatch, N.O. (Ed.) (1988). *The Professions in American History*. Notre Dame, IN: University of Notre Dame Press.

Heppner, P.P., Kivlighan, D.M. Jr., & Wampold, B.R. (1991). *Research Design in Counseling*. Monterey, CA: Brooks/Cole.

Holt, R.R. (1963). Two influences on Freud's scientific thought: A fragment of intellectual biography. In: R.W. White (Ed.), *The Study of Lives*. New York: Atherton Press.

Holt, R.R. (1973). On reading Freud. In: C.L. Rothgeb (Ed.), *Abstracts of the Standard Edition of the Complete Psychological Works of Sigmund Freud*. New York: Jason Aronson.

Horney, K. (1937). *The Neurotic Personality of Our Time*. New York: Basic Books.

Horney, K. (1939). *New Ways in Psychoanalysis*. New York: Norton.

Horney, K. (1950). *Neurosis and Human Growth: The Struggle Toward Self-realization*. New York: Norton.

Horney, K. (1967a). The denial of the vagina. In: H. Kelman (Ed.), *Feminine Psychology*. (pp. 147–161). New York: W.W. Norton. (Original work published in 1933.)

Horney, K. (1967b). The flight from womanhood. In: H. Kelman (Ed.), *Feminine Psychology*. New York: W.W. Norton. (Original work published in 1926.)

Horney, K. (1967c). Inhibited femininity: Psychoanalytic contribution to the problem of frigidity. In: H. Kelman (Ed.), *Feminine Psychology* (pp. 71–83). New York: W.W. Norton. (Original work published in 1926–1927.)

Horowitz, M. (1976). *Stress Response Syndromes*. New York: Aronson.

Horvath, A. (1981). An Exploratory Study of the Working Alliance: Its Measurement and Relationship to Outcome. Unpublished doctoral dissertation, University of British Columbia, Brunaby, British Columbia.

Horvath, A., & Greenberg, L. (1989). Development and validation of the Working Alliance Inventory. *Journal of Counseling Psychology*, **36**, 223–232.

Horwitz, L. (1974). *Clinical Prediction in Psychotherapy*. New York: Jason Aronson.

Hoshmand, L.L.S.T. (1989). Alternate research paradigms: A review and teaching proposal. *The Counseling Psychologist*, **17**, 3–80.

Howard, G.S. (1984). A modest proposal for a revision of strategies for counseling research. *Journal of Counseling Psychology*, **31**, 430–432.

Howard, G.S. (1985). Can research in the human sciences become more relevant to practice? *Journal of Counseling and Development*, **63**, 539–544.

Howard, G.S. (1986). The scientist–practitioner model in counseling psychology: Toward a deeper integration of theory, research, and practice. *The Counseling Psychologist*, **14**, 61–105.

Howard, G.S., Nance, D.W., & Meyers, P. (1986). Adaptive counseling and therapy: An integrative, eclectic model. *The Counseling Psychologist*, **14**, 363–442.

Jacobs, M. (1988). *Psychodynamic Counseling in Action*. London: Sage Publications.

Jacobson, E. (1964). *The Self and the Object World*. New York: International Universities Press.

Jennings, B., Callahan, D., & Wolf, S.M. (1987). The professions: Public interest and common good. *A Hastings Center Report Special Supplement/February 1987*. New York: The Hastings Center.

Jones, E. (1963). *The Life and Works of Sigmund Freud* (Vol. 1). New York: Basic Books.

Jordan, A.E., & Meara, N.M. (1990). Ethics and the professional practice of psychologists. *Professional Psychology*, **21**, 107–114.

Jung, C.G. (1968). *Analytical Psychology: Its Theory and Practice*. New York: Pantheon.

Kahn, E. (1985). Heinz Kohut and Carl Rogers: A timely Comparison. *American Psychologist*, **40**, 893–904.

Keith-Spiegel, P., & Koocher, G.P. (1985). *Ethics in Psychology*. New York: Random House.

Keithley, L.J., Samples, S.J., & Strupp, H.H. (1980). Patient motivation as a predictor of process and outcome in psychotherapy. *Psychotherapy and Psychosomatics*, **33**, 87–97.

Kelly, G.A. (1955). *The Psychology of Personal Constructs*. New York: Norton.

Kernberg, O. (1976). *Object Relations Theory and Clinical Psychoanalysis*. New York: Aronson.

Kernberg, O. (1978). *Borderline Conditions and Pathological Narcissism*. New York: Jason Aronson.

Kernberg, O. (1980). *Internal World and External Reality*. New York: Aronson.

Kernberg, O., Burstein, E.D., Coyne, L., Appelbaum, A., Horwitz, L., & Voth, H. (1972). Psychotherapy research project. *Bulletin of the Menninger Clinic*, **36**, 1–275.

Kerr, A.E., Patton, M.J., Lapan, R.T., & Hills, H.I. (1991, August). *Interpersonal Correlates of Narcissism in a Group of Adolescents*. Poster session presented at the Annual Meeting of the American Psychological Association, San Francisco, CA.

King, P.T. (1965). Psychoanalytic adaptations. In: B. Steffler (Ed.), *Theories of Counseling* (pp. 91–139). New York: McGraw-Hill.

King, P.T., & Bennington, K.F. (1971). Psychoanalysis and counseling. In: B. Stefflre & W.H. Grant (Eds.), *Theories of Counseling* (2nd edn.) (pp. 177–243). New York: McGraw-Hill.

King, P.T., & Neal, R. (1968). *Ego Psychology in Counseling*. (Guidance Monograph Series). New York: International Universities Press.

Kitchener, K.S. (1984). Intuition, critical evaluation and ethical principles. *The Counseling Psychologist*, **21**(3), 43–55.

Klein, M. (1949). *The Psychoanalysis of Children*. London: Hogarth Press. (Original work published in 1932.)

Kohut, H. (1966). Forms and transformations of narcissism. *Journal of the American Psychoanalytic Association*, **14**, 243–272.

Kohut, H. (1971). *The Analysis of the Self*. New York: International Universities Press.

Kohut, H. (1977). *The Restoration of the Self*. New York: International Universities Press.

Kohut, H. (1974/1978a). A note on female sexuality. In: P. Orenstein (Ed.), *The Search for the Self: Selected Writings of Heinz Kohut: 1950–1978* (Vol. 2, pp. 783–792). New York: International Universities Press.

Kohut, H. (1974/1978b). The self in history. In: P. Orenstein (Ed.), *The Search for the Self: Selected Writings of Heinz Kohut: 1950–1978* (Vol. 2, pp. 88»–782). New York: International Universities Press.

Kohut, H. (1984). *How Does Analysis Cure?* Chicago: University of Chicago Press.

Kokotovic, A.M., & Tracey, T.J. (1990). Working alliance in the early phase of counseling. *Journal of Counseling Psychology*, **37**, 16–21.

Koles, M.R. (1981, August). Scales to measure client cognitive operations. In: M.J. Patton (Chair), *Scaling Counseling Outcomes: A Multivariate Strategy*. Symposium conducted at the Annual Convention of the American Psychological Association, Los Angeles, CA.

Koles, M.R. (1982). The Construction of Scales to Measure Change in Client Cognitive Operations. Unpublished master's thesis, University of Utah, Salt Lake City, UT.

Kunce, J.T., Cope, C.S., & Newton, R.M. (1989). *Personal Styles Inventory: Interpretation Guide and Scoring Directions*. Columbia, MO: Educational and Psychological Consultants.

Langs, R. (1973). *The Technique of Psychoanalytic Psychotherapy* (Vols. 1 and 2). New York: Aronson.

Lapan, R.T., & Patton, M.J. (1986). Self-psychology and the adolescent process: Measures of pseudoautonomy and peer group dependence. *Journal of Counseling Psychology*, **33**, 136–142.

Laughlin, H.P. (1979). *The Ego and its Defenses*. New York: Jason Aronson.

Lennard, H.L., & Bernstein, A. (1960). *The Anatomy of Psychotherapy: Systems of Communication and Expectation*. New York: Columbia University Press.

Lerman, H. (1985). Some barriers to the development of a feminist theory of personality. In: L. Rosewater & L.E. Walker (Eds.), *Handbook of Feminist Therapy: Women's issues in Psychotherapy* (pp. 5–12). New York: Springer.

Lerman, H. (1986). From Freud to feminist personality theory: Getting from here to there. *Psychology of Women Quarterly*, **10**(1), 1–18.

Lewis, H.B. (1986). Is Freud the enemy of women's liberation? In: T. Bernay and D.W. Cantor (Eds.), *The Psychology of Today's Woman: New Psychoanalytic Visions* (pp. 7–35). Hillsdale, NJ: Analytic Press.

Loevinger, J. (1976). *Ego Development: Conceptions and Theories*. San Francisco: Jossey-Bass.

Luborsky, L., Crits-Cristoph, P., Alexander, L., Margolis, M., & Cohen, M. (1983). Two helping alliance methods for predicting outcomes of psychotherapy: A counting signs vs. a global rating method. *Journal of Nervous and Mental Diseases*, **171**, 480–492.

Luborsky, L., McLellan, T., Woody, G., O'Brien, C., & Auerbach, A. (1985). Therapist success and its determinants. *Archives of General Psychiatry*, **42**, 602–611.

Maccoby, E.E. (1990). Gender and relationships: A developmental account. *American Psychologist*, **45**, 513–520.

MacIntyre, A. (1966). *A Short History of Ethics: A History of Moral Philosophy from the Homeric Age to the Twentieth Century*. New York: Collier Books.

Mahler, M.S., Pine, F., & Bergman, A. (1975). *The Psychological Birth of the Human Infant*. New York: Basic Books.

Mahoney, M.J., & Lyddon, W.J. (1988). Recent developments in cognitive approaches to counseling and psychotherapy. *The Counseling Psychologist*, **16**, 190–234.

Malan, D.H. (1963). *A Study of Brief Psychotherapy*. New York: Plenum Press.

Malan, D.H. (1976). *The Frontier of Brief Psychotherapy: An Example of the Convergence of Research and Clinical Practice*. New York: Plenum Press.

Mann, J. (1973). *Time-limited Psychotherapy*. Cambridge, MA: Harvard University Press.

Marmor, J. (1974). *Psychiatry in Transition*. New York: Brunner/Mazel.

Masterson, J. (1983). *Countertransference and Therapeutic Technique*. New York: Brunner/Mazel.

Matlin, M.W. (1987). *The Psychology of Women*. New York: Holt, Rinehart and Winston.

May, W.F. (1984). The virtues in a professional setting. *Soundings*, **67**, 245–266.

Meara, N.M. (August, 1987). Discussant remarks. In: M.J. Patton (Chair), *Key Elements of the Psychoanalytic Counseling Interview Process*. Symposium presented at the Annual Convention of the American Psychological Association. New York, NY.

Meara, N.M. (1990a). Science, practice, and politics. *The Counseling Psychologist*, **18**, 144–167.

Meara, N.M. (1990b). Selected theoretical and philosophical aspects of counseling psychology: A personal view. *Newsletter of the Journal of Philosophical and Theoretical Psychology*, **9**(2), 48–52.

Meara, N.M., & Schmidt, L.D. (1991). The ethics of researching counseling/therapy processes. In: C.E. Watkins & L.J. Schneider (Eds.), *Research in Counseling* (pp. 237–258). Hillsdale, NJ: Laurence Erlbaum Associates.

Menninger, K. (1958). *Theory of Psychoanalytic Technique*. New York: Harper Books.

Michigan University, Institute for Human Adjustment (1950). *Training of Psychological Counselors: Report of a Conference Held at Ann Arbor, Michigan, July 27 & 28, 1949, and January 6 & 7, 1950*. Ann Arbor, MI: University of Michigan Press.

Millon, T. (1983). *Millon Multiaxial Clinical Inventory Manual* (3rd edn.). Minneapolis: National Computer Systems.

Mitchell, J. (1974). *Psychoanalysis and Feminism*. New York: Random House.

Monte, C.F. (1987). *Beneath the Mask*. New York: Holt, Rinehart and Winston.

Moras, K., & Strupp, H.H. (1982). Pre-therapy interpersonal relations, a patient's alliance, and outcome in brief therapy. *Archives of General Psychiatry*, **39**, 405–409.

Moseley, D.C. (1983). *The Therapeutic Relationship and Its Association with Outcome*. Unpublished master's thesis, University of British Columbia, Vancouver, Canada.

Nachmann, B. (1960). Childhood experience and vocational choice in law, dentistry, and social work. *Journal of Counseling Psychology*, **7**, 243–250.

Napoli, D.S., (1981). *Architects of Adjustment: The History of the Psychological Profession in the United States*. Port Washington, NY: National University Publications, Kennihat Press.

Nunnally, J. (1978). *Psychometric Theory*. New York: McGraw-Hill.

Osipow, S.H. (1980). *Manual for the Career Decision Scale*. Columbus, OH: Marathon Consulting and Press.

Patton, M.J. (1978, August). A multivariate model of the counseling process. In: J. Gavelek (Chair), *Problems in Constructing a Model of Counseling*. Symposium conducted at the Annual Convention of the American Psychological Association, Toronto, Ontario, Canada.

Patton, M.J. (1980a, January). *Who's Borderline: A Comparison of the Theories of Kernberg and Masterson*. Paper presented at the Oliver Wendall Holmes Seminar, Granite Community Mental Health Center, Salt Lake City, UT.

Patton, M.J. (1980b, June). *Alcoholism and Drug Abuse as Narcissistic Behavior Disorders*. Paper presented at the University of Utah School on Alcoholism and Other Drug Dependencies, Salt Lake City, UT.

Patton, M.J. (1981a). *Devaluing and the Borderline Client*. Paper presented at the Psychology Service Training Lecture Program, Salt Lake Veterans Administration Medical Center, Salt Lake City, UT.

Patton, M.J. (1981b, August). Developing a multivariate model of counseling processes. In: M.J. Patton (Chair), *Scaling Counseling Outcomes: A Multivariate Strategy*. Symposium presented at the Annual Convention of the American Psychological Association, Los Angeles, CA.

Patton, M.J. (1982a). A methodological preface to research on counseling. *The Counseling Psychologist*, **10**, 23–26.

Patton, M.J. (1982b). Counseling psychology at the interface. Review of J.M. Whiteley & B.R. Fretz (Eds.) (1980), *The Present and Future of Counseling Psychology*. Monterey, CA: Brooks/Cole. *Contemporary Psychology*, **26**, 475–476.

Patton, M.J. (1984). Managing social interaction in counseling: A contribution from the philosophy of science. *Journal of Counseling Psychology*, **31**, 442–456.

Patton, M.J. (1987, August). An Heuristic model of the psychoanalytic counseling interview. In: M.J. Patton (Chair), *Key Elements of the Psychoanalytic Counseling Process*. Symposium conducted at the Annual Convention of the American Psychological Association, New York.

Patton, M.J. (1989). Problems with and alternatives to the use of coding schemes in research on counseling. *The Counseling Psychologist*, **17**, 490–506.

Patton, M.J. (1991). Qualitative research on college students: Philosophical and methodological comparisons with the quantitative approach. *Journal of College Student Development*, **32**, 389–396.

Patton, M.J., Connor, G., & Scott, K.J. (1982). Kohut's psychology of the self: Theory and measures of counseling outcome. *Journal of Counseling Psychology*, **29**, 268–282.

Patton, M.J., & Robbins, S.B. (1982). Kohut's self-psychology as a model for college-student counseling. *Professional Psychology*, **13**, 876–888.

Patton, M.J., & Sullivan, J.J. (1980). Heinz Kohut and the classical psychoanalytic tradition: An analysis in terms of levels of explanation. *Psychoanalytic Review*, **65**, 365–388.

Patton, M.Q. (1990). *Qualitative Evaluation and Research Methods*. Newbury Park, CA: Sage.

Paul, H. (1985). Current psychoanalytic paradigm controversy: A Horneyan perspective. *American Journal of Psychoanalysis*, **45**, 221–233.

Peabody, S.A., & Gelso, C.G. (1982). Countertransference and empathy: The complex relationship between two divergent concepts in counseling. *Journal of Counseling Psychology*, **29**, 240–245.

Pepinsky, H.B., & Pepinsky, P.N. (1954). *Counseling Theory and Practice*. New York: Ronald Press.

Pepinsky, H.B., & Patton, M.J. (Eds.) (1971). *The Psychological Experiment: A Practical Accomplishment*. Elmsford, NY: Pergamon.

Pepinsky, P.N. (unpublished manuscript). Worlds of Common Sense: Equality, Identity, and Two Modes of Impulse Management.

Polkinghorne, D.E. (1984). Further extensions of methodological diversity for counseling psychology. *Journal of Counseling Psychology*, **31**, 416–429.

Pope, K.S., & Vasquez, M.J.T. (1991). *Ethics in Psychotherapy and Counseling: A Practical Guide for Psychologists*. San Francisco: Jossey-Bass.

Principles Concerning the Counseling and Therapy of Women (1979).*The Counseling Psychologist*, **8**(1), 21.

Rapaport, D. (1959). The structure of psychoanalytic theory: A systematizing attempt. In: S. Koch (Ed.), *Psychology: A Study of Science* (3rd edn.). New York: McGraw-Hill.

Robbins, S.B. (1980, December). *Scaling a Client's Reduction in Successful Adaptive Response Patterns*. Paper presented at the Annual Conference of the Utah Psychological Association, Salt Lake City, Utah.

Robbins, S.B. (1983). Constructing measures of narcissism and their relation to career development (Doctoral dissertation, University of Utah). *Dissertation Abstracts International*, **44**, 1976B.

Robbins, S.B. (1986, August). (Chair) *Contributions from Contemporary Psychoanalysis to Counseling Theory, Research, and Practice*. Symposium presented at the Annual Conference of the American Psychological Association, Washington, D.C.

Robbins, S.B. (1987a, August). The role of contemporary psychoanalysis in counseling psychology. In: W. Rowe (Chair), *Counseling Psychology and Psychoanalytic Thought: Implications and Applications*. Symposium presented at the Annual Conference of the American Psychological Association, New York.

Robbins, S.B. (1987b). Predicting change in career indecision from a self-psychology perspective. *Career Development Quarterly*, **36**, 288–296.

Robbins, S.B. (1989). Role of contemporary psychoanalysis in contemporary psychology. *Journal of Counseling Psychology*, **36**, 267–279.

Robbins, S.B., & Jolkovski, M. (1987). Managing countertransference feelings: An interactional model using awareness of feelings and theoretical framework. *Journal of Counseling Psychology*, **35**, 325–329.

Robbins, S.B., & Patton, M.J. (1985). Self-psychology and career development: Development of the superiority and goal instability scales. *Journal of Counseling Psychology*, **32**, 221–231.

Robbins, S.B., & Patton, M.J. (1986). Procedures for the construction of counseling outcome rating scales. *Measurement and Evaluation in Counseling and Development*, **19**, 131–140.

Robbins, S.B., Payne, C., & Chartrand, J. (1990). Goal instability and later life adjustment. *Psychology and Aging*, **5**(3), 447–450.

Robbins, S.B., & Schwitzer, A. (1988). A validity study of the self-scales as predictors of women's adjustment to college life. *Measurement and Evaluation in Counseling and Development*, **21**, 117–122.

Robbins, S.B., & Tucker, K. (1986). Relation of goal instability to self-directed and interactional career workshops. *Journal of Counseling Psychology*, **33**, 418–424.

Robbins, S.B., & Von Galambos, V. (1988). Implementing a time-limited treatment model: Issues and solutions. *Professional Psychology*, **19**, 53–57.

Robertellio, R.C. (1978). The occupational disease of psychotherapists. *Journal of Contemporary Psychotherapy*, **9**(2), 123–129.

Robinson, F.P. (1950). *Principles and Procedures of Student Counseling*. New York: Harper and Brothers.

Rogers, C.R. (1951). *Client-centered Therapy*. Boston: Houghton Mifflin.

Rogers, C.R. (1957). The necessary and therapeutic conditions of therapeutic personality change. *Journal of Consulting Psychology*, **21**, 95–103.

Rosenbaum, M. (Ed.). (1982). *Ethics and Values in Psychotherapy: A Guidebook*. New York: The Free Press.

Sacks, H., Schegloff, E.A., & Jefferson, G. (1974). A simplest systematics for the organization of turn-taking in conversation. *Language*, **50**, 696–735.

St. Clair, M. (1986). *Object Relations and Self Psychology: An Introduction*. Monterey, CA: Brooks/Cole.

Sampson, E. E. (1977). Psychology and the American ideal. *Journal of Personality and Social Psychology*, **35**, 767–782.

Sampson, E. E. (1988). The debate on individualism. *American Psychologist*, **43**, 15–22.

Sayers, J. (1986). *Sexual Contradictions: Psychology, Psychoanalysis and Feminism*. London: Tavistock.

Scher, M., Stevens, M., Good, G., & Eichenfield, G. (Eds.) (1987). *Handbook of Counseling and Psychotherapy with Men*. Newbury Park, CA: Sage.

Schmidt, L.D. (1977). Why has the professional practice of psychological counseling developed in the United States? *The Counseling Psychologist*, **7**, 19–21.

Schutz, A. (1966). In: I. Schutz (Ed.), *Collected Papers III: Studies in Phenomenological Philosophy*. The Hague: Martinus-Nijhoff.

Schutz, A. (1967). In: M. Natanson (Ed.), *Collected Papers I: The Problem of Social Reality*. The Hague: Martinus-Nijhoff.

Scott, K., & Robbins, S.B. (1985). Goal instability: Implications for academic performance among learning skill students. *Journal of College Student Personnel*, **26**, 129–134.

Segal, S.J. (1961). A psychoanalytic analysis of personality factors in vocational choice. *Journal of Counseling Psychology*, **8**, 202–210.

Segal, S.J. (1965). Use of clinical techniques for structuring feedback in vocational counseling. *Personnel and Guidance Journal*, **43**, 876–878.

Showalter, E. (1982). Feminist criticism in the wilderness. In: E. Abel (Ed.), *Writing and Sexual Difference* (pp. 9–35). Chicago: University of Chicago Press.

Shreve, B., & Patton, M.J. (1988, August). *Shame-proneness Among Suicidal Persons: Psychometric Properties of the Shame-proneness Scale*. Poster session presentation at the Annual Meeting of the American Psychological Association, Atlanta, GA.

Sifneos, P.E. (1968). 'The motivational process': A selection for prognostic criterion for psychotherapy of short duration. *Psychiatric Quarterly*, **42**, 271–280.

Sifneos, P. (1972). *Short-term Psychotherapy and Emotional Crisis*. Cambridge, MA: Harvard University Press.

Smith, L., & Robbins, S.B. (1988). Validity of the Goal Instability Scale (modified) as a predictor of adjustment with retirement-aged adults. *Journal of Counseling Psychology*, **35**, 325–329.

Sterba, R. (1929). The dynamics of hate dissolution of the transference resistance. *Psychoanalytic Quarterly*, **9**, 363–379.

Sterba, R. (1934). The fate of the ego in analytic therapy. *International Journal of Psychoanalysis*, **15**, 117–126.

Stone, L. (1954). The widening scope of indications for psychoanalysis. *Journal of the American Psychoanalytic Association*, **2**, 567–594.

Strachey, J. (1934). The nature of the therapeutic action of psychoanalysis. *International Journal of Psychoanalysis*, **15**, 127–139.

Street, D.L. (1990). An Examination of the Relationship of Narcissism and Social Variables to Bulimia. Unpublished master's thesis, University of Missouri, Columbia, MO.

Strong, S.R. (1968). Counseling: An interpersonal influence process. *Journal of Counseling Psychology*, **15**, 215–224.

Strong, S.R. (1991). Theory-driven science and naive empiricism in counseling psychology. *Journal of Counseling Psychology*, **38**, 204–210.

Strupp, H.H., & Binder, J.L. (1984). *Psychotherapy in a New Key: A Guide to Time-limited Dynamic Psychotherapy*. New York: Basic Books.

Strupp, H., & Hadley, S. (1979). Specific vs. non-specific factors in psychotherapy: A controlled study of outcome. *Archives of General Psychiatry*, **36**, 1125–1136.

Sullivan, J.J. (1959). From Breuer to Freud. *Psychoanalysis and the Psychoanalytic Review*, **46**, 69–90.

Sullivan, J.J. (1968). Franz Brentano and the problem of intentionality. In: B.B. Wolman (Ed.), *Historical Roots of Contemporary Psychology*. New York: Harper & Row.

Super, D.E. (1955). Transition: From vocational guidance to counseling psychology. *Journal of Counseling Psychology*, **2**, 3–9.

Tennov, D. (1976). *Psychotherapy: The Hazardous Cure*. Garden City, NY: Anchor Press.

Thompson, C. (1964). Penis envy. In: M. Green (Ed.), *On Women* (pp. 73–78). New York: Basic Books.

Tinsley, H.E.A., & Harris, D.J. (1976). Client expectations for counseling. *Journal of Counseling Psychology*, **23**, 173–177.

Tinsley, H.E.A., & Weiss, D.J. (1975). Inter-rater reliability and agreement of subjective judgments. *Journal of Counseling Psychology*, **22**, 358–376.

Tracey, T.J. (1986). Interactional correlates of premature termination. *Journal of Consulting and Clinical Psychology*, **54**, 45–51.

Truax, C., & Carkhuff, R. (1967). *Toward Effective Counseling and Psychotherapy*. Chicago: Aldine.

Tryon, G.S. (1990). Session depth and smoothness in relation to the concept of engagement in counseling. *Journal of Counseling Psychology*, **37**, 248–253.

Tucker, K.R. (1982). The Construction of Scales to Measure Client Change in Social Relations. Unpublished master's thesis, University of Utah, Salt Lake City, UT.

Turner, R. (1972). Some formal properties of therapy talk. In: D. Sudnow (Ed.), *Studies on Social Interaction* (pp. 367–396). New York: Free Press.

Valliant, G. (1977). *Adaption to Life*. Boston: Little, Brown.

Walsh, M.R. (Ed.) (1987). *The Psychology of Women: Ongoing Debates*. New Haven: Yale University Press.

Westfall, R.(1964). *Symptom Formation: The Relationship Between External Factors and Internal Conflicts*. Paper presented to the San Francisco Psychoanalytic Institute, San Francisco, CA.

Westkott, M. (1986). *The Feminist Legacy of Karen Horney*. New Haven, CT: Yale University Press.

Williams, R.H. (1940). The method of understanding as applied to the problem of suffering. *Journal of Abnormal and Social Psychology*, **35**, 367–385.

Winnicott, D.W. (1953). Transitional objects and transitional phenomena. *International Journal of Psychoanalysis*, **34**, 89–97.

Winnicott, D.W. (1958). The capacity to be alone. *International Journal of Psychoanalysis*, **39**, 416–420.

Winnicott, D.W. (1965). *The Maturational Processes and the Facilitating Environment: Studies in the Theory of Emotional Development*. New York: International Universities Press.

Wright, D.E. (1980). The Construction of Scales to Measure Counselor Interventions. Unpublished doctoral dissertation, University of Utah, Salt Lake City, UT.

Zetzel, E.R. (1956). Current concepts of transference. *International Journal of Psychoanalysis*, **37**, 369–376.

Author index

Subject index

Resistance (*cont.*)
  functions of, 202–203, 204–205, 206
  manifestations in the interview,
    83–84, 207–222
    fears of
      counseling, 207–212
      counselor, 210–211
      process, 208–209
      reasonable ego, 211–212
    general indicators, 212–218
      acting out, 216–217
      behavior, 216–218
      discussion topic, 214–216
      language, 212–214
    through defenses, 218–222
  techniques for dealing with, 168–169,
    222–231
    allowing to increase, 224–225
    analyzing, 227–235
      clarification, 227–229
      interpretation, 229–231
    demonstrating (confrontation),
      225–227
    identifying, 223–224
  theoretical considerations, 203–207

Scientific principles of explanation, *see*
  Levels of explanation
Scientist–practitioner model, 305–306,
  336–337
Self, 51, 175
  adult, cohesive, 53, 55–60, 64, 285
  bi-polar, 51, 59, 285
  break-up of, 55–56, 57
  grandiose or mirroring selfobject, 52,
    55, 56–58, 60–61, 285
  idealized selfobject (or target),
    52–55, 59–61, 285
  infantile self and its selfobjects,
    51–52, 55–56, 58
  self-selfobject relations, 51–52, 54,
    55, 58, 59
  transmuting internalization, 55, 57
Self psychology theory, 10, 11, 17, 23,
  47–64
  and feminist theory, 273–274,
    278–283
  applications to the counseling of
    women, 283–286
  development of self, 51–60
    grandiose line of development,

      56–58, 61, 63–64, 283–284,
      325, 329–333
    idealized line of development,
      58–60, 61, 63–64, 283–285,
      325, 329–333
    measurement in, 325–328, 329–336
  disturbances of self, 60–64, 171
Sexuality, 11, 15, 30, 73, 169, 170, 215,
  220
  female, 273
  in anal stage, 35
  in latency period, 38–40
  in oedipal stage, 35–37
  in oral stage, 33
  in puberty, 39–40
  libidinal development, 32
  libido, 29, 47
    narcissistic libido, 48
  role in development of neurotic
    symptoms, 10
  sexual impulse, 12
Shame, 37–38, 74, 205, 209, 220
  shame-proneness, 23, 61, 333–336
Superego, 36–37, 38, 40, 42
Symptom formation, 28, 29, 42, 105,
  165, 166, 168, 169, 173, 190
  see also Compromise formation

Tension gradient, 59
Termination, 90, 264–265
  premature, 208
Therapeutic alliance, *see* Working
  alliance
Therapeutic context, 73–74
Transference, 15, 16, 23, 48, 85–86, 97,
  100, 125, 145, 174, 175, 215, 230
  and ethical principle of fidelity, 296
  defined, 5
  idealized, 61
  mirroring, 61
  narcissistic or selfobject, 48
  neurosis, 99

Unconscious, the, 10, 14, 15, 49, 86
  and feminism, 269, 272
  and resistance, 206, 217, 229

Women, *see* Psychoanalytic counseling
  of women

DATE DUE

MAY 1 5 1994

DIS MAY 1 4 1994

NOV 2 9 1995

JUL 0 1 1996

FEB 1 3 1998

APR 2 5 2005

DEMCO, INC. 38-2971